America's Moment : 1918

Books by Arthur Walworth

SCHOOL HISTORIES AT WAR

BLACK SHIPS OFF JAPAN

CAPE BRETON: *Isle of Romance*

WOODROW WILSON: *American Prophet*
(awarded the 1958 Pulitzer Prize in biography)

WOODROW WILSON: *World Prophet*

AMERICA'S MOMENT: 1918

AMERICA'S MOMENT:1918

*American Diplomacy
at the End of World War I*

☆ ☆ ☆ ☆ ☆

ARTHUR WALWORTH

W · W · NORTON & COMPANY · INC · NEW YORK

Copyright © 1977 by W. W. Norton & Company, Inc. All rights reserved.
Published simultaneously in Canada by George J. McLeod Limited,
Toronto. Printed in the United States of America.

FIRST EDITION

Library of Congress Cataloging in Publication Data

Walworth, Arthur Clarence, 1903–
America's moment, 1918.
Bibliography: p. 291
Includes index.
1. United States—Foreign relations—1913–1921.
2. European War, 1914–1918—Influence and results.
3. Wilson, Woodrow, Pres. U.S., 1856–1924.
I. Title.
E768.W34   1977   940.3'22'73   76–24836
ISBN 0–393–05591–4

1 2 3 4 5 6 7 8 9 0

To the memory of Charles Seymour
and to the other men of good will
who helped me to know and to understand

Contents

America's Moment : 1918

☆ I ☆

America—the "Associated Power"

In October 1918, as the first great war of the century neared its end, social and political turmoil was shaking the foundations of the defeated countries. In Central and Eastern Europe the fall of empires left a vacuum. There was poverty, famine, and a political disintegration such as modern Europe had not known.

In contrast with the limited conflicts of the preceding hundred years, this had been a mass slaughter. Civilians in the path of ruthless military machines were victims of atrocities. People who had thought themselves secure against violence were torpedoed and bombed. The horror of total war shocked men who had considered peace to be the normal state of society and had thought it impossible for such folly to exist.[1]

Europe, in the view of Thomas G. Masaryk, was "a laboratory resting upon a vast cemetery."[2] The opportunity that lay before the statesmen of the victorious Allied Powers as they surveyed the havoc was Olympian. They were in theory masters of the world, commanding dominant armies as well as fleets that ruled the seas. What now would they do with their victory? Would its fruits overbalance the awful reckoning of losses?

The minds of many of their peoples were weary and possessed by old grudges, a lust for vengeance, and a greediness for spoils. The

---

1. John Buchan, *A History of the Great War, 4* (Boston, 1922), 422; Pierre Renouvin, *La Crise Européenne et la Grande Guerre,* 5th ed. (Paris, 1969), pp. 742–43, *Les Crises du XXe Siècle, 1,* pp. 130–31; A.J.P Taylor, *The First World War: an Illustrated History* (London, 1963).

When the place and year of publication of a title are omitted, see Bibliography (p. 290). Abbreviations used in the footnotes are listed on page 286.

2. Quoted in Maurice Baumont, *La Faillite de la Paix, 1918–1939,* p. 8.

war had been fought, according to the slogan of the president of the United States, "to make the world safe for democracy." But would the governments of the democratic powers have the wisdom to make the world safe?

The fact that "the people" had now come to power was to give to the peacemaking of 1919 a different character from that of the settlement arrived at by the ministers of European monarchs in 1815. It would be difficult for the leaders to temper the popular passions of the hour and yet retain parliamentary support. The Western nation-states still had a measure of cohesiveness and stability, but the elected officials could not be sure that their several peoples would follow their leadership. The human spirit rebelled against the rigid disciplines of wartime. There was a pervading impulse to throw off the bonds of traditional morality, to venture and experiment in political change. Violent strife between classes threatened to follow the four years of bloody conflict among nations. Statesmen were alarmed by reports that the revolutionary Soviet government in Russia was carrying on active and subversive propaganda not only in Germany, Switzerland, and Scandinavia, but even in France, Italy, and Great Britain.

The menace of revolution cast its shadow over Washington. President Wilson told his cabinet that Bolshevik agencies were sending funds into Germany, Hungary, and other countries to encourage class warfare generally.[3] He recognized that even in America civil order was threatened by the unrest that came with war-weariness.[4]

The president used the word "outrageous" when he denounced the Russian Soviet government for asserting that the peoples of the democracies were being exploited for the imperial purposes of capitalists.[5] The Soviet leaders had released for publication in Western newspapers the texts of certain agreements made by the diplomats of the Allied Powers with a view to strengthening the alliance against Germany and dividing the spoils of war. These pacts, negotiated in secrecy and kept from public view in accord with the tradition of the old diplomacy of Europe, would transfer certain peoples from one sovereignty to another without their consent.

The British prime minister, David Lloyd George, responding to demands from Labour for specification of constructive proposals for

3. Franklin K. Lane, *The Letters of Franklin K. Lane,* ed. by A.W. Lane and L.H. Wall, p. 298.

4. Ray Stannard Baker, *Life and Letters, Armistice 1918,* Potomac edition vol. 7 (designated hereafter as "Baker") p. 482, fn.; interview with Sir William Wiseman, Wiseman pa., Yale House Collection (designated hereafter as "Y.H.C.").

5. Wiseman interview, Jan. 23, 1918, Balfour pa., 49741, British Museum.

peace, felt it necessary to make a strong avowal of liberal purposes.[6] These were: first, the overthrow of Prussia and, inversely, the guaranteeing of democracy for the German people as for others; second, the liberation of occupied nations—first Belgium and then those of Eastern Europe; and third, the abolition of international war by a joining of democratic and independent nations, including Germany, in a concert and community of power that would supplant the old practice of balancing power.[7] Informed that Wilson intended to define war aims, Lloyd George determined to be the first to speak out.[8] He prepared a declaration for delivery at a meeting of trades-union delegates on January 5, 1918. His text was a synthesis of Liberal and Labour proposals and discussions that had been going on in the war cabinet for nine months and took account of reports from committees representing the whole empire.[9]

Lloyd George insisted on three essentials of a lasting peace: "first, the sanctity of treaties; secondly, a territorial settlement based on the right of self-determination or the consent of the governed, and lastly . . . the creation of some international organization to limit the burden of armaments and diminish the probability of war." He accorded the right of self-determination to the inhabitants of the German colonies as well as to the peoples of Europe. As for the secret treaties made under the stress of war necessity, he said that they would not "prevent a free discussion between the Allies as to their future, as the Russian collapse had changed all the conditions."[10] He declared that Russia could be saved only by its own people. Insisting on restoration of seized territories and reparation for damages, he denied any intent "to shift the cost of warlike operations from one belligerent to another." Although he said that the adoption of democratic institutions by Germany would make it easier to negotiate a peace, he did not demand any change in the Imperial constitution or any disintegration of the German state. Acknowledging the existence of the new diplomacy of propaganda that the Bolsheviks were practicing, the prime minister showed little sympathy for their espousal of "open diplomacy."

However, Lloyd George's speech did not entirely satisfy British

---

6. For the considerations that moved Lloyd George to speak out, see Sterling J. Kernek, *Distractions of Peace during War*, pp. 72–73.

7. W.M. Jordan, *Great Britain, France, and the German Problem*, pp. 3–5.

8. Wiseman's note on ms. of *The Intimate Papers of Colonel House, 3,* ch. 11, Seymour pa., Y.H.C.

9. Lloyd George, *The Truth about the Peace Treaties, 1,* 94.

10. Balfour stated in the House of Commons on June 20, 1918, that the secret treaties were "no obstacle to peace" and the Allies would listen to "reasonable suggestions." Harold W.V. Temperley (ed.), *A History of the Peace Conference at Paris, 1,* 190.

radicals. They still looked to Wilson for leadership in creating a world free from war as well as from social injustice. The Allied governments welcomed the moral support of the American president, as well as the material aid that his nation was able to provide. They were dependent upon the United States for provisions and munitions. The volume of American exports during the war was huge, and this had brought about a radical change in the relative financial positions of the nations. At the end of hostilities London would no longer be the cosmic banking center, and the American Treasury would control the finances of much of Europe. Its stock of gold had almost doubled since 1914 and amounted to nearly half of the world supply. The British Treasury owed it several billions of dollars and in turn had loaned billions to Continental powers. Not only were the depleted European treasuries unable to repay short-term loans, but the depreciation of their currencies made further credits necessary to finance imports of food and of the new materials needed to revive industrial production to a point where it could be taxed so that funds might be available for the settlement of debts in the future. The American republic had risen to a position of power as Europe consumed itself.

Woodrow Wilson had observed the tide of history at the turn of the century, remarking that the United States was then stepping into "the arena of the world." He was not unaware of the confusion of motives that influenced the nation's foreign relations, perceiving in his people "a great ardor for gain" and also "a deep passion for the rights of man." During his first year in the presidency he had given little attention to foreign affairs except for relations with Mexico, where he found his obligation to protect American property and his antipathy to immoral rulers were in conflict with his desire to let native peoples work out their problems without foreign intervention. His difficulties with Mexico had confounded European diplomats who were accustomed to deal with de facto governments without too close scrutiny of their moral credentials.

The American people, restrained by a tradition of isolation, were inclined at the beginning of Wilson's presidency to regard international law as, in the words of Elihu Root, "a rather antiquated branch of useless learning, diplomacy as a foolish mystery, and the foreign service as a superfluous expense."[11] At the outset the president found it difficult to persuade men of high caliber and sufficient means to serve abroad. Most of the envoys had not been required to solve critical questions. These amateurs were usually ill prepared to

---

11. Walter Millis, *Road to War* (New York, 1935), p. 9.

deal with the professional diplomats of Europe, who generally functioned with precision, tact, and mutual understanding. Even for the key position of secretary of state, the president had to appoint a party man to whom he was politically indebted and who had few qualifications. In the absence of assistance that he considered competent, Wilson came to accept responsibility for foreign policy.

Neither Wilson nor Secretary of State Bryan gave serious study to problems that European diplomats faced in 1914, nor did they know much about them.[12] At the outset Wilson realized that not the least part of the difficulty was going to be the satisfaction of opinion in the United States and the full performance of what he conceived to be its duty as the only powerful neutral. For more than two years Wilson had devoted himself to keeping his country out of war. At the same time he explored possibilities of ending hostilities through mediation. He tried to defend the rights of American shipping on the high seas, denouncing British seizures of contraband goods almost as fervently as he condemned German drownings of noncombatants. He seemed, Prime Minister Lloyd George wrote, "so studiously unpleasant to both sides that statesmen of the fighting alliances never were quite sure where his sympathies lay."[13] He felt that neither alliance was solely to blame for the outbreak of the war, and he refrained from judgments on the question of responsibility.

For a time after the United States declared war the president concentrated his moral fervor against the "military masters" of Germany. He staked the achievement of his goal as peacemaker for the world upon an Allied victory and the opportunity he hoped it would give to take the lead in a peace conference that would realize his ideals. However, he became handicapped in effecting his exalted mission when his facility in shifting from a policy of "peace without victory" to one of crushing the German militarists led Allied officials to scorn him as a "righteous self-deceiver." His sudden change of tone when he entered the war had given credence to old assertions of political enemies and others that he was an opportunist, and dishonest.[14]

The resentment of critics abroad did not deter the American prophet (if indeed he was aware of it) from proclaiming the popular creed that was called for to meet the political necessity existing at the

---

12. Woodrow Wilson (designated hereinafter as "W.W.") to Walter Hines Page, October 28, 1914, Wilson pa., Library of Congress (Designated hereinafter as "L.C."), 2.

13. David Lloyd George, *War Memoirs, 2,* p. 662; Charles Seymour, *The Intimate Papers of Colonel House, 2* (hereinafter designated as *"I.P."*), pp. 395, 407.

14. See Patrick Devlin, *Too Proud to Fight,* pp. 622, 679.

beginning of the year 1918. He was embarrassed by the publication of the secret treaties.[15] Although the United States had not been a party to them , it was an associate of the powers that conceived them. When the Soviet government denounced the treaties, Wilson was urged to react positively and constructively. He was advised that English Liberals would readily accept his leadership because they would find in his doctrines an invaluable support for their domestic policies. Moreover, pleas came from American agents in Russia for a statement of America's good faith that they could give to the Soviet leaders, who were about to open peace talks with Germany at Brest-Litovsk.

In response to the challenge President Wilson delivered on January 8 the most significant of all statements of war aims.[16] Praising the speech that Lloyd George had given three days before as "spoken with admirable candor and in admirable spirit," he set forth what he called "a provisional sketch of principles" that dissociated his nation from the purposes of the secret treaties.[17] By this and subsequent declarations he projected the American political tradition into a faith for all peoples. His creed appealed to liberal opinion in the Western democracies, which already had been drawn to him by his record of progressive reform in the United States.

In the drafting of this bold speech the president drew upon the work of a body of scholarly advisers known as "The Inquiry."[18] In a memorandum dated December 22, 1917 scholars of The Inquiry set forth the objectives, assets, and liabilities of the United States. Outlining a "programme for a diplomatic offensive," the report recommended that American policy play upon both the hopes and the fears of the German people by holding before them the alternatives of world collaboration and economic constriction. "This is our

---

15. On May 18, 1917, A.J. Balfour, foreign secretary of Great Britain, had given the text of most of the pacts to Wilson, who had responded with a handwritten letter in which he said he would study the documents with interest. W.W. to Balfour, May 19, 1917, Public Records Office, London (designated hereinafter as "P.R.O."), FO/800/208. Balfour recorded that he "handed" Wilson, confidentially, copies of all secret treaties sent to him from London, but possibly did not reveal the arrangements for the transfer of German rights in Shantung to Japan. Ms. by Balfour, N.D., Balfour pa., 49734; *I.P.*, *4*, p. 365; Mary Reno Frear, "Did President Wilson Contradict Himself on the Secret Treaties?" *Current History* vol. xxx, no. 3, (June 1929), pp. 435–43.

16. Wilson wanted to "innoculate the left Socialists and syndicalists against the mounting Soviet propaganda." Arno J. Mayer, "Historical Thought and American Foreign Policy in the Era of the First World War," in Francis L. Loewenheim (ed.), *The Historian and the Diplomat.* pp. 82, 86.

17. See Appendix (p. 275) for the Fourteen Points, and also for the four supplementary principles set forth on February 11, 1918.

18. See below, page 75 ff.

strongest weapon," the report stated, "and the Germans realize its menace." It should not be surrendered until Germany accepted terms of peace that assured the attainment of American objectives. Another part of the memorandum and a revision of it outlined peace terms on eight issues involving boundaries in Europe. A paragraph suggested that out of the existing anti-German alliance a league of nations was already developing.[19]

The prescriptions for peace that Wilson advanced differed in some respects from those of Lloyd George; but the variances were glossed over on both sides of the Atlantic in the interest of wartime unity.[20] The president, like Lloyd George, accepted nationalism as the dominating political force of the century and invoked the principle of self-determination. He made a special point of disarmament. Another point expressed friendship for the Russian people and for any government that ruled Russia with their consent. Of the "provisional" Fourteen Points that he proclaimed, those that he later described as "essentially American" were: (1) "open covenants of peace, openly arrived at"; (2) "absolute freedom of navigation upon the seas"; (3) "the removal, so far as possible, of all economic barriers"; and (4), Point Fourteen, "a general association of nations under specific covenants for the purpose of affording mutual guarantees of political independence and territorial integrity to great and small states alike." It was his view that this last point was the paramount prescription for an enduring peace and one that provided for the enforcement of many of the others.[21]

The Fourteenth Point evoked a warm response from idealists seeking a new world order as an alternative to suicidal warfare. Aware that patriotism was "not enough," they hoped that common standards of justice might come to supersede national interests. The age-old concept of war as a means by which contending nations could settle a dispute without disturbing their neighbors was yielding to a twentieth-century belief that a resort to force was such a threat to the very existence of mankind as to make it an offense against

19. The memorandum of Dec. 22, 1917, with marginal notes by Wilson, is printed in Ray Stannard Baker, *Woodrow Wilson and World Settlement, 3,* pp. 23–41. A revision, dated Jan. 2, 1918, is in The Inquiry papers, Y.H.C. Gelfand comments that the memorandum was based on insufficient study. See Lawrence E. Gelfand, *The Inquiry,* pp. 136–50). For an account of the drafting of the Fourteen Points, see Charles Seymour, *American Diplomacy during the World War,* ch. 7.

20. See Kernek, pp. 73–77, for an analysis of the differences and the reactions.

21. "A League of Nations was the fundamental war aim; the rest were only machinery to provide a clean foundation for it . . . it was the only practical ideal before the world, in the sense that it was the only one which met the whole needs of the case" Buchan, pp. 156–57.

common morality.[22] On both sides of the Atlantic there was questioning of the adequacy of the traditional diplomacy of Europe, which by professional negotiations had succeeded for a century in balancing power and averting a general war but had not been able to avert the fatal clash of opposing alliances in 1914.[23]

Elihu Root, the elder statesman of the Republican Party, wrote in August of 1918:

> The view now assumed and generally applied is that the use of force by one nation toward another is a matter in which only the two nations concerned are primarily interested, and if any other nation claims a right to be heard on the subject it must show some specific interest of its own in the controversy. That burden of proof rests upon any other nation which seeks to take part if it will relieve itself of the charge of impertinent interference and avoid the resentment which always meets impertinent interference in the affairs of an independent sovereign state. . . . The requisite change is an abandonment of this view and a universal, formal and irrevocable acceptance and declaration of the view that an international breach of the peace is a matter which concerns every member of the Community of Nations—a matter in which every nation has a direct interest and to which every nation has a right to object. . . . the practical results which will naturally develop will be as different from those which have come from the old view of national responsibility as are the results which flow from the American Declaration of Independence compared with the results which flow from the Divine Right of Kings. . . .[24]

Several leaders of English liberal thought, writing at the end of the war upon the idea of a league of nations, proclaimed that in 1914 the world awoke out of a dream of intensified nationality to a new system of realities that was entirely antagonistic to the continuance of national separations. Pointing to the facilitation of human intercommunication in the years since 1900, they asserted that such a phenomenon must lead to political consequences equally revolutionary. It seemed conceivable that habits of thought might develop that would give effective sanction to an international organization. They were encouraged in their belief by a conviction that the alter-

---

22. Devlin, *Too Proud to Fight,* pp. 595–96.
23. During the war specific proposals were put forward in Germany by the government (see Ralph H. Lutz, *The Fall of the German Empire, 1914–1918,* 2 [Stanford, 1932] pp. 860–68) and by the Bund Neues Vaterland, at Paris by a journal, *La Paix par de Droit,* and at the Hague by l'Organisation Centrale pour une Paix Durable, the creation of Dutch and Swiss nationals. Seven plans for international peace were described in Leonard S. Woolf (ed.), *The Framework of a Lasting Peace* (New York, 1917).
24. *I.P., 4,* pp. 43–44.

native to a mutual assumption of responsibility, in view of the nature of modern warfare, was mutual destruction.[25]

Sir Edward Grey, foreign secretary at the beginning of the war, had emphasized at the time of the Balkan crisis in 1912, and again when disaster threatened in July of 1914, that it was necessary to revive the Concert of Europe and to give it facilities for constant consultation among the powers to keep the peace. Seeing in President Wilson a leader for whom men would die,[26] and conceiving that a league of nations could result in American participation in a system that would perpetuate the best traditions of the British Empire, Grey called this the "pearl of great price" in the peace settlement.[27] British liberals believed that a league should not only restrain its members from war but should promote cooperation in every sphere of international relations. Thus there might rise—like British law, on a foundation of human need and experience—a great structure of international tradition. Labour leaders took a part in promoting the cause, and organizations were formed to further it.[28]

In the past the prime guarantee of peace among sovereign states had been the existence of treaties negotiated and sustained by the national ministries of foreign affairs and their diplomatic services. There was no supreme authority endowed with effective means of enforcing a treaty's behests or of adjudicating violations of what passed for international law. Jurists made a pithy comment: Where no writ runs there is no law. (An eminent scholar has written: "Law . . . seeks to correct human weaknesses; diplomacy accommodates them. Between the two there is an inevitable strain, and at a certain tension law breaks.")[29]

---

25. H.G. Wells, in collaboration with Viscount Grey, Lionel Curtis, William Archer, H. Wickham Steed, A.E. Zimmern, J.A. Spender, Viscount Bryce, Gilbert Murray, *The Idea of a League of Nations* (Boston: 1919).

26. According to Frank I. Cobb, Grey once said to Gilbert Murray that Wilson was "a leader he could die for." Cobb journal, Wilson pa., series 14, file 19.

27. Grey to House, Aug. 10, 1915, *I.P., 2*, p. 87. "The establishment and maintenance of a league of nations such as President Wilson has advocated," Grey wrote, "is more important and essential to a secure peace than any of the actual terms of peace that may conclude the war; it will transcend them all." Pamphlet "League of Nations," May 11, 1918, London.

28. See H.R. Winkler, "The Development of the League of Nations Idea in Great Britain, 1914–1919" (microfilm, University of Chicago Library, 1947); *The League of Nations Movement in Great Britain, 1914–1919,* New Brunswick N.J., 1952); and Philip Noel Baker, "The Making of the Covenant from the British Point of view," ms. in possession of the author. *Cf.* below, p. 269.

29. Percy E. Corbett, *Law and Society* (New York, 1951) pp. 13–14; *Law in Diplomacy* (Princeton, 1959), p. 272.

Venturesome idealists of several nations had long endeavored to
discover in "international law" an instrument that might serve to
regulate the relations of one sovereign state with another. With this
end in view American delegates shared between 1898 and 1914 in
sixteen nonpolitical conferences with other nations.[30] Representatives of the United States took part in two peace conventions at
The Hague, in 1899 and 1907. After abstaining from voting on a
disarmament resolution on the ground that it was solely a European
issue, and after insisting on excluding from adjudication any disputes that involved the Monroe Doctrine, they agreed to their nation's participation in a Permanent Court of International Arbitration.

At The Hague it was suggested that a more or less general acceptance might lend the quality of positive law to certain rules of national conduct that had been either formally agreed upon or generally
accepted by the civilized states of the world. Liberals stressed the
need for a political body in which governments might regularly
discuss threats to the peace, and where, in times of crisis, states contemplating aggression would come face to face with moral pressure
and perhaps a threat of economic or military coercion.

The liberals seized upon the vast progress already made in the
processes of government and put their trust in the immediate possibility of further improvement. It seemed obvious that in the growing
complexity of the modern world, the cost of war, in both life and
treasure, had for all time destroyed its utility as an instrument of national policy and had tainted all armed aggression by the state with
an aspect of crime. To many liberals the union of the nations in a
covenant to keep the peace seemed imperative as the next step in the
forward march of civilization. They saw in the final collapse of the
ancient dynastic structure of Europe the advent of democratic institutions and the free expression of a worldwide public opinion in the
interest of a lasting peace for the benefit of all mankind.

The conservatives, however, accepting the postulate that human
nature is far from perfect, depended on that little wisdom with
which man had governed his world. They put trust in the customary
ways of doing things that long experience had shown to be acceptable. An all-embracing alliance to enforce peace seemed to them to
be premature, and they judged humanity at large still to be too
varied in race and language, too diverse in ways of thought and life,
to allow a parliament of the world to function by the voluntary submission of the minority to the will of the majority. They were con-

---

30. Bemis, *The United States as a World Power* (New York, 1955), p. 102.

vinced that a power of veto would have to be retained by each of a league's sovereign members if the international body was to have the consent and loyalty of all. In their view the utopian vision of lasting peace that a league conjured up was vitiated by the very existence and the certain abuse of veto power that each nation would feel that it must retain.

From this dilemma the conservatives saw no ready escape. They feared, perhaps above all else, that the very fact that a league existed might serve to beguile the Western democracies to disarm to a degree that might endanger their existence. Minds not easily unsettled by the tragedy of world war and the consequent popular clamor for reform and innovation noted that historical precedent was lacking for an effective political confederation of all nations. In the United States many were reluctant to yield up even the smallest part of that full sovereignty that the Founding Fathers had labored to attain and had so successfully achieved. The last of the President's Fourteen Points, on which he depended above all others as a basis for American leadership of the postwar world, evoked sincere philosophical doubts among wise men in both the United States and Europe.

The ideal of a world polity had long fascinated Woodrow Wilson. He recognized in a "league of nations" the sort of great cause on which he depended in political leadership. In 1915 he had worked on a text for a pan-American pact whereby the nations of the Western Hemisphere would undertake mutually to guarantee political independence and territorial integrity under republican forms of government, to settle boundary disputes by direct negotiation or by arbitration, and to prevent the fitting out of revolutionary expeditions against the governments of other states. In 1918 Wilson sought to apply the substance of this project to the entire world.[31] By autumn of that year he conceived of a league of nations as the main compensation to be sought for the suffering of the war, and the very center of the peace agreement.[32] Until the war came to a close, how-

31. On April 5, 1918, Wilson revealed his tentative thoughts on an international organization in a letter to the editor of the *Spectator,* St. Loe Strachey (Beaverbrook Library, London). In remarks to Mexican editors at the White House on June 7, 1918, he traced the transfer of his own thinking from the Pan-American Pact to a world-wide compact. Reviewing his proposals for an agreement among nations of the Western Hemisphere, he went on to say: "I must admit that I was ambitious to have the states of the two continents of America show the way to the rest of the world as to how to make a basis of peace."

32. "The Attitude of the U.S. and Woodrow Wilson," Wiseman's conversation with Wilson, Oct. 16, 1918, Y.H.C. For contemporary American interpretations of the history, philosophy, and possibilities of the league ideal, see Stephen P. Duggan (ed.), *The League of Nations* (Boston, 1919).

ever, the president, fearful of sponsoring any specific proposal for a league that might become a target for criticism, avoided discussion of details. While Wilson kept his own counsel, other political leaders of the nation formulated plans.[33]

Edward M. House, who was Wilson's privy counselor, was in touch with the thinking of British and French proponents of an international organization,[34] received a copy of recommendations made to the British government by an official committee of which Lord Phillimore was chairman. He found a sympathetic correspondent in the person of Lord Robert Cecil who, inspired by the ideals of his father, the third marquess of Salisbury, and by a religious nature that made him deplore the brutality of the blockade that he was obliged as a cabinet minister to enforce, was fervently devoted to the cause of peace and, as he said, "violently in favor" of the Phillimore plan.[35] House forwarded his views to Wilson.[36]

The president advised against immediate publication of the Phillimore report and against any discussion of it in Parliament that might bind the British government even informally before there was a full interchange of British and American views.[37] Not wishing to appoint a committee to consult with British experts, he preferred to wait to discuss the matter with Lloyd George, who he felt would

---

33. Taft to Bryce, Dec. 5, 1918, Bryce pa., *10*, pp. 107 ff., Bodleian Library, Oxford, the diary of Edward M. House (hereinafter designated by "House diary"), Jan. 13, 1918, Y.H.C.; *I.P. 4*, pp. 12–17, 15, 16, 43–47; Baker, pp. 38, 43, 59; memo., Apr. 12, 1918, J.B. Moore pa., box 1, L.C. See Ruhl J. Bartlett, *The League to Enforce Peace* Chapel Hill, 1944).

34. See Wilton B. Fowler, *British-American Relations, 1917–1918,* pp. 205, 207, 215–16.

35. David Cecil, *The Cecils of Hatfield House* (London, 1973), pp. 294 ff; Kernek, p. 42. On May 17, 1917, Lord Robert Cecil, sending copies of a tentative Phillimore report to House, wrote to Wiseman: "It seems very important that we should as soon as possible clear our ideas on this subject." Wiseman pa.

36. House to W.W., Aug. 9, 1918, Y.H.C. See Baker, *Woodrow Wilson and World Settlement, 3,* pp. 67–78. The British committee made its first report on March 20, 1918. The final report was sent to the president by the British Embassy and acknowledged by him on July 3. See George W. Egerton, "The Lloyd George Government and the Creation of the League of Nations," *American Historical Review, 79, 2,* (April 1974), 428–29. "House . . . tells me he will keep you fully informed. . . . Wilson recognizes the practical difficulties far better than most people suppose." Dispatch for Lord Robert Cecil from Wiseman, July 17, 1918, Wiseman pa.

37. Dispatch, British Foreign Office (designated hereinafter as "F.O.") from Wiseman, July 16, Wiseman pa.; British War Cabinet (designated hereinafter as "B.W.C.") minutes, Oct. 2, 1918, P.R.O., Cab/23/8.

House advised Reading to ask his government not to publicize the Phillimore report. "I do not want them to anticipate the President," House wrote in his diary on July 28. Following the advice of its envoy at Washington, the British government decided to respect Wilson's wish. See Kernek, pp. 92–93.

share his opinions. But in mid-August of 1918 he said he was willing to talk with anyone the British government wished to send him.[38] At that time he considered a proposal for a league constitution that he had asked House to draft, and suggested many changes. Then Wilson did no more work on the project until January of 1919.[39] Meanwhile British and French advocates of a league developed plans for an organization that would meet the particular concerns of their governments.

Wilson had been advised by The Inquiry that he should satisfy the desires of both Allies, to a large extent, by means of a league "for common protection, for the peaceful settlement of international disputes, and for the attainment of a joint economic prosperity."[40] In his concern for the common good of all nations the President refused to consider the proposed league in terms of benefits to particular nations. Mistrustful of the Allied statesmen, he had acted early in 1918 to assert the independent position of his government. When on February 4 the Supreme War Council released a statement of a political nature, Wilson instructed the American "observer" to object to any such release unless the American government was consulted or it was made clear that the United States was not a party to the statement.[41]

Stephanne Lauzanne of *Le Matin,* a French propagandist in the United States, had foreseen friction at the peacemaking when, on April 8, the president disclosed what he called "the real inside of his mind" to a group of journalists from Western Europe. "At the Peace Conference . . . ," Wilson said,

> it will be necessary to repair all past injustices, but I shall never permit anyone to put into practice a policy of plunder. I shall not suffer the annexation of territories against the wishes of their inhabitants. If this happens I shall leave the Conference. As far as I am concerned this principle demands no exceptions, even in colonial matters. . . . I shall not allow anyone to interfere in the internal af-

---

38. Dispatch, Murray from Wiseman, Aug. 10, Wiseman pa.; Reading from Wiseman, Aug. 16, 1918, in Fowler, pp. 278–80.

39. House called his draft a "covenant" because of Wilson's fondness for the word, and adopted many ideas that appeared in a paper finished by his legal adviser, David Hunter Miller, on July 14, 1918. It included a provision for an international court of justice, which Wilson struck out. House drew upon suggestions of Lord Robert Cecil, Lord Grey, Root, Taft, Lowell, and the Phillimore committee. *I.P., 2,* 337, *4,* 6–9, 17–50.

40. Inquiry memorandum of Dec. 22, 1917. See Egerton, 419–37.

41. "A Note on the Working of the Supreme War Council 1917–18," HMG doc. Secret 16311, Charles Webster pa. U491/25/70, London School of Economics Library.

fairs of other states. Nobody has the right to get anything out of this war.[42]

This Paris editor concluded that the president's vanity no longer recognized any limit and he thought he could "play professor for a world empire."

Wilson was sometimes immoderate, too, in his remarks on the policies of Great Britain, whose blockade of Germany during the early years of the war had resulted in interference with American trade that angered him.[43] On August 21, House warned against hurting British *amour propre* so deeply that liberals in England might turn against him.[44] In response to a suggestion by House, the British government had released Lord Reading from his duties as chief justice so that he might bring his talent for negotiation to bear upon critical problems in Washington.[45] House, foreseeing that there would be a general election in Great Britain at the end of the war, tried to induce the British envoy to urge Lloyd George to bring into service more ministers who would be in harmony with Wilson's ideals for peace.[46] However, Reading, returning to London, learned that the British Cabinet had been informed that Wilson was declaring that Great Britain should get no benefits from its war efforts.[47]

In Europe diplomats long accustomed to seek reasonable and precise accommodations of national interests wondered how the American prophet could carry out a pledge to make peace without "any kind of compromise or abatement" of his principles.[48] In their view

---

42. Lauzanne, "Un Universitaire: President Wilson," in *Les Hommes que j'ai vus, souvenirs d'un journaliste* (Paris, 1920), p. 93, trans. by John L.B. Williams, *Great Men and Great Days* (New York, 1921), p. 89. The infelicitous remarks quoted by Lauzanne appear in Swem's transcript of this interview in the Swem papers in the Princeton University Library, but some do not appear in the version printed in Baker, pp. 79–80.

43. Burton J. Hendrick (ed.), *The Life and Letters of Walter Hines Page* (Garden City, N.Y., 1926), 2, p. 347; Gelfand, pp. 15–16; Devlin, *Too Proud to Fight,* pp. 502 and passim.

44. House diary, Aug. 21, 1918.

45. Sir Arthur Willert, *The Road to Safety,* pp. 117–18 and Notebook "I", p. 27, Y.H.C.

46. House diary, July 28, 1919.

47. "Of course I am combatting acceptance," Reading wrote, "but it is creating impressions, and I cannot myself leave entirely out of account other statements made." Telegram to Wiseman from Reading, Aug. 16, 1918, P.R.O., FO/800/US93. Later, Reading reported that several British requests had been turned down by the United States government for reasons that sometimes seemed unconvincing. Cable, Wiseman from Reading, Aug. 28. "I am persistently pressing the President's views . . . ," ibid., Sept. 12, 1918, Y.H.C.

48. Speech of Sept. 27, 1918, Ray Stannard Baker and William E. Dodd (eds.), *The Public Papers of Woodrow Wilson* (hereinafter designated as *"P.P."*) 5, p. 255.

the young nation in the West was asserting itself more strongly than behooved a land that for more than two years had escaped the burden of battle and piled up vast wealth while the Allies poured blood and treasure into a desperate struggle with the common enemy.

European veterans of wartime diplomacy were disturbed by the prospect that peacemaking might fall under the control of a man of whom they knew little and who seemed to be an extreme idealist and maybe even a visionary. All could applaud his pious, conventional wish for a "just and permanent settlement" and some could share his sympathy for small nations and his general vision of a league to preserve peace. But for the development of an adequate policy toward Russia and for the settlement of questions of reparation and boundaries, they found little hope in formulas that they suspected were drafted without adequate understanding of conditions in Europe. There seemed to be too much chance that Wilson's program for peacemaking, set forth in cogent language but with imprecision, would give rise to divergent interpretation and to deception.

Nevertheless, as Europe suffered the attrition of war and the potential of the United States increased,[49] it was politic for European leaders who were skeptical of Wilson's creed to weigh the effect of their words and acts on Washington. They did not venture to speak publicly in opposition to the general principles of the president. They kept in mind the vast power of the United States and their dependence on its economic strength. They were aware of the value of Wilson's creed as a weapon of psychological warfare within the German and Austrian empires. Moreover, they continued to appreciate the appeal of the American doctrine to elements of their peoples who might otherwise accept the creed of Lenin.[50] In England both Liberal and Labour leaders proclaimed the necessity of maintaining peace by international institutions.[51] In France the leftist press and radical minorities in the Chamber of Deputies criticized the government and a mutiny broke out among disillusioned soldiers. In Germany a bloc in the Reichstag demanded parliamentary government and a declaration of democratic war aims.

During the autumn Samuel Gompers, president of the American

---

49. See Renouvin, *Crises du XXe Siècle, 1,* pp. 130–33.

50. "Even if the President had not had American power behind him, it would have been difficult to disavow him without provoking malaise in the minds of a large part of the population in France, Great Britian and Italy." Pierre Renouvin, *L'Armistice de Rethondes,* p. 209.

51. On September 19 a Labour Conference in London endorsed Wilson's Fourteen Points as a basis for peace. A week later the minister of labour urged the cabinet to give attention to preparing a detailed plan for a league of nations. Paper circulated by George Barnes, Sept. 28, 1918, P.R.O., G.T. Series, Cab. 24/65/5815.

Federation of Labor, traveled to England, France, and Italy and made an effort "to allay a disquieting unrest"[52] and to turn the thought of the workers away from revolutionary channels. Wilsonism, however, rather than American trade unionism, was now the new thing around which all who were discontented with the old order could foregather.[53] Nevertheless Colonel House, who kept closely in touch with liberal thinking, warned Wilson that the support of labor in England and France was "uncertain and erratic" and not powerful enough to compel reactionaries to yield to American purposes at the peace conference.[54] Lloyd George, Clemenceau of France and Sonnino of Italy were the men who would have to be reckoned with there.

On September 27, after Austria-Hungary had asked for peace terms and when Germany was about to do likewise, Wilson continued to speak in handsome generalities. Summing up his idealistic program in an address in New York, he proclaimed that the world did not want peace "terms" but the "final triumph of justice and fair dealing." He called for "perfect unity of purpose and of counsel," and invited Allied leaders to respond frankly. Lord Robert Cecil privately praised this speech as "the finest description of our war aims yet uttered;"[55] but Foreign Secretary Balfour, speaking in public three days later and recognizing the necessity of creating a league of nations, asserted the importance of complete victory and a rearrangement of the map of the world that would be in line with British policy and would give the league "a clean slate" on which to work.[56]

The president made his assertions, as he had those in addresses earlier in 1918, without full consideration of the views of the states

---

52. Report of Consul Tracy Lay on the status of socialism, Oct. 28, 1918, National Archives (hereinafter designated as "N.A."), Record Group (hereinafter designated "R.G.") 59, document 851.00/59; W.H. Buckler to I. Laughlin, Oct. 29, 1918, Wilson pa., 5B. According to Buckler, who accompanied him, Gompers spent two weeks in France and ten days in Italy, testified that American workers were solidly loyal to their government, and "served as a real mascot," establishing friendly relations with responsible Labour and Socialist organizations in the Allied nations. Buckler to Brent Keyser, Nov. 2, 1918, Bowman pa., Eisenhower Library, The Johns Hopkins University, file 1.

Gompers helped to combat pacifism in the ranks at an inter-Allied Labor Conference in September 1918, where the program of Wilson was heartily applauded. Wiseman to Murray, Aug. 30; Murray to Wiseman, Sept. 9 and Oct. 1, 1918, Wiseman pa.

53. Cole (ed.), *Beatrice Webb's Diaries* (London, 1952), p. 105.

54. House to W.W., Sept. 3, 1918, Y.H.C.

55. Cable, Cecil to House, Sept. 28, 1918, *I.P., 4,* p. 72.

56. J.B. Scott (ed.), *Official Statements of War Aims and Peace Proposals,* Dec. 1916–Nov. 1918, Washington, D.C., 1921, pp. 407–9.

that had contributed most to the defeat of the common enemy. He was confident of the adequacy of America's material power to command the acquiescence of the exhausted combatants of Europe.

The American prophet of peace stood aloof and independent. The leader who talked most about "common counsel" continued to be difficult to consult. The leverage that built up from his detachment had been achieved only at the risk of misunderstanding and even hostility. "It was a very narrow line," H.G. Nicholas has written, "that separated the disinterestedness of a spokesman for humanity from the presumption of an intruder who had come late into the conflict and, by the terrible accountancy of war, had bought his seat at the peace conference at a discount."[57]

---

57. H.G. Nicholas in J. Joseph Huthmacher and Warren I. Susman (eds.), *Wilson's Diplomacy,* pp. 80–81.

☆ II ☆

Wilson, the Arbiter of Peace

The remote moral position in which Wilson held the United States, irritating though it was to the Allied governments, served well in bringing about an armistice. When in October both the German and Austrian governments came to the president with proposals for peace negotiations based on his conditions, the president was able to bring the fighting to an end within six weeks. He had put forth in his idealistic program such principles as the defeated peoples could grasp in an effort to escapt utter humiliation. "We have no jealousy of German greatness," he had said in his Fourteen Points speech, "and there is nothing in this programme that impairs it. . . . We wish her only to accept a place of equality among the peoples of the world . . . instead of a place of mastery." A month later he had declared that there should be "no annexations, no contributions, no punitive damages."[1] Depending on the prestige that he had built by his speeches, the president took full responsibility for conducting negotiations. He achieved his end not by conference or conversation but by writing masterful notes to which he gave publicity. Confident that there were moral forces within the Central Empires that would welcome his ideals, he adhered persistently to his liberal platform.

Wilson wished to protect the military advantage of the Allies and at the same time to prevent the ravaging of enemy lands. He was determined to avoid any statement that might harden resistance to the point of desperation.

On the other hand, the president had left no doubt of his detestation of the militarists who ruled Germany. After the Germans, on March 3 at Brest-Litovsk, had forced a humiliating settlement on

---

1. *P.P., 5,* pp. 161,180.

Russia while professing a desire to make a fair peace, he spoke out more than once against the "aggrandizement" and "selfish ambitions" of the military masters. In his address of September 27 he said that it would be impossible to come to terms with such dishonorable men. He warned that Germany would "have to redeem her character." But in his soul, hatred and distrust mingled with a determination to rise above the dictates of Old Testament practice and to act in a Christian spirit.

When a note came to Washington from Berlin on October 6, requesting "the immediate conclusion of a general armistice" and asking the president to invite all belligerents to discuss a peace based on his program, no understanding had been reached with the Allies. The European leaders were not fully informed of Wilson's intentions. Reports of their unhappiness had been coming to Washington for some weeks from American officials in France. As early as August, General Tasker H. Bliss, the military representative of the United States on the Supreme War Council, reported that political issues were injecting themselves into the military deliberations and his English colleagues wished to have an understanding among the Allies while there was still enough pressure from the enemy to hold them in a united front. On August 22 Bliss wrote to Secretary of War Newton D. Baker that his English colleagues told him plainly that in their belief no one but the United States could lead in a get-together movement.[2]

The president rejected a suggestion that he consult the Allies before replying to Germany. He explained that the German note was too vague to justify reference to the European governments, and moreover, such a course would cause a delay that would damage the martial spirit of the army and the public.[3] On October 8 he sent off a note that he had prepared in consultation with House.[4] It asked three questions: Would Germany agree to base negotiations on the principles he had set forth? Would the Germans consent immediately to withdraw their forces everywhere from invaded territory?

---

2. This letter was forwarded to the president on Sept. 17. Baker, pp. 348–50.

3. Telegram, Barclay to F.O., Oct. 9, 1918, Balfour pa., 49741, British Museum; House diary, Oct. 24, 28, 1918, Y.H.C.; dispatch, Wiseman from Reading, Oct. 12, 1918, Y.H.C.

4. House thought Wilson's draft too mild to satisfy Americans who demanded unconditional surrender. "He did not realize," House wrote, "how war mad our people have become. This, I thought, had to be taken into consideration, but not, of course, to the extent of meeting it where it was wrong." House diary, Oct. 9, 1918. Only a few weeks before, House had criticized Senator Lodge for "helping the German military party to sustain itself through the winter" by his insistence on crushing Germany. Diary, Aug. 25.

Did the new chancellor speak "merely for the constituted authorities of the Empire who have so far conducted the war"?

The State Department, in order to appease Americans who demanded unconditional surrender on the part of Germany, confidentially asked journalists to insist that this note was no reply to the German overture and in no sense a commitment on the part of the president, but merely an inquiry preliminary to a reply.[5]

The statesmen of the Allies, however, were not satisfied by this interpretation of the independent action of the American government. Jealous of their right to take part in negotiations for ending the fight of which their peoples had borne the brunt, they saw a possibility that Wilson's response might give to Germany a chance to get rid of its emperor, alter its constitution, and withdraw its armies, only to regroup them and prepare for more fighting. Moreover, it seemed to Prime Minister Lloyd George that Wilson's note implied that he would recommend an armistice if the Fourteen Points were accepted, and thus Great Britain, which totally rejected the curb on its maritime operations imposed by Point II, might be put in the embarrassing position of standing in the way of an ending of hostilities. Lord Robert Cecil warned against any commitment to the position that no peace could be made with the Hohenzollerns, and there was a reluctance to try to arrange Germany's internal affairs.[6]

In contrast with the standoffish attitude of Wilson, the leaders of the Allies had learned to take counsel together. The exigencies of the war had led them to depend less on their diplomatic corps than on their own political instincts. When they heard of Germany's appeal to Washington, the premiers were meeting at Paris with no Americans present, and had just drawn up conditions for an armistice with Turkey, which they decided not to make known to Wilson immediately.[7] They asked their generals at Versailles to prepare in

---

5. Dispatch, Tardieu (at New York) to Ministère des Affaires Étrangères (designated hereinafter as M.A.E.), Oct. 9, 1918, Archives Diplomatique du M.A.E., À paix, A1017.1, fascicule (designated hereinafter as "f.") 45.

6. Maurice Hankey, *The Supreme Command, 1914–1918, 2,* 854; Minutes of the Imperial War Cabinet (designated hereinafter as "I.W.C."), Oct. 11, Minutes of the B.W.C., Oct. 11, 15, 1918; Pierre Renouvin, *L'Armistice de Rethondes,* pp. 134–35; English minutes and French procès-verbal for meeting of premiers, Oct. 9, 1918, Archives Historiques du Ministère de Guerre, Château de Vincennes, "Fonds Clemenceau" (Designated hereinafter as "F.C."), 6N69, "Negotiations de Paix."

7. The European premiers wished "to keep President Wilson's fingers out of the Turkish pie." Stephen Roskill, *Hankey: Man of Secrets, 1,* pp. 606, 608–9. Although the United States was not at war with Turkey, the British Foreign Office thought Washington should be kept informed, and therefore the suggested armistice terms were eventually delivered to Wilson on October 19, five days after he had received an ap-

consultation with naval experts a statement of terms for Germany that would guarantee security and that they could present to Wilson in case he insisted on generalities that they thought vague.[8]

Arthur Hugh Frazier came into the meeting of the three premiers to find out why they were conferring outside the Supreme War Council and what they were saying.[9] He reported to Washington that there was an undercurrent of hurt pride. Frazier, a career diplomat, had been assigned to special missions of Colonel House during the war, and had served as "diplomatic liaison officer," not a participant, at sessions of the Supreme War Council.[10] He was Wilson's ear but not his voice. House wrote of him: "He had enjoyed long personal contact with the prime ministers and ministers of foreign affairs of the Allied governments and they held him in such esteem as to be willing to share with him their conferences."[11] However, Lord Robert Cecil reported that Frazier had been "waiting about outside the doors . . . to pick up crumbs of information" which were not given to him.[12] The president, suspecting that he might give offense by listening in by deputy on conversations in which he was unwilling to take part, had once suggested that if Frazier detected such a feeling on the part of Clemenceau, it might be well for him tactfully to withdraw.[13]

The premiers were indeed resentful of Wilson's refusal to call his nation an "ally" or to send a duly accredited representative to speak with authority on his behalf while he seemed to expect to be kept fully informed. Lloyd George remarked that it was the president's own fault if he was not properly represented; and Clemenceau said: "He wishes to remain isolated and superior. He is Jupiter."[14] But the

---

peal from Turkey for intercession. The British Cabinet advised the president to tell the Turkish government to apply for an armistice to the forces opposing them. On the thirty-first the United States government did so. But the armistice of Mudros had been signed the day before. See Sterling J. Kernek, *Distractions of Peace during War,* pp. 100–101.

8. French procès-verbal, Oct. 7, 9, 1918, F.C., 6N69. See Sir Frederick Barton Maurice, *The Armistices of 1918* (London, 1943), pp. 29 ff., and David F. Trask, *The U.S. in the Supreme War Council,* p. 154. A copy of the document prepared by the military and naval advisers entitled "Avis Collectif: Étude des conditions d'un armistice avec l'Allemagne et l'Austrie-Hongrie" is in F.C., 6N72. A note from Foch proposed conditions less harsh than those recommended by the advisers. See Guy Pedroncini, *Les Négociations Secrètes pendant la Grande Guerre,* pp. 99–100.

9. Roskill, *1,* p. 608.

10. Cable, Bliss to House, Feb. 27, 1918, Y.H.C.

11. *I.P., 4,* p. 228.

12. Telegram Derby to Drummond, Oct. 7, 1918, Balfour pa., 4973.

13. W.W. to House, March 20, 1918, Y.H.C.

14. British and French procès-verbaux of meetings of Oct. 6, 7, 1918.

Europeans were too tactful to give Frazier more than a hint of the depth of their feelings.[15]

Lloyd George, piqued because the press had been given Wilson's note before it was communicated to the premiers, was disposed to speak out before the Germans could embarrass the Allied governments by replying affirmatively to the president's questions. Clemenceau, however, accepted with appreciation the strong position in which Wilson had put the Allies. The president's note, he said, "commits us to nothing and leaves us time to turn to our military men. . . . The Germans would seize upon the first word we said as evidence that we are responsible for the continuation of the war." He was willing to accept Lloyd George's desire to send a cautionary note to Wilson, but warned against any publicity for the message that might offend the president.[16]

Accordingly, a formal note was addressed to Wilson from the prime ministers of Great Britain, France, and Italy. It held that the conditions of an armistice could be fixed only after consultation with military experts and in accordance with the military situation. The message made it clear that the evacuation of territory invaded by the Germans would not be an adequate guarantee against a revival of hostilities.[17] Actually, as Orlando pointed out on October 9, Wilson had set down evacuation not as a condition of an armistice but as the condition under which he would agree to propose to the Allies a discussion of the possibility of an armistice. Nevertheless, Lloyd George continued to complain of the president's independence, feeling that he himself was "left out in the cold."[18]

The president was as distrustful of the talks in Paris as were the European premiers of his correspondence with Germany. Terms proposed by the generals might lay a basis of peace that could not be altered easily. In particular, to police the banks of the Rhine might

15. Roskill, *1*, 608. Premier Orlando of Italy expressed the sense of the meeting when he said: "One must do nothing that might offend the United States." French procès-verbal, Oct. 6, 1918.

16. French procès-verbaux of meetings of Oct. 8, 9, 1918.

17. Frazier to State Dept., dispatches of Oct. 8, 9, 1918, *Papers Relating to the Foreign Relations of the U.S.* (hereinafter designated as *F.R.*), *1918, I, 1,* 345–46, 351–54.

18. Cable, Sir Arthur Murray to Wiseman, Oct. 23, 1918, Wiseman pa., Y.H.C. See Riddell, George Allardice, Baron, *Lord Riddell's Intimate Diary of the Peace Conference and After,* entry of Oct. 13, 1918.

General Sir Henry Wilson recorded the discussions in the British Cabinet in his diary: "Lloyd George took the line that we pandered and bowed too much to President Wilson. Bob Cecil and Bonar Law [Lord Privy Seal] were all in favor of conciliating him. I agree with Lloyd George, and am certain that a few good home truths would do the President good." Charles E. Callwell, *Field Marshall Sir Henry Wilson, 2,* p. 134.

give France a hold that it would be difficult later to break and that might goad Germany to violent vengeance.

However, General Bliss, too ill to attend a meeting of the military representatives, independently informed the premiers in writing that he personally agreed with the report of his European military colleagues.[19] But he did not sign their report, and in a personal letter to Secretary of War Baker he said he could not do so because it would commit the president to a policy that Wilson had already decided he could not adopt.[20]

Wilson was fearful that the Allies might come to an agreement without consulting him, and that the terms drafted by the military men at Paris might put the enemy in fear of extermination and make them fight on in desperation. He was very perturbed and discussed Bliss's report with Secretary of State Lansing and Chief of Staff Peyton C. March. The envoys of the Allied governments were asked for an explanation of what Lansing characterized as the "extraordinary procedure" of the premiers.[21] At the same time the French ambassador, Jules Jusserand, was told that Wilson misunderstood the situation as a result of maladroit drafting of Bliss's report.[22]

At this point the diplomats of the Allies sought to assure the president that their governments were merely going through the routine usual when wars reached an end. They denied that they had come to any definite agreement on armistice terms. Balfour explained in a personal note to the president that there had been merely a discussion of what terms would be proper in case there was an armistice. In other communications he suggested that, first, it be made clear to the Germans that an armistice could be granted only on terms that would make it impossible for them to resume hostilities, and, second, that the British government would "object most strongly" to some of the Fourteen Points and probably would have to insist on additional

---

19. Bliss liked to think that he had more independence of political action than his military colleagues. "Fortunately for me," he wrote in his diary on January 1, 1919, "the American Government was too far away for restrictive intervention and I consequently was left with a free hand." Nevertheless, he wrote about October 8, 1918, to the premiers of France, Great Britain and Italy: "I, personally, concur [in the "Avis collectif" of the military representatives] . . . but must await the instructions of my government for which I have cabled before signing it." Doc. in F.C., 6N72.

20. Bliss to N.D. Baker, Oct. 9, Bliss to War Dept., tel. no. 244, Oct. 8, 1918, Wilson pa., 2, L.C.

21. Polk diary, Oct. 9, 1918 Y.H.C.; Lansing desk diary, Oct. 9, 1918, L.C.; dispatch, Barclay to F.O., Oct. 9, 1918, Balfour pa., 49748.

22. Dispatch, Jusserand to M.A.E., Oct. 17, 1918, Archives du M.A.E. À paix, A1017.1, f. 45, doc. 13.

conditions.[23] The British wished to reserve their freedom of action in the peacemaking and to negotiate immediately for agreement on questions in doubt.

Jusserand, acting by virtue of seniority as spokesman at Washington, presented the views of the European premiers. He learned from Secretary Lansing that Wilson was *"très choqué"* because the Allies had prepared armistice terms, and that the president had said that if the American people knew how far the Allies had gone it would be impossible to resist a demand on their part for the recall of American troops from Europe.[24] The French ambassador went to the White House and reported that in a long conversation (which Jusserand described as very friendly) the president made it clear that he agreed with the Allies that the withdrawal of German troops would not be sufficient for the granting of a truce. Wilson expressed regret at the action of the Allied premiers and spoke of the importance of withholding from his people any suggestion of a forthcoming armistice that might weaken their morale. When the ambassador remarked that it was essential that the United States be represented in the councils at Paris by someone who knew the president's mind and could take an effective part in decisions,[25] Wilson explained that such an agent might be too much influenced by his surroundings and unable to speak as an American. Jusserand responded that it was not impossible to find a man of the necessary savoir faire and political sense who could negotiate while keeping directly in contact with the president. Wilson promised to consider this advice seriously; and the ambassador left with the impression that the misunderstanding had been cleared up.[26]

Actually, two days later Wilson indicated in a talk with Colonel House that he was still "much exercised," not only because the Supreme War Council had acted without consulting him, but because he thought it a mistake for anyone to go into details at this time

23. Wiseman to Reading, Oct. 10, 1918, Balfour pa., 44741; Wiseman from Reading, Oct. 12, 1918, Y.H.C.; Lansing to W.W., Oct. 13, 1918, Wilson pa., 2; Hankey, pp. 855–56; cable, Reading for Wiseman, Oct. 13, 1918, Y.H.C.; telegram for Reading from Barclay, Oct. 16, 1918, P.R.O./800/US/90; Minutes of the B.W.C., Oct. 11, 21, 1918.

It seemed to the editor of *The Times* that Balfour maintained "the sound Anglo-American point of view" when the "peculiar temperament" of Lloyd George raised a "real risk" of friction. Dawson to Willert, Oct. 4, 1918, Willert pa., Y.H.C.

24. Jusserand to Diplomatie, Paris, Oct. 9, 1918, Archives du M.A.E., À paix, A1017.1, f. 45.

25. The Allied premiers had agreed to ask for an American consultant who had the confidence of the United States government and could inform them of its views. French procès-verbal, Oct. 9, Annexe II.

26. Several dispatches, Jusserand to M.A.E., Ministère to Jusserand, Oct. 11, 12, 1918, Archives du M.A.E., À paix, A1017.1, f. 45.

about armistice terms.[27] Nevertheless Wilson's second note to Berlin, dispatched on October 14 after the German government had responded favorably to his three questions, reflected the counsel that came to him from abroad as well as from advisers at Washington.[28] It stated that no armistice would be granted that did not, in the judgment of the military advisers, provide "absolutely satisfactory safeguards and guarantees of the maintenance of the present military supremacy of the armies of the United States and of the Allies in the field."[29] In spite of this promise, however, the Allied ministers were still fearful that Germany would not understand that it must give up certain territory, such as Alsace-Lorraine.[30]

On the day this note was sent a step was taken toward closer rapport with the Allies. There was at the moment no American ambassador in England and no British ambassador in the United States. Walter Hines Page, scornful of House[31] and so pro-British that he had lost Wilson's confidence, was too ill to function at London.

At this juncture the Allied chiefs requested that Wilson send House to Europe. The Europeans felt they could negotiate with him in a way that would smooth over jealousies and misunderstandings.[32] Wilson naturally turned to House, his representative in earlier missions to Europe, to undertake this delicate assignment, giving him credentials that made him virtually an attorney for the president. A secret code was arranged for their communications, and as the men parted Wilson said, "I have not given you any instructions because I feel you will know what to do."[33]

Wilson was not accustomed to rely upon the counsel of the secretary of state. Robert Lansing was learned in international law and experienced in its practice, yet the president thought him stupid, and too fearful of the opinion of the electorate. When Wilson characterized a speech by Lansing as "too flat-footed," House wrote:

---

27. House diary, Oct. 13, 1918; Polk diary, Oct. 11, 14, 1918.

28. House diary, Oct. 15; Josephus Daniels diary, Oct. 13, 14, 1918, L.C.

29. In the cabinet meeting of October 15 Balfour criticized Wilson's second note to Germany, calling it "one of the most humorous documents ever produced." The foreign secretary said the president was "a first-rate rhetorician and a very bad draftsman," and noted the inconsistency of Wilson's resolve to destroy arbitrary power in Germany and his laissez-faire policy toward Russia. Keith Middlemas (ed.), *Whitehall Diary, 1,* London, 1969, p. 68.

30. Kernek, p. 99.

31. "They are laughing at the 'empty House' here," Ambassador Page had written in his diary on Feb. 9, 1916, Page pa., Houghton Library, Harvard University. Also see ibid., Feb. 13, 18, 1916. House had found Page so uncooperative that he felt it necessary to act without the ambassador and to refrain from telling him what was done for fear he would take offence. House diary, Aug. 24, 1918.

32. See below, p. 38.

33. House diary, Oct. 15, 1918.

"That is the trouble with Lansing. He has never had, and never can have, the diplomatic touch."[34]

When a final note came from Berlin that seemed to indicate capitulation, the president, lacking House's advice, undertook to get opinions of foreign diplomats. In a talk with Jusserand on the twenty-first, he weighed the relative advantages of a Hohenzollern or a Bolshevist government in Germany. The former would not be strong, he said, and the latter would be incapable of paying reparations.[35]

On October 22 he took the cabinet into his confidence. Reflecting the elemental feelings of the American people, to which political opponents were appealing vigorously, some of the men called for unconditional surrender. Wilson spoke of the force of public opinion. The hysteria of die-hards, he said, might make him take to a "cyclone cellar" for forty-eight hours; but labor was asking why Americans should fight on for the imperialist purposes of Europeans. To a suggestion that the publishing of peace notes without the consent of the Allies might seem to them a form of coercion, Wilson replied that they needed to be coerced. It was agreed that American influence on the peace could be greater at present than later; for the national aims of the several Allies would be asserted more strongly as victory became assured.[36]

The president's third and last note went off to Berlin on October 23. It stated that he deemed it his duty to repeat that "the only armistice he would feel justified in submitting for consideration would be one which should leave the United States and the Powers associated with her in a position to enforce any arrangements that may be entered into and to make a renewal of hostilities on the part of Germany impossible." The president insisted that if the United States government must deal with "the military masters and the monarchical autocrats of Germany . . . it must demand, not peace negotiations, but surrender."

He outlined a definite course to end hostilities:

> Having received the solemn and explicit assurance of the German Government that it unreservedly accepts the peace terms laid

34. House diary, Sept. 24, 27, Oct. 13, 1918. House recognized that Lansing's ideas were "good along certain lines, especially as to techniques." Diary, Oct. 13, 1917.

35. Jusserand to M.A.E., Oct. 21, 1918, Archives du M.A.E., À paix, 1017.1, f. 45, p. 22.

36. Franklin K. Lane, *The Letters of Franklin K. Lane,* ed. by A.W. Lane and L.H. Wall, pp. 293–96; Daniels, Josephus, *The Cabinet Diaries of Josephus Daniels,* ed. by E. David Cronon pp. 342–44.

down . . . and that this wish and purpose emenate . . . from ministers who speak for the majority of the Reichstag and for an overwhelming majority of the German people: . . . the President . . .
feels that he cannot decline to take up with the Governments with
which the Government of the United States is associated the question of an armistice. . . .

The President has, therefore, transmitted his correspondence
with the present German authorities to the Governments with
which the Government of the United States is associated as a belligerent, with the suggestion that, if those Governments are disposed
to effect peace upon the terms and principles indicated [the Fourteen Points and supplementary principles], their military advisers
and the military advisers of the United States be asked to submit to
the Governments associated against Germany the necessary terms
of such an armistice as will fully protect the interests of the peoples
involved and ensure to the associate Governments the unrestricted
power to safeguard and enforce the details of the peace to which
the German Government has agreed, provided they deem such an
armistice possible from the military point of view.

On the same day copies of the note and the previous correspondence with Germany were transmitted to the Allies, without any
recommendations of specific armistice terms. They were asked to
take the matter under consideration and to communicate their views
to the American government. Secretary Lansing wrote: "I wish to
point out . . . that the President has endeavored to safeguard with
the utmost care the interests of the peoples at war with Germany in
every statement made in the enclosed correspondence, and that it is
his sincere hope that your Government will think that he has succeeded and will be willing to cooperate in the step which he has
suggested."[37]

The press of France and Great Britain were almost unanimous in
approving this note.[38] Lloyd George liked its tenor, although it did
not eliminate fears of a challenge to British sea-power. The Cabinet,
which took the view that the Allies would not be committed to the
Fourteen Points if Wilson accepted the German proposals, decided
that Balfour should notify the United States that Great Britain could
not agree to the doctrine of "freedom of the seas"; but Lord Reading had warned of the importance of cordial relations with Wilson
and it was decided the next day that Balfour should not send a tele-

---

37. *F.R., 1918, Suppl. 1, 1,* 381–83; Lansing desk diary, Oct. 23, 1918.
38. Pierre Renouvin, *L'Armistice de Rethondes,* pp. 134–35. On the views of the
Allies of Wilson's notes, see V.H. Rothwell, *British War Aims and Peace Diplomacy,* pp.
252, 255 and Kernek, pp. 96–100.

gram he had drafted, but that he and Lloyd George should make the British position perfectly clear at the Peace Conference.[39]

Wilson had carried through a strategy of peacemaking that at once met the military necessities and challenged both sides to accept his program. Within five days he had replies from both the enemy and the associated powers.[40]

At Berlin officials were depending on President Wilson to extricate their people from the morass of hopelessness into which they were falling as their military machine collapsed. The president's independence of action was therefore most welcome. "The United States alone can bring help and save the world from worse misery," wrote Count von Bernstorff, who had been ambassador at Washington, to House.[41] The new political regime of Prince Max of Baden, declaring the military power to be now subject to it, replied to Wilson on October 27 with an assertion that the German people were in control of their government, actually and constitutionally. In expressing interest in an armistice as "the first step towards a peace of justice, as decided by the President in his pronouncements," the message reminded Wilson of the responsibility toward Germany that he assumed by accepting the original German proposal that his principles serve as the basis of the peacemaking.

Simultaneously with his correspondence with Germany the president was exchanging peace notes with Austria-Hungary. In the past he had held various views about the future of the peoples of that state. On December 4, 1917 he had said to the Congress: "We do not wish in any way to impair or to rearrange the Austro-Hungarian Empire." In his Point Ten he went only so far as to say: "The peoples of Austria-Hungary, whose place among the nations we wish to see safeguarded and assured, should be accorded the freest opportunity of autonomous development." Very reluctant to permit propaganda that would encourage revolutionary activity, Wilson had cautioned the State Department against any sanction of "irresponsible agents" in the Hapsburg empire.[42]

---

39. Minutes of the B.W.C., Oct. 22, 24, 25, 26, 1918, Curzon pa., India House Library, box 72, F/12/132; brief for the Cabinet, "The President's message of Oct. 23, 1918," Balfour pa., 49699. For the opinions of British ministers of Wilson's policy, see Harold I. Nelson, *Land and Power*, pp. 69–72, and Sir Winston L.S. Churchill, *The Aftermath*, p. 99.

40. The answer of the Allies was a draft of military and naval terms for an armistice, which House received from Clemenceau and forwarded to Washington on the twenty-seventh. See below, p. 42.

41. Von Bernstorff to House, Oct. 11, 1918, Y.H.C.

42. For example, Secretary Lansing had received a veto from the President of a proposal by Congressman Fiorello LaGuardia, on duty in Italy as a captain in the Sig-

As the year 1918 progressed, however, it seemed less important to consider the possibility of a separate peace with the Hapsburg government. The future seemed to lie in the hands of Masaryk of Czechoslovakia, Paderewski of Poland, and other spokesmen for the "oppressed nationalities" that received encouragement from blood brothers who had migrated to the United States.[43] The president had consented to a statement released by Secretary Lansing on May 29, announcing the sympathy of the United States for the "national aspirations" of the Slavs. Lansing had made it clear on June 28 that the United States government took the position that all branches of the Slav race should be completely free from German or Austrian rule.

On October 19, replying to a second appeal from Vienna for an armistice, the president reaffirmed this policy. He was now willing to accept a breakup into native states, and at the same time he assured the French government that he would respect its desire that no encouragement be given to any merger of Austria with Germany.[44] He wrote thus to Vienna:

> the Government of the United States has recognized that a state of belligerency exists between the Czecho-Slovaks and the German and Austro-Hungarian Empires and that the Czecho-Slovak National Council is a *de facto* belligerent government clothed with proper authority to direct the military and political affairs of the Czecho-Slovaks. It has also recognized in the fullest manner the justice of the nationalistic aspirations of the Jugo-Slavs for freedom. The President is, therefore, no longer at liberty to accept the mere "autonomy" of these peoples as a basis of peace, but is obliged to insist that they, and not he, shall be the judges of what action on the part of the Austro-Hungarian Government will satisfy their aspirations and their conception of their rights and destiny as members of the family of nations.

This statement, in conjunction with the proclamation by the Hapsburg emperor of a plan for autonomy and federation, encouraged

nal Corps, that he join with a Hungarian politician in instigating revolution in Budapest. Lansing, by Wilson's direction, notified the Embassy in Rome that the United States government did not want "anyone associated with it to be in any way associated with efforts towards revolution in Austria-Hungary," W.W. to Sec. State, Jan. 1, Lansing to T.N. Page, Jan. 5. 1918, N.A., RG 59, 864.00/20.

43. See below, ch. XI.

44. Jusserand to M.A.E., Oct. 12, 1918, Archives du M.A.E. À paix, 1918–20, A 1017.1, f. 45. Wilson's respect for the French apprehension was perhaps not made clear to Clemenceau, who was annoyed by the president's independent note to Vienna. Minutes of the B.W.C., Oct. 22, 1918, Curzon pa. Lloyd George again thought that Wilson was unfair in putting the Allies in an embarrassing position.

insurgent forces that broke up the empire beyond mending. On October 27 Vienna responded to the adverse tide of battle by asking for armistice terms.[45]

Thus Wilson's program of peace, set forth in eloquent messages during the last ten months of the war in response to the challenge of social revolution, provided the basis on which the enemy agreed to end hostilities. But if the president was to be the arbiter of peace, the Allies had still to be persuaded to respond favorably to a condition set forth in his note of October 23: that the presentation of military terms to the enemy would be contingent upon a disposition on the part of the Allies "to effect peace upon the terms and principles indicated."

The independence that had characterized the action of the United States government had provoked questioning in Europe of the disinterestedness of the "associated Power." The American army fought valiantly but preferred to operate under its own flag, and only dire necessity had brought it to accept a French commander-in-chief. The Americans supplied vast riches and used these ingeniously to produce the engines of war. They preferred to employ wealth and machinery in ways of their own devising and immense credit balances arose in their accounts. When their charity spanned the ocean and nourished millions of innocent victims of warfare, it was their own administrators who directed the distribution of their own products. President Wilson was insisting that the United States stand aloof from the alliance with which he made common cause against the Central Powers. His goals were peaceful and ecumenical; but to attain them he would use, if necessary, the material power of his nation. Its president might even hope to bring about a *pax Americana*.

The battle-hardened statesmen of Europe raised their eyebrows. In the proud, independent voices that came from across the ocean French leaders detected echoes of the "troublesome and garrulous patriotism" of which Tocqueville wrote. It seemed to Clemenceau, who had lived in the United States for a few years after the Civil War, spoke its language, and knew its people well, that though they were descended from most of the races of the world, they were "26,000 times more proud of being American than the Frenchman

---

45. Arthur J. May, *The Passing of the Hapsburg Monarchy*, 2 (Philadelphia, 1966), pp. 764–72, 797, 821; Victor S. Mamatey, *The United States and East Central Europe, 1914–1918*, pp. 333–34. See below, pp. 49–50. "Wilson's notes were undoubtedly the foremost instrument of Austria-Hungary's downfall." Robert W. Seton-Watson, *Britain and the Dictators*, p. 50.

of being French."[46] The prospect of conciliatory negotiation was not brightened by the fact that wartime leaders of the Allies disliked the American president and Lloyd George mistrusted him as a political rival.[47]

---

46. Jean Martet, *Le Silence de M. Clemenceau* (Paris, 1929), p. 95; *Georges Clemenceau* (New York, 1930), p. 59.

47. House diary, Aug. 22, 1918; telegram, Derby to Drummond, Oct. 7, 1918, Balfour pa., 49738.

The Diplomacy of Colonel House

Despite the skepticism with which European leaders regarded the diplomacy of Wilson, his principles had become popular religion in Western Europe, a creed to which the forces of Good could rally to joust with Evil. In the view of Walter Lippmann, observing public opinion in France and England, the president was "a figure of mystical proportions, of really incredible power but altogether out of reach."[1] No one who spoke for the United States at Paris at the end of the war would be able to renounce the ideals that had served so well to bring the struggle to a victorious end and that now might exalt the president as the ethical arbiter of the world. By his speeches and notes he had added moral authority to the stark reality of America's economic and military potential; and the past aloofness of Americans from treaties among European governments gave them stature now as mediators without prejudice.

It was to require all the tact and good will of Colonel House, however, to soothe the irritation of the leaders of the Western Allies at the independent and admonitory attitude that the American president had taken. House had noted, when Lloyd George and Wilson vied for leadership of liberal thought at the beginning of 1918, that it was "not so much general accomplishment that those in authority seem to desire as accomplishment which may redound to their own personal advantage." House was fully aware of the rivalry for political dominance,[2] and had worked faithfully with Foreign Secretary

---

1. Lippmann to Mezes, Sept. 5, 1918, Mezes pa., Butler Library, Columbia University.
2. House diary, Jan. 3, 1918, Y.H.C. See Sterling J. Kernek, *Distractions of Peace during War*, p. 110 and note 5.

Balfour, through Reading and Wiseman, to overcome its menace to Anglo-American understanding.

Edward M. House had made a reputation for sagacity as a friendly counselor to governors of Texas, and for his services received the honorary title of "colonel." Ambitious to play an impresario's role in the drama of history, he made himself agreeable to the president by supplying reliable information, by insinuating advice without offense, by expressing dissent usually by silence, and by taking care not to oversell himself or his ideas.

After a talk with Wilson on October 14, the "colonel" wrote: "I have a feeling that not until we are together again will I meet a mind so sympathetic with my own. He has his weaknesses, his prejudices and his limitations like other men, but all in all Woodrow Wilson will probably go down in history as the great figure of his time, and I hope, of all times." One could expect that the president's counselor would share in the glory.

After America's entry into the war Wilson had concentrated on the immediate necessity of military victory while House pursued preparations for peacemaking. A liberal by instinct, the colonel hoped to use leftist movements for the promotion of the constitutional government that he envisioned for Germany, and even for Russia.[3] He was in some doubt as to the length to which the president would go to force the Allies to accept the principles that he avowed. Eager to ascertain to what extent Wilson would want the Allies to be apprised of his intentions, House arranged to have him talk with Sir William Wiseman, who acted in liaison between the British Foreign Office and the White House.[4] Wiseman, who came to enjoy the confidence of Wilson and House more than any other foreign diplomat, perceived a necessity for great patience in dealing with the United States. "The American nation," he wrote,

> is making its first appearance as a great world-power. They have been flattered unduly by each of the Allies in turn, and will no doubt receive a subtle form of flattery from the enemy. We must remember that after peace is signed we shall by no means have finished with America. We shall not even have finished with President Wilson. During the difficult period of reconstruction, it will be nec-

---

3. House diary, June 28, 1918. See Norman Gordon Levin, *Woodrow Wilson and World Politics.* House thought the president was brusque and offensive to socialist and labor groups when Wilson pleased die-hards by rejecting an Austrian peace feeler in September.

4. House recorded that he arranged Wilson's conversation of October 16 with Wiseman "in order to find how much [of] his mind the President wished disclosed to the British and other Allied governments." Diary, Oct. 22, 1918.

essary for the two nations to work together in harmony. . . . In
spite of jealousy and misunderstanding, the British and American
peoples believe in the same things and follow the same ideals."[5]

Wiseman suggested to Wilson that he might profit by taking counsel with the Allied governments, which were studying the effect of
the peace notes on the Germans and on their own peoples. The
president replied that he was always willing to consult but time and
distance made it almost impossible. He was therefore sending
House, he said, and he wished to remind those who called for the
colonel's services abroad that he himself would now have no one
with whom to take counsel.[6]

House sailed for France on October 18, before the president had
concluded his exchange of notes with the German government. He
was accompanied by Wiseman, who went to London to continue to
advise his government on American affairs during the peacemaking.
Residing in the same apartment house in New York, these friends
had worked unofficially and effectively to serve the common cause
of victory and Anglo-American understanding. Each received valuable information from the other. Wiseman had come to feel that
House and Wilson regarded him as perhaps their chief source of information.[7]

House, as he crossed the Atlantic with Wiseman, questioned the
effectiveness of the president's peace note of the twenty-third. He

---

5. Six-page paper by Wiseman, "The Attitude of the U.S. and of President Wilson towards the Peace Conference," undated, Wiseman pa., Y.H.C.

6. Wiseman to Reading, cable, Oct. 16, 1918, Y.H.C.; House diary, Oct. 22, 1918.

7. Wiseman to Murray, Sept. 4, 1918, Y.H.C.; Wiseman to the writer, April 21,
1960. See Wilton B. Fowler, *British-American Relations, 1917–1918,* and Patrick Devlin,
Too Proud to Fight, 609–13; Sir Arthur Willert, *Washington and Other Memories,* pp.
91–92.

House recorded in his diary on Nov. 10, 1917: "Balfour offered me the freedom
of the Foreign Office, stating I might have any papers they had no matter of how confidential a nature. As a matter of fact, I get everything they have from Sir William
Wiseman and others." This may have been true at that date; but Wiseman's correspondence with Sir Arthur Murray in the autumn of 1918 shows that he was sifting
his correspondence with increasing care before showing items to House. Cable, Murray from Wiseman, Oct. 4, 1918, Y.H.C.

Wiseman regarded House as "almost a father." Wiseman to the writer. "I think
he [House] shows me everything he gets, and together we discuss every question that
arises." Wiseman to Drummond, April 27, 1918, Balfour pa., 49741, British Museum.
Wiseman impressed upon Murray "the importance of keeping control of this within
our own group—I mean, you and I and Reading." Wiseman to Murray, Sept. 27,
1918, Y.H.C.

"Most unorthodox . . ." was Foreign Secretary Balfour's comment to Murray on
this procedure, "but what does that matter? Anything that helps us to work with the
President and the President with us is helping to win the war, and personal feelings
and jealousies do not count." Arthur Cecil Murray, *At Close Quarters,* p. 18.

regretted that Wilson had "gone into a long and effusive discussion . . . a reckless and unnecessary gamble" that might result in a stiffening of German resistance. House had advised Wilson to reply to the first German note by saying merely that he would confer about it with the Allies, and the colonel had not been happy about the independent reply that he and the president had drafted.[8] House did not conceal his opinion from his British friends. General Haig wrote in his diary on October 26: "I lunched with Colonel House and others. He struck me as natural, sincere, and capable. He criticized the President's Note to Germany, and said that had he been at home he would have advised the president to have merely replied that he was passing the German request for an armistice to his allies for consideration."[9]

In undertaking to maintain liaison with the Allies and to project American ideals into the peacemaking Colonel House took the weight of a chaotic world on his slender shoulders, and with a commission more vague than any that a careful attorney would accept.[10] In addition to the suspicions and jealousies that had been festering for months at the top level on both sides of the Atlantic,[11] he had to reckon with two other menaces to peace.

One was the flickering flame of Prussian aggression. There was a widespread feeling that Junkerism was not dead. Germany's neighbors feared that in a few years it would again try to grind them under its heel. This was a familiar peril and the French generals had definite plans to deal with it.

More difficult to assess was the menace that loomed east of Germany. No such massive threat to the stability of European society had appeared since the French revolution. Having a propagating vitality that could leap national boundaries, it threatened to fill all political vacuums with regimes that would challenge the philosophies of state and church. The Bolshevik party, which wielded absolute power after satisfying the elemental urge of the Russian people for peace, had deeply offended the Western Allies by withdrawing from what the latter conceived to be a common crusade against German militarism. And the new regime compounded the offense by issuing insulting manifestoes.

The German Foreign Office undertook to exploit the political situ-

8. *I.P.*, *4*, 75; House diary, Oct. 9, 1918.

9. House diary, Oct. 22, 24, 1918; Robert Blake (ed.), *The Private Papers of Douglas Haig* (London, 1952).

10. F. L. Warrin, Jr. to the writer.

11. "Political and international jealousies . . . created situations which only the highest diplomatic skill could smooth over; and this was where House was at his best." Wiseman to Seymour, criticizing the ms. of *I.P.*, Y.H.C.

ation. On October 13 Wilhelm Solf, the new secretary of state for foreign affairs, suggested to his diplomatic agents in the Eastern border states that they should inspire the citizens there to protest against the withdrawal of German troops in view of the possibility that the Bolshevists would move in.[12] British Military Intelligence intercepted Solf's message and sent a copy to the American State Department, and Secretary Lansing immediately conferred with an assistant about what he set down as "Solf's duplicity." To Wilson every word of the message seemed to breathe Prussian trickery and deceit.[13]

Another instance of the enemy's strategy came to the attention of the Americans when the Austrian government requested that, because of Bolshevist movements in the Ukraine, their troops be allowed to remain in that region to preserve order until forces of the Allies arrived. House reported this to Wilson, explaining that the British had not yet expressed their view and the French government opposed the Austrian plan, fearful that it would "constitute a point which the Germans might make use of." House himself was so moved by the prevailing dread of bolshevism[14] that he told the French foreign minister that, while making no promises, they should allow the Austrians to remain for the moment until more was known about the situation; and the president cabled his approval of this course.[15]

Wilson addressed his cabinet at some length on November 5 about the possibility of revolutions in Europe as a result of Bolshevik propaganda. He asked Lansing to find out whether American diplomats could induce European governments to seize Bolshevist funds and expel agitators. His concern deepened when radical factions in Germany tried to usurp power. During the week preceding the signing of the Armistice the German state appeared to be breaking up.

12. Solf to Foreign Office representatives in Helsinki, Riga, Vilna, Warsaw, Tiflis, Kiev, Oct. 13, 1918. Solf's message explained that the German Foreign Office would have to take a hands-off position in order to avoid suspicion of double-dealing. Notifying the army's high command of what he had proposed, Solf recommended that the execution of so delicate a maneuver should be managed exclusively by political agencies. Ludwig F. Schaefer, "German Peace Strategy in 1918–1919," p. 26.

13. Lansing desk diary, Oct. 14, 1918, L.C.; Wiseman interview, Oct. 16, 1918, Y.H.C.

14. General Bliss observed on November 10: "The political leaders here have been unanimous in their feeling of dread of a Bolshevik revolution in Germany." Frederick Palmer, *Bliss, Peacemaker*, p. 350.

15. Baker, p. 560; House to W.W., Nov. 7, 1918, Wilson pa., 5C, L.C. Willert recorded that in his first talk with House at Paris the colonel stressed the danger of bolshevism above all else, and said that a barrier of European self-respect must be interposed at all costs. Sir Arthur Willert, *The Road to Safety*, p. 175; House diary, Dec. 9, 1918.

Sailors revolted in the seaports; a rebellion at Munich under a communist leader led to the proclamation of a republic in Bavaria; Kaiser Wilhelm abdicated and fled to Holland; and councils of workers and soldiers took over government in many localities. Panicky fears excited in Western Europeans and in Americans could be exploited by German and Austrian diplomats by the mere mention of "bolshevism," which actually was scarcely less repugnant to the socialists now in power in Berlin than to the democratic statesmen of the West.[16]

William C. Bullitt, a young liberal attached to the State Department, advised that in order to break the movement toward bolshevism it was "necessary to support the moderate socialists throughout Europe."[17] He argued that social democracy was destined to prevail. On November 8 he suggested that House should ask Lloyd George and Clemenceau to consult with their Labour leaders and cooperate with the German socialists in an orderly transition as a means of thwarting bolshevism. Forwarding this suggestion to Wilson on the ninth, Secretary Lansing wrote that despite "a certain force in the reasoning," he opposed "compromise with any form of radicalism" and thought it unwise to give special recognition to a particular class of society as if it possessed exceptional rights. The president did not act upon Bullitt's suggestion.[18]

Wilson and House felt that a compassionate peace was to be preferred to a harsh settlement that might result in political vacuums in Central Europe that would invite bolshevism. Unless quick decisions encouraged civil order it seemed possible that the writ of the victors might not run in Eastern Europe. House mentioned his apprehension in his first meeting at Paris with Clemenceau and Lloyd George. The latter admitted that there was danger in England,[19] and both thought that anything might occur in Italy.[20]

---

16. See Pierre Renouvin, *L'Armistice de Rethondes,* pp. 71–88, and Richard M. Watt, *The Kings Depart,* pp. 109, 185–200, 217.

17. Bullitt to Lansing, Nov. 2, 1918, N.A., RG59, 862.00/7.

18. Wilson pa., 2 and letter-press book. See Arno J. Mayer, *Politics and Diplomacy of Peacemaking,* pp. 61–68, 254–59.

19. For evidence of the fear of British officials of a revolution in England, see Howard J. Elcock, *Portrait of a Decision,* pp. 13, 39, 57.

20. House diary, Oct. 29, 1918. Frank I. Cobb wrote in his journal on October 26 of "the disquieting possibility that if Germany is pushed to extreme lengths, there may be a German Bolsheviki, which would inflict more injury upon Europe than German militarism has been able to accomplish." L.C.

It was the opinion of William G. Sharp, the American ambassador at Paris, that the military victory and the absence of famine made a successful Bolshevist movement "quite impossible" in France. He reported to the State Department on Nov. 12, 1918: "There may be friction and agitation of labor and peasants, but no revolution." N.A., RG 59, 861.00/3206.

By working unobtrusively and by taking advantage of the authority that accrued to the president in time of war, House managed to escape formal interrogation by legislators,[21] though the very air of mystery that he cultivated gave a shadow of the sinister to his public image. Wilson, fearing to commit himself to specific peace plans that the press might misrepresent and partisan opponents might attack, and apprehensive lest his secretary of state and ambassadors might blunder, trusted implicitly in this friend on whom they had long depended.

House stepped into the service of his country without the experience commanded by European diplomats. He had not traveled extensively on the Continent and at first had few acquaintances abroad. In previous missions to Europe he had pursued the informal methods that he had found effective in American politics. It was often not clear to what extent he acted on instructions from the White House and how far he went in presenting personal views to which he expected to commit the president. Wilson had perceived that House had a remarkable faculty for taking a detached point of view and fixing upon the really important questions.[22]

It was House's desire to take part in mutual accommodations by gentlemen of honor in the interest of maximum safety and prosperity for all. Received by European statesmen because he was the confidant and spokesman of the president, he impressed them by his good sense, discretion, and friendliness. He appealed to their better nature without offensive reproof, attempting to make them see that mutual sacrifice of national interests would result in a world order in which all would benefit. He won the trust of British leaders whose immediate responsibility to parliament exerted a certain restrictive influence from which the American chief executive was relatively free. They revealed to him not only their own minds, but proceedings of their cabinet. In some instances the Foreign Office departed so far from its tradition as to consult this foreigner about intimate questions of policy and personnel.[23]

---

21. "Sending . . . Mr. House to Europe brought active remonstrance on the ground that the Constitution had been violated," Henry M. Wriston, *Executive Agents in American Foreign Relations* (Baltimore, 1929) p. 205. Actually because House was not technically an officer of the government confirmation of his appointment by the Senate was not required.

22. Wiseman's "Notes on Interview with the President, Jan. 23, 1918," Balfour pa., 47941.

23. Typescript by Wiseman clipped to letter, Wiseman to House, Sept. 1, 1927, Y.H.C.; Wiseman and Hankey to the writer. "Everyone from Cabinet ministers down appealed to House when things went wrong." Willert, *Road to Safety,* p. 173. "It is to House that a great deal of the credit is due for the fact that the wartime collaboration

Dedicated to the furtherance of Wilson's leadership, and with a full comprehension of the suspicions and jealousies that had muddied American relations with the Allies during the war, House landed at Brest on October 25. He was accompanied by his son-in-law and secretary, Gordon Auchincloss, an attorney who had worked in the State Department for more than a year under Counselor Frank L. Polk, for whose appointment in 1915 House had been responsible.[24] These men operated efficiently and in close confidence, exchanging dispatches that constitute a substantial record of the work of Colonel House at Paris. House had as advisers General Tasker H. Bliss, Admiral William S. Benson, chief of naval operations, those judgment and extreme modesty House valued highly,[25] young Joseph C. Grew of the State Department, and Frank I. Cobb, liberal editor of the New York *World* and a man under consideration as successor to the ailing Walter Hines Page as ambassador at London.[26]

When House reached Paris, on October 26, events both military and diplomatic were giving promise of an ending of the martial deadlock that had drained the strength of the European powers for more than four years. On the Western front the British armies were gaining ground in the north, the Americans were advancing in the center, and the French were planning a massive thrust through Lorraine. On the day after House's arrival General von Ludendorff resigned his command and Berlin sent a favorable response to Wilson's third and final peace note.

The French people, on whose soil most of the blood had been shed and most of the damage to property done, were about to feel themselves released suddenly from what had come to seem an eternal purgatory. Millions of their young men had been killed or maimed, and the citizens had suffered from financial constriction and economic shortages. They held the "Boches" responsible for their plight, and their mood at the end of October was not one to

---

between the two countries functioned as well as it actually did." Inga Floto, *Colonel House in Paris,* p. 26.

24. House diary, Sept. 23, 1915.

25. Letter, House to Seymour, May 3, 1933, Y.H.C.; House diary, Oct. 15, 1918; Seymour to the writer.

26. House and Secretary of State Lansing preferred John W. Davis, who became Page's successor at the end of 1918. Wilson hoped that Cobb would act as director of publicity at the peace conference. See below, p. 262n.

House also had the services of Major Stephen Bonsal, a journalist who, according to his chief, "knew the world from North to South and from East to West and spoke many alien tongues." Delegates who came to Paris to plead national causes were placed under his intelligent care. Bonsal and Frazier translated for House, and later for Wilson, See *I.P. 4,* 228, and Stephen Bonsal, *Suitors and Suppliants,* pp. 6–7.

respond readily to Wilson's pleas for compassion and forebearance.
They demanded compensation from the enemy for horrible and unprecedented suffering in behalf of what they conceived to be the
cause of all civilization; and they insisted that a repetition of the ca-
tastrophe be prevented. It was hoped that the Americans, who had
suffered far less, would act with sympathy for these claims, which
the French concept of human justice held legitimate.

Upon his arrival House was briefed by General Bliss, who said that
his experience had taught that little could be accomplished in formal
meetings of the Supreme War Council and that it would be necessary to talk with the European leaders individually and commit them
to the American program.[27] Yet when the American "colonel" appeared in Paris he was regarded with some misgivings on the part of
French officials. The Quai d'Orsay was informed by Ambassador
Jusserand that House was "not entirely apart from such tendencies
as one finds frequently among humanitarians, pacifists, intellectuals,
and socialists" who would exonerate the German people of the
crimes of their rulers. Jusserand, on guard against American influence that might soften the conditions of armistice and peace, had
warned Wilson that the hearts of the Germans did not change as fast
as their Constitution.[28] Opinion in the Chamber of Deputies tended
to regard Wilson as pro-German.[29]

House presented himself to President Poincaré, whom he thought
a very intelligent man but a "bitter-ender,"[30] and learned that this
punctilious conservative did not consider that the colonel was properly accredited as an ambassador by the extraordinary papers that
Wilson had given him. Of one of the documents that House presented, Poincaré wrote on October 28: "[This] is a kind of circular
addressed by President Wilson to the whole world and couched in
the most autocratic terms."[31]

However, House was received warmly by the premier of France,
of whose ability he formed a high opinion. House wrote in his diary

---

27. Bliss to N.D. Baker, Oct. 27, 1918, Bliss pa., box 74.

28. Dispatches, Jusserand to Pichon, Oct. 14, 15, 1918, Archives du M.A.E., À
paix, A1154.1, f. 154–55.

29. According to the Socialist leader, Longuet, he and the Marquis de Chambrun
were the only members of the Chamber who did not share in the prevailing opinion
of Wilson. Record of conversation of House with Longuet and Cachin, Nov. 16, 1918,
Y.H.C.

30. Grew diary, Oct. 28, 1918, Joseph C. Grew pa., Houghton Library, Harvard
University.

31. Raymond Poincaré, *Au Service de la France, 10,* 395. For the texts of House's
commission as "Special Representative of the U.S. in Europe in matters relating to the
war," and of Wilson's appointment of him as "personal representative," see *I. P., 4,*
87.

of the French leader on November 29: "It seems to me now that Clemenceau is one of the ablest men I have met in Europe. . . . There can be no doubt of his great courage and unusual ability." The dynamic veteran of French politics who in his seventy-eight year was president of the Council of Ministers, was a relentless force in inter-Allied councils. "The Tiger" feared neither God nor devil, loved his country passionately, and hated the Germans. His heart beat with those of his countrymen who felt that they were fighting for elemental human rights against the might of arrogant aggressors whose "necessities" knew no law. He saw on the one side the peoples who sought to enslave, on the other the free peoples who were ready to sacrifice their lives in order to remain masters of their own affairs at home and abroad.[32]

Clemenceau sought for France no continental hegemony but, first and always, as much security as could be gained in a fluid, changing world. For him the great fact of recent history was the triumph of the principle of nationalities. A member of the National Assembly in 1871, he had signed the French protest against the annexation of Alsace and Lorraine by Germany. Clemenceau desired now to redeem this loss and to punish the Germans who bore responsibility for World War I; yet he felt that Germany, like other nations, had a right to live. He envisioned no sure or permanent equilibrium, under either a concert or a balance of powers. Peace, he once said, "leaves us plenty of burdens, vexations, difficulties, miseries. They will last a long time, alas. Mankind will not change for some time to come. Besides, all existence is nothing but a struggle. No matter. *Il faut agir.*"[33]

Wilson's creed elicited no enthusiasm from the Tiger of France, who had in fact criticized it in the press. He found in it, he said, "a certain number of abstractions that might fall in the domain of Utopia." But he had refrained from taking issue with Wilson.[34] Clemenceau knew that his prime purpose, French security, could be realized best with American aid.[35] The United States must be compensated in some way for its part in the common victory; and if this could be done with no cost and perhaps some profit to France, well and good. Clemenceau had a pleasant recollection of his dealing with the colonel at the inter-Allied conference at Paris a year earlier. The two

---

32. André Tardieu, *The Truth about the Treaty,* p. 79.
33. Jean Ratinaud, *Clemenceau,* p. 217. On the strength of national feeling in the belligerent countries, see Pierre Renouvin, *Le Traité de Versailles,* ch. I.
34. Ratinaud, pp. 189, 218–19.
35. Clemenceau recognized that the United States was "the world's strongest nation—at least potentially." Wythe Williams, *Tiger of France,* (New York, 1949), p. 182.

men very quickly formed a friendship that endured to the end of
their lives and was to serve as a basis for effective understanding between their governments at times of crisis during the peacemaking.

On October 26 Clemenceau welcomed Wilson's agent with open
arms and intimate confidences that the American found flattering.
"He seems genuinely fond of me," House recorded in his diary on
the twenty-sixth. "He spoke in acrimonious terms of Lloyd George
and of the British generally. He said they did not tell the truth, and
he remarked: 'Lloyd George sends his orders to me from time to
time.' He also said: 'I wonder how I keep my temper.' It was news to
me that he did."

Clemenceau gave to House, in deepest secrecy, terms that Marshal
Foch had presented for an armistice. No one had seen these, he said,
not even President Poincaré, and they were to be revealed to no one
but President Wilson. House tucked the document under his pillow
that night, placing a sailor on guard at each door of his room. The
next day he sent a summary of Foch's terms to the White House with
the first of a series of messages to be exchanged in private code during the weeks when Wilson and House were separated.[36]

The paper given to House by Clemenceau had been drafted by
the generals and admirals in response to Wilson's final peace note of
October 23.[37] On the twenty-fifth Marshal Foch had invited American, British, and French generals to put their ideas in writing. Foch

---

36. Joseph C. Grew, *Turbulent Era, 1,* 342. Communication between Wilson and
House was confused by garbling of their messages. See W. Stull Holt, "What Wilson
Sent and What House Received," *American Historical Review, 65;* 3 (April 1960),
569–71. A code that Wilson and House used in 1915 had been cracked without great
difficulty by British Naval Intelligence. Devlin, p. 455.
    During the pre-armistice talks House and Admiral Benson had recommended to
Washington that communications could be handled most efficiently by the navy; but
Lansing, after talking with the president, instructed that the State Department should
retain control. Polk to Embassy for Auchincloss, Oct. 31, N.A., RG 59, 033.1140/2L;
Lansing, desk diary, Oct. 30, 31, 1918.
    In mid-November a plan was agreed upon by the Army Signal Corps and the
Navy. Cable, House to Sec. State, Nov. 15, 1918, copy in Wilson pa., 50. A month later
Auchincloss, urging Polk to secure the best treatment possible for the Navy, commented: "No fear of the Navy running away with organization inasmuch as Army has
almost done so already." Telegram secret for Polk only from Auchincloss, Auchincloss
diary, Dec. 15, 1918, Y.H.C. Confusion continued until the American Commission to
Negotiate Peace reached Paris. See various messages between Auchincloss and the
State Department, Nov. 1918, Auchincloss diary. The writer has found no evidence to
support Floto's suggestion (p. 68) that House's use of navy personnel reflected a wish
to be independent of Secretary of War Baker. There were as many army as navy
officers on House's staff (lists of personnel in Y.H.C.). The use of yeomen of the Navy
as clerks possibly resulted from House's confidence in Admiral Benson.
    37. See above, p. 27.

himself did not share the extreme views of compatriots who advocated the annexation by France of German territory on the left bank of the Rhine.[38] The conviction that was uppermost in Foch's mind from the first, and was never dislodged, was that France could not feel secure unless Allied armies occupied the left bank and certain bridgeheads across the river.[39]

On the 26th the president addressed a letter to General Pershing, the commander of the American forces overseas, questioning the advisability of requiring the occupation of bridgeheads, and calling such a step "practically an invasion of German soil." Wilson wanted to make demands strong enough to prevent a renewal of hostilities by Germany, yet not so strong as to humiliate the German people and thus "throw the advantage to the military party." Conscious now of the importance of a balance of power—a principle that he had repudiated more than once[40]—he expressed concern that the Allies should not achieve such a preponderance as would make a real peace impossible. He insisted in a cable to House on a moderate and reasonable armistice, because it seemed certain that too much success or security on the part of the Allies would make a genuine peace settlement exceedingly difficult.[41] Through Secretary of War Baker, Wilson suggested that Pershing confer with House on all phases of the subject and "feel entirely free" to apprise the president of any consideration.[42]

Pershing immediately took his chief at his word. Without consulting House, he reported to Washington that on his own responsibility he had handed to the Supreme War Council a letter in which he set forth the bright prospects of the moment for complete military victory and urged that the situation be exploited to force unconditional surrender by Germany.[43]

Secretary of War Baker and General March, chief of staff, were

---

38. See Renouvin, *Traité de Versailles*, p. 14.

39. Report of Bliss to Sec. State, Feb. 6, 1920, *F.R., Lansing pa., 2*, 291–92; Tasker H. Bliss, "The Armistices," 513 ff.; Ferdinand Foch, *Mémoires, 2,* 283; Gabriel Terrail, *Les Négociations Secrètes et les Quatre Armistices,* pp. 221–22.

40. In an address before the Congress on Jan. 22, 1917 Wilson had said: "There must be, not a balance of power, but a community of power," *P.P. 4,* p. 410. In his address of Feb. 11, 1918 he spoke of the "The great game, now forever descredited, of the balance of power." Ibid., *5,* pp. 182–83.

41. There are discrepancies between the text of what Wilson sent (in the Wilson pa., 2), and House's transcription (in Y.H.C.) These were such as to leave House in the dark as to the president's precise position with respect of the views of Foch.

42. Baker, pp. 520–22.

43. Baker, p. 532. See Frank E. Vandiver, *Commander-in-Chief-Commander Relationships: Wilson and Pershing,* Rice University Studies, vol. 57, *1* (Winter 1971), 74.

indignant at what seemed to them a confusing intrusion by a general who was giving a military opinion that had political implications.[44] Pershing's proposal, had it been made public, would have played into the hands of those American critics who were plaguing the administration with demands for "unconditional surrender."[45] Wilson was disturbed. He pointed out to Secretary Baker that he had invited advice by Pershing directed to himself, not to the Supreme War Council. However, when Baker drafted a letter of reproof for the president's signature Wilson preferred to leave the matter in the hands of House.[46] The president was inclined to credit reports from unofficial observers that Pershing was "glory mad" and thirsting for vengeance, and had been responsible for unnecessary American casualties.[47] A message of October 27 from House informed the president that Clemenceau and Foch thought Pershing was handling the American forces badly and was losing more men than necessary. Rumors reached the Wilsons that Pershing was ambitious to be president, and Mrs. Wilson was persuaded this was the case.[48]

Colonel House was as astonished as his associates at Washington when Pershing handed to him a copy of his letter to the Supreme War Council. The general seemed to be trespassing on the province of diplomacy, and House was now put in the mediating position that he had thus far managed to avoid.[49] The colonel immediately laid the letter before Clemenceau and Lloyd George. The French premier read it carefully and exclaimed, "Theatrical!" Lloyd George's comment was "Politics!" And House agreed.[50]

House thought that Pershing had made a fool of himself and gave evidence of ambition for the presidency. The colonel reported—"laconically," Wilson thought—that the matter had been straightened out. Pershing still insisted that his opinion was "based on military considerations" and not political ones.[51]

---

44. Francis B. Lowry, "The Generals, the Armistice, and the Treaty of Versailles, 1919," p. 74.

45. See above, pp. 19n., 20.

46. Letter, W.W. to N.D. Baker, Nov. 1, 1918, N.D. Baker pa., L.C.

47. Edith Benham, diary letter, Dec. 5, 1918. Helm pa., L.C.

48. Raymond B. Fosdick to the writer. Though some American journals mentioned Pershing as a candidate for the presidency, the general professed embarrassment at the idea. Pershing pa., scrapbook and diary, L.C.: Frazier to House, Sept. 12, 1918, Y.H.C.; House diary, Oct. 30, 1918.

49. When in May of 1918 Lloyd George had asked for an American representative on the Supreme War Council, House commented: "What Lloyd George wants is someone to overrule Pershing." *I.P., 3,* 447–48.

50. Pershing to House, Oct. 22, 30 Nov. 6, 1918; copy of Pershing's letter to the Supreme War Council with House's annotation, Y.H.C.

51. John J. Pershing, *My Experience in the World War, 2,* 368; House diary, Oct. 30; Grew diary, Oct. 30, 1918. House recorded in his diary on November 2 that

It was necessary also to deal with dissenting views of General Bliss, the "permanent military representative"[52] attached to the Supreme War Council, who had taken alarm at the growing tendency of Allied militarists to plan aggressive action in secondary theaters in which their nations had special interests. Bliss noted "a curious revival of French ambitions" in regard to the East, the Near East, and the German colonies.[53]

A student of the Greek and Latin poets and of Oriental botany, and an authority on military history, Bliss had what Secretary Baker described as "a brooding intelligence." He was gruff and shy, and a stern disciplinarian. At times he blew off steam in what he called "a good cussing bee." Out of respect for his ego House circumspectly refrained from revealing the extent of the power that he exercised in the name of the president.[54]

Refusing, as he put it, "to abdicate the functions of the mind," Bliss ventured to express to the secretary of war his belief that the armistice terms should be limited, as nearly as could be, to the entire disarmament and demobilization of all enemy forces on land and sea, in the belief that peace terms could be imposed immediately thereafter. He desired this not to humiliate Germany, but as a practical step toward the disarmament of all nations and as "the only way to get a complete surrender" and thus create a state of security from which a lasting peace might come. In his opinion disarmament, as advocated in the president's Point Four, must be effected immediately, while the peoples were receptive, the prestige and influence of the United States was predominant, and the European governments might not be able to block it.[55] Partial disarmament of Germany as proposed by Foch now appeared to be too lenient, because it would leave a potential military menace that would haunt and distract the minds of the peacemakers. It seemed to Bliss that Germany believed its military position was hopeless, else its government would not have asked for an armistice; and this being the case more severe terms would prove as acceptable as those of Foch.[56] Bliss recommended

---

Pershing apologized for not consulting him before writing the bothersome letter. "The fact that he had submitted it to the War Department modified the matter," House wrote.

52. Bliss diary, Jan. 1, 1919, L.C.

53. Bliss to Newton D. Baker, Oct. 9, 1918, signed copy in Wilson pa., 2.

54. House told Bliss that he was in Paris only to confer with the Europeans as on previous missions. Seymour's notes on a talk with General Bliss, June 22, 1928, Y.H.C.

55. Report by Bliss to Sec. State, Feb. 6, 1920, *F.R., Lansing pa., 2*, 293; Frederick Palmer, *Bliss, Peacemaker*, pp. 339–43.

56. *I.P., 4*, 147.

that the United States act swiftly and forcefully to put forward its own views of a just settlement, including Wilson's idea of rational and general disarmament. He thought that the Allied governments, realizing that their people were ripe for this doctrine, would listen.[57]

When Bliss pressed his views on Foch, and asked what guarantee there was that Germany would not rearm its concentrated army, the marshal replied that his own less severe terms would be enough to paralyze the enemy's military power. Lord Milner, one of the most forceful members of the British Cabinet, did not doubt that the Germans would accept complete disarmament, but then talked at length about Russia and suggested that it might not be wise to lay Germany open to Bolshevik invasion.[58] To the argument that the German army should be left strong enough to put down a revolution, Bliss replied that the army was quite as likely to become revolutionary as any other element.[59] He thought there was no present danger of Soviet action in Germany by force of arms. However, on October 28 the British military men sent to House an unfavorable report of Bliss's ideas.

House, having confidence in the military judgment of Foch, discussed the opinions of Bliss in the Supreme Council, and no action was taken on them. Had the recommendations of the American generals for unconditional surrender been accepted it is possible that the peacemakers could have avoided a succession of crises that arose in the ensuing months when the armistice terms had to be renewed while delicate discussions of final peace conditions were under way.[60]

As the representative of the president, Colonel House was sought out by many callers. On the day of his arrival he engaged in a long series of interviews. Distinguished Americans and foreigners, including newsmen, came to his door. According to his record he "did a great deal of talking," in an effort "to frame the case as the president wished it.[61]

---

57. *I.P., 4,* 114–16, 145–47. Bliss's message to Secretary Baker went to the desk of the president; and Bliss set down his ideas in a memorandum, of which he sent a copy to House.

58. *I.P., 4,* 116.

59. Bliss to N.D. Baker, Nov. 10, 1918, Bliss pa.

60. Bliss commented in a memorandum of June 14, 1928: "The Allies became obsessed with a fear that Germany would rearm herself to such an extent, at least, as would make her very formidable, and for months this fear haunted the Peace Conference." *I.P., 4,* 115. "The one great error in the armistice, as now admitted by thinking men generally in Europe," wrote General Bliss in retrospect, "was in the failure to demand complete surrender with resulting disarmament and demobilization. The situation would have compelled acceptance of this condition by the Germans." "The Armistices," 520; *F.R., Lansing pa., 2,* 293.

61. House Diary, Oct. 26, 1918.

Diplomacy was to House neither a profession nor a means of livelihood. It was essentially a game such as he had played in Texas and
Washington, and the prize at stake was enduring fame. He now had
the supreme opportunity of which he had dreamed, the chance he
had longed for to go down in history. The Europeans respected his
acumen and sought his advice partly because of his closeness to the
powerful president of the United States, partly because his counsel
was believed to be, in the words of Walter Lippmann, "a little nearer
this world than the President's and a good deal nearer heaven than
that of Lloyd George and Sonnino."[62]

The colonel had learned much during the war about the political
behavior of the Allied statesmen, and had found it not much different from that of old friends in Texas. He made it his business,
before going into conferences at Paris, to know what each man was
thinking and what he would say; and he docketed this knowledge,
filed it in a mind that he kept uncluttered by minor worries, and
used it to direct his argument skillfully. Distilling the essential points
into as few words as possible, he spoke quietly and deliberately, gaining emphasis by pointing a finger at the man addressed. He tried to
commit individuals to his views before they met in a formal council.

The premiers conferred with House at his residence at 78 rue de
l'Université, or at the office of Clemenceau or that of Foreign Minister Pichon. The political leaders of the Allies—Clemenceau of
France, Lloyd George of Great Britain, and Orlando of Italy—
belonged to a new school of European negotiators. For almost a year
they had met frequently. Under the stress of the desperate combat
in which their nations were engaged, they had worked out a modus
vivendi, and they derived exceptional authority from their vigorous
leadership during a war that threatened the very existence of their
democracies. National passions often erupted in their conversations;
but in the necessity of averting defeat they had learned to exchange
insults without drawing blood.

The morning meetings in Paris were in preparation for deliberations in the afternoons at Versailles, where the Supreme War Council met, enlarged by the presence of representatives from Japan,
Belgium, and Serbia. These formal sessions sat in the Trianon Palace Hotel, at a large mahogany table that ran the length of the room.
Long speeches were ruled out and the number of voices was strictly
limited. The foreign secretaries attended, as well as generals and ad-

---

62. Describing House's position as "that of the Human Intercessor, the Com-
forter, the Virgin Mary," Lippmann wrote: "To him the weak, even in principle, can
go and be listened to kindly." Lippmann to Mezes, Aug. 5, 1918, Y.H.C.

mirals. The European leaders had the aid of competent diplomatic
staffs while Colonel House, sitting on one side of the table at the
center, represented the United States with his military and naval advisers. Clemenceau, whose arms and shoulders waved when the discussion turned acrid, held in his gray-gloved hands a paper cutter
with which he rapped on the table to demand silence. He spoke
sharply to cut off rambling talk. A.J. Balfour, gentle and courteous,
walked about the table to hear better,[63] and strove to perpetuate the
traditions of British diplomacy in a strange new world. Sir Maurice
Hankey, secretary of the British war cabinet, was assiduous, as he
had been in earlier meetings of the Supreme War Council, in keeping records and preparing resolutions.[64]

The decisions made informally in Paris were subject to review and
amendment at Versailles. Thus the pre-armistice negotiators fell immediately into a pattern of action that grew out of necessity and
usage rather than from executive planning. The procedure set a
precedent that was to be followed by the peace conference itself.

The pressure for immediate decisions was imperative in the last
week of October, when the enemy powers were seeking armistice
terms and the policy to be followed toward any one of them was contingent not only on dealings with the others but on the interests of
the various triumphant states. The victorious statesmen were
beginning now to relax their united efforts to subdue Germany and
their thoughts were turning toward their relationships one with another. Differences that had been suppressed during the fighting
could no longer be easily passed over. House and his advisers had
been aware for some months that divisive tendencies among the victors could be exploited by the enemy even in defeat.[65]

House began conversations with the French and the British premiers on October 29, and immediately the bases for armistices took
shape.[66] The colonel, sitting quietly while Clemenceau and Lloyd

---

63. Palmer, p. 353; Grew, p. 352.

64. "I ran the conference as usual," Hankey recorded in his diary on November
4. "I drafted every resolution." Stephen Roskill, *Hankey, 1,* p. 627.

65. Bowman to House, Aug. 30, 1918, Inquiry pa., Y.H.C.

66. Use has been made of the various records of the pre-armistice meetings that
are described in Floto, pp. 282–83, n. 175, except that Paul Mantoux's procès-verbal
has been read in the original, in the Bibliothèque de Documentation Internationale
Contemporaine, rather than in the transcript in the Loucheur papers. Madame Mantoux has written the following description of her husband's work: "He dictated the
record from his rough notes—taken in view of immediate oral translation—day after
day, habitually on the morning following each meeting. The typewritten copies were
probably submitted to him before being released, and he would then insert an omitted sentence, or make some correction." Letter to the writer, Sept. 18, 1973. The notes
of Aldrovandi-Marescotti, printed in *Guerra Diplomatica,* have been consulted.

George wrangled wittily over conditions for a truce with Turkey,[67] explained that this question did not concern the United States, which had not been at war with Turkey.[68] The armistice of Mudros was concluded on October 30. An armistice with Bulgaria had been signed on September 30. The United States took part in neither.

On October 30 the work on the German armistice was interrupted by news that Austria was requesting terms for an immediate truce. The day before,, Wilson had discussed with his cabinet a note from Vienna that accepted his conditions and asked him to bring about an armistice forthwith.[69]

The Italian government pressed for a simultaneous conclusion of armistices with Germany and with Austria, and its ambassador at Washington sought unsuccessfully to enlist American support for this procedure.[70] Lloyd George insisted that one could not determine how hard to press Germany until it was known whether Austria's resistance was broken.[71] It was decided to act immediately to set final terms for Austria-Hungary, based on recommendations of the military advisers. The Italian commander was to deliver them directly to the Austrian high command. House thought that by using this military channel they could avoid controversial discussion of Italian claims before the capitulation of Austria was assured.[72] Although he made an effort to exclude from the armistice any clause that would permit occupation "to preserve order" and thus give Italy grounds for sending troops to Fiume, he was unsuccessful.[73] In his eagerness to avoid friction and delay he did not reach any understanding as to the relation of the limits of the military occupation to the boundaries that would be required by an application of Wilson's principle of self-determination.

On the afternoon of November 3, without waiting for advice from Washington, the Allies concluded the armistice of Villa Giusti, by

---

67. Clemenceau seemed to be thinking in terms of the Second Empire; and Lloyd George, House recorded, bandied words "like a fishwife." House diary, Oct. 30, 1918.

68. See above, p. 20n.

69. See above, p. 30.

70. Ambassador di Cellere presented the Italian plea to Secretary Lansing in a note of October 30. The latter forwarded this to the president the next day and asked for instructions. N.A. RG 59, 763.72119/2554½; Polk diary, Oct. 29, 1918, Y.H.C. Italy feared that if the armistice with Germany was concluded first, Austria's army would be strengthened by the acquisition of three Austrian divisions then in France as well as German units in an Austrian disguise. Renouvin, *Armistice de Rethondes,* p. 210.

71. Renouvin, *Armistice de Rethondes,* p. 208.

72. House to W.W., Oct. 30, 1918, Baker, 7, 532.

73. See below, p. 163.

which Austria yielded to Italy the right to occupy such points as
might be deemed necessary to conduct military operations and to
maintain order. Germany now clearly faced a threat of invasion
from the south by Italian armies, in addition to the menace posed by
French forces in the Balkans that had been released from battle
when Bulgaria and Turkey left the war.[74] Terms similar to those accepted by Austria were imposed hastily on November 13 upon
Hungary, which declared its independence. In these armistices,
negotiated by military men at the fronts, there was no commitment
to Wilson's program for peace, although in asking the president on
October 27 to act to end the fighting the Austro-Hungarian government accepted his principles.

The Allied leaders were now the more inclined to feel that Germany would accept terms at least as severe as those that Marshal
Foch submitted. Nevertheless, they still held back from demanding
unconditional surrender and total disarmament.

On the morning of October 31 Foch came himself to the formal
session of the Supreme War Council to explain and defend his plan
for occupation of the left bank of the Rhine and three bridgeheads
and for the delivery by the Germans of large quantities of military
matériel.[75] He made it clear that he was satisfied that his terms
would give the security that France demanded, and therefore no
man had the right to cause one more drop of blood to be shed.[76]
Clemenceau supported the marshal, declaring that neither the
French army nor the Chamber of Deputies would accept less. He
gave his word of honor, however, that France would end the occupation as soon as Germany fulfilled the conditions of peace. At this
Lloyd George, whose government opposed any plan that might result in an independent "buffer state" on the left bank,[77] yielded and
accepted Foch's terms as satisfactory in general.

---

74. General Bliss took part in the preparation of an Allied plan for an attack on
Germany through Austria (see U.S. Grant III, "America's Part in the Supreme War
Council," *Records of the Columbia Historical Society, 29–30* (1928), p. 334. The plan (see
Bliss, "The Armistices," 510) was accepted by the S.W.C. on November 4 (Minutes,
Y.H.C.). The military advisers were ordered to examine the possibility of taking steps
immediately to send a force including Czechs from the Western front to Bohemia and
Galicia to prepare those countries against a possible German invasion, to establish
airdromes from which Germany could be bombed, and to prevent the export of coal
and oil to Germany and make these commodities available to the Allies.

75. Foch's final plan, as transmitted to Clemenceau on October 26, is in Tardieu,
pp. 62–64.

76. *I.P., 4,* 91.

77. Balfour thought the creation of a buffer state "a rather wild project" in which
Paul Cambon, French ambassador at London, appeared to have little faith. (Elcock,
p. 10.)

According to Clemenceau's biographer, the French premier persuaded House in a private talk to agree to Foch's plan, despite Wilson's objection to the occupation of bridgeheads. House had just received a message from a secret agent in Berlin on whom he relied. It reported that Prince Max was "playing politics." The liberal chancelor was said to be unwilling to risk his own political demise and that of the monarchy by agreeing to a surrender, and to be hopeful that the terms to be proposed by the victors would be so severe that he could convince the German people that Wilson's profession of liberalism, in which Prince Max actually had little confidence, was indeed unreliable, and therefore they must fight to the death.[78] However, even at the risk of playing into the hands of Prince Max, House did not try to alter Foch's terms. Insisting that no more should be taken from Germany than was absolutely necessary for the security of France, he wanted the Allies to assume full responsibility for the military conditions, as they did in the armistice with Austria-Hungary. He honored the pledge of Clemenceau that occupying forces would be withdrawn when Germany complied with the prescribed conditions.

The terms that were approved on November 4, substantially as Foch presented them, charged him with the enforcement of the armistice and gave him discretion with respect of minor technicalities. The occupation was to continue until Germany met the demands for reparation that were to be made in the peace treaty. Thus a military lever was established that was to be pressed a month later to force additional concessions.[79]

The naval conditions were the subject of debate in several sessions. The political leaders and Foch thought that Germany should be required to surrender its submarines, since these had grievously hurt the Allies; but they hesitated to demand its warships at the risk of prolonging the fighting. The president gave instructions that "all armed vessels should be held in trust" and the Allies should not "go too far in demanding excessive security."[80]

The British Admiralty, however, unwilling to accept the substitu-

---

78. Report from "the colonel's secret agent in Berlin," Oct. 28 [1918], Bonsal pa., L.C., box 24, "Notes" folder. Bonsal did not identify this "agent," but wrote that House "set great store upon" his reports.

House's informant reported that General Ludendorff, determined to avoid odium for his acknowledgment of military defeat, and encouraged by a belief that morale in the army was improving, was now inclined to continue hostilities. On Ludendorff's vacillation, see Watt, p. 146.

79. See below, p. 103.

80. Daniels, Josephus. *The Cabinet Diaries of Josephus Daniels,* ed. by E. David Cronon, p. 345.

tion of international surveillance for the sea power that they asserted Britain had "exercised beneficially for centuries," hoped that by the accession of German battleships they might restore strength lost during the war. The Allied Naval Council, sitting at London, objected to the drafting of naval measures by Foch. It adopted stiff terms that were presented by British authorities, who feared that later in the peace talks, when Wilson's principles came into play, it might be hard to obtain the surrender of the German fleet. The Naval Council forwarded its conditions to the Supreme War Council and explained that it acted on the assumption that Germany was completely defeated.[81]

House told the first lord that he was willing to accept the proposals of the British Admiralty.[82] However, restrained by a message received from the president on October 29, he stood aside while Lloyd George presented a formula that was adopted.[83] It provided that all of Germany's submarines should be surrendered and brought to Allied ports. Designated warships were to be interned in neutral ports and put under surveillance of the Allies and the United States, with German caretakers aboard. Their ultimate disposition was to be decided by the peace conference. Admiral Benson and the American naval planners were given the impression that the Allied Powers hoped to add German ships to their fleets, and they suspected that there had been secret talks about this matter among officials of France, Great Britain, and Japan.[84]

The British admirals found the compromise unsatisfactory and opposed it when it was discussed at Versailles on November 4. However, the Naval Council, "withholding its approval," submitted to the will of the Supreme War Council. Lloyd George explained to his cabinet that the terms agreed upon would avoid making it unnecessarily difficult for Germany.[85]

"The conference at Versailles was tedious and lasted from three to six o'clock," House wrote in his diary on November 4. "To me the most amusing incident was the determination of Balfour, Milner, Sir Eric Geddes, and Admiral Hope to throw the responsibility of the modified naval terms upon Lloyd George. They openly repudiated his views and said they acquiesced under compulsion. It gave an in-

---

81. Three statements of the Allied Naval Council, Y.H.C. See Stephen Roskill, *Naval Policy between the Wars* (New York, 1968), pp. 74, 81, and David F. Trask, *Captains and Cabinets*, pp. 334–35, 343–48.

82. House diary, Nov. 4, 1918.

83. The moderate terms suggested by the president are summarized in Trask, *Captains and Cabinets*, pp. 330–31; and see pp. 336–37.

84. Ibid., pp. 350–54.

85. Minutes of the B.W.C., Nov. 4, 5, 1918, P.R.O., Cab/23/13.

sight into how thoroughly they dislike him and upon what thin ice he skates."

When it appeared that no neutral port was available, the Naval Council, sitting at London with Admiral Sims representing the United States, decided on November 13 that American and Allied representatives should be attached to the British Grand Fleet to take part in an internment at Scapa Flow.[86] Seven months later the admirals were to have an opportunity to criticize the compromise of the statesmen, when the German crews opened the cocks in the interned vessels and sank them.

As in the case of the military conditions, House was willing for the most part to leave the framing of the naval terms to the experts in whom he had confidence. He fully comprehended the delicacy of the matter. Two years later he wrote:

> The outstanding problem was to have the terms cover what must be practically unconditional surrender without imperiling peace itself. . . . Germany was retreating in an orderly fashion and no one could say with certainty that she would not be able to shorten her line and hold it for months. If she had done this and we had failed to make peace when she had accepted the President's terms there would have been a political revolution in every Allied country save the United States. . . . This was all known to us in Paris, and it was as delicate and dangerous a situation as was ever given to a group of diplomats to solve. As it was, the European military and naval advisers were satisfied, and the outcome was the ending of the world war."[87]

Satisfied that the exactions of the generals and admirals were not so strict as to drive Germany to desperation and a refusal to sign an armistice, House reserved the bargaining power of his government for a campaign for realization of the prime American objective: the acceptance of Wilson's program of peace, and thus of his leadership in the postwar world. At the end of the pre-armistice meetings he cabled to the president: "I am now busy bringing every force to bear to help win a people's victory."[88]

---

86. Roskill, *Naval Policy*, p. 75.

The Austrian armistice provided for the surrender of the emperor's fleet to the Allied and Associated Powers, but on October 31 the Austrians turned it over to the Yugoslav National Committee at Pola. See below, p. 162.

87. Philadelphia *Public Ledger*, Nov. 11, 1920.

House suggested that the Germans be given a little more than three days to ask for armistice terms; but Clemenceau insisted on a three-day limit, with Foch empowered to designate the moment at which the period should begin. French procès-verbal, Nov. 4, 11:00 A.M.

For the texts of the armistices, see Harry R. Rudin, *Armistice 1918*, pp. 404–11, 426–32.

88. House to W.W., Nov. 5, 1918, Y.H.C..

☆ IV ☆

House's "Victory"

Colonel House had foreseen, and had warned Wilson, that as the Allied armies advanced, the president's influence would wane. During his first two days at Paris, when General Ludendorff's resignation was accepted and the pressure of American arms on the Lorraine front threatened to force a German withdrawal to the Rhine, House perceived that his prediction was all too prescient.[1]

Wilson himself, remote from the councils at Paris, already had noted the drift and felt that the disposition to make "an absolutely and rigorously impartial peace" was "growing less and less on the other side of the water." He told his cabinet that in the peacemaking, Americans must never do the things that they condemned.[2]

The reprehension that sustained his pulpit and that he had directed toward the enemy was now felt again by the Allied Powers, as it had been before the entry of the United States into the war. The European statesmen were not comfortable under the censure of the American prophet. Differences and tensions that had been submerged by the necessities of warfare and by the rapture of victory could be expected to surface soon.

American news correspondents warned House that the one definite policy of the Allies was to take the control of the peace negotiations out of the hands of President Wilson.[3] Actually French diplomats, accustomed to the discreet reticence of practitioners of the "old diplomacy," observed that the public was attracted by Wilson's eloquence, and feared that the Allied governments would lose the support of their peoples. Apprehensive also that Wilson would fulfill

---

1. House diary, Oct. 28, 1918, Y.H.C.
2. W.W. to Dr. E.P. Davis, Oct. 26, 1918, Wilson pa., 2 L.C. Josephus Daniels, *The Cabinet Diaries of Josephus Daniels,* ed. by E. David Cronon, p. 341.
3. House to Lansing, Oct. 29, 1918, *F.R., 1918, I, 1,* p. 113.

the German hope for soft conditions of peace, the French foreign ministry was unprepared to accept blindly any principles that were stated in general terms and were open to divergent interpretations. Moreover, it seemed illogical that Wilson should act as both belligerent and arbiter.[4]

On his first day in Paris House learned from Sir William Wiseman, who came from London to keep open their channel of information, that the British Cabinet had stormy discussions in which Wilson's demand for "freedom of the seas" was questioned. British diplomats, noting that the president failed to demand terms that would plainly demonstrate the defeat of the Germans, found that the American program seemed inadequate, unprecedented, and also at variance with the maritime, colonial and economic policy of Great Britain.[5] Wiseman, aware of the full force of the opposition, thought it impossible to persuade the Allies to agree to an armistice based on the Fourteen Points; and House feared that this might be true.[6]

Nevertheless, House undertook to force the acceptance of Wilson's creed as the philosophical basis for peace. Wishing to give precision to the American program, which he admitted had been presented in the president's speeches in such broad terms as to permit almost any exaction on Germany that anyone might suggest,[7] he arranged for the drafting of an interpretive commentary on each of the Fourteen Points.[8] He had assistance from Walter Lippmann[9] and from Frank I. Cobb. On October 29 House cabled the draft of the commentary to Wilson for "correction and revision." The president replied the next day that the paper was a satisfactory interpretation of the principles involved, but "details of application mentioned should be regarded as merely illustrative suggestions and reserved for the peace conference."[10] With this paper on the table House tried to persuade his European colleagues to make commit-

---

4. Dispatches, P. Cambon to M.A.E., Oct. 26, Archives du M.A.E., À paix, A1017. 1, f. 46, doc. 70; M.A.E. to Jusserand, Oct. 29, 1918, ibid., A 1163, f. 199.

5. "Memorandum on President Wilson's Speeches as a Basis of Negotiations," P.R.O., FO/general/002; David Hunter Miller, *My Diary, 2,* 59 ff.; Stephen Roskill, *Hankey, 1,* pp. 611, 613.

6. According to Grew's record House, regretting that the president had not acted before the exchange of notes with Germany to bind the Allies to the Fourteen Points, was "a little worried" as to whether Clemenceau and Lloyd George would repudiate them. Grew diary, Oct. 29, 1918, Joseph C. Grew pa., Houghton Library, Harvard University.

7. See Inga Floto, *Colonel House in Paris,* pp. 50–51 and n. 196.

8. See Appendix pp. 275–84.

9. "Lippmann wrote the commentaries on all the points save that which called for the creation of a league of nations," John L. Snell, "Wilson on Germany and the Fourteen Points," *Journal of Modern History* 365. The commentaries were a condensation of The Inquiry's memorandum of Dec. 22, 1917. See above, p. 6.

10. *F.R., 1918, suppl. I, 1,* p. 421.

ments that it would be difficult for them to put aside later. The interpretations of the Fourteen Points presented in this document made some concessions to the war aims of the Allies.

At the first meeting of the negotiators, on October 29, the Europeans immediately questioned the wisdom of binding themselves to Wilson's points as a basis for peace. The views of the Allied leaders had changed little since their discussions of the German overture of October 8.[11] Lloyd George still feared that if terms of armistice were proposed in accordance with Wilson's plan, and without reservations, Germany would conclude that the Allies had accepted all of the president's points and principles. "Should we not make it clear to the German Government," he asked, "that we are not going in on the Fourteen Points?" Although he had written a letter to Clemenceau advising the acceptance of Wilson's terms,[12] he now announced he would "put quite clearly the points that he did not accept." Clemenceau was not ready to commit himself; and Sonnino, the Italian foreign minister, asked with a trace of sarcasm for "the five more and the others."

And so the statesmen read and discussed the points, one by one, referring to House's commentary when it seemed desirable. Both Clemenceau and Lloyd George questioned Point One. They said emphatically that they could not agree never to make a private or secret diplomatic agreement of any kind. Such understandings were the foundation of European diplomacy, and everyone knew that to abandon secret negotiations would be to invite chaos. To this House replied by referring to the explanation given in the commentary: there was no intention to prohibit confidential talks on delicate matters, but only to require that treaties resulting from such conversations should become "part of the public law of the world."

Moving on to Point Two, the statesmen found themselves embroiled in arguments that lasted for days and were indeed to crop up persistently until the end of the peace conference. "Freedom of the seas" was a topic that provoked loose thinking and looser talk, both in the United States and in Great Britain. David Hunter Miller, House's legal adviser, thought the phrase a "mysterious slogan that may mean anything but more probably and usually nothing at all."[13] Nevertheless any mention of it roused patriotic fervor on both sides of the Atlantic.

All through its history the United States had strongly resented interferences with its ships by warring powers. In 1907 at the Second Hague Conference the government of Great Britain, for which the

---

11. See above, p. 21.
12. Joseph C. Grew, *Turbulent Era, 1,* 342.
13. David Hunter Miller, *The Drafting of the Covenant, 1,* 50.

right of blockade had long been an essential weapon in war with Continental powers, and the United States government, which had insisted on enforcing a blockade against the Confederacy during the Civil War, had made an effort to reach a comprehensive understanding on maritime law. An international prize court was set up to hear appeals from national prize courts. However, when the naval powers met the next year and attempted to codify the law of blockades in a Declaration of London, the British and American governments failed to accept it. Moreover, Wilson had been unable to persuade Great Britain to abide by its provisions during the period of neutrality. In the absence of any authority to unify, enforce, or amend a code that would take precedence over the decisions of national courts, the rules of blockade had remained, according to Lord Devlin, "almost as unreal as the rules of jousting and very much less precise." The statesmen, having no sure legal solutions, had been forced to use diplomatic and political recourses in efforts to maintain a modus vivendi. As early as 1915 House had discussed with Sir Edward Grey the possibility of developing new provisions for the immunity of neutral shipping; and House had been aware then that if he pressed England too hard its resentment would be felt in the peacemaking.[14]

At the outbreak of the war the battle fleet of the United States had not been in the same class with that of Great Britain. In campaigning for reelection in 1916, however, Wilson advocated that his nation construct "the most adequate" navy in the world, and soon the Congress approved the largest building program ever authorized by the legislature of a nation not at war. The United States laid plans for the construction of a two-ocean fleet within three years. In July of 1918 the Navy Department was instructed to lay the keels of the new ships "as soon as practicable." Moreover, the Navy was developing a second three-year program that would give the nation a force stronger than any yet planned by Great Britain. Meanwhile the American merchant tonnage grew rapidly, and before the fighting ended, the United States suddenly found itself a first-class power on the seas and a challenger to the long-standing supremacy of Great Britain. Insistence on a strong navy appealed to American officials as a way to protect the growing merchant marine and the expanding commerce of the United States, as well as a means of forcing Europeans to accept the new order proposed by Wilson. Secretary Daniels conceived that the building program would provide "a good instrument to use at the Peace Conference."[15]

---

14. See Lord Devlin, *Too Proud to Fight*, ch. 6 and pp. 273, 278, 314.
15. Daniels, *Cabinet Diaries*, pp. 341, 350. See Floto, p. 42 and sources cited, and George T. Davis, *A Navy Second to None* (New York, 1940), pp. 238–42. On December

In some quarters American opinion regarded the British Navy as a potential foe. Many British patriots reciprocated this fear, and felt that the United States was ungrateful in attacking the maritime power by which Great Britain had defended not only itself but its allies. Having just fought off the challenge of Germany they now looked upon the United States as another potential rival on the seas.[16] Why, it was asked, was a huge navy necessary to a great military power that was strategically invulnerable? In the case of Great Britain, however, naval supremacy seemed essential both as a means of defense against a blockade of the British Isles and as a weapon for enforcing the sort of blockade that had contributed vitally to the present victory and could help to consolidate it.[17] Moreover the British held that their navy could serve the world under a league of nations by helping to maintain an open door for trade and free transit.

Frank I. Cobb, noting that the question of freedom of the seas became acute almost overnight in October, undertook what he called "an old-fashioned job of reporting" in London. He found that British officials attributed the prevailing commotion largely to a speech in which Chairman Edward Hurley of the U.S. Shipping Board said that the United States intended to build "the greatest merchant marine in the world." Aware of "tremendous propaganda" in England, Cobb thought that Lloyd George was using the issue in his campaign for the forthcoming election.[18]

On October 16 Wilson had told Wiseman that he was appreciative of the policing role of the British Navy and had no wish to weaken it, but rather to use it in connection with a league of nations. He said that the submarine introduced a new element in naval warfare and

2 the president recommended to the Congress "the uninterrupted pursuit" of a new program submitted by the secretary of the navy, with this warning: "It would clearly be unwise for us to attempt to adjust our programs to a future world policy as yet undetermined."

16. "Coming from a President who was regarded as the hope of the world and from a nation which claimed that it fought only so that mankind might start a new era of world solidarity, our naval program aroused amazement and consternation abroad," Davis, pp. 244–45.

17. "The Blockade," Keynes wrote, "had become by that time a very perfect instrument. It had taken four years to create and was Whitehall's finest achievement; it had evoked the qualities of the English at their subtlest. Its authors had grown to love it for its own sake; it included some recent improvements, which would be wasted if it came to an end; it was very complicated, and a vast organization had established a vested interest. The experts reported, therefore, that it was our one instrument for imposing our Peace Terms on Germany, and once suspended it would hardly be reimposed," John Maynard Keynes, *Two Memoirs,* p. 24.

18. Cobb journal, Nov. 1, 2, 1918, Wilson pa., 14. See below, p. 149. Hurley's intemperate speech was reported in *The New York Times* on August 24 and, according to Cobb, was misrepresented by "certain British shipping journalists." On Anglo-American naval rivalry, see David F. Trask, *Captains and Cabinets,* pp. 357–58.

this required a modification of international maritime law. He remarked also that many nations, great and small, were irritated by the feeling that their sea-borne trade could develop only with the permission of Great Britain, and he thought that the deep-rooted cause of the war had been the prevalence of this feeling in Germany. It seemed to him that the old definition of blockade should be revised, and the extent of territorial waters enlarged. The president, presenting his opinion in interviews with the first lord of the admiralty and with Ambassador Jusserand, recognized the peculiar necessities created by the insular position of Great Britain, but protested against the tactics that had been used in enforcing the blockade of Germany.[19] He told Jusserand that the peace treaty should provide for a special conference that would define maritime law in the light of new conditions and provide for enforcement by a league of nations.[20]

In his Point Two the president offered what he considered an international guarantee of Britain's lifeline by a league of nations in which the British Empire would participate. Despite the fact that the United States, after it entered the war and shared in enforcing the blockade, had adopted some of the objectionable British practices,[21] the president now insisted that the rights of neutrals must be asserted vigorously. Point Two called for "absolute freedom of navigation upon the sea, outside territorial waters, alike in peace and in war, except as the seas may be closed in whole or in part by international action for the enforcement of international covenants." On October 29 Wilson cabled to House: "League of Nations underlies freedom of the seas and every other part of peace program."

Colonel House stood firmly on a position that was precisely defined. The American commentary explained that there would be "no serious dispute" in the event of a war directed against an outlaw nation by an international league because "complete non-intercourse" with that nation would be required of all members. But as for a war

---

19. The president's remarks to Geddes led the latter to report to Lloyd George that Wilson's views on the subject were "obviously unformed." Geddes to P.M., Oct. 13, 1918, Wiseman pa., Y.H.C. Wilson's remarks to Wiseman were known to Lloyd George. Because the Cobb-Lippmann commentary seemed less conciliatory, some of the British diplomats surmised, erroneously, that freedom of the seas was "a pet fad of House" and of greater concern to him than to Wilson. Maurice Hankey, *The Supreme Command*, p. 859. See Snell, pp. 364–69.

20. Dispatch, Jusserand to A.E., Nov. 5, 1918, Archives du M.A.E. À Paix, 1163.2, f.199, p. 61.

21. Lord Devlin has pointed out that the United States government, having become a belligerent, followed the practices of the British blockade and found the idea of a "black list" especially appealing, issuing one that contained the names of sixteen hundred firms in Latin America. Devlin, p. 519.

in which the league might choose to remain neutral: "The rights of neutrals shall be maintained against the belligerents, the rights of both to be clearly and precisely defined in the law of nations." House conceived his proposition to be "simply the combination of the British proposal . . . and the American proposal . . . which had been advanced at the Hague Conference in 1907."[22]

House had already made it clear that unless the United States could get assurance against a repetition of the British violations of American neutrality in 1915 and 1916, his government would have to build a navy that could protect its trade. He let Lloyd George know, through Wiseman and Reading, that in the future British rule of the seas would be no more acceptable than Germany's attempt to dominate the Continent. Alluding to the fact that the United States had more men and wealth than Great Britain, he warned of the threat that competition in naval building would pose. He told Reading that Great Britain was not to be feared because eventually its territory would be reduced to the British Isles.[23]

In the first formal discussion of Point Two on October 29 Lloyd George, who did not himself feel strongly about freedom of the seas but was instructed by the War Cabinet not to await the peace conference to repudiate this point plainly, spoke with spirit against it.[24] "It means that the power of blockade goes," he said. ". . . My view is that I should like to see this league of nations established first before I let this power go. If the league is a reality, I am willing to discuss the matter." The extreme to which opinion in the British armed services went is illustrated by an entry of November 9 in the diary of Sir Henry Wilson, British chief of staff, who after reading intercepted messages between House and Wilson, wrote: "I believe Wilson to be an unscrupulous knave and a hater of England and House to be a poor miserable fool."[25]

House, who had no objection to British naval superiority provided neutral rights were respected, gave assurance that the United States did not ask abolition of blockades, but merely insisted on their regu-

---

22. *I.P., 4,* 164, 185, 193. For House's views, see Edward M. House, "The Freedom of the Seas," *The Contemporary Review.*

23. House diary, October 28, 1918. Stephen Bonsal recorded that he heard the colonel say to Reading on October 28, "with a suave, ingratiating smile: 'I do not believe that the United States will submit to Britain's domination of the sea any more than she has to Germany's domination of the land. I hope Britain will be brought to recognize this, our position, and soon. If not, we had better stop talking right now.' " Unpublished ms., Bonsal pa., box 24, L.C.

24. Roskill, *Hankey, 1,* 621, 623. Lloyd George had admitted earlier to House that freedom of the seas was at least debatable. House diary, Jan. 15, 1916.

25. Cited in Floto, p. 280.

lation by law. He found himself in a minority of one. Clemenceau, skeptical, and Sonnino, unsympathetic, had reservations of their own for which they wanted the support of Lloyd George, and their tone was barbed with irony.[26] Sonnino thought that Wilson should be told that it was impossible to agree on a peace program while drafting an armistice.

At this juncture House made a bold threat. "Take care," he warned, "that the President doesn't say: 'The Allies did not accept my Fourteen Points; that puts an end to my correspondence with them. Now it remains to be seen whether I ought to continue negotiations with the Central Powers.' " It was thus made clear that a separate peace between the United States and Germany might result.[27]

In justification of this dire warning House cabled to the president: "Unless we deal with these people with a firm hand, everything we have been fighting for will be lost."[28] The colonel reported that his statement had a very exciting effect on the Allied ministers, and that Balfour warned against any breach that Germany might exploit. Actually, however, the British statesmen thought House's threat was an unauthorized bluff. Lloyd George remarked that the British government would regret it if the United States made a separate peace but would go on fighting; and Clemenceau supported him.[29] At this juncture House suggested that France, Great Britain, and Italy get together to limit their acceptance of the Fourteen Points, and he offered to leave the room while they conferred. Until they stated their conditions, he said, it was futile to talk of an armistice.[30] Lloyd George then proposed that each nation should frame its reservations to the Fourteen Points and see the next day whether all could not agree on a common draft.

After the discussion on the twenty-ninth House told his advisers what had taken place and sought their counsel, and the next day he cabled Wilson to suggest that the president play upon Allied fears of

---

26. Hankey, *Supreme Command*, p. 860. Hankey recorded: "Clemenceau looked unutterable things when Colonel House spoke in hushed tones of what the President thinks." Roskill, *Hankey, 1*, 623.

27. French procès-verbal, Oct. 29, 1918, Mantoux pa., B.D.I.C.; Hankey, p. 860; Stephen Bonsal, *Unfinished Business*, pp. 3–4, translated from Aldrovandi-Marescotti, *Guerra Diplomatica*, p. 190. Eye witnesses did not agree as to House's manner of speaking. Aldrovandi wrote: "a man without nerves . . . serene and courteous". Hankey wrote in his diary: "House looked very sick." Roskill, *Hankey, 1*, 623.

28. House to W.W., Oct. 30, 1918, Y.H.C.

29. Hankey, p. 860; Roskill, *Hankey, 1*, 623. Lloyd George assured the Imperial War Cabinet on November 5 that Great Britain would continue the war rather than give way on the issue of freedom of the seas. Minutes, Nov. 5, 1918, P.R.O., Cab/23/17.

30. French procès-verbal, Oct. 29, 1918.

American withdrawal of economic support: "I would suggest that you quietly diminish the transport of troops giving as excuse the prevalence of influenza or any other reason but the real one. I would also suggest that you begin to gently shut down upon money, food, and a little later raw material."[31]

On the thirtieth the British had a draft ready to which they hoped all could subscribe. This document[32] declared willingness to make peace on the terms laid down in the president's various addresses, but subject to a reservation of "complete freedom" at the peace conference on the topic of freedom of the seas.[33]

House feared a flood of reservations from the other Allies. The essential American aim, he perceived, must be to reach an understanding with the British on the point that they challenged with the greatest vigor. Once accord was established on freedom of the seas, Lloyd George might then help to persuade Clemenceau and Orlando to accede to the entire memorandum of the thirtieth. House immediately telegraphed the text of the British document to the president, advising that Wilson accept it without alteration if the Allies adopted it.

The president was meanwhile sending messages to House that suggested that he resented the questioning of his program. If it was the purpose of the Allied statesmen to nullify his influence, a garbled cable of October 29 said, "force the purpose boldly to the surface" and "let me speak of it to all the world as I shall."[34] The next day another message came, in which the president proclaimed that it was his solemn duty to authorize his agent to say to the Europeans that he could not "consent to take part" in negotiating a peace that did not include freedom of the seas, because the United States government was pledged to fight not only to do away with Prussian militarism but with militarism everywhere.

The tone of these communications brought a cautioning message from House. "It is exceedingly important," it said, "that nothing be said or done at this time which may in any way halt the Armistice which will save so many thousands of lives. Negotiations are now proceeding satisfactorily."[35] After receiving this Wilson reaffirmed

---

31. Grew, *1*, 347; House to W.W., Oct. 30, 1918, Y.H.C. Wilson's transcription places the phrase "a little later" after "suggest," *F.R., 1918, Suppl. I, 1*, 424.

32. See below, p. 70.

33. The memorandum drafted on October 30 contained also a clarification of Wilson's declaration that invaded territories should be restored.

34. The quoted words reached House unchanged except for the substitution of "Council" for "surface." Transcription in Y.H.C.

35. "Everything is changing for the better since yesterday," House cabled, "and I hope you will not insist upon my using your cable except as I may think best. If you

his position, but added: "Of course, I depend upon your discretion to insist at the right time and in the right way." The president required a clarification of the British memorandum of the thirtieth before he decided whether it was acceptable or whether he should take up the matter with a Congress that would have no sympathy whatever with the spending of American resources to perpetuate British control of the seas. Thus Wilson put weight in the club that his agent was holding over the heads of the Europeans. His cable concluded with a pat on the back for the colonel: "I am proud of the way you are handling things."[36]

When these presidential messages reached Paris, House's task was both complicated and eased. He had to satisfy a proud and sensitive chief as well as a reluctant prime minister, and both were responsible to irrational national sentiment. Above all he must maintain liaison and do nothing to prevent the conclusion of an armistice. Assured of backing from Washington, he kept up pressure on British officials.[37] He said that all hope of Anglo-Saxon unity would end unless they made reasonable concessions. He again clearly stated the position of the United States. Wiseman, having to deal with naval officers who came from London breathing fire, and fully aware that the controversy over sea power threatened to break up the conference, worked for an understanding and gave House a report on progress with his own people.

In a meeting at his residence on November 3, House read to the premiers a tempered paraphrase[38] of one of Wilson's insistent messages, explaining that the president did not object to the principle of blockade. But he said that the law governing it would have to be altered and asked for an understanding among themselves on the principle of freedom of the seas before they talked with the Ger-

---

will give me a free hand in dealing with these immediate negotiations, I can assure you that nothing will be done to embarrass you or to compromise any of your peace principles. You will have as free a hand after the Armistice is signed as you now have." *I.P., 4,* 74.

36. Wilson's texts of the cables quoted above are printed in Baker, pp. 429–39. House's transcriptions are in Y.H.C..

37. House's diary tells us he spent "almost every minute" of free time in discussing Point Two with British leaders. Heavy losses on the American battlefront spurred his efforts. House diary, entry of Oct. 29 (actually Oct. 30; see Floto, p. 285, ns. 204ff.); entries of Nov. 2, 3, 1918.

In a conversation with Lord Reading, who explained that the British people regarded the high seas as their private property, House remarked that if he were a British statesman he would not hesitate to tell the truth to the people and explain where their isolated, nationalistic thinking would lead them. "I let him know," the colonel recorded in his diary on November 4, "that it was not my intention to budge and that I had the backing of the President."

38. See Floto, p. 286, n. 247.

mans. Wilson's message made it clear that he could not recede from the "essentially American terms in the program:" Points One, Two, Three, and Fourteen.[39]

Lloyd George thought the president obdurate. Adroitly trying to avoid the stigma of sole objector, he suggested that freedom of the seas was a question for France and Italy as well as for Great Britain. But Clemenceau, with whom House had been talking persuasively, broke in with: "I do not see any reason for not accepting the principle. We accept." And then turning to Lloyd George: "You do also, do you not?"

The prime minister bade them face political realities. Freedom of the seas had "got associated in the public mind with the blockade," he said. "It's no good saying I accept the principle. It would only mean that in a week's time a new prime minister would be here who would say that he could not accept this principle. The English people will not look at it. On this point the nation is absolutely solid." House thought he had never seen Lloyd George so agitated.[40]

Unable to get unqualified acceptance of Point Two, House had asked Wiseman to work out "something anodyne." Now he agreed to settle on a compromise that seized upon a thought expressed to Wiseman by the president two weeks before.[41] It was arranged that the question could be discussed among themselves at the peace conference without including Germany in the talks. The prime minister, yielding nothing substantial but consenting to humor the Americans by leaving the vital question open, set down the understanding in a note to House, who insisted that it be addressed to him personally and not to Washington.[42]

House transmitted Lloyd George's letter to the president, specify-

---

39. See *I.P., 4*, pp. 182–83.
40. *I.P., 4, p.* 184. "Notes of a Conversation at the Residence of Col. House," Nov. 3, Y.H.C.; House diary, Nov. 3, 1918.
41. See above, pp. 58–59. Sir Arthur Willert, *The Road to Safety*, p. 163. "Actually it was Sir William Wiseman who worked out the compromise." Seymour's note on memo. of Feb. 20, 1953 signed "W.W.," Y.H.C.
42. House diary, Nov. 4, 1918; *I.P. 4,* 184–85.

Paris, November 3, 1918

My dear Colonel House:

I write to confirm the statement I made in the course of our talk this afternoon at your house when I told you that 'we were quite willing to discuss the Freedom of the Seas in the light of the new conditions which have arisen in the course of the present war.'

In our judgment this most important subject can only be dealt with satisfactorily through the freest debate and the most liberal exchange of views.

I send you this letter after having had the opportunity of talking the matter over with the foreign secretary, who quite agrees.

Ever sincerely,
D. Lloyd George

ing that it should not be published unless necessary. "If I do not hear from you to the contrary," the colonel's message concluded, "I shall assume that you accept the situation as it now is. This I strongly advise. Any other decision would cause serious friction and delay." Wilson assented, while resolving to pursue the question later and win the members of a league of nations to his position.[43]

Thus the statesmen of the West, meeting in secrecy and speaking with good will, frankness, and with due regard for political realities, deferred discussion of the most dangerous of the differences between the United States and British governments. House, although failing to attain the declaration of principle from the British that Wilson wanted, succeeded in averting a complete impasse.[44] The controversial issue of freedom of the seas, which was a symbol of material conflict between the nation that had been the world's greatest power and the nation that was about to succeed to that role, defied rational treatment and remained to complicate the deliberations of the peace conference. It was perhaps partly in compensation for Clemenceau's support in this controversy with the British that House acquiesced in the French plan for the Rhineland.[45]

The way was now clear for acquiescence of the Allied statesmen in another point that Wilson considered to be "essentially American," and the one that he thought fundamental to the entire peace settlement—the call for a general association of nations to keep the peace. Cables from the president kept this ideal in the forefront. A letter from Lord Robert Cecil warned Wilson that the desire to create a league would meet opposition from bureaucrats and militarists in Europe, that some people thought that the Germans would exploit such a league, "lulling us and others to sleep, and then falling on us when we have disarmed."[46]

On October 30, the president made it clear to House that he could not participate in a settlement that did not include a league of nations because peace would be without any guarantee except universal armament, which would be intolerable. Vital to the founding of a strong league, in House's view, was the maintenance of close rela-

---

43. Baker, 457; Daniels, *Cabinet Diaries*, pp. 346–47.

44. House recorded that he "brought Lloyd George to terms." Ten years later he wrote: "We had the whip hand then and I pushed our position to the limit." House to Bonsal, March 17, 1929, Bonsal pa. However, a Canadian historian has written that House "suffered a severe defeat" and "Lloyd George and Balfour secured at Paris a substantial victory." Harold I. Nelson, *Land and Power*, pp. 84n., 85.

45. Cf. above, p. 51. Floto, pp. 53–54, 60.

46. Willert, *Road to Safety*, pp. 154–55. For a time the code word of the British Foreign Office for a league of nations was "Christian Science."

tions among the United States, Great Britain, and the Dominions.

The ministers meeting at Paris knew that many liberals in Western Europe were calling for an international association, and they saw no harm in gratifying the Americans. Although they would have preferred to make the league a sort of postscript to the peace treaty, they nevertheless accepted Point Fourteen, Clemenceau giving notice at the same time that France would not participate in the near future in any association that included Germany. Thus by November 4, the last day of the pre-armistice sessions, the first and last of the four points that Wilson thought "the essentially American terms" were approved as bases of peace, and another, Point Two, was admitted to the agenda of the peace conference.

Point Three advocated "the removal so far as possible of all economic barriers and the establishment of an equality of trade conditions." This matter was as provocative of national rivalry as the question of sea power.

A southern Democrat and an admirer of the Manchester liberals, Wilson had established freer trade than any American president since the Civil War, and had expressed the traditional opposition of his people to commercial discrimination. As the pre-armistice talks began, Democratic politicians in the United States asked for an interpretation of Point Three. They feared that their opponents in the coming Congressional election might win votes by alleging that the president would commit the United States to international free trade. Wilson therefore set forth his views fully in a letter to Senator Simmons on October 28:

> I of course meant to suggest no restriction upon the free determination by any nation of its own economic policy, but only that, whatever tariff any nation might deem necessary for its own economic service, be that tariff high or low, it should apply equally to all foreign nations; in other words, that there should be no discriminations against some nations that did not apply to others. This leaves every nation free to determine for itself its own *internal* policies, and limits only its right to compound those policies of hostile discriminations between one nation and another. Weapons of economic discipline and punishment should be left to the joint action of all nations for the purpose of punishing those who will not submit to a general program of justice and equality.
>
> The experiences of the past among nations have taught us that the attempt by one nation to punish another by exclusive and discriminatory trade agreements has been a prolific breeder of that kind of antagonism which oftentimes results in war, and that if a permanent peace is to be established among nations every obstacle

that has stood in the way of international friendship should be cast
aside. . . . American business has in the past been unaffected by a
policy of the kind suggested and it has nothing to fear now from a
policy of simple international justice. . . .

House's commentary on Point Three propounded the same policy, limiting its application to states belonging to a league of nations,
and calling for a "fair and equitable understanding as to the distribution of raw materials." The colonel had occasion to refer to this
interpretation at a formal meeting of the Supreme War Council on
November 1. Lloyd George, fearful that the victors would have to
endure shortages while the enemy was supplied, asked for clarification. House dodged detailed discussion, except for assuring Belgium
and France of the raw materials needed for reconstruction. Remarking that it was his understanding that Point Three had been accepted by the Allies, he pleaded that he was not prepared to discuss
the question immediately but would be glad to consider it more
closely. Clemenceau relieved his embarrassment by saying that discussion would be postponed until further conversations were held
with House on the subject.[47]

It was equally difficult to define any general American policy with
respect to another economic question of vital political interest to the
European statesmen: reparations. The president had spoken of "restoring" Belgium and occupied portions of France and of the Balkan
Allies; but he had given no hint as to how and to what extent this
should be done.

In the eyes of businessmen in Belgium, Great Britain, France, and
Italy, their countries had suffered attrition in order to save the
world, including the United States, from the ravages of a victorious
Germany. They hoped after the war to regain both their strong posi-
tions in the markets of the world and much of their real wealth.
They expected to do this through seizures of German colonies, German gold, and German machinery. "The most terrible of accounts
between peoples has been opened," Clemenceau told the French
Senate on September 17. "It shall be paid." Posters blossomed out in
Paris immediately after the armistice: *"Que l'Allemagne paye d'abord!"*
The British memorandum of October 30 stated: "The Allied Governments understand that compensation will be made by Germany
for all damage done to the civilian population of the Allies and their
property by the forces of Germany by land, by sea, and from the
air."

---

47. French procès-verbal, Nov. 1, 3:00 P.M. On trade rivalry between the United
States and Great Britain see below, p. 233.

The matter came up on November 1. France and Belgium, the nations that had suffered the greatest damage, wanted to make provision in the armistice terms for restitution. House discouraged this, saying that General Bliss called his attention to the fact that insistence on restitution would "make an extremely great delay necessary," so that the armistice would "never end." Nevertheless when Clemenceau said that the French people were demanding an understanding on this matter, and asked for recognition of the principle of German responsibility, House, seeing that this seemed vital to the Europeans, acceded. It was agreed finally that Germany was not to remove public securities while the armistice lasted, and was to make "immediate restitution of the cash deposit in the National Bank of Belgium and, in general, all documents, specie (including Rumanian and Russian gold), stocks, shares, paper money, together with plans for the issue thereof affecting public or private interests in the invaded countries."

The next day the French secured the inclusion of a general financial clause of far-reaching significance. This reservation provided that "any subsequent concessions and claims by the Allies and United States remain unaffected." French spokesmen at the peace conference were to find this useful in justifying demands beyond the provisions of the armistice or the Fourteen Points.

House had received little counsel on the matter from Wilson. By his silence the president seemed to assent to the statement in the British memorandum of October 30 that Germany would have to provide compensation for all damage done to civilians and their property. House feared that if the reckoning were made too severe, the Germans would conclude that they were to lose their means of livelihood and therefore would fight on in desperation.

From the discussion House understood that the major Allied Powers held Germany responsible only for *direct* damage to civilian populations, and his interpretation was validated years later by Lloyd George's secretary, Philip Kerr.[48] However no precise definition was given to the key phrase in the British statement of October 30 that required restoration of damages. Every government was free to bring its own interpretation to the peace conference. As a result of this imprecision the Allies were able later to propose exactions upon

48. *See* the comment of Kerr (later Lord Lothian) in Charles Seymour, *American Diplomacy during the World War,* p. 391. Lloyd George wrote: "The Allies . . . had no intention of putting forward any demand which would include the costs of the war." David Lloyd George, *The Truth about the Peace Treaties, 1,* 81. On November 3 Hymans of Belgium asked for "a more ample phrase than merely 'damages to the civilian population,' " but Lloyd George insisted that they should not put into the armistice terms anything that would lead Germany to suppose that the victors wanted a war indemnity. Harry R. Rudin, *Armistice 1918,* p. 281.

Germany that were harsher than any that they dared to suggest before the enemy surrendered, exactions that violated the principle that the United States wished to apply to the economic settlement.

The discussions in the pre-armistice sessions brought out other questions about the Fourteen Points.

Hymans asked for a reservation on Point Five that would protect Belgium's rights to its colonial domain. Here he found the interpretation of the American commentary reassuring: There was no intention of reopening all colonial questions, but only of applying Wilson's principles in adjusting the claims created by the war. The question of trusteeships under mandates from a league of nations, which was sure to involve conflicts between American concern for the will of native populations and the commitments made by the Allies in secret treaties, was not formally discussed.

In a private conversation with House, Lloyd George suggested protectorates by the Great Powers over various pieces of the German and Turkish empires. When it was proposed that the United States become trustee for German territory in East Africa, House discouraged the idea of mandates for his nation. In a report to Washington he remarked: "The British would like us to accept something so they might the more freely take what they desire."[49] According to the prime minister, House said that America could not administer colonies, its experiment with the Philippines had not been a great success. The colonel spoke of "a special knack for handling colonies, which did not interfere with the population, and which allowed them to go their own way."[50]

The formal sessions closed without recognition of a reservation that Sonnino presented with respect of the new boundaries of Italy. To avoid controversy that would delay the armistice and perhaps befog essential American purposes, House was reluctant to come to grips with territorial questions. He warned that any essential change in the Fourteen Points would require the president to make a new declaration before the Congress, and he agreed with Clemenceau and Lloyd George in opposing any Italian reservation in connection with the German armistice.[51] In spite of House's warning, however, Sonnino insisted on making a reservation in connection with the armistice with Germany rather than that with Austria-Hungary. He read a statement on Point Nine, but little attention was paid to it.[52]

---

49. House to Lansing, Oct. 30, 1918, *F.R., 1918, I, 1,* p. 424.

50. Lloyd George, *Truth about the Peace Treaties, 1,* p. 115.

51. Rudin, pp. 277, 280; *I.P., 4,* p. 177.

52. French procès-verbal, Oct. 30, 1918. Bonsal, who was present as House's interpreter, recollected in his diary on April 23, 1919: "Apparently nobody heard him, perhaps because no one was paying attention to Italy at the moment." Stephen Bon-

At their last pre-armistice meeting, on November 4, the Allied premiers came to a decision as to their answer to Wilson's note of October 23. Approving the final draft of military and naval terms that Foch was to offer to Germany, they concluded a pre-armistice agreement among the victors by accepting the British memorandum of October 30, thus adopting Wilson's principles as the basis for peacemaking, with two reservations.[53] They authorized House to send the armistice terms and the memorandum of agreement to the president. They asked that Wilson forward the memorandum to the Germans, but not the military terms, which they were to get from Foch. The president was to inform the Germans that if after reading the pre-armistice agreement they still wanted a truce they should send envoys to Marshal Foch. House apprised Wilson by cable, very explicitly, of what was expected of him; and on November 5 the president played the part assigned, dispatching a note to Berlin containing the memorandum of agreement.

Tardieu, French high commissioner in the United States, had recommended that the French statesmen act favorably on the Fourteen Points. He suggested that they could thus help the election campaign of the Democrats, from whom he thought France would gain most in the peacemaking.[54] However, if the Allied ministers hoped that by their acquiescence in Wilson's program they might strengthen his hand at Washington, they were disappointed. On the day on which the president sent his note to Berlin the American voters gave the Republicans a majority of the seats in the Senate.[55]

Within a week the fighting was over. The German emperor having abdicated, coalition of Socialists authorized unconditional acceptance of the armistice proposal. A commission from Berlin sought terms from Foch, raising the menace of famine and bolshevism and asking modification of the blockade so that their people might have

---

sal, *Suitors and Suppliants,* p. 102. The British minutes did not record the reservation. Its text is reproduced in Aldrovandi-Marescotti, *Guerra Diplomatica,* p. xxxi.

53. The text of the reservations, as printed in the French procès-verbal of November 4, is: "They [the Allied governments] must point out, however, that clause two, relating to what is usually described as Freedom of the Seas, is open to various interpretations, some of which they could not accept. They must therefore reserve to themselves complete freedom on this subject when they enter the Peace Conference. Further, in the conditions of peace laid down in his address to Congress of January 8, 1918, the President declared that invaded territories must be restored as well as evacuated and freed. The Allied Governments feel that no doubt ought to be allowed to exist as to what this provision implies. By it they understand that compensation will be made by Germany for all damage caused to the civilian population of the Allies and their property by the aggression of Germany by land, by sea, and from the air."

54. Dispatch, Tardieu (N.Y.) to Clemenceau and Pichon, Nov. 1, 1918, Archives du M.A.E., À paix, A 1159, f.197.

55. See below, pp. 112–13.

food. Foch consented to slight alterations in the exactions, and the armistice was signed at Rethondes on November 11.[56]

The end came so suddenly that the German people scarcely realized that they had suffered a military defeat.[57] Civilians and their property were not injured. No representative of the high command was at Rethondes to surrender a sword. Soldiers marched home with their arms. The commission that was to supervise the armistice set up its headquarters not in Germany's capital, but at Spa in Belgium. The victors had spared the Germans from fully experiencing the bitterness of defeat.

The triumphant peoples welcomed the armistice as the advent of enduring peace. Londoners reveled in a violent rapture. Parisians romped like children in the Place de la Concorde. The fighting was over, men could come home from the trenches and from prison camps, the wheels of industry could turn again, the fields could be cultivated—and the defeated enemy would be expected to pay for damages suffered.

House was jubilant, and so was Wilson, over what they regarded as an American triumph in the pre-armistice negotiations. They rejoiced immoderately in the concessions made by Europeans who in their hour of exhaustion were dependent on the material strength of the United States. House did not undervalue his persuasiveness, reinforced though it was by circumstances; and the colonel seemed untroubled by the possibility that the European negotiators might not precisely share his view of what they had agreed to. Cabling to the White House on November 5 that they had won a "great diplomatic victory," House expressed doubt whether any of the Allied statesmen with whom he had been dealing quite realized how far they were now committed to the American program for peace. To Bonsal he confided in "graveyard" secrecy: "I think the President is in a stronger position than if the Fourteen Points had received a blanket endorsement. The fact that these two half-way reservations have been made, and the right reserved to discuss them later on, demonstrates that twelve of the Fourteen Points have been accepted."[58]

---

56. House agreed with Clemenceau that a marginal note on revictualing, which was granted by Foch, did not invalidate the German signature of the armistice. House to W.W., Nov. 9, 11, 1918, Wilson pa., 5C. See Edward F. Willis, "Herbert Hoover and the Blockade of Germany, 1918–1919," in *Studies in Modern European History in Honor of Franklin Charles Palm*, pp. 270–71.

57. On the conclusion of the armistice and the question of its timeliness, see Pierre Renouvin, *L'Armistice de Rethondes*, pp. 236–67. Clemenceau stated on February 5, 1919 that if the Supreme War Council had known the exact condition of the enemy's forces, it would have imposed far harder conditions. Ibid., p. 267.

58. Bonsal's unpublished ms., Bonsal pa., box 24; House diary, Nov. 4, 1918.

In his diary House wrote on November 4:

> Wiseman and many other friends have been trying to make me
> believe that I have won one of the greatest diplomatic triumphs in
> history. That is as it may be. The facts are that I came to Europe
> for the purpose of getting the Entente to subscribe to the Presi-
> dent's peace terms. I left a hostile and influential group in the
> United States saying they did not approve the President's terms and
> they were trying to incite not only the people of America but the
> Allies to repudiate them. On this side, I find the Entente govern-
> ments as distinctly hostile to the Fourteen Points as our opponents
> at home. The plain people[59] generally both in America and in
> Europe are, I think, with the President. . . . Our armistice to Ger-
> many carries with it the approval of the President's January 8th
> address. . . . I have had to persuade; I have had to threaten, but
> the result is worth all my endeavors.

Auchincloss sent off to Counselor Frank L. Polk an even rosier
view of his father-in-law's achievement. "You have no idea how skillfully the colonel conducted himself during the ten days of the negotiation. . . . George and Clemenceau scrapped like wildcats at one
meeting while we looked on and cheered inaudibly. . . . As usual
the colonel is the confidant of each of the prime ministers; . . . each
plays just as close to the colonel as it suits his purpose at the time and
no closer." The glow of success went to the head of this ardent
young man. "Before we get through with these fellows over here,"
he wrote in his diary, "we will teach them how to do things and to do
them quickly."[60]

In the United States the New York *Herald* expressed the prevailing opinion when it described the signing of the armistice as an "immense diplomatic success." Wilson was made less vulnerable to political attack. The imprecision and inconclusiveness of the
interpretation of the Fourteen Points that the Allies had accepted,[61]
and the dubious extent of their commitment, were overlooked in
the general rejoicing over the ending of the war.

"At this moment," according to Pierre Renouvin, Wilson seemed
to "emerge from the test triumphantly." The French historian wrote
a half-century afterwards: "He has led to his views a public opinion
that was at first pointed towards unconditional surrender. He has

---

59. House's faith in the "plain people" was sustained at this juncture by expressions of good will from important French groups of laborites and liberals. Stephen
Bonsal, *Unfinished Business*, p. 4.
60. Auchincloss diary, Nov. 5, 10, 1918, Y.H.C.
61. See Geoffrey Bruun, *Clemenceau*, pp. 174–75.

not yielded to senatorial opposition. He has sustained his refusal to consult his European allies and yet he has finally got their consent. . . . He has maintained his general direction in accord with the principles that he declared. Actually, he has imposed his arbitration."[62]

In the long view of history the jubilation of the Americans and of their leaders over the apparent acceptance of Wilson's program seems premature. Operating within the limits of what he regarded as "the possible" and moderating the acerbity of the president's tone as well as the extreme views of advocates of unconditional surrender, House had not forced the conferees to accept a strict application of Wilson's Fourteen Points. This might perhaps have been done with more prospect of success before rather than after the fighting ended, although with some risk of prolonging the war.

Actually the pre-armistice agreement was only a declaration, grudgingly approved by the Allies, that in general Wilson's principles would be the basis of peace. The Germans, by accepting the declaration's invitation to ask Foch for armistice terms, seemed to acknowledge the declaration. They were aware of the specific interpretations of the Cobb-Lippmann commentary, although this had not been revealed to them by their enemies. The German news service had intercepted and decoded the wireless message that transmitted the commentary to Wilson; and officials at Berlin made a careful study of its content and seem to have been influenced in making policy by its provisions.[63]

The pre-armistice agreement was based upon an interpretation of the Fourteen Points that modified their application and that was in Wilson's own view merely a presentation of "illustrative suggestions," subject to review at the peace conference. Moreover there had been no action at Paris to supplement the armistices with Austria, Hungary, Turkey, and Bulgaria with any commitment to the American program. If there was any triumph of good diplomacy, its essence was not an American "victory" but rather the taking of a step by all parties toward the ultimate necessity of accommodating conflicting national programs. It was important to the cause of peace that Colonel House had succeeded in establishing rapport with the political chiefs who had led the Allied nations to victory.

---

62. Renouvin, *Armistice de Rethondes,* pp. 136–37. Bernadotte E. Schmitt wrote: "Woodrow Wilson's performance in October 1918 . . . is without parallel in the history of diplomacy." "With How Little Wisdom . . . ," *American Historical Review, 66:* 2 (Jan. 1961), 315. "Wilson had achieved a brilliant diplomatic success," Seymour, p. 325.

63. Klaus Schwabe, *Deutsche Revolution und Wilson-Frieden,* pp. 177, 220, and footnotes.

☆ V ☆

The Americans Improvise

The Allied leaders had been persuaded to give qualified approval to the Fourteen Points by two considerations: their desire to end the fighting quickly, and their dependence on the moral and material power of the United States. After the truce took effect the first of these considerations no longer existed. In order to exploit the second, the American government might have done well to pursue its advantage while the Europeans were still somewhat dazed from the shocks of warfare and fearful of a social upheaval.

The Americans did not immediately exploit their fortunate position, however. Their hesitation has been set down by a British scholar as "one of the amazing features of this post-Armistice period."[1] Actually the armistice had come with a suddenness that took the war leaders of the Allies by surprise and left them gasping.[2] Each day's urgent business and the vast task of demobilizing the machines of war diverted attention from the quest of lasting peace. With every day's delay it became more difficult to build an enduring order upon the prevailing uncertainties.

---

1. F.S. Marston, *The Peace Conference of 1919,* p. 31. See Charles Seymour, "Secret Treaties and Open Covenants," in *These Eventful Years,* (London, 1924), p. 223; Edward H. Buehrig (ed.), *Wilson's Foreign Policy in Perspective,* p. 26; and Harold Nicolson, *Peacemaking,* pp. 47–56.

"The historian may well ask whether the postponement of the mutual consideration and determination of post-war policy, whether by reason of the fear that differences might arise prejudicial to the common war effort, or upon other grounds, amounted to anything more than a manifestation of weakness inherent in a democratic form of government, a disinclination on the part of men inured to the politics of self-governing states to accept responsibility in circumstances in which such acceptance might equally well be postponed." F.L. Warrin, Jr. to the writer.

2. "The governing minds among the Allies never expected the war to end in 1918." Winston Churchill, *The Aftermath,* p. 14.

Woodrow Wilson kept in touch with the negotiations in Europe only spasmodically and superficially. His "one-track mind," about which he often joked and that House privately lamented, occupied itself with duties nearer home. Many of the precious hours that he did devote to foreign affairs were squandered in decoding the secret cipher of House's cables, a task that might well have been assigned to a trustworthy expert. He gave the State Department little knowledge of the line of action he proposed to follow in the peacemaking. In fact, he did not take pains to develop tactics that would effectively exploit the leadership that he held. He was content to entrust this responsibility to House.

Arrangements had been taking shape in the United States for more than a year for the organization and briefing of an American delegation at the peace conference. The president had discussed this matter with House even before the United States entered the war.[3]

A committee of the State Department had been making preparations for the peace conference in the domain of international law.[4] However, the department could provide few experts on the past and current affairs of European and Asiatic countries. The American diplomatic and consular services, only recently organized on a permanent basis with secure tenure, had dealt chiefly with government bureaus and business agencies abroad and contained few men versed in those facts of geography, history, economics, and military strategy that would influence the fundamental decisions of a peace conference. Wilson had decided, therefore, to form an independent body of able specialists; and he gave the colonel a mandate to make plans to formulate the American case for a peace conference "with a full knowledge of the position of all the litigants."[5]

---

3. House wrote in his diary on March 19, 1917: "I shall try to have an effective organization to help influence members of the [peace] conference towards proper solution of the problems. . . . I should want to have information just as available as if in a library," but through people instead of books. Ten days later House gave his views to Wilson and found him receptive. House diary, Y.H.C.

4. The members of the committee, appointed on Feb. 11, 1918, were David Hunter Miller, Lester H. Woolsey, and James Brown Scott, solicitor of the State Department, 1906–10, and a technical delegate to the Second Hague Conference. On preparations initiated by Secretary Lansing see Lawrence Gelfand, *The Inquiry*, pp. 25ff.

5. On August 7 Felix Frankfurter, then a special assistant to the secretary of war, sent to Secretary Lansing from Paris a recommendation that since special committees in France were making preparations for a peace conference, men in the United States should undertake similar studies. House, getting Frankfurter's ideas directly, regretted that "little or nothing" was being done. House to W.H. Buckler, Aug. 21, 1917, Y.H.C. Frankfurter's written suggestions went to Wilson, and a week later the president informed Lansing by letter that he had read the ten-page memorandum "with a great deal of interest." N.A., RG 59, docs. 851.00/ 261/2 and 27 1/2.

Secretary Lansing seemed to accept the situation with good grace,[6] but among officials of the department jealousies were awakened that were to persist through the peace conference at Paris. The creation of a new and separate organization and a lack of contact with it became a source of annoyance to officials.[7]

House acted promptly to organize the band of scholars that the president commissioned, taking men from universities as well as from the Department of State. Some donated their services; some had to submit to loyalty investigations by the Department of Justice. Known collectively as "The Inquiry"—a name thought unlikely to arouse premature expectations of peace among the populace—these experts worked as secretly as possible.[8]

House, determined not to "allow the ignoble element to run away with the situation as they had done in Russia,"[9] thought it wise to enlist the aid of a moderate liberal. With this in view Walter Lippmann was made secretary of The Inquiry.[10] The title of "director" was given to Sidney R. Mezes, president of the College of the City of New York and brother-in-law of Mrs. House. David Hunter Miller, an able member of the New York Bar and a partner of House's son-in-law, directed studies of international law and undertook to effect liaison with the State Department, where he served as "special assistant." He reported to House that he tried to see Lansing every week, as the colonel instructed, with the result that The Inquiry gradually came to work "in very close touch" with the State Department. Plans of organization, an outline of work, and proposals for expenditures went to the secretary of state.[11] Nevertheless, House recorded in his

---

6. House diary, Sept. 13, 1917; Baker, 7, 275. Wilson wrote to House on September 19, 1917: "Lansing is not only content that you should undertake the preparation of data for the peace conference but volunteers the opinion that you are the only one to do it." Y.H.C.

7. William Phillips, *Ventures in Diplomacy,* p. 93; Phillips record, OHRO, Butler Library, Columbia University; Phillips to the writer, May 22, 1954; Gelfand, pp. 23–26, 28, 30. James T. Shotwell recorded that there was "naturally a feeling of antagonism, not to say of jealousy, on the part of State Department officials," and especially the secretary of state, because House had The Inquiry under his personal direction. Shotwell record, OHRO, Butler Library, Columbia University, p. 91.

8. Sidney E. Mezes, "A Brief Account of the Origin and Development of The Inquiry," Inquiry pa. Y.H.C. See Gelfand, pp. 13–31, and Shotwell's account of the beginning of The Inquiry, Shotwell record, pp. 77–8.

9. House diary, Feb. 24, 1918.

10. Colonel House explained to Isaiah Bowman that he had chosen Lippmann, who was editor of the *New Republic,* to represent "liberal" opinion because of his influence and because he was "the least vocal of that crowd." Bowman's "Notes on The Inquiry," Nov. 30, 1918, Bowman pa., file 1, drawer 1, Eisenhower Library, Johns Hopkins University. Much of this document appears in Gelfand, pp. 350–53.

11. Robert Lansing, *The Peace Negotiations,* p. 18; report of Miller to House, June 7, two letters, Miller to House, June 28, 1918, Inquiry pa. On Miller's work, see Gel-

diary on July 23 that Phillips William, an assistant secretary of state, informed him that House's men were "building up too much of an organization within the Department" about which the other officials were not informed. "I rather believe this is true," the colonel wrote.

There was historical precedent for the use of expert consultants at international conferences; but The Inquiry was unusual in that it began work far in advance of the conference that it was to serve.[12] It carried into world affairs the progressive urge for social planning that had led to the creation of administrative commissions at Washington. For months the output was disappointing. Deadlines were disregarded, some reports were sketchy drafts. Not many of the men were experts in the fields to which they were assigned. Indeed few were available who understood the racial and religious tensions in the Middle East and Africa and their bearing on international politics. Nor did they have an adequate understanding of the character and psychology of the Europeans and Asiatics with whom the peace delegates would have to deal. Specialists were selected largely for their general capacity and scholarship and for their ability to write reports well.[13]

The subjects of study were chosen with a view to providing information relevant to any question that might arise. A majority had to do with boundaries, and considered not only those of the German, Austrian, and Turkish empires, but the whole network of Balkan frontiers as well. Each report dealt with a limited geographical area and approached its subject from a specific point of view: historical, sociological, economic, or political.

The Inquiry did not try to synthesize the area studies in such a way as to prescribe measures of greatest benefit to Europe as a whole. Nor did it attempt to reconcile and assign relative weight to the recommendations resulting from the various approaches to each subject. It suffered from lack of effective leadership or control by Wilson, House, and the Department of State.[14]

The director, Sidney Mezes, could not convince the scholars that

---

fand, pp. 301–2, and John P. Posey, "David Hunter Miller at the Paris Peace Conference."

12. Norman L. Hill, *The Public International Conference* (Stanford University, 1919); pp. 37–43, cited in Gelfand, p. 34.

13. James T. Shotwell, *At the Paris Peace Conference,* pp. 83 ff.; Gelfand, p. 113 and supra; *F.R., PPC, 1,* p. 87. See Charles Seymour's comments on members of The Inquiry, *Letters from the Paris Peace Conference,* pp. xxiv–xxx.

14. Gelfand, 181–90, 225. "The Inquiry's operations frequently reflected lack of money but also lack of foresight. . . . Too much was attempted." Ibid., pp. 113, 315–16. In all, The Inquiry had a collection of some two thousand documents, only about 30 percent of which were the products of its members. Ibid., pp. 113, 183–87, 315–16.

he himself had sufficient intellectual capacity to direct their studies. Soon he was head of the organization in name only.[15] House did not remove his wife's brother-in-law, on whose personal loyalty he could rely entirely, but allowed Isaiah Bowman, a prominent geographer, to take executive responsibility. In August Bowman became the driving force, responsible for men, money, and plans. Lippmann resigned to undertake propaganda work in Europe for the Army. An able research committee undertook direction of the work, the appropriation from the president's special funds doubled, and cooperating government bureaus speeded their part in the program.[16] The scholars supplemented their studies by talks with officials of the Allies and with leaders of nascent nations.

Plans for tentative boundaries were worked out in detail and sent in November of 1918 to House, who already had read some of the reports and offered suggestions. The studies on Russia, Africa, and the Pacific Islands were little used; those on Latin America, which were more costly than all others combined, were used not at all;[17] but the information on Europe proved to be of great value. A series of base maps made it possible to meet the cartographic needs, from day to day, of various committees of the peace conference.[18]

Both the State Department and The Inquiry had taken steps to keep posted on the preparations of the Allied governments. Secretary Lansing sent to American embassies in the capitals of the Allies, on November 27, 1917, a request for intelligence about the men who would probably be chosen as peace delegates.[19]

Douglas Johnson, an instructor in physiography at Columbia, had been commissioned by the Army War College and instructed to

---

15. Mezes seemed to scholars unable to understand the rudiments of international usage and problems. Shotwell record, pp. 77–80; Gelfand, pp. 350–55; Geoffrey J. Martin, *Mark Jefferson: Cartographer,* p. 169. However, after several talks with Mezes at New York, Emmanuel de Martonne, secretary of the French Comité d'Études, found him to be a sound and reserved administrator, with an intellect inferior to those of the professors of The Inquiry but with some knowledge of European questions and willing to acquire more. "Rapport sur le Comité d'Enquête," Archives du M. A.E., À paix, vol. 161.

16. Bowman to Clive Day, Nov. 4, 1918, Inquiry pa. The members of the research committee were Bowman and professors Haskins of Harvard, Young of Cornell, and Shotwell of Columbia. When conflicts among the personnel arose, House or Bowman resolved them. F.L. Warrin, Jr. to the writer.

17. The work on Latin America continued into 1919. House ordered that all work at New York be ended on January 31. Miller to Polk, Jan. 15, 1919, N.A., RG 256,184.83/12, 12½, 13A, 15.

18. Isaiah Bowman, "The Inquiry," J.T. Adams (ed.), *The Dictionary of American History, 3,* New York, 1940, p. 124.

19. Lansing to embassies in Allied capitals, Nov. 27, 1917, N.A., RG 59, 763.72119/1002a.

make a study for The Inquiry of the relation of military strategy to the defining of national boundaries after the war. He was to observe the organization, technique, and output of foreign specialists who were assembling data. Going to Europe in March of 1918, Major Johnson talked with many of these men and visited most of the battle fronts.[20] He proposed the creation of a center in which the national programs could be correlated in advance of the peace conference, hoping thus to dispel the attitude of suspicion and distrust that he found in certain circles at London and at Paris. Johnson informed House on May 1 that Balfour wanted the "peace data" that had been collected by British experts to be exchanged for similar studies of The Inquiry. In France he found some sympathy among members of the Comité d'Études.[21] But officials who feared to risk controversy over incendiary issues did not take the work of this "college professor" seriously. Ambassador Walter Hines Page, for example, brushed him off as "a very nice fellow who doesn't at all see the absurdity of his errand."[22] However, Bowman put a high value on Johnson's work, and House read his reports with satisfaction.[23]

Walter Lippmann, undertaking a mission of propaganda abroad and coordinating his work with that of Johnson, was less successful in being of service. Commissioned a captain in the Army's intelligence, he reported to House that officials of the foreign offices of the Allies were eager to work with The Inquiry, and that he himself wished to attempt "subtly" to promote the cause of a league of nations. Lippmann sent dispatches to the State Department that were critical of propaganda of the Committee on Public Information.[24] The censure reached the president and was resented by George Creel, director of the C.P.I., who had the confidence of Wilson. House, after receiving a letter from the president asserting that

---

20. D. Johnson's instructions, Inquiry pa. Mezes encouraged Johnson to be "merely receptive" and to refrain from expressing opinions. Mezes to American Embassy, Paris, for Johnson, telegram, n.d., Inquiry pa.; reports of Johnson to Bowman and House from London. Inquiry pa., box 1.

21. Martonne described Johnson as *"un esprit solide et un ami de la France."* "Rapport sur le Comité d'Enquête." Studies in progress in France and Great Britain preparatory to peacemaking are described by Gelfand, pp. 175–83.

22. Page diary, April 13, 1918, Page pa., Houghton Library, Harvard University. "This is House . . . of course," Page wrote. "House and Evangeline are innocent twins."

23. Bowman to Col. John M. Dunn, October 30, 1918, Bowman pa., file 1, drawer 3.

24. Lippmann wrote to Mezes that appointees of the C.P.I. were making "a tragic and grotesque effort to interpret the soul of America," and that many a diplomat had been "bitten in an attempt to control the uncontrollable Creel." Lippmann to Mezes, Sept. 5, 1918, Mezes pa., Butler Library, Columbia University.

Lippmann's judgment was "most unsound, and therefore unserviceable" in matters of propaganda, wrote to warn Lippmann to refrain from saying or cabling anything of a critical nature, and urged him to remain in Europe.[25]

Actually there was little conferring of the advisers of the various peace delegations until the Americans reached Paris and came to grips with the specific questions of the settlement. However, Emmanuel de Martonne, secretary of the French Comité d'Études, talked with the men of The Inquiry and was convinced that House was above all a man of good sense. He shared the relief expressed by Bowman at the departure of Lippmann, whose concern for self-determination suggested a plebiscite for Alsace-Lorraine, which France expected to regain unconditionally.[26]

By the time of the armistice The Inquiry, although possessing a vast number of British and French studies, was not well posted on the information that came to the State Department from its embassies. Its own periodic reports of progress went to the president and the secretary of state. According to House, Wilson preferred everything to go to him first rather than to the State Department. "Later I got him to agree. . . . ," House wrote, "for Mezes to keep in touch with Lansing, but the President added 'and also with me.' I shall arrange this and shall endeavor to give Lansing a larger and larger part."[27]

After taking ship for Europe, House sent a wireless message asking that Mezes organize The Inquiry for service at Paris. Bowman suspected that House had lacked courage to inform him face to face of this move, which seemed to Bowman to undermine the authority that House had given to him.[28]

In a conference of October 24th, Lansing suggested to Mezes that the staff of The Inquiry was inexperienced in practical dealing with foreign questions and there were better men in the State Department. Although Lansing gave the impression that he might "try to get more of his men and to influence the composition of the secre-

---

25. W.W. to House, Aug. 31; House to Lippmann, Sept. 6, 1918, Y.H.C.

26. Martonne, "Rapport sur le Comité d'Enquête," pp. 1, 11. Martonne came to an understanding on all important points with Professor Charles H. Haskins of Harvard, who was in charge of the study of the question of Alsace-Lorraine, and whom he set down as "very sympathetic to France." He recorded that though the French committee had sent all of its works to House, it was not possible to get all the American documents until the last two months of 1918.

27. House diary, October 13, 1917. "Ordinarily, Inquiry members received from the State Department information they requested. It was not furnished voluntarily," Gelfand, p. 106.

28. "Statement made by Dr. Bowman on the organization of The Inquiry" (notes taken March 14, 1932). See also Bowman's "Notes on the Inquiry," Gelfand, p. 358.

tariat," Mezes assured House that in their talk "everything was entirely friendly."[29]

The next day Mezes sent to Lansing a copy of a diagram of organization for the American delegation with his own interpretations of it. After a cabinet meeting on the twenty-ninth the secretary of state left the chart with the president, and Wilson immediately returned it with this comment:

> I think the enclosed much too ambitious a program, and I would be obliged if you would have a simpler one worked out in the meantime telling Mezes that it is so unlikely that anything but main territorial, political and racial questions at issue will be settled at the Peace Conference and practically so certain that all detailed discussions of financial and commercial and other similar arrangements will be delegated by the conference to special conferences or commissions, that I think he ought to plan only to carry the men and materials with him which will be serviceable in settling the main questions, together of course with the necessary clerical aid. The Department itself in the meantime can work out the necessary minimum personnel and organization.[30]

Lansing acted to carry out the president's wishes. After a talk with Bowman and in consultation with Mezes he cut down the staff of The Inquiry from the seventy-five contemplated by House to twenty-three, and it was decided that Bowman should serve as "chief territorial specialist."[31]

Counselor Frank L. Polk was distressed by a lack of coordination. On October 28 he told Secretary Lansing that House, who had been communicating directly with the President in a private code, had not sent a report of his work through the regular channels of the State Department, and that this was bad practice. However Mezes sent reports on the work of The Inquiry to House through the department. The first was blocked by the president; and Mezes, informed of this by Polk, sent a second and wrote to House: "Evidently cabling must be very circumspect and colorless from my end. . . . On one point (they were too polite to mention) they are right, . . . It's the old point of our relationship and the hold for criticism it gives and

---

29. Mezes to House, Oct. 26, 1918, Inquiry pa., series I, box 2, Y.H.C.

30. W.W. to Lansing, Oct. 29, 1918, *F.R., PPC, 1,* p. 113. Lansing sent Mezes a copy of Wilson's reply and Miller took it to House, at Paris. Mezes to House, Nov. 1, 1918.

31. Statement made by Dr. Bowman on the reorganization of The Inquiry. (Notes taken March 14, 1932.) Of about 150 who had taken part in the work of The Inquiry not more than 35 served at the Peace Conference. Gelfand, pp. 183, 318.

will increasingly as the rush for the bandwagon grows. . . . That is
why in my second try I mention Bowman."[32]

When the peace mission finally embarked for Europe, on December 3, the president noted with surprise that the delegates were
so numerous. He had denied himself the pleasure of appointing his
son-in-law, Francis B. Sayre, while House had taken along a son-in-
law[33] and Mrs. House's brother-in-law. Each was accompanied by his
wife, contrary to a general order issued by the president, who himself was to enjoy the company of Mrs. Wilson. Exceptions were made
also in the cases of Mrs. Miller, Mrs. Lansing, and Mrs. Grew.[34]

In the days following the armistice the demands upon House, as
spokesman for the president, were many and diverse. He was the
target of all who sought American aid or favor. He approached the
peacemaking in the same spirit in which his nation plunged into the
war. Ambassador Gerard had predicted at Berlin, when the Kaiser
asked him with what weapons Americans might hope to fight, that
they would "invent something." Now the resourceful Texan undertook to improvise an organization to make peace.

He established rapport with the American embassy at Paris and
was shown all of its outgoing telegrams.[35] For matters of organiza-

32. Lansing desk diary, Oct. 28, 1918; letter and cable Mezes to House, both
Nov. 2, 1918, Y.H.C. In the cable Mezes said: "If you need them some men with a few
draughtsmen and translators could be sent over in Bowman's [sic]."

33. Auchincloss fully realized that it would be "immensely improper" for him, as
House's son-in-law, to serve as secretary of the American Commission to Negotiate
Peace and was aware that such a mistake might provoke a bitter attack and an inves-
tigation by the Congress. Auchincloss diary, Nov. 14, 1918, Y.H.C.

A professor of law at Harvard, Sayre had canceled other plans in order to work
for The Inquiry at New York. A memorandum dated Nov. 1, 1918 indicates that as of
that date Sayre was to go to Paris with The Inquiry, Miller pa., box 83, folder I, 12,
L.C. Wilson vetoed the idea and advised Sayre to accept the decision without protest.
Sayre to the writer. Sayre wrote to House: "He [Wilson] felt that if I went over, my
relationship to him might give the opposition some handle of attack (in spite of the
fact that I was going without salary), and he therefore asked me not to go. . . . I had
hoped so much to have had a hand in helping to overthrow some of the reactionary
forces at the Peace Conference." Letter, Nov. 30, 1918, Y.H.C.

Professor Sayre made an analysis of past peace treaties and also of the policies
and practices of international organizations that had functioned in limited areas, such
as the Postal Unions. As a result he challenged what he called "perhaps one of the
oldest and most securely established principles of diplomatic procedure"—the principle of unanimity, which deprived the majority in international congresses of power to
bind the minority. Francis B. Sayre, Experiments in International Administration (New
York, 1919); Sayre to Miller, Dec. 3, 1918, Miller pa., box 84, II, 21.

34. The exclusion of wives was to cause much embarrassment. Some of the most
valuable advisers balked at going abroad without consorts. Lansing cabled to House:
"Department having serious difficulties with wives of Army officers. . . . Any exception created tremendous problems." Auchincloss diary, Nov. 19, 1918.

35. Telegram for Polk, signed "House," Nov. 16, 1918, Auchincloss diary. Of
William G. Sharp, the American ambassador to France, House wrote during the pre-

tion he depended chiefly on Joseph C. Grew, whom he had asked to accompany him to Europe and whom Lansing appointed secretary general of the United States Commission to Negotiate Peace. Grew was a young man who had served in the embassies in Germany and Austria during the war before relations were broken. Thereafter he was chief of the Western European Division of the State Department, where he became familiar with the inner workings of what he had regarded as "a big mysterious machine or secret society." He went to Paris with an understanding of many of the difficulties to be met and with an impatience of red tape. He looked forward to the peace conference as "the great event of this age or of any age," and he regarded House's little advance group as trail blazers seeking to clear a road to peace. He honored the colonel as "the Head Pioneer."[36]

With Major Willard Straight, a young liberal of great charm and ability who was appointed as executive officer, Grew drew up a provisional chart and began work. Immediately, however, these men fell ill with the influenza that was then ravaging the Western world. Straight died. House, Wiseman, and Ambassador Sharp were stricken. House's secretary, thinking the atmosphere the "most depressing" he had ever been in, wrote: "Everyone around seems to have something the matter with him."[37]

Grew recovered in a week and, after making inquiries among ranking Americans at Paris, tentatively selected heads for various bureaus. Keeping his office open every day but Sunday, he held daily meetings to discuss the efforts of the bureaus and to coordinate them.[38]

To lodge the American delegates the Hotel Crillon on the Place de la Concorde was requisitioned. An urgent request by Ambassador

---

armistice meetings: "His judgment is keen and his appreciation of the various currents of French opinion acute." *I.P., 4,* p. 226.

36. Joseph C. Grew, *Turbulent Era, 1,* pp. 328–32. House and Bliss thought that Grew ought to have a title as impressive as that of the corresponding British official, who was known as "superintending ambassador." They noted that some of the military officials at Paris misunderstood the prerogatives of a mere "secretary." To make Grew an ambassador would be to rank him equally with the American plenipotentiaries. When the matter was put to the president he approved the rank of minister with the designation of "supervising director." Grew decided to keep also the title of "secretary," which he thought dignified enough. Ibid., 371–72; House to Lansing, Dec. 12, 1918, Y.H.C. Auchincloss reported to Polk that House wanted to cut loose from detailed preparations for the conference and that therefore he did his "best to turn over every bit of the work [to Grew] except that which pertained to the colonel personally." Auchincloss to Polk, Nov. 21, 1918, Y.H.C.

37. Auchincloss diary, Nov. 23, 1918.

38. Grew, pp. 369–73. Minutes of the meetings in Grew's office, Nov. 25–Dec. 12, 1918, are in N.A., R.G. 256, doc. 184,00101. "Grew . . . and the entire staff came in from time to time for information and advice." House diary, Dec. 7, 1918.

Sharp caused it to be vacated under French direction, the hundreds of occupants being given only twenty-four hours to get out.[39] But the Crillon was not big enough to house the mushrooming body of American peacemakers. Grew cabled to the State Department that three buildings were full and yet another might be needed.[40]

House, detached from all permanent bureaus of his government and responsible only to the president, moved on December 7 into the Crillon. His office became an agency for international negotiation that was without precedent.[41]

One of the practical questions that had to be settled was that of a site for the peace conference. Wishing to escape the nationalistic atmosphere that prevailed in the capitals of the belligerents, he agreed with Lloyd George upon Geneva.[42] At first Wilson preferred Lausanne because of its pro-Ally sympathies. However, Ambassador Jusserand talked persuasively with him. Warning of the "inconvenience" of meeting in Switzerland "in a center of espionage without an equal in the world," Jusserand begged Wilson not to reject Paris and Versailles, where treaties pertaining to the independence of the United States were signed.[43] On November 8 Wilson cabled to House: "On second thought it occurs to me that Versailles may be the best place for the peace conference where friendly influences and authorities are in control rather than Switzerland which is saturated with every poisonous element and open to every hostile influence in Europe." Although he felt that the president did not appreciate the French influences that they would have to contend with at Versailles, House yielded to Clemenceau's wish. Thus it was ordained that Clemenceau, and not Wilson, would as host be the presiding officer at the peace conference.[44] Since the living accommodations at Ver-

---

39. William G. Sharp, *The War Memoirs of William G. Sharp,* p. 390; Auchincloss diary, Nov. 29, 1918; F.L. Warrin, Jr. to the writer, June 1962.

40. Grew to Sec. State, Dec. 7, 1918, N.A., RG 256,184/35A; minutes of Dec. 3, ibid., 184,00101/1. The American quarters were described by Nicolson as "a ramshackle office stretching out over Maxims." *Peacemaking,* p. 223.

41. See below, pp. 257–61.

42. Stephen Roskill, *Hankey, 1,* 622; House diary, Oct. 29, 1918.

43. Dispatches, Jusserand to Pichon, Jusserand to M.A.E., Nov. 5, 1918, Archives du M.A.E., A paix, A 1000.1, f.30.

44. House diary, Nov. 8; W.W. to House, Nov. 7, 14, 1918 Y.H.C. The State Department was seriously concerned by the presence in Switzerland of revolutionary committees from central and eastern Europe. Lansing to House, Nov. 9, 1918, N.A. RG 59, 763.72119P43/284b. See Arno J. Mayer, *Politics and Diplomacy of Peacemaking,* pp. 347, 352–53.

Lloyd George said to Wiseman: "I never wanted to hold the Conference in his [Clemenceau's] bloody capital. Both House and I thought it would be better to hold it in a neutral place, but the old man wept and protested so much that we gave way." Wiseman diary, Jan. 29, 1919, Wiseman pa., Y.H.C.

To prepare British opinion to meet Wilson's wish, House induced Lord North-

sailles were inadequate, the delegates took up residence in Paris and found it convenient to hold most of their meetings there.

The question of an official language remained open until the meetings began in January. Before the war European diplomats had taken it for granted that French was their common tongue; and the Quai d'Orsay now argued that the language used should be that of the city in which the conference met.[45] However, House thought that since almost all delegates would understand English, France should make a concession. Wilson, whose political strength depended in large measure on his eloquence and who felt that he did not have a "suitable confidential force" of translators, wanted to negotiate in English, which, he reminded House, was the diplomatic language of the Pacific. Balfour, foreseeing difficulty in persuading France to yield, suggested that Clemenceau be asked whether both English and French might serve as official languages. Clemenceau, who understood English, consented, and eventually the conference adopted this arrangement.[46]

Noting excessive claims for reparation that were being advanced in the Allied nations, House apprised Wilson of the importance of having a technical study of the actual damages to property in Belgium and France. He set army engineers to work on such a project, only to have it pointed out later by his American colleagues that such a study was "a great waste of time and expense." [47]

---

cliffe to print an editorial in *The Times* of November 11 advocating Versailles as the site of the conference. *I.P., 4,* pp. 218–19; Stephen Bonsal, *Suitors and Suppliants,* p. 12. On November 20 Ambassador Derby informed House that the British government agreed to hold an inter-Allied conference at Versailles, but would not commit itself as to the site of the final conference. Derby-House corres., Y.H.C. Nicolson wrote, in retrospect: "One of the greatest misfortunes of the last Peace Conference was that it took place in Paris. It was impossible for even the most minor official to remain uninfluenced by the tenseness of the atmosphere which prevailed." *Peacemaking,* "Introduction 1943," p. xxiv.

45. "Conversations Berthelot-Frazier," Nov. 21, 1918, Archives du M.A.E., À paix, A1000. 1, f.30; Raymond Poincaré, *Au Service de la France, 11,* 49.

46. *I.P., 4,* pp. 228, 236–37. Cable, W.W. to House, Nov. 23, 1918, in Auchincloss diary; telegram, Wiseman to Drummond, Nov. 24, Drummond to Wiseman, Nov. 26, 1918 Y.H.C.; F.O. to Derby, Dec. 30, 1918, Y.H.C.; House diary, Jan. 7, 1919. The final understanding provided that proceedings should be conducted in French and English on equal terms, and that conclusions should be first drafted in French but English-speaking delegates should be bound only by the English version, which would be of equal authority with the French. Memo of Jan. 15, 1919 signed by Balfour, Wilson pa., 5B, L.C.

47. *F.R., PPC, 1,* pp. 303–4. The president authorized the expenditure of such additional funds as were required for the project directed by General McKinstry. W.W. to Sec. War, Jan. 14, 1919, Wilson pa., 5B. On February 7 at the daily meeting of the American Commission to Negotiate Peace McKinstry's work was set down as "a great waste of time and expense, inasmuch as the American government had no interest in the division of whatever sum Germany would be able to pay." It was decided to

House worked to end censorship and was able to advise Wilson before the end of November that both the French and the British government agreed to stop political interference with press dispatches to the United States.[48] Then he effectively urged the American newsmen at Paris to take advantage of this by sending home dispatches that would strengthen the president's hand. The colonel's faith in the fundamental rightness of popular opinion was strong. He cultivated friendships with publicists and diplomats who could help Wilson's cause.[49]

It was understood among scholars in the United States[50] that the work of ending a war consisted of two parts: the making of a preliminary agreement as to essentials; and then the drafting of a treaty implementing the agreement by men of special technical skill and knowledge of international law, who prepared their cases with full regard to considerations of history and jurisprudence.

House, realizing that the pre-armistice meetings had accomplished much of the necessary groundwork, advocated the immediate writing of a treaty that would impose military terms, conditions for reparations, and tentative boundaries. Such a procedure, he argued, would do more than anything else to reduce the dangers of anarchy and rampant nationalism in Central Europe.[51] Haunted by the men-

---

communicate this opinion to the president and to ask whether he wanted McKinstry's work to continue. Minutes of the ACTNP, Feb. 7, 1919, *F.R., PPC, 11, 24*.

48. In a cable of November 19 Wilson asked House to press "very earnestly and very promptly" with the British and French authorities the removal of political censorship of news dispatches. House sent a paraphrase of the president's message to Pichon, who responded affirmatively the next day, November 21. Auchincloss diary, Nov. 19–21, 1918. On the twenty-fourth Wiseman informed Drummond, at London, of the French response, and said that House was asking whether the British government would not take the same action. Telegram, Wiseman to Drummond, Nov. 24, 1918, P.R.O., FO/800/US/98. Drummond replied: "We are obliged on national grounds to maintain censorship control of military and naval matters and of certain aspects of finance and economics but political censorship as you and I understand it has been entirely removed." Telegram, Drummond to Wiseman, Nov. 27, 1918, Wiseman pa. Wilson's cabinet agreed that like Great Britain and France the United States should continue commercial censorship, which the War Trade Board desired, until conditions were normal. Daniels diary, Nov. 12, 1918, L.C. cf. below, pp. 236–37n.

49. For example, House invited Wickham Steed, Northcliffe's editor, to assist "in an honorary capacity as adviser on Central and South European Affairs." Steed recorded: "I was warmly attached." *Through Thirty Years, 2*, p. 250.

50. See Charles C. Hyde, professor of international law at Northwestern University and author of monographs on international law for the State Department for the use of delegates to the peace conference, "The Preparation of the American Delegates to the Peace Conference," J.B. Moore pa., box 167, "Wilson" folder, L.C.

51. House's desire for an immediate conference to settle essential matters was supported by a memorandum of October 28 from General Bliss. *I.P., 4*, p. 145. Looking back later from a perspective of ten years, House wrote in justification of his instinct to follow the traditional procedure:

ace of bolshevism, he wrote in his diary a week after the armistices: "I am trying to frighten those who are endeavoring to postpone the congress. I am telling them the people will soon begin to murmur."

The unofficial channel of communication that House had established with the British Foreign Office remained open. Miller talked daily with Wiseman, who was eager to bring together House and Foreign Secretary Balfour to discuss the really important points on which American and British policies might differ.

It was a cardinal principle of the British Foreign Office that delay would prove fatal.[52] A month before the armistice they produced plans for negotiations with Germany to settle fundamental questions arising out of the war, as a preliminary to a peace conference. They pointed out the advantage of a definite treaty of peace that would make it possible for demobilization to proceed rapidly. The Foreign Office was prepared to supply qualified negotiators to deal with the inevitable questions of the peacemaking, expeditiously and concurrently. They conceived that it was in the interest of their country to work with the Americans along the general lines laid down by Wilson, while endeavoring at the same time to give effect to the time-honored British policies of maritime supremacy, a balance of power on the Continent and demilitarization of the Channel coast, preservation of civil order, and open facilities for trade. The British diplomats were willing to attempt to respect the principle of national integrity and also the doctrine of self-determination, difficult though it would be in application.[53] The Foreign Office was inclined to act as it thought best, and to take the consent of the Parliament and the public for granted.

Lloyd George, however, was not ready to get on with the peacemaking. He was preoccupied with the strengthening of imperial ties

---

In retrospect, it seems that this course might have saved the debacle of the Continental European currencies. It might have avoided the long years of delay in the adjustment of reparations. . . . In all probability, the United States would have ratified both treaties, surely the first, and such a commitment would have all but ensured ratification of the second. President Wilson probably would not have continued in Paris after the preliminary peace was made, and he would thus have been spared the heart-breaking task laid upon him from January to June. . . . Both the Allies and the Central Powers would have been already pledged to it [the League of Nations] in the preliminary treaty. . . . With a preliminary treaty ratified, he would in fact have been in even a stronger position. *I.P., 4,* pp. 202–4.

52. Lord Hardinge, *Old Diplomacy,* p. 229.

53. Hardinge p. 230; two printed memos., n.d., filed under Dec. 1918, P.R.O., Cab/29/52, 53. A commission of British scholars, set up in the winter of 1916–17 as an adjunct of the Foreign Office, produced 163 handbooks filled with information that might be useful in making peace. The British reasons for supporting self-determination are explained in V.H. Rothwell, *British War Aims and Peace Diplomacy,* pp. 288 ff.

and with plans for calling a general election that could be expected
to reaffirm his position as a popular and victorious war leader. His
experience during the war, when in order to evolve overall strategy
and control he had to contend with archaic protocol, bureaucratic
stuffiness, and the ambitions and jealousies of small men, had led
him to share Clemenceau's feeling that war was far too important to
be entrusted to the military. He was likewise distrustful of the capacity of diplomats to make an adequate peace. Moreover, before undertaking the peacemaking he wanted an opportunity to cross-ex-
amine Wilson personally and induce him to define precisely the four
points that the president regarded as "essentially American."[54]

Veterans of the Foreign Office distrusted certain personal friends
and publicity men who were close to Lloyd George, just as officials in
the State Department at Washington looked askance at emergency
wartime organizations that they could not control. The men who
knew the prime minister well thought him open-minded and acces-
sible, ready to argue any point and to listen to disagreeable fact. Professional diplomats, however, noted that until he became prime minister at the end of 1916 Lloyd George showed no deep interest in
foreign affairs. Though superb as an advocate of policy before the
electorate, he seemed unwilling to create or consistently pursue a reliable course. Critics thought him vain, imprecise, and far too self-
serving in his aims. These were shortcomings that diplomats of the
old school loathed. It seemed to the men of the Foreign Office that
insufficient account was being taken of their work and that Lord
Hardinge, the permanent undersecretary who had it in charge, was
to be slighted at the Peace Conference.[55] The career men, profes-
sionals who were fluent in French and had a deep knowledge of the
processes of negotiation, resented the transfer of traditional
prerogatives of their office to a private secretariat that Lloyd George
set up at 10 Downing Street and that became known as the "Garden
Suburb." At least one distinguished diplomat, Sir Arthur Murray,
noted a tendency for foreign policy to be conducted with no fixed

---

54. After an interview with the prime minister, Frank I. Cobb of the *World* reported to House that the British government had no intention of attending a formal
peace conference for several months and that the procrastination was due entirely to
considerations of finance, trade, and industry. Cobb to House, Nov. 16, 1918, Y.H.C.
See Chapter 14 of this volume. Auchincloss attributed to all the Allies a desire to work
out reconstruction problems in the war boards before they were abolished. Diary,
Nov. 15, 1918. Marston (p. 34) has cited "other forces tending to delay the conclusion
of peace."

55. Diary of Sir James Headlam-Morley, Jan. 19, 1919, in the possession of Prof.
Agnes Headlam-Morley. See Roskill, *2,* 24. Of the British delegation of about four
hundred people at Paris, only eighteen were on the staff of the Foreign Office. Hardinge, p. 231.

principles, to lack stability of purpose, and to become increasingly opportunistic and hand-to-mouth.[56]

Neither at Paris nor at London was it indicated in November at precisely what point the inevitable pourparlers should become a formal conference. The machinery was at hand in the Supreme War Council and the steering committee of premiers for a resumption of the pre-armistice discussions, and House was ready to fall in with some such program. In earlier centuries the diplomats of Europe could have proceeded expeditiously about their business, with the assurance that only their chiefs had to be pleased and the people would accept and endure. Now it was necessary to satisfy popular opinion that was critical, demanding, and sometimes ill-informed and arrogant. In November of 1918 the victorious political leaders were not ready to proceed with the dispatch that the professional diplomats urged. And it would require several weeks for some of the Japanese delegates to make the long voyage to Paris.[57]

House was not able to arrange for the preliminary peace that he and the professional diplomats of England and France envisioned, but he still entertained hope that a conference of the victorious powers might meet before the year's end and agree on the essential terms to be presented to the enemy. House argued at great length with Léon Bourgeois, the chief French proponent of a league of nations, about what seemed to him the main problem of the peace conference: the treatment to be accorded to the enemy. To Stephen Bonsal, his interpreter, House appeared "determined—even boisterous" as he advocated that Germany be given a voice in the peace talks at the earliest moment possible and be brought into a league of nations. "If we leave her out we will be giving her a free hand," he said. "We must bring her into the new world order and we must hold her to it not by chains . . . but by her appreciation of where her advantage would lie."[58] If Germany became an outcast it might start a rival league that would result in a struggle for supreme power. However, Bourgeois, advocating an international army for the league of nations, insisted that Germany must be punished and accepted into the family of nations only when humbled.

Acting with the tremendous prestige of Wilson's backing, House had now become so confident of his competence that he wished he

56. Arthur Cecil Murray, *At Close Quarters*, p. 71.

57. Polk reported to the American Commission that the head of the Japanese delegation, Marquis Saionji, would leave Japan with his suite on January 14, 1919, and arrive in Marseilles "early in March." Dispatch, Jan. 8, 1919, Wilson pa., 5B.

58. Bonsal diary; House diary, Dec. 5, 1918.

were chairman of an American peace commission, with Secretary of the Treasury McAdoo and Herbert C. Hoover as his associates. Thinking in terms of American politics, he wrote in his diary: "The distribution politically would have been perfect. Texas, New York, and California, with Hoover as the Republican member. . . . If I could have had these two men and . . . only these, I would have been willing to guarantee results."[59]

Every day of delay was eroding the common height of triumph on which the victorious governments stood. Bonsal wrote on November 19: "The hot fit is over, and the satisfaction that we all felt on Armistice night was fading fast. . . . The colonel's desk is piled high with reports of unpleasant incidents that presage bitter discussion and future conflicts. . . . Only ten days have passed and with the pressure of danger Wilson's omnipotence has passed also. New claims and new interests are being presented of which we know little, and of which the powers we have brought into the haven of victory think we know nothing at all. Some of our people are beginning to say that Wilson should have made hard-and-fast agreements with the powers while the eventual issue hung on the balance."[60] In the city of Paris, at the beginning of December, "peace" was so much in jeopardy that General Bliss wrote to advise his wife that it was hardly safe for her to come over until "things settle down a bit."[61]

---

59. House diary, Dec. 3, 1918. House recognized that Hoover and McAdoo alike craved full authority to act. Diary, Jan. 10, 1919.
60. Stephen Bonsal, *Unfinished Business*, pp. 5–7.
61. Letter, Dec. 1, 1918, Bliss pa., L.C.

☆VI☆

The Allies Meet at London

While the American and British spokesmen refrained from promoting any essential negotiating in the last weeks of November, French officials were vigilant to prevent any softening of the policy of the victors toward the enemy. They were active in planning a peacemaking that would protect the interests of France.

A month after the signing of the armistice with Germany it was clear that French opinion demanded compensation for the nation's unprecedented sacrifices. The people were in no mood to forgive and forget. There were indications that the Chamber of Deputies would accept nothing less than the repayment of all costs of the war, annexation of the Saar valley, and permanent policing of the Rhineland by an international force. On November 13 the French ambassador at Washington warned the president against any undue indulgence of the Germans. He was particularly averse to the admission of Germany to a league of nations until after a trial period.[1]

A French high commission had been sent to the United States to direct propaganda; and on Armistice Day its head, André Tardieu, reported to Clemenceau that largely due to the work of his agents the people of the United States entirely accepted the demand for the return of Alsace-Lorraine to France.[2] A member of the commission, Louis Aubert, informed the foreign ministry at Paris that "trustee-

---

1. Dispatch, Jusserand to Pichon, Nov. 15, Archives du M.A.E., À paix, A1154.1, f.155; ibid., Nov. 14, 15, À paix, 1017, f.48; ibid., Dec. 1, 1918, À paix, A 1163, f.199. A plea published by Grey in the summer of 1918 for the admission of Germany into a league of nations had provoked a storm of protest in the French press. Stephen Bonsal, *Unfinished Business,* p. 19.
2. Tardieu to Clemenceau, Nov. 11, 1918, Archives du M.A.E., À paix, A 1025.1.

ship" was a word familiar to American men of affairs and might persuade them to agree to "mandates" under a league of nations. American consent to the occupation of the right bank of the Rhine might be facilitated by the use of the word "neutralization." Moreover, the argument of "compensation" for war damages might be the key to the approval by the United States of France's claim to the subsoil rights in the Saar basin.[3] Tardieu and Aubert returned to Paris before the peace conference began and, working in liaison with the American delegates, made good use of the knowledge that they had gained in the United States and of the respect in which they were held by Colonel House and his friends.[4]

In November the French officials were vigilant to prevent any rift between the Allies and the United States that might be exploited by the enemy. They had reason to be concerned.

The socialist ministers who took over the German government were hostile to extremists[5] and, depending on Marshal Hindenburg and General Groener to preserve order, put faith in President Wilson's proclamation of a "peace without victory" and strove to prepare for the election of a constitutional assembly that would confirm their leadership. The German Foreign Office, believing that harsh conditions of the truce had been forced upon Wilson by the Allied governments, repeatedly pleaded to the State Department for a policy that would mitigate the suffering of the people of Germany and would render them less susceptible to revolution. The Germans sought a moderation of the armistice terms by identifying the aspirations of their own democracy with the program of Wilson.[6] Their strategy won some sympathy in the United States as well as in England.

On November 13, two days after the signing of the armistice, House transmitted to Washington a request by Clemenceau that the German government be notified that it must now address its communications to the Allied governments as well as to the United

3. Aubert realized that it might be difficult for France to follow acquisition of the subsoil rights in the Saar with political acquisition of the region. The large German population, he warned, might make it very hard, though not impossible in the course of time, to get the consent of the people of the Saar to French rule. *"Note sur les Travaux de L'Inquiry et sur les Solutions de paix Américaines,"* Dec. 11, 1918, signed "L.A.," Archives du M.A.E., À paix, vol. 161.

4. F.L. Warrin, Jr. to the writer. "Tardieu appears to be rendering very useful services to the various boards and missions in France." Frazier to House, Oct. 3, 1918, Y.H.C.

5. "Soviets being started all over Germany. Everyone here fearing Bolshevism and its spread through Germany and France to England." Straight diary, Nov. 10, 1918, Croly transcript, John M. Olin Library, Cornell University.

6. Ludwig F. Schaefer, "German Peace Strategy in 1918–1919," pp. 46–48, 64.

States. Advised by House to comply with this request, the State Department did so. Moreover, in response to a German proposal of "a central diplomatic agency" to which appeals might be sent, the department pointed out that the Supreme War Council was such an agency.[7] Thus the divisive strategy of the German foreign ministry was quickly and effectively countered.

Nevertheless the State Department was not insensitive to the plea of the provisional socialist government at Berlin for support against communist rivals. Secretary Lansing, alarmed by the menace, wrote more than one note to the president on the subject.[8] He reported that the Spartacists were gaining headway and that there were many advantages in doing what one could to strengthen the tentative regimes at Berlin and Munich that were "in the hands of good men—moderate social democrats." On Armistice Day, addressing the Congress, Wilson spoke of the intention of the victors to provide food for those peoples who chose "the way of self-control and peaceful accommodation." After a talk with Wilson, Lansing sent a message to House:

> The President is impressed with the wisdom of a suggestion which has recently come to him from more than one quarter, namely that the German authorities be notified that there can be no official dealings with them on the part of the other Powers in connection with the final settlements of the peace until a constituent assembly has been brought together and a definite form of government agreed upon and set up.

This American proposal of an intrusion into the domestic politics of a sovereign state, which grew out of fear that resulted from exaggerated notions of a danger of a communist revolution,[9] was given no support by Europeans who had confidence in the political stability of the German people. When House took up the matter with the Quai d'Orsay he received this reply:

> Intervention of this kind in German internal policy might perhaps be a delicate matter . . . we would take the risk, by bringing pressure of that kind to bear, [of halting] the federalist movement which is taking shape in Germany, while our interest in maintaining peace must suggest to us a hope that the centralist tendencies which were those of Prussia may fail. It further seems to M. Pichon that

---

7. *F.R., PPC, 2,* pp. 17–20, 38–39, 43–45.
8. Lansing to W.W., Nov. 9, Wilson pa., 5A, L.C.; ibid., Nov. 18, 25, 1918, file 2.
9. "In retrospect the danger of bolshevization of Germany seems to have been overestimated." Schaefer, p. 49.

action of this character would seem premature, for there would be objection to our enemies organizing before we were afforded, by a complete carrying out of the clauses of the armistice now underway, the indispensable guarantees against any possible resumption of hostilities.[10]

House was informed by Ambassador Derby on December 12 that the British government was "in general agreement" with the views of the French.[11]

A month after the armistice it was clear to at least one of the officials at Berlin that the American government would act only in concert with the Allied Powers. Count von Bernstorff, formerly the German ambassador at Washington and now head of a bureau for peace negotiation in the Foreign Office, wrote: "Any further pleas to Wilson that he influence the Allies towards moderation must remain unsuccessful because the Americans fear the odium of being classified as pro-German."[12]

The French Ministry of Foreign Affairs, receiving expert advice from a small, compact Comité d'Etudes, undertook to play its part in advancing the peacemaking by circulating a precise plan. The first version was dated November 15 and the second, varying somewhat, November 21. This masterpiece drew four general conclusions from the precedents of the great peace congresses of the nineteenth century. It proposed sixteen rules of procedure to govern the work of the forthcoming conference, recommended a preparatory commission of plenipotentiaries to work out an organization, and very fully outlined an agenda for a preliminary conference that would not include representatives of the enemy. Three basic principles were to be: self-determination and protection of minority rights; renunciation of secret and sectional treaties; and the inviolability of Allied territory as of August 1, 1914. Rejecting the Fourteen Points as too vague, it would give priority to the fulfillment of a joint declaration of war aims that the Allies had issued on January 10, 1917 and that provided that the complete reckoning "would be set forth in detail,

10. The paragraphs above are based on dispatches in *F.R., PPC, 2,* pp. 88–107.
11. Derby–House correspondence, Y.H.C.
12. Bernstorff dreamed of becoming a Talleyrand at the peace conference, and hoped that House would receive him under the same terms of confidence as those under which they worked in the United States in 1916 in attempting to end the war. Schaefer, pp. 46–48, 64; "memo. for Col. House" signed "Lincoln Eyre," Wilson pa., 5B. According to a report from the American chargé at Copenhagen, Bernstorff said if he went to the peace conference and found that House's opinion of him had changed, he would feign illness and leave for Berlin immediately. *F.R., PPC, 2,* p. 122. See below, p. 210 and note.

with all the reservations and equitable indemnities for harm suffered, at the moment of negotiation of the peace."[13]

The document reflected the traditional French desire for a federalized Germany and a weakening of the centralized state that Bismarck had consolidated in 1871 at the expense of France. The peace conference should hear the claims of the new states of Poland and Czechoslovakia, in view of the collapse of Russian power. "Essential problems" must be solved "in order to reconcile the necessary strategic guarantees with the principles of rights of peoples"; Alsace-Lorraine and the Saar basin must become French and the left bank of the Rhine must be neutralized under a "special military regime."

On November 15 House dispatched the French plan to the secretary of state, tentatively omitting a sentence that would have offended Wilson deeply.[14] The sentence read: "Nor can the fourteen propositions of President Wilson be taken as a point of departure, for they are principles of public law, by which the negotiations may be guided, but which have not the concrete character which is essential to attain the settlement of concrete provisions." House also withheld several paragraphs relative to the work of the congresses of Vienna, Paris, and Berlin. In his role of catalyst of peace he saw no reason to introduce elements that might rouse the ire of a prophet who thought the nineteenth-century congresses had been reactionary and even wicked. Wilson, under the influence of historians who condemned the peacemakers of 1815 for their failure to anticipate the strength of the forces of liberalism, nationalism, and industrialism, insisted that no "odor of the Vienna settlement" should come into the forthcoming discussions at Paris, "not even by reference."[15]

---

13. F.S. Marston, *The Peace Conference of 1919*, pp. 35–38; David Hunter Miller, *My Diary, 2*, docs. 4, 5.

14. Miller, *My Diary, 2*, docs. 13, 14. In forwarding a second version of the French plan to the State Department on November 21 House included the offending sentence.

In a document found among Wilson's papers the substance of the French plan is outlined, with comment in typewriting other than that of the president's machine. Wilson pa., 5A.

Secretary Lansing, questioning the practicability of some of the president's principles, and particularly that of self-determination, set down his own views briefly in a memorandum. It was his opinion that the peoples wanted justice and peace and the prevalence of democracy would be enough to attain these goals; that a league of nations needed no sanction or executive functions; that territorial expansion was legitimate where the inhabitants were half civilized; and that conflicting territorial claims could be settled by diplomacy or by a court. Lansing, private memoranda, entries of Oct. 29, 30, Nov. 18, 1918, Lansing pa., microfilm L.C.; William E. Rappard, "W.W., La Suisse et Genève," *Centenaire Woodrow Wilson, 1856–1956*, p. 43.

15. Hajo Holborn, "The Reasons for the Failure of the Paris Peace Settlement," *Henry Wells Lawrence Memorial Lectures*, p. 3.

The president was both suspicious of Allied diplomacy and disinclined to develop a precise American plan of procedure. He ignored an invitation from House for "any modifications, additions, or suggestions" that Washington might care to make with respect of the French proposals. When the State Department sent the French plan to the president on November 16 with a list of thirty-three questions that should be considered, there appears to have been no response from the White House. Two days later Lansing wrote to ask to what extent the president would recognize the secret treaties and, so far as is known, Wilson did not answer.[16] Unfortunately, as later events were to show, the Americans failed to take advantage of the clause in the French plan that proposed a denunciation of treaties. This clause, had Wilson seized upon it, might have required the victorious Powers, by reason of their participation in a general peace conference, to waive rights under the secret agreements that were in conflict with Wilsonian principles.

A third and final version of the French plan proposed that Wilson's principles, "not sufficiently defined in their character to be taken as a basis for a concrete settlement of the war even if appealed to as they have been admitted by the Allies," were to "resume their full strength in the matter of the future settlement of public law." The Quai d'Orsay, now rejecting the Allied declaration of January 10, 1917 along with the Fourteen Points as adequate bases for a peace conference, proposed the ending of a state of war by a preliminary treaty that would prepare a foundation for a general congress. Three nineteenth-century precedents were cited—The Paris Treaty of May 30, 1814, the protocol signed at Vienna on February 1, 1854, and the Treaty of San Stefano, signed March 3, 1878.

The conditions of the preliminary treaty were to be imposed on the enemy without any discussion with them. In accord with a stipulation that had been inserted in the second draft, Germany would be forced to legitimize the exactions of the peace treaty as just punishments for violation of the laws of nations and for crimes against humanity. However, the French diplomats, though using the word "indemnity," did not go so far in demanding reimbursement for costs of war as radical legislators were advocating. Emphasis was placed on the ending of the state of war before a league of nations was organized.[17] Jusserand delivered the final version of the French plan

---

16. Lawrence E. Gelfand, *The Inquiry*, p. 259. The list of thirty-three questions is in the Wilson pa., 5A.

17. For the third draft of the French plan see Ray Stannard Baker, *Woodrow Wilson and World Settlement*, 3, 55–63. The three drafts of the French plan have been analyzed by Robert C. Binkley in "New Light on the Paris Peace Conference," *Political Science Quarterly*, pp. 340–49.

to the State Department on November 29, conscious that it would be in harmony with the wishes of the most active friends of France in America and also with the demand of Senator Lodge for "a preliminary entente" so firm that there would be nothing to arbitrate between victors and vanquished.[18]

The precise plan of the Quai d'Orsay proved to be no more than window-dressing. Wilson was cold to any of the propositions that he may have read. He mistrusted any written formulation of agenda. Moreover he was unwilling to appear to forsake the popular crusade that he was leading and to run the risk that the French would secure the assent of the peace conference to a practical settlement that might in fact confirm some of the provisions of the secret treaties that the French plan appeared to renounce.

Wilson was not in sympathy with the sentiment of the French. Making a brief speech at their embassy soon after the armistice at a celebration of the occupation of Strasbourg he made an infelicitous remark. As a boy, he said, his heart "bled for the sundered provinces. How wonderful it would have been could I have then known that I was to live to go to France as her victorious friend and to play the leading part in their restoration." It seemed to Frenchmen that their stout-hearted *poilus* had played the leading part in making possible the return of Alsace and Lorraine. A secretary of the embassy interpreted Wilson's careless remark as evidence of megalomania.[19]

At Paris the French plans for a peacemaking were given close scrutiny by the Americans, who perceived the menace posed to Wilson's program. House asked David Hunter Miller[20] for a critique, warning him against subservience to precedent. Miller thereupon drafted a paper that emphasized the importance of a peace congress in which there would be "open discussion" of terms with represen-

---

18. Dispatch, Jusserand to M.A.E., À paix, A1025.1.

19. Sir Arthur Willert, *The Road to Safety,* p. 167. "The French Embassy here [in Washington] is far from being in close relations with the Administration." Wiseman to Murray, Sept. 14, 1918, Wiseman pa., Y.H.C.

20. Miller, who was House's chief legal counselor, was without experience in diplomacy. He was respected for his industry and integrity and for his ability to draft polished legal documents. He joined Gordon Auchincloss, his junior partner, in Paris on November 19. Frank L. Warrin, Jr., also a partner, and Professor Manley O. Hudson accompanied him as assistants. The three produced a large volume of pertinent documents. They prepared a memorandum on the peace settlement of 1871, approved Grew's plans for organizing the American commission, fed material on disarmament to General Bliss, supplied studies on the league of nations and a draft of an agreement for its establishment, and summarized for House a French paper entitled *"Projet des Préliminaires de Paix avec Allemagne."* This French project was issued informally by the ambassador and chargé at London. Miller regarded it as a *"balon d'essai"* of the Quai d'Orsay. Miller, *My Diary, 1,* Nov. 19–Dec. 10, 1918; *2,* docs. 7, 10, 28–29, 37–38, 46–48, 50–54, 58.

tatives of the Central Powers. It advocated an informal pre-agreement among the Allied and associated powers as an "essential prerequisite" to the peacemaking.[21] It went beyond the French proposals by suggesting that the Great Powers confer with each small nation that wished to plead its case and, after study and discussion, arrive at principles of settlement to be submitted for the approval of the conference. Miller kept in mind the responsibility that the United States felt for the interests of the states of Latin America.[22] His paper was received by the Allies with a silence that did not denote assent.

It was apparent, at the end of 1918, that the careful reasoning of diplomats and legal counselors would yield whenever it conflicted with purposes that the political chiefs held to be essential to their leadership. Like Wilson and Lloyd George, Clemenceau took little interest in the details of organization and procedure in the peacemaking. French elections on November 16 had put the old man firmly in the saddle. He resolved to hold the reins of power in his own hands as tightly in the peacemaking as in the war. Vexed by President Poincaré, he made it plain that he alone would exercise the responsibility of speaking for France. He intimated that he might resign if Poincaré interfered. "His rule in France is absolute," House wrote in his diary.[23] As minister of war as well as president of the Council of Ministers, Clemenceau held the generals in leash. He bade Marshal Foch to confine himself to military matters and told him that in planning to send Allied troops to Eastern Europe as a

---

21. As early as June 28, 1918 Miller had written a paper entitled "Preliminary Peace Agreement or Protocol," and suggested that, as a sort of constitution or fundamental law for the peace conference, a preliminary understanding would be of prime value. "It is not necessary for a Protocol to be ratified as a treaty is ratified," he wrote, "for it is a preliminary and not a final agreement." Inquiry pa., box 28, folder 21, Y.H.C. Miller thought that the negotiation of a formal peace treaty without any such preliminary agreement would be "hardly possible owing to the circumstances and magnitude of this war." Among Miller's papers is a forty-five-page document entitled "Form and Procedure of the Peace Conference." This was submitted to a Committee on International Law in the summer of 1918. D.H. Miller pa., box 83, folder I, II, L.C.

22. Informed by a cable from Polk (Dec. 7, 1918) that Ambassador da Gama of Brazil was eager, for political reasons, to have his country represented at the preliminary conference, House replied immediately: "I will press the matter. . . . There is considerable opposition here to bringing into the preliminary Conference any but the Great Allied Powers and the United States." Y.H.C. The State Department had notified da Gama in November that it thought it unnecessary for Brazil to be represented at the preliminary meetings, but that he should go to the peace conference. Lansing to Embassy, Rio de Janeiro, Nov. 19, 1918, N.A., RG, 59, 763.72119/262. A Brazilian delegation arrived at Paris early in January, and in April its head, Pessôa, was elected president of Brazil.

23. Jean Ratinaud, *Clemenceau*, pp. 205–26; House diary, Oct. 26, 1918, Y.H.C.

barrier against communism he was attempting something that Napoleon had not been able to accomplish.[24]

Clemenceau informed Jules Cambon, who had served as France's ambassador in Washington and in Berlin, that he had his ideas on two or three essential points and the rest did not matter. When Cambon suggested that everything depended on diplomatic method, and referred to the precedent of Talleyrand at the Congress of Vienna, Clemenceau called him an old bewigged stickler of a diplomat. "Those fellows did a pretty good job of it all the same," Cambon replied, "and I hope we may do as well.[25] His brother, Paul Cambon, French ambassador at London, advised Clemenceau not to imitate the thorough preparations of the British Foreign Office for the peacemaking, which he thought would obscure the major points on which the premiers ought to agree.[26]

Believing the tie of kinship among the English-speaking peoples might work against the interests of France, Clemenceau sought an *adhésion de principe* with the Americans. Pleading the legitimacy of the French demands, he begged that House would commend the case of France to Wilson.[27] House responded with a promise of sympathy, but he made no commitment with respect of the French claim to the Saar basin, since this would violate Wilson's Point Eight. In reporting to the president he avoided the irritation that would result if he mentioned the French territorial demands. He cabled on November 9: "Clemenceau asked Pichon who was present to be a witness to the promise that he would never bring up any matter at the Peace Conference that he had not first discussed with us, and the inference was clear that if we disagreed he would yield to our wishes and judgment." To this Wilson responded with formal cordiality.[28]

At the same time a French diplomat was pursuing a policy of reaching a separate understanding with the British.[29] While Clemenceau was professing to House a desire for French-American accord,

---

24. Jere C. King, *Clemenceau vs. Foch,* Harvard Historical Monograph no. 44 (Cambridge, Mass., 1960).

25. Geneviève R. Tabouis, *The Life of Jules Cambon* (London, 1938), p. 318; Jules Cambon, "La Paix," *Revue de Paris.*

26. Paul Cambon, *Correspondance, 3,* 283.

27. House diary, Nov. 9, 1918; Raymond Poincaré, *Au Service de la France, 10,* 420.

28. Cables in Baker, pp. 575, 580, 592. In a talk with House at the end of November, Clemenceau again asserted France's claim to the Saar basin, presenting a map of the region. House diary, Nov. 30, 1918.

29. In mid-October, when the French government had proposed a joint approach to an interpretation of the Fourteen Points, Lord Robert Cecil wrote: "It is part of the policy of the French government to detach us from the U.S.A. and bring us into the European fold." P.R.O., FO/371/3444, minute on doc. 173395, cited in V.H. Rothwell, *British War Aims and Peace Diplomacy,* pp. 253–54.

the French ambassador in London was working to bring about an Anglo-French understanding without American participation. Paul Cambon urged Clemenceau to make a preliminary peace at once and to skip the question of a league of nations, which violated his pragmatic philosophy.[30] He even adumbrated a future war to the death in which England and France would oppose the United States and Germany. Returning from Paris with a note that was to serve as a basis for conversations,[31] Cambon went so far as to propose to Foreign Secretary Balfour that they arrive at a peace settlement without consulting Wilson and with a view to presenting it to him as a fait accompli. The ambassador wished to avoid a détente that might oblige the two Allied governments to seek a *point d'appui* in the United States. He professed to have Clemenceau's support for his proposition.[32] The possibility of connivance among the Allies without regard to Wilson, which the American president had recognized some weeks before,[33] was now an imminent threat; but there is no evidence that House, relying implicitly on the good faith of Clemenceau and Balfour, took this possibility seriously.

House's confidence in Balfour was fully justified. The foreign secretary, true to the policy of bringing the United States into a position of responsibility for the peace, insisted upon the participation of the Americans in the making of all final decisions.[34] Reporting Cambon's proposal to Lloyd George, Balfour wrote: "I am convinced that, from the point of view of immediate diplomacy, Cambon's policy is little short of insanity. . . . House is undoubtedly anxious to work with us as closely as he can and it would be fatal to give him the impression that we were settling, or had the least desire to settle, great questions behind his back."[35] The Foreign Office replied to Cambon's proposal thus: "The Royal Government shares the opin-

---

30. Cambon thought Wilson "a vague dreamer" who had "an imagination sailing before every wind." Keith Eubank, *Paul Cambon* (Norman, Okla., 1960), p. 192.

31. Fleuriau (London) to "mon cher ami," Nov. 29, 1918, Archives du M.A.É., À paix, A1160.6, f.198, pp. 203–6.

32. In a letter of November 14 Cambon informed Clemenceau of a talk with Lloyd George two days before in which he advocated a close understanding. He did not say that he had told the British premier that Clemenceau favored an understanding apart from the United States; and we have no evidence that Clemenceau went as far as Cambon indicated in his talk with Balfour. Cambon, *3*, 282–83. Cf. below, p. 102.

33. See above, p. 23.

34. If there was to be any two-party understanding before the final settlement, Balfour preferred that it should be with the United States rather than with France. Rothwell, pp. 253–54.

35. Balfour to Lloyd George, Nov. 29, 1918, Lloyd George pa., F/3/3/45, Beaverbrook Library, London.

ion that the arrival of President Wilson will permit the four Powers
to set among themselves the peace conditions." It was suggested that
there should be two congresses, the first to meet immediately and
determine what the relations of the states in the war should be, and
the second to consider a constitution for a new international organization.[36]

Whatever Clemenceau's part may have been in the overture of
Cambon, the premier pursued the policy of seeking an understanding with the British government. He proposed to Lloyd George
that they meet with Orlando of Italy either at Paris or at London to
arrange for a peace conference.[37] He made this proposal on November 15, the day on which his foreign ministry issued its first
peace plan.[38]

Lloyd George planned a meeting in London on December 1 and
invited House to attend. The latter, however, told by both Clemenceau and Ambassador Derby that Lloyd George was arranging the
conference "purely for election purposes,"[39] chose to remain in
Paris. The president had expressed his opposition to any "general
conference" among the victorious powers that might make of a "general peace conference" a mere formality.[40] House was unwilling to
expose himself to the sort of examination of American policy that
Lloyd George was planning. Probably to assure Wilson that no important steps would be taken before the president could participate,
the colonel reported that Clemenceau was willing to wait for the
German revolution to "settle down for a while," and was suggesting
to Lloyd George only that "preparatory memoranda" be drawn
up.[41]

Before departing for London Clemenceau took pains to reassure
House, giving his word of honor that he would discuss no question
of any importance with Lloyd George, that if the British appeared to
demand too much he would oppose them, and that France would

---

36. Note of Nov. 30, 1918, Archives du M.A.E., À paix, A1160.6, f.198, pp.
207–29. Wiseman informed Miller that the Foreign Office had declined a French
suggestion of a two-party understanding. Miller, *My Diary, 1,* 163.

37. Telegram, Clemenceau to Lloyd George, Nov. 15, 1918, F.C. 6N72, "Négociations de Paix."

38. Jean Jules Henri Mordacq, *Le Ministère Clemenceau,* (Paris 1921), *3,* 6.

39. House diary, Nov. 19, 30, Dec. 4, 1918. Lloyd George sent this message
to House on November 25: "Monsieur Clemenceau is coming to London on 1st December and I earnestly hope you will be able to come also, as a number of urgent
questions require discussion. As I shall not be able to attend any conferences in Paris
before the election of December 14th, this is especially important." Y.H.C..

40. Cable, W.W. to House, Oct. 31, 1918, Baker, 7, 539.

41. Cables, House to W.W., Nov. 15, 16, 1918, Wilson pa., 2 and 5C.

always be willing to submit its claims to the peace conference. House reported this pledge to the president and did not question its sincerity.[42]

Still afflicted by the prevailing influenza, House gave this as an excuse for remaining in Paris. He asked Miller to accompany Wiseman to London as an observer only, instructed to express merely tentative and personal views and bring back full reports.[43] House urged Wiseman to be sure to "pin down" Lloyd George to some election pledges, particularly with respect of a league of nations.[44] No one was delegated to represent the United States officially at this important conference—an omission that Lloyd George ascribed to Wilson's "suspicious nature."[45] General Bliss got no satisfaction when he notified House that the Allied governments would have military representatives at the London conference and the United States would have none unless House appointed one.[46]

At the conference of premiers that met at London on December 2 and 3, Lloyd George alluded to Cambon's desire to act independently of the Americans. After the conferees expressed regret at the absence of House the question of the role of the United States in the peacemaking was discussed. Clemenceau remarked that the kings of Belgium, Greece, and Italy must be feted at Paris and therefore the preliminary conference that he envisaged could not conveniently assemble until January. This would give Wilson a chance to visit the devastated regions of France, which he understood, wishfully and erroneously, to be what the president desired.[47] When Lloyd George said that it would be difficult to make Wilson wait until January and Balfour mentioned a wish of House that the talks begin on De-

42. House diary, Nov. 30, 1918; cable, House to W.W., [Nov. 1918.] Y.H.C.

43. F.L. Warrin, Jr., to the writer; John P. Posey, "David Hunter Miller at the Paris Peace Conference, Nov. 1918–May 1919," p. 9; House diary, Dec. 1, 1918. House cabled to Wilson on November 27: "I replied that while I hoped to be present it would depend on my doctor's decision. I think it wise, for reasons other than those presented by my physical condition, not to go to London for this conference." *F.R., PPC, 2*, p. 637. Lloyd George was aware that House had other reasons. Roskill, *Hankey: 2*, 30.

44. House diary, Dec. 1, 1918.

45. House to W.W., disptach of Nov. 30, 1918, Auchincloss diary, Y.H.C. and N.A., RG 59, 763.72119/9191; David Lloyd George, *The Truth about the Peace Treaties,* p. 138. Frank I. Cobb, calling on House, found him weakened by illness and depending on Clemenceau's promise that nothing of importance would happen at London. It seemed to Cobb that Clemenceau was "a great little humorist." Cobb Journal, Nov. 29, 30, 1918, L.C.

46. Bliss to Newton D. Baker, Dec. 9, 1918, Jan. 11, 1919, Bliss pa., L.C.

47. Wilson did not wish to see the devastation. See below, p. 140. Clemenceau was perhaps misled by House in the interest of good public relations and with a hope of inducing Wilson to comply with the French desire.

cember 16, Clemenceau replied that the president's time would not be wasted while he waited.

Lloyd George brought up the question of the cost of enforcing the armistice. If the United States took no part in the occupation after three months, he said, it would leave the Allies with the whole charge. "I'll have a question to put to Wilson," said Clemenceau. "He says he's not an ally, but an associate. What is the difference? . . . If President Wilson after his comparatively small losses in the war, is not ready to bear his part of the costs of peace, what must we do?"[48]

At the London conference, with no American military representative present, Marshal Foch was authorized to extend the German armistice for one month beyond its expiration on December 17. Foch was satisfied that the enemy were in fact disarmed, that if their government balked he had only to give an order and his troops would overrun Berlin and Munich. Asked by Lloyd George how he would reconcile his proposal for French control of all of the left bank of the Rhine with Wilson's principles, he replied that since Germany had proved that its signature on a treaty was untrustworthy, it was "necessary to take material precautions," and the erection of a military barrier on the Rhine was the obvious one. He proposed to conciliate the populace by economic benefits and by the advantage of affiliation with the victorious powers.

Foch succeeded in bringing about a renewal of the armistice that imposed new conditions. A clause was added giving the victors the right to occupy, on six days' notice, the neutral zone on the right bank north of the bridgehead at Cologne. A financial protocol was signed, binding the German government not to dispose of hard assets without the consent of the Allies, and to take steps promptly toward restitution for securities lost or stolen in invaded regions and for goods sequestered to the detriment of nationals of Allied countries. At the same time the Germans were given some reason to hope that the peacemaking would proceed rapidly; and in order to get food they agreed to put their merchant marine under the control of the victors as soon as they received assurance that the vessels, which Foch promised would remain German property, would be allowed to carry German crews and fly the German flag. This assurance was not received for almost three months.

Foch assumed control of the International Armistice Commission

48. French procès-verbaux of meetings of Dec. 2, 3, 1918, F.C., 6N72. Neither the British nor the French minutes corroborate a statement attributed to Wiseman in the diary of Auchincloss (entry of Jan. 12, 1919) to the effect that Clemenceau proposed an alliance among the Allies without regard to the United States and directed against Germany.

at Spa, where, in semidiplomatic negotiations during the next half-year, representatives of the Allies and of Germany worked out details of the execution of the terms.[49]

In other than military matters the conferees at London felt that they could make only tentative arrangements. Discussing the question of Russia, they concluded only that they could reach no decision without the participation of the United States.[50] They agreed to the holding of an inter-Allied conference at Versailles at the earliest date possible and the signing of a preliminary treaty there that the Germans could consider with the privilege of proposing changes. The Great Powers, of which Japan was now deemed to be one, were to have five delegates each. Representatives of the smaller Allied states would be present only when questions of special interest to them were discussed, and new states would be allowed to present their claims. The sentiment of Lloyd George in favor of a trial of the ex-Kaiser received endorsement; and it was agreed that if Holland refused to deliver him it should be denied a seat in the league of nations.[51]

With respect to reparations, the conferees agreed that each of the victorious governments should prepare its claim and that an inter-

---

49. *Conversation entre M. Lloyd George et Foch,* Dec. 1, 1918, 5:00 P.M., F.C., 6N72, f. 267; Raymond Recouly, *Foch,* p. 52; Lloyd George, *Truth about the Peace Treaties,* p. 135; Edward F. Willis, "Herbert Hoover and the Blockade of Germany," in *Studies in Modern European History in Honor of Franklin Charles Palm,* p. 278.

The performance of the Germans in carrying out the provisions of the armistice is analyzed in Samuel G. Shartle, *Spa, Versailles, Munich,* pp. 48–65. Gen. Rhodes was chief of the American delegation at Spa until December 22, when he was injured in an airplane accident and was succeeded by Gen. Barnum. The chairman of the commission, Gen. Nudant, was Foch's appointee and, determined to treat the Germans severely, assumed an uncompromising leadership. Ibid., pp. 27, 38, 66. Foch threatened to extend the area of occupation if the Germans continued to procrastinate in handing over war matériel.

According to Shartle, chief of staff of the American contingent, The French . . . hatred of the Germans was not concealed and they exacted their dues. . . . The Germans were in general truculent. Well aware of the disaster they had suffered, these educated Germans on the Armistice Commission endeavored by any and every means to minimize its results for their nation—by arguments, protests, complaints, memorials, propaganda, tears, and bluster. . . . Perhaps the records . . . contain more dissertations on "bolshevism" and its dangers to Germany than on any other subject." Ibid., pp. 66–67.

After reading the records of the German Foreign Ministry, Schaefer concluded that the German delegation at Spa used the negotiations to complain against Allied "injustices" and to secure control over their own foreign office. Erzberger, head of the delegation, adopted a policy of trying to ingratiate Germany with the victors. He wrote and spoke in favor of a league of nations. Schaefer, pp. 69–72.

50. "Allied Conversations in the Cabinet Room," Dec. 1–3, 1918, P.R.O., Cab/23/17.

51. French procès-verbal of meeting of Dec. 2, 1918, 11:00 A.M.

Allied commission of experts should consider the demands and also the capacity of the enemy to make payments. Miller conferred with John Maynard Keynes, British expert, and Paul Cravath, representing the United States Treasury. They agreed that Germany's capacity to pay was based on "real surplus earning power," and that this should not be impaired by breaking the will of the people to work.[52] Miller transmitted to House a warning by Keynes that the French were demanding a huge indemnity that was to be the basis for continued occupation and ultimate acquisition of the Rhine provinces.[53]

The statesmen at the London meeting took it for granted that the establishment of a league of nations would be an essential part of the settlement. Neither Clemenceau nor Sonnino, the most forceful of the Italian statesmen, had faith in the efficacy of an international body, but they realized that the ideal was riding on a strong current of popular opinion. British diplomats understood that the functions of a league must be agreed on before specific territorial solutions could well be arrived at. Conferring with Miller, they insisted that it was essential to reach an understanding with the United States in advance. They wished to establish contacts with American experts, but they gave no encouragement to the idea of drafting a preliminary treaty, and left Miller convinced that it would be necessary for President Wilson to have his own program and priorities of subjects for discussion. To maintain liaison it was arranged that Wiseman go to Paris soon as Balfour's adviser on American affairs;[54] but there was still no British ambassador at Washington.[55]

Clemenceau, true to his promise to House, joined with Balfour in overcoming the annoyance of Lloyd George at Wilson's aloofness and his naval policy. The British premier complained that Wilson talked much about disarmament and began by having an appropriation made that would double the number of American warships. Nevertheless he was brought to agree that the resolutions of the London Conference must be subject to American approval. It was understood that the advice of the president would be respected as to the date of convening with him. All conclusions involving the United States were to be reserved except those requiring immediate action,

52. Miller, *My Diary, 1,* Dec. 5, 1918.
53. *F.R., PPC, 2,* pp. 582 f.
54. Miller, *My Diary, 1,* Dec. 5, 1918, *2,* docs. 36–37; Marston, p. 45.
55. Arthur Willert, Washington correspondent of the London *Times,* warned the Foreign Office that the atmosphere in the United States was "not altogether healthy" because of commercial jealousy and "a lot of nasty, hostile gossip" among American junior officials, and he advised that an ambassador was needed. Willert to Wiseman, Nov. 15, 1918, Willert pa., Y.H.C..

such as a decision to create a commission of four admirals to deal with an immediate threat of fighting in the Adriatic region.[56] The Europeans directed Balfour to send a report of the proceedings to House.[57] Accordingly a telegram went to the colonel, asking him to approve as many of the resolutions as possible.

In acknowledging Balfour's report House protested, in a white lie, that it was "a great disappointment" to him not to be able to go to England. The colonel was kept fully informed of the thinking at London by Miller; he also had accounts from Clemenceau and Sonnino, as well as from Lord Derby. His confidence in the cooperation and integrity of Balfour and Clemenceau had been justified, and he had avoided contamination by presence at negotiations with respect of enemy territory that Wilson might have regarded as unclean.[58]

House immediately sent a report of the proceedings to the president and asked for a prompt reply. He told Wilson that he was taking the responsibility of informing the Allies of substantial American agreement with the military and naval decisions, and with the resolution on reparations.[59] He reserved American judgment on the question of trying the ex-kaiser, having had word that the president was "at a loss to suggest" what should be done. He asked that Wilson authorize him to agree to measures for the occupation of enemy territory and to a decision not to object to "any international labor or any other conference in relation to the peace conference" being held in a neutral country. And he proposed amendment, in line with an American plan for relief, of a resolution that referred the question of victualling the enemy to "a special commission."[60]

House's report to the president reached him aboard the *George*

---

56. See below, p. 162. It was left to Hankey and the other secretaries to select the exceptions. Roskill, 2, p. 30.

57. "Allied Conversations in the Cabinet Room"; French procès-verbaux, Dec. 2, 3, 1918.

58. Miller, *My Diary, 1,* entry of Dec. 2; House diary, Dec. 5, 1918; telegram from the Foreign Office, presented by Lord Derby to House on December 5, summarized in *I.P., 4,* 247–49.

59. *I.P., 4,* 249.

60. Auchincloss diary, Dec. 6, 1918; *F.R., PPC, 1,* p. 342; Roskill, 2, pp. 20, 29. On the American program of relief, see below, Chapter 13.

Wilson had pointed out that there were "serious disadvantages" in having the kaiser, who had taken refuge in Holland, so near to Germany and "the center of intrigue." cable, W.W. to House, Nov. 22, 1918; Y.H.C. Sonnino opposed trying the kaiser, and Clemenceau expressed himself as mildly in favor. House diary, Dec. 5, 1918. Jules Cambon warned against any action that might lift William II out of his wretched exile in Holland and make him a martyr. Cambon thought it important to avoid differentiating, as Wilson had done, between the emperor and the German nation or releasing the latter from its own responsibility by punishing its leader. Tabouis, *Cambon,* pp. 319–20.

Washington, en route to Paris.[61] Wilson discussed the matter with Secretary Lansing and sent a response that was both prompt and decisive. One of the London resolutions called for a "preliminary peace treaty" to be "signed at the inter-Allied Conference at Versailles." The president envisioned only informal talks among the victorious powers before a formal conference, including the enemy,[62] would meet to make a peace for all the peoples of the world. It was "imperative" in order to prevent misunderstanding, he notified House, that final conclusions as to the London resolutions should be withheld until his arrival at Paris.

Colonel House was troubled by the fact that France was the strongest military power in Europe, if not in the world, and therefore might upset any balance of power on the Continent in the future. Reflecting upon this he wrote in his diary on January 3, 1919:

> Every day now there is an indication that she [France] intends to assert herself as the dominant Continental Power. I do not think it is realized by the rest of the world that this war leaves France the only great military power in Europe. . . . This fact must be reckoned with. . . . I see many evidences that the English are concerned and do not like the prospect. . . . On the other hand it is to be remembered that France is a nation of less than forty million people and cannot go far alone.

The aggressive conduct of Foch at the renewal of the armistice disturbed House. On December 19 he sent Frazier to call on Foreign Minister Pichon to express surprise that the marshal had dealt with the Germans on the thirteenth without consulting the political leaders who had authorized the original armistice, and who would make the peace. To this representation Pichon replied that even the French government had not been consulted because this matter had been placed in the hands of Foch and of the members of the Armistice Commission. The foreign minister pointed out that the change in terms giving the Allies the right to occupy the neutral zone on the right bank of the Rhine on six days' notice was made merely to insure the carrying out of the original armistice.[63]

Before the end of the year the commanders of the victorious armies received from Foch a suggestion as to the contributions that

---

61. Dispatch, House to Sec. State, Dec. 6, 1918, endorsed "repeated to the *G.W.*, Dec. 7, 11 A.M., 1918," N.A., RG 59, 763.72119/32211/2; Lansing desk diary, Dec. 8, 1918.

62. Wiseman interview, Oct. 16, 1918, Wiseman pa., Y.H.C..

63. Notes of a conversation between Pichon and Frazier, Dec. 19, 1918, Y.H.C.

each might make to the force to be maintained against Germany. Arguing that "the most elementary prudence" demanded that the victors remain in condition to face a possible resumption of hostilities, he added that the force of arms would be the best argument in imposing their will upon the enemy. The marshal suggested quotas for Belgium, France, Great Britain, and the United States.[64]

Asked by Foch for his opinion, General Pershing observed that American soldiers merited special consideration because of the greater distance that separated them from home. He thought that the marshal's suggestions put a burden upon the United States that was out of proportion to the small size of the sector to be occupied, and he suggested an American share much less than that proposed. Reporting Foch's proposal to the War Department, Pershing renewed a previous recommendation that all American troops be taken out of Europe at the earliest moment possible. This was necessary to comply with the law under which most of them had been drafted.[65] It was planned to reduce the American Expeditionary Force to twenty combat divisions by March 1, to fifteen by April 1, and about ten by May 1.[66] Pershing explained to Foch that the American national army could legally be held in service for only four months after the signing of peace.[67]

No significant number of American soldiers left Europe during the month following the close of hostilities, and at the end of that period Foch insisted that no more should be sent home until peace was signed.[68] A month later General Bliss reported to the American peace commission that the French High Command was only too willing to occupy German territory alone but the French people would not allow enough men to be held in service to permit this, and therefore it was desired that 1,200,000 American troops be held in France.[69] But by the end of 1918 there was a general demand by American citizens that they return at once, and the War Department was determined to bring them back as soon as ships could be found.

House refused to allow his friendly relation with Clemenceau to be impaired by altercations among the generals. When Pershing asked him to intercede to settle a controversy with Foch about the

64. The number of American divisions had been fixed at thirty, and was reduced to twenty-five in February. James G. Harbord, *The American Army in France, 1917–1919* (Boston, 1936), p. 548.

65. Pershing diary, boxes 4–5, Pershing pa., L.C.; entry of Dec. 12, 1918; copies of Pershing's correspondence sent to House by Gen. McAndrew, chief of staff, Dec. 31, 1918, Y.H.C.

66. Hayes to General Churchill and Grew, Jan. 7, 1919, *F.R., PPC, 2*, pp. 57–58.

67. Pershing to House, Dec. 30, 1918, Y.H.C.

68. Pershing diary, Dec. 8, 1918.

69. Minutes of the ACTNP, Jan. 4, 1919, Grew papers, Houghton Library, Harvard University.

allocation of troops to occupy Koblenz,[70] House thought Pershing was "making much out of nothing," and when he discussed the matter with Clemenceau the two statesmen agreed that it was too trivial to disturb their governments.[71]

In the month that passed after the signing of the armistices little progress was made in furthering American influence on the peace-making. The right of the United States to participate in decisions had been safeguarded by the hard sense of Balfour and Clemenceau, who clearly saw Europe's need for American wealth and power as a guarantee of security in the future. House had been equally realistic in appreciation of the fact that the common good, as well as the welfare of the United States, would best be served by maintaining a relation of confidence with the wisest and most reliable of the Europeans. He resolved to appear quite open and frank in his dealings with them and to continue to do what he could to convince them that President Wilson was less austere than his public policies and speeches had suggested. Two American publicity men came for luncheon on December 5 and told House that British and French agents were watching him and knew everything that was going on. Recording this in his diary, he was able to persuade himself that he never said or did anything that he was unwilling that they should know. "It is the only way to win in the long run and it is so much pleasanter," he wrote.

70. Early in December, Pershing and Foch found themselves at loggerheads over the occupation of Koblenz. The marshal wished to assign two French units to join the American troops in this area. In his diary Pershing set this down as "a political scheme . . . to give the Germans the impression of the importance of the French in these affairs and to minimize the American effort." Colonel Mott, the American military attaché at Paris, made efforts through General Weygand to dissuade Foch, but he was not successful. Weygand angrily denied that Foch could be moved by political considerations. Pershing diary, Nov. 29, 30, Dec. 6, 1918; Mott to Pershing, Nov. 30, Dec. 1, 1918, box 141, Pershing pa. Mott's arguments were set down in a long letter of Dec. 1, 1918 to the headquarters of Foch, whom Mott found "very old, tired, and irritable" and better approached by letter than in person, Y.H.C. See Francis B. Lowry, "The Generals, the Armistice, and the Treaty of Versailles, 1919," pp. 129 ff.

71. Declaring that this was the first that he had heard of it, Clemenceau said that the desires of Pershing should be met, and that he would telephone to Foch. On the next day Clemenceau told President Poincaré of House's intercession and said, *"Je n'en ferai rien."* House diary, Dec. 4, 5, 1918; Poincaré, *Au Service de la France, 10,* entry of Dec. 6, 1918.

Pershing, resenting the shortness of the American line in comparison with those of the British and French, complained to Clemenceau of Foch's stubbornness. But the French premier jollied him and asked whether the American himself was not possibly "a little stubborn at times," and on December 11 Pershing reported to House that the differences were at an end. On lower levels friction continued, Pershing diary, Dec. 1, 5, 7, 8, 9, 10, 11; Mott to House, Dec. 3, 1918, Y.H.C.; Foch to Pershing, translation of letter and telegram, Dec. 9, 1918; Pershing to Foch, Dec. 11, 1918, Dickman to Pershing, Dec. 17, 1918, Pershing pa., boxes 75, 373. See D.H. Miller pa., box 89, IV, 5.

☆VII☆

Wilson Undertakes
"Summit Diplomacy"

At the very time of the signing of the armistice with Germany, and during the preceding weeks, the president was beset with political opposition at home. Unfortunately he supplied grounds for damaging criticism when he allowed himself to be persuaded by Democratic politicians to plead publicly for votes for men of his own party in the Congressional elections on November 5.

If the voters returned a Republican majority to the Senate, Henry Cabot Lodge would become chairman of the Committee on Foreign Relations, and would then be in a position to obstruct ratification of any treaty of peace the president might make. Lodge had long been on guard against the tendency of idealists to promise more than was practicable. He feared that this proclivity, applied to international treaties, might lead more often to war than to peace. Not an isolationist, and willing that the United States should make some commitments in an effort to prevent future wars, he could applaud the purpose of a league of nations. Nevertheless, he felt that such an international body as Wilson envisaged was not the best means of preserving peace. He put his trust in a continuance of the wartime association of the United States with the Allies, and he was jealous of the sovereignty of his country.[1] Lodge devised a strategy to counter what he thought to be political exploitation of an unsound doctrine.

"Now the strength of our position," he wrote to Senator Beveridge, a fellow Republican, "is to show up the impossibility of any of the methods proposed and invite them, when they desire our support, to produce their terms. They cannot do it. . . . If they do form

---

1. On October 14 Lodge had written to Bryce: "We have got a good league now—the Allies and the United States. As Roosevelt said the other day, it is a going concern. "Letter in the Bryce pa., Bodleian Library, Oxford University.

anything that involves control of our legislation, of our armies and navies, or the Monroe Doctrine, or an international police force, and that sort of thing, then our issue is made up and we shall win."[2]

Wilson confessed that he looked forward with "genuine anxiety" to the part that Lodge, a man whom he heartily disliked, would play in a Senate controlled by Republicans.[3] Importuned by Democratic congressmen to make a public appeal that would help all candidates of the party, the president finally agreed to do so. He mentioned the matter to House, who had at first been in favor but now was cool to the idea.[4] The colonel thought it undignified for the president to indulge in electioneering. However, Wilson had good precedents.[5]

Wilson issued an appeal to the voters on October 25: "Not for my own sake," he said, "or for the sake of a political party, but for the sake of the nation itself, in order that its inward unity of purpose may be evident to the world." A Republican victory, he declared with a frankness that would soon become embarrassing, would "certainly be interpreted on the other side of the water as a repudiation" of his leadership. Only five months earlier, he had said to the Congress: "Politics is adjourned."[6] Among the candidates for election were Republicans who had been loyal to the president and Democrats

---

2. John A. Garraty, *Henry Cabot Lodge,* p. 347. See Lloyd E. Ambrosius, "Wilson, the Republicans, and French Security after World War I," *Journal of American History,* 59; 2 (September 1972): 342.

3. G.W. Anderson to W.W., Nov. 14; W.W. to G.W. Anderson, Nov. 18, 1918, Wilson pa., *2,* L.C. Wilson's personal feeling was reciprocated by Lodge. Garraty, pp. 312, 346.

4. House diary, Sept. 24, 1918, Y.H.C. In the summer of 1918 the executive committee of the Democratic National Committee was unanimous in directing its chairman, Vance McCormick, to take up with the president the writing of an appeal for the election of Democrats to the Congress. Advised by House that it would be wise to issue such an appeal, McCormick found the president willing. McCormick to Gavin McNab, Sept. 9, 1924, Y.H.C.

On October 25 House wrote in his diary: "He [Wilson] mentioned, the last time I was in Washington, that he thought of making an appeal. I made no reply, which always indicates to him my disapproval." A year later House adjudged Wilson's appeal to have been "as great a political blunder as he has made." Had he not made it, House thought, he would have "won handsomely." Diary, Oct. 26, 1919.

For a summary of the advice of Wilson's counselors, see Baker, 513–14. Also see John M. Blum, *Joe Tumulty and the Wilson Era* (Boston, 1951), pp. 157 ff.

5. Lincoln and McKinley had spoken out in times of crisis against divided councils and changing leadership; Lodge had made a similar appeal before the congressional election of 1898 (Springfield *Republican,* Oct. 27, 1898), and Roosevelt in 1906, when there was no war emergency, had written a letter stressing "the urgent need" to keep a Republican Congress in power (to James E. Watson, Aug. 18, 1906, T. Roosevelt pa., reel 342).

6. Actually politics was not adjourned during the war. See Seward W. Livermore, *Woodrow Wilson and the War Congress, 1916–1918* (Middletown, Conn., 1966), pp. 206–47.

who had been disloyal. But Wilson's appeal seemed, unfairly, to equate disloyalty with Republicanism.

Theodore Roosevelt, contemptuous of Wilson's leadership and bitterly critical of his policies, saw a "splendid opening." Making the most of it, he charged the president with putting personal advantage above loyalty to the nation and damned him with a barrage of lurid adjectives. Roosevelt united with ex-President Taft in a counterappeal to "all Americans who are Americans first." Wilson's plea to the voters revived Republican efforts to picture him as a dictator who sought autocratic power through emergency legislation and who had appointed House to negotiate an armistice secretly and without reference to the Congress. The attack gained momentum when Secretary Lansing admitted to a friend that the president had not consulted his Allies about his peace correspondence with Germany. This news reached the ear of Roosevelt and added volume to his thunder.[7]

In the voting on November 5 the Democratic party lost control of both the Senate and the House of Representatives. This defeat would, in the words that Wilson had written only a fortnight before, "oblige all action to be taken amidst contest and obstruction." Although the tenure of the president himself was not affected and sophisticated Europeans knew that he was still a powerful figure, the result of the election could, as he himself had said, "be interpreted . . . as a repudiation" of his leadership. After the defeat (to which other factors contributed),[8] House wrote in his diary on November 7: "I am afraid it will make our work harder at the peace conference, and heaven knows, it will be hard enough." He hoped that Wilson would revamp his cabinet, call in Democratic leaders of the House of Representatives (in addition to Carter Glass, who became secretary of the Treasury), and reach an understanding with the Senate Committee on Foreign Relations.[9]

---

7. T.R. to Taft, Nov. 2, 1918, Taft pa., reel 322, Lansing "leaked" the information to Gus Karger, a journalist, from whom it went to Taft and then to Roosevelt.

Roosevelt ridiculed the "fourteen scraps of paper" as symbols of "the conditional surrender of the United States." He assailed the president's course as "dangerously near to being treacherous diplomacy," and expressed the hope that the Senate and "all other persons competent to speak for the American people" would "emphatically repudiate" Wilson's program. Alice Longworth, *Crowded Hours* (New York, 1933), p. 273; J.J. Leary, Jr., *Talks with Theodore Roosevelt* (Boston, 1930), p. 329; William H. Harbaugh, *Power and Responsibility* (New York, 1961), p. 515.

8. See Selig Adler, "The Congressional Election of 1918," *The South Atlantic Quarterly* 36:4 (October 1937), pp. 447 ff. Lloyd George remarked on November 10: "The elections show that America is not behind Wilson," George Allardice, baron, Riddell, *Lord Riddell's Intimate Diary of the Peace Conference and After*, p. 380.

9. Memo by Seymour of a talk with House, March 17, 1920, Y.H.C.

The returns came to Wilson on the very day on which he was rejoicing with his cabinet over the tentative acceptance of the Fourteen Points by the statesmen at Paris and over the fixing of armistice terms to which he thought the Germans would assent. Asked whether he would resign if the vote went against him, he explained that the world's need for American leadership prevented this. He would have to try to attain the objects for which the nation went to war, he said. When told that his people did not understand the momentous issues of peace, he replied that some day he would have to tour the country to educate them.

Woodrow Wilson's reaction to defeat never had been meek. His sensitivity had been a priceless asset in conducting the delicate maneuvers that had brought the war to an end; but it made him bleed too easily when he was checked in the prosecution of a cause to which he had dedicated himself. He conceived himself now as a crusader fighting against odds. Assuring his daughter, Mrs. Sayre, that he was not at all dismayed or disheartened by the outcome of the election, Wilson wrote on November 13: "I think the Republicans will find the responsibility which they must now assume more onerous than joyful, and my expectation is that they will exercise it with some circumspection. I shall see to it that they are put in a position to realize their full responsibility and the reckoning in 1920 may hold disappointing results for them."[10] His suspicions became sinister, his secrecy regarding affairs of state grew into almost an obsession, and his resistance to counsel that ran counter to his prophetic impulse was strong.[11]

The president spoke earnestly[12] of both the obligations and the opportunities of the peacemaking. He felt that he was personally bound to redeem the pledges with which he had inspired men to

---

10. W.W. to Mrs. Sayre, Nov. 13, 1918. Wilson pa., 2. Apropos Wilson's feeling at this time about seeking a third term, the following quotation from the diary of Charles S. Hamlin, a prominent Democrat and a member of the Federal Reserve Board, is significant. "I said to Tumulty—'If Wilson has to withdraw from Paris, and the Senate Republicans are charged with breaking up the peace of the world, the President would have a great issue with which he might be reelected.' Tumulty replied enthusiastically—'That is correct.' He left no doubt in my mind that the president desired a renomination." Hamlin diary, Dec. 18, 1918, L.C.

11. Wilson's stenographer has recorded that he was instructed to take the president's state papers home to copy and grew accustomed to sleeping with a message and a gun under his pillow. Swem book ms., Swem pa., Princeton University Library. "He asked no advice—only information," Swem wrote, "and had a fundamental conviction that where responsibility is, there the decision must be."

12. W.W. to Homer Cummings, Nov. 11, 1918, Cummings diary, R.S. Baker pa., L.C.

give their lives. He held himself accountable too for the realization of the promises that he had made to all humanity. He conceived that the United States had no interests save those that it shared with all nations: to suppress chauvinistic aggression, despotism, trade wars, and other phenomena that might disturb the peace. He hoped that national ambitions might give way before the overriding requirements of the common welfare of mankind, and he saw clearly that the great power that could lead most effectively toward a new order was the one that was most disinterested.

It seemed to be Wilson's duty, as president of this power, to play an effective part in the peacemaking. Indeed he had been reconciled to entry into the war by a prospect that afterwards America could fulfill what he believed to be its historic mission.[13] During the prearmistice meetings he had cabled to House: "I assume that the Allies cannot honorably turn the present discussions into a peace conference without me." [14] He told Ambassador Jusserand that he wanted very much to make the trip to France and the Constitution did not forbid it, and that preliminary talks might begin before he arrived. He was not sure he could remain at Paris until the end of the conference, which he thought might last three or four months because of the thorny nature of certain questions.[15]

Wilson had advice from David Hunter Miller as to the legality of such a step. No American president had ever gone overseas during his term of office. Moreover, in 1913 the Congress had put in an appropriation bill an amendment that forbade the executive to attend any international conference without the specific authority of law. However, Wilson declared this an utterly futile statute and beyond the powers of the Congress; and Miller advised that his presence at the peace conference was "not only within his functions under the Constitution, but . . . also a solemn duty imposed upon him." There would be no question of his ability to perform his duties, and none of his powers would devolve upon the vice-president.[16]

---

13. Lord Devlin has written that in 1917 Wilson's need of a dominating place at the peace conference was "the strategic objective of his foreign policy." Patrick Devlin, *Too Proud to Fight*, p. 679.

14. Baker, p. 529.

15. Jusserand to M.A.E., Nov. 5, 1918, Archives du M.A.E., À paix, A1000.1, f.30.

16. The quotation is from a letter from Miller to House, Oct. 8, 1918, covering a forty-two-page brief developing the case. Wilson pa., 2. See David Hunter Miller, "Some Legal Aspects of the Visit of President Wilson to Paris," *Harvard Law Review*, 51–76. On the other hand George W. Wickersham, who had been attorney general under Taft, released the opinion that if Wilson left the country he would cease, ipso facto, to be president. When Wiseman and House had encouraged Wilson to go to England in the summer of 1918, advisers in Washington opposed the idea, fearing that the absence of the president would emphasize the overcentralization of the gov-

It was a decision of great moment. Seldom has a president received so much advice from friends, so much obstruction from foes. Opinion in Congress opposed a presidential venture abroad and almost everyone in the Department of State wished Wilson would not go, or at least would depart from the peace conference after giving it his blessing in the opening session.[17] The members of his cabinet held diverse views. There was a division too in public opinion. Liberals and idealists, at home and abroad, looked to him to champion their causes at Paris; the *Manchester Guardian* described him as "the only statesman of the first rank who has concerned himself seriously to think out any policy at all." And at the same time reactionaries, fearing that he would be soft towards Germany, hoped that he would stay at home.[18]

For several days after the armistice the president pondered. He had received an encouraging message from General Bliss: "I wish to God that the President himself could be here for a week. I hear in all quarters a longing for this. The people who want to get a rational solution out of this awful mess look to him alone. . . . In this dark storm of angry passion that has been let loose in all quarters I doubt if any one but he can let in the light of reason."[19]

However, it was upon House that Wilson depended chiefly for counsel. He had no negative reply to the cable in which he assumed that he would take part personally in "the real settlement" and therefore he took it for granted that his pressence would be expected at the peace table. On Armistice Day he let House know that he was in no hurry to depart, and suggested that it might be "wise and necessary" to postpone the conference until there were governments in Germany and Austria-Hungary that could enter into binding agreements. In response to a request from House for the immediate fixing of a date he cabled that he expected to sail on December 3, after delivering his annual message to the Congress, and that he

---

ernment in the hands of one man. Dispatch for Drummond from Wiseman, June 30, 1918, Wiseman pa., Y.H.C.

17. William Phillips, *Adventures in Diplomacy*, p. 93.

18. See George Bernard Noble, *Policies and Opinions at Paris, 1919*, pp. 95ff; Arthur Walworth, *Woodrow Wilson, 2*, 207; "On the President's Going to the Peace Conference," Lansing's private memoranda, Nov. 18, 1918, L.C.; also letters, Key Pitman to W.W., Nov. 15, 1918, *F.R., PPC, 1*, pp. 132–34, and Curzon to Lloyd George, in William Maxwell Aitken Beaverbrook, *Men and Power 1917–1918*, p. 385. David Lawrence wrote to Wilson on Oct. 30, 1918 to report that Mark Sullivan, a fellow journalist and a critic of the administration, had just returned from Europe and believed that Wilson could poll more votes in England than Lloyd George and more in France than Clemenceau. Three days later the president replied: "This is certainly good to hear." Wilson pa., 2.

19. Bliss to N.D. Baker, Oct. 23, 1918, Bliss pa., L.C., box 66; Frederick Palmer, *Bliss, Peacemaker*, p. 343.

would attend the peace conference only if the prime ministers of the Allied governments were present. "I assume also that I shall be selected to preside," his message said.[20]

Wilson's obvious inclination to go to Paris raised serious difficulties. Clemenceau, wishing to keep President Poincaré out of the peace talks, notified House that it would be impossible to admit one chief of state to the conference without admitting all.[21] Lloyd George also had reservations about a presidential visit. He did not like to contemplate the political effect of eloquent speeches in Europe by Wilson.[22] He was willing that the president attend a preliminary conference provided he would not take part in the essential negotiations.[23] A different opinion prevailed in the Foreign Office among young men who were excited by Wilson's vision of a new order.

Colonel House was aware of the views of the European leaders, and also with press opinion, which was divided. The view prevalent at Paris was that if the president did go abroad he should not stay long.[24] From London came the trenchant advice of Frank I. Cobb. The editor, who had at first wanted Wilson to attend the conference, now warned that by going to Paris he would cease to be a great arbiter of human freedom and would become only a negotiator with one vote, his eloquence smothered by translations of his words and by a biased press. Friction and endless controversy could easily grow out of personal contacts with political leaders who were jealous and suspicious of him. There was danger, Cobb wrote, that they would "miss no opportunity to harass him and wear him down." At Washington the president could sit as a revered, dispassionate judge, and if necessary put his case before all humanity by an appeal to the Congress over the head of the peace conference. At Paris he would be an advocate fighting on enemy soil.[25]

House, feeling the force of these arguments, found it difficult to join with the British or French leaders in making definite plans. On the day after the signing of the armistice he suggested to Ambas-

---

20. Baker, pp. 579, 585.

21. House to W.W., Nov. 15, 1918 Y.H.C.; F.S. Marston, *The Peace Conference of 1919*, p. 32.

22. In February of 1917, when his prime object was to induce Wilson to bring the United States into the war, Lloyd George had said to Ambassador Page that he wanted the president to take part in the peacemaking, where no one could have so commanding a voice. Devlin, p. 647.

23. Cobb journal, Nov. 11, 13, 14, 15, 1918, Wilson pa., file 14; Sir Arthur Willert, *The Road to Safety*, pp. 161–62.

24. Willert, p. 162; Palmer, *Bliss*, p. 343.

25. *I.P., 4*, pp. 210–12. Wilson's coming to Europe, Cobb wrote on November 13 in his journal, "would be another colossal blunder. Reading and Wiseman wholly agree with me." Wilson pa., 14, file 19.

sador Derby that an inter-Allied conference convene to arrange peace terms and agree on a date and conditions for negotiating treaties with the enemy. House explained that if the president was to attend, the conference could not meet before December 16. On the other hand, if he decided not to come, they could convene as soon as colleagues arrived from the United States; and in that case House would welcome preliminary talks. Even if the president chose to participate and thus restricted his agent's freedom to act, the colonel was willing to talk things over with any British official who might visit Paris.[26] House told Derby that there would be no differences between the United States and England if he could deal with men like Grey, Balfour, and himself. Derby agreed heartily and thus, House thought, showed his dislike of Lloyd George.[27]

A year before the United States entered the war House had begun to consider the peace conference; and his thought at that time was that the president should preside and be the only American delegate.[28] But the colonel's contact with the realities at Paris altered his view. The change was gradual. For a time it seemed possible that Wilson might follow the course taken by European rulers at Vienna in 1814, remaining outside the conference room but in close touch with the plenipotentiaries.[29] The colonel was convinced, after the discussions with the European premiers in the pre-armistice meetings, that the president's temperament was ill suited to the give-and-take of diplomatic business. Now a participant in official action rather than merely a critic and counselor, House shared Secretary Lansing's distress at Wilson's secretiveness and imprecision, which he had lamented more than once.[30] He had noted that the president

---

26. Lord Derby reported House's views to the F.O. and sent House a copy of the dispatch. The colonel found it inaccurate in respect of its report of his advice to the president. Derby to House, Nov. 12, 1918, enclosing copy of telegram of same date; House diary, Nov. 12, 1918.

Derby transmitted to Balfour, "privately," views expressed by House on a league of nations. Derby to House, Nov. 18, 1918 Y.H.C. In his diary House wrote: "Derby is not the cleverest man in the world, but he is honest and a gentleman, and I would prefer dealing with that kind of person even though we do not always agree." Entries of Nov. 19, 1918.

27. House diary, Dec. 11, 1918.

28. House diary, March 19, 1916.

29. Immediately after the signing of the armistice House sent this message to Wilson: "I shall count on your sailing December third. . . . The Peace Conference will probably be called for December sixteenth but there need be no active sessions for a week or ten days. This time could be used for inter-Allied conferences. Please let me know whether I can plan according to this schedule." Baker, pp. 582–83. At the same time he wrote in his diary: "We want the President at any time he can come, but probably not to sit in the negotiating sessions." Entry of Nov. 12, 1918.

30. House diary, August 19, Sept. 8, 1918. "The President expects me to keep absolutely abreast of both domestic and foreign situations, and, in addition to that, he

seemed incapable of handling two great questions of state at the same time. The negotiations at Paris would require a sort of mental juggling that would keep many issues constantly in the air.

With these misgivings House cabled a report, on November 14, of the sentiment of the statesmen of the Allies:

> Clemenceau has just told me that he hopes you will not sit in the congress because no head of a State should sit there. The same feeling prevails in England. Cobb cables that Reading and Wiseman voice the same view. Everyone wants you to come over to take part in the preliminary conference. It is at these meetings that peace terms will be worked out and determined just as the informal conferences determined the German and Austrian armistices. It is of vital importance, I think, for you to come as soon as possible, for everything is being held in abeyance. . . . In announcing your departure I think it is important that you should not state that you will sit at the Peace Conference. That can be determined after you get here.[31]

In other cables, which were seriously garbled in transmission, House repeated the suggestion that the president wait until his arrival in France to assess the situation and decide just what part he would take.[32] House took pains to disavow responsibility for the unpleasant advice that he had felt constrained to send despite his personal inclination to the contrary. For him, the ideal arrangement would be to have the president at hand, but not as a participant in negotiations.[33]

Secretary Lansing, when Wilson discussed the question with him, objected bluntly to the trip abroad and saw the president's face set

expects me to read his mind and know what conclusions he has come to or will come to under certain conditions. . . . It is hardly fair to me, and less fair to him. If my advice is as valuable as he seems to think, he ought to know that it would be more valuable if he informed me oftener as to his reactions upon what I advise."

31. *I.P.*, 4, pp. 212–13.

32. This is probably the only idea that came through clearly in cables of Nov. 15 and 16. House's texts in Y.H.C. and Wilson's transcriptions in Wilson pa., 2.

33. Noting that Wilson was "evidently worried" by his negative advice, the colonel wrote in his diary: "It seems clear to me that he should come over and decide for himself. Personally, I want him because if he were not here I would have the burden to bear without being able to direct matters alone as I have up to now." Apparently he feared that if the president were not present the State Department would be in control and would make it very difficult to carry out Wilson's program.

Young Willard Straight, taken into House's confidence, wrote in his diary in one of the last entries before he fell sick and died: "I think he [Wilson] wants to come. It's obvious the others don't want him to. They're afraid of him. House is afraid of the rest of the American mission." Straight was so overcome by House's personal kindness, and by the colonel's account of "putting over" the American program in the pre-armistice negotiations, that he wrote: "Old E.M. is a perfect wonder." Straight diary, Nov. 16, 1918.

firmly.[34] House's rebuff to an enterprise that Wilson anticipated as both a source of gratification and a fulfillment of a solemn duty aroused both suspicion and intransigence. In his reply the president did not mince words. House's message had upset "every plan . . . made," and thrown him into "complete confusion." He inferred that the English and French leaders wished to exclude him from the meetings as a means of "pocketing" him, out of apprehension that he might lead the smaller nations against them. He feared that if he stayed outside the meetings he would be "merely the center of a sublimated lobby" to which all weak parties would resort, and there would be exactly the same jealousy that was excited when the Germans addressed themselves exclusively to him. "I play the same part in our government that the prime ministers play in theirs," he cabled to House. "The fact that I am head of the state is of no practical consequence. [No point of] dignity must prevent our obtaining the results we have set our hearts upon and must have." Then he added a sentence that showed how far, in House's absence, he had fallen out of touch with opinion at Washington: "It is universally expected and generally desired here that I should attend the conference." He urged House to be very shy of European advice. "Give me your own independent judgment after reconsideration," he said.[35]

On November 18 the president announced to the public that he would depart immediately after the convening of the Congress on December 2. The next day he cabled assurance to House that if Clemenceau was uneasy about the presidency of the conference, he would be glad to propose that the French premier preside. House and Clemenceau discussed a procedure similar to that followed at the pre-armistice meetings; and the colonel gave assurance that, far from being hard to get along with, Wilson was a gentleman and more amenable to advice than any public man to whom he had been close. In the end Clemenceau withdrew his opposition to Wilson's presence in the essential sessions.[36]

Few decisions of a twentieth-century president have been the subject of more criticism and speculation than Wilson's determination to go to Paris in 1918. It is doubtful that without the full weight of his presence the Americans would have exerted an influence upon the peacemaking commensurate with the power that the nation held. By

---

34. Lansing, *The Peace Negotiations*, p. 22.

35. The message that Wilson wrote and sent on November 16 is printed in Baker, pp. 585–86. The quoted passage does not vary significantly in the text of House's transcription except that the three bracketed words are replaced by, "I object very strongly to the fact that."

36. House diary, Nov. 30, Dec. 5, 1918. See below, p. 145 and note.

remaining in Washington the president would have disappointed
those who looked to him for strong leadership toward a new world
order, and the difficulties of trans-Atlantic communication might
have delayed the proceedings at Paris.[37] After the peace conference,
Foreign Secretary Balfour affirmed an opinion he held before the
conference, that, being a clumsy machine, "it would not have run at
all had the President been compelled to contribute *his* most important share of the common work from the White House 3,000 miles
away."[38]

By meeting on a "summit" with European leaders who under the
stress of war had resorted to this style of diplomacy, Wilson helped
set a twentieth-century precedent for repeated violations of the
maxim of Philippe de Comines, the fifteenth-century diplomat:
"Two great princes who wish to establish good personal relations
should never meet each other face to face but ought to communicate
through good and wise ambassadors."

In breaking with tradition President Wilson ran the grave risk of
further shaking his political position, already unstable in the United
States, in the trying negotiations that were to come. A statesman
more aware of the pitfalls ahead would perhaps not have dared to
set out on so bold and perilous a mission.

---

37. See Arno J. Mayer, *Politics and Diplomacy of Peacemaking,* pp. 354–55; Charles
Seymour, "Woodrow Wilson: A Political Balance Sheet," *Proceedings of the American
Philosophical Society,* 137; and Richard M. Watt, *The Kings Depart,* pp. 40–41. The
debate on Wilson's decision to go to Paris is summarized in Thomas A. Bailey's *Wood-
row Wilson and the Lost Peace,* pp. 71–86. American journals expressed the gratifi-
cation of the public and stressed the leading role that the president would play at the
Peace Conference. See the *New York Times,* Dec. 5, and article by "ex-attaché," in the
Washington Post, Nov. 17, 1918.

38. Letter, Balfour to Close, Sept. 13, 1919, Wilson pa., 4, file 324c.

☆VIII☆

The Argosy of Peace

The initial opposition of the Europeans to Wilson's participation in
the peace talks further irritated the wound that he had suffered in
the Congressional election. Frustrated both abroad and at home, his
sense of mission grew and he assumed an air of confidence and competence. He boasted to a Swiss scholar that he was "stubborn . . .
but worldly wise" and confessed that he hoped to "run it all" at Paris
without hurting the feelings of the Allies. He knew that the peacemaking would be "a long rocky road," filled with rivalries and suspicions; but still he hoped to extend the Monroe Doctrine to the world
and to make of it "not a big-brother affair, but a real partnership"
for mutual protection.[1]

To help him establish American leadership amidst the controversies that he foresaw, Wilson felt that he must have aides who would
be loyal to his platform and would be helpful in winning its acceptance. It had been his custom, in the political battles of his career, to
choose some popular cause to fight for, to plead it both publicly and
privately, and to overcome opposition by every practical means. He
had already singled out from the Fourteen Points four "essentially
American terms."[2] Hoping that his platform would be adopted as
that of all mankind, he desired no advice from American political
leaders who had not approved it. Coping with the ideas of foreigners would be difficult enough. The American front must be
unified and unyielding.

House in this respect seemed irreplaceable. Wilson was dubious
about the value of Lansing to his enterprise; but he had decided that

1. William E. Rappard, "Woodrow Wilson, La Suisse, et Genève," *Centenaire
Woodrow Wilson,* pp. 51–53.
2. Cf. above, p. 64.

he must take the secretary of state.[3] Secretary of the Treasury McAdoo, Wilson's son-in-law, thought the president should not go to Paris and wished to go himself, feeling that he could adequately represent the position of the United States on matters of finance. Wilson's abhorrence of nepotism, however, which had led him to forbid the employment of another son-in-law, Francis B. Sayre, prevented such an appointment.[4] McAdoo resigned from the Treasury, and it seemed wise that the secretary of war, Newton D. Baker, remain on duty at Washington. Instead of Baker, Wilson appointed General Bliss, nominally a Republican and the military representative at the Supreme War Council. House considered this the best choice, thinking Bliss scholarly, statesmanlike, and free from "the army point of view," but so little known in the United States that he was no political asset to the president. In the opinion of Wilson the general was a statesman of mature judgment.[5]

For the fifth place Wilson sought a Republican who would support his principles. He was urged by many advisers to appoint ex-President Taft or Elihu Root, a former secretary of state, as men of sufficient stature to rise above party feeling. Taft's influence upon the public and Root's prestige among senators were considerable. But Wilson felt that their views diverged so far from his that they could not be useful in Paris. House, who recommended the appointment of one or both to a commission of seven, thought that in passing them by Wilson "made again one of his common mistakes."[6]

The president was hard put to find a Republican whom he could trust always to act cooperatively. He considered several names. He inclined toward men experienced in peace negotiations but apparently gave no consideration to John Bassett Moore, who had been secretary of the commission that negotiated peace with Spain at Paris in 1898. Professor Moore, whom Wilson had drawn from a chair at Columbia University to serve as counselor of the Depart-

---

3. Lansing desk diary, Oct. 14, L.C.; House diary, Oct. 15, 1918, Y.H.C.

4. See above, p. 82 and note. House diary, Oct. 13, 1918; copies of letters in Auchincloss diary, Dec. 16, 20, Y.H.C.; McAdoo to W.W., Oct. 26, Wilson pa., file 2, L.C.; memo. of Oct. 24 to McAdoo signed by four assistant secretaries, "Peace Mission" file, Bureau of Accounts, U.S. Treasury Dept.; cable for Glass from House, Dec. 26, 1918, *F.R., PPC, 2,* p. 546.

5. Benham diary letter, Dec. 5, 1918, Helm pa., L.C.

6. House diary, Dec. 1: House to W.W., Nov. 30, 1918, Wilson pa., file 2.

Declining to appoint Root to the Permanent Court at The Hague, Wilson wrote to Lansing on Sept. 13, 1918: "Frankly, I think Mr. Root is past his period of active usefulness." Wilson pa., 2. See Philip C. Jessup, *Elihu Root* (New York 1938), *2,* pp. 79–81.

Wilson described Taft as "a fine, honest man" whose amiability made it impossible for him "to stand hitched" and "who wobbles all over the place." George Creel, *Rebel at Large,* p. 253.

ment of State, had been disgusted by Bryan's partiality to "deserving Democrats" and by Wilson's policy toward Mexico, and had resigned in 1914. He was so far out of sympathy with the president that he probably could not have served him well. Moore complained especially of the policy proclaimed by Wilson on March 11, 1913: that American opinion of the character of foreign governments should be a criterion for diplomatic recognition. By American opinion, Moore thought, Wilson meant his own opinion—a position as "arrogant" as it was "ridiculous."[7]

Wilson authorized Lansing to offer appointment to Justice Day of the Supreme Court, who as secretary of state had been a peace commissioner in 1898; but Day, after talking with Chief Justice White, declined.[8]

Thereupon the president discussed the name of Henry White with Lansing, and learned that he had the support of Secretary Baker. Lansing drew out White's opinions on the Fourteen Points and found them sympathetic. After eliciting from Lansing an explanation of Wilson's views on a league of nations, trade relations, and freedom of the seas, White agreed to serve.[9] He had been conspicuous for judicial poise during the period of American neutrality, and had served Wilson by informing him of gaucheries of Ambassador Gerard at Berlin and by transmitting reports of British liberal opinion that came to him from London from his half-brother, W.H. Buckler.

Thus the president at last appointed an experienced diplomat to the American Commission to Negotiate Peace. Henry White had served as senior American delegate at the Algeciras Conference in 1906.[10] He had a happy faculty for bringing men together and rec-

7. J.B. Moore papers, Box 167, "W" folder, L.C. Moore wrote to Lansing that he had an "intimation" from the Chinese government that it would like to make him one of its delegates at the peace conference, and that he would not serve in this way unless the president permitted him to do so. He was told that the president considered that it would be quite improper, and replying on November 2, somewhat hurt, he cited the tradition of service to Chinese governments by American advisers. Moore to Lansing, Oct. 24, Lansing to Moore, Oct. 30, 1918, Lansing pa., vol. 39, L.C.

8. William R. Day to W.W., Nov. 14, 1918, *F.R., PPC 2,* p. 159.

9. Lansing desk diary, Nov. 13, 14, 18, 19, 20, 1918, microfilm, L.C. White's daughter had married a German officer. Lansing thought it wise to ascertain from Ambassador Jusserand whether this relationship would prejudice White's position at the peace conference in the eyes of the French government.

10. White, representing President Theodore Roosevelt, introduced proposals that contributed to a settlement at Algeciras. In a Senate debate on ratification of the Act of Algeciras, Roosevelt was accused of ignoring the counsel of the Founding Fathers and of exceeding his constitutional authority. Lodge vigorously defended the administration and the treaty against Democratic criticism; but the Senate insisted on a reservation asserting that the United States would not depart from its tradition of noninvolvement in European affairs.

onciling differences among them. He hoped that he would be able to serve similarly at Paris, where he would meet Balfour and other old friends. His appointment pleased Root. Theodore Roosevelt, who had called White "the most useful man in the entire diplomatic service," wrote to Lodge that he was "simply overjoyed." White had lived abroad for years, however, and had little influence in the Republican party.[11] Counselor Frank L. Polk protested against the appointment, but Wilson explained that it was the best that he could do since he could not trust other prominent Republicans.[12] House thought it "a great mistake to have three Democrats and two near-Republicans" on the peace commission.[13]

No senator was to be included. Moreover, the commissioners and indeed all the delegates were appointed as executive agents, not subject to approval by the Senate. Wilson explained that the Senate was an independent body and it did not seem fair to impair its freedom of action by appointing men as negotiators, responsible only to him and compensated at his will, who would eventually have to sit in the Senate and judge a treaty they had helped to make.[14] Wilson lacked confidence in the chairman of the Committee on Foreign Relations, Gilbert M. Hitchcock. Indeed, the president had tried to remove him from that office, and at one time had characterized him and the other Democratic members as "a rum lot."[15]

In failing to establish an understanding with the Committee on Foreign Relations, Wilson fell short of the view he had presented while he was president of Princeton. The Convention of 1787 intended, he had then explained, that the Senate should advise the president as to treaties "in the spirit of an executive council associated with him upon terms of confidential cooperation"; and it was the president's privilege, best policy, and plain duty to deal with the Senate on that basis. "If he has character, modesty, devotion, and insight as well as force, he can bring the contending elements together into a great and efficient body of common counsel." But at the same time Wilson had pointed out that the president "need disclose no step of negotiation until it is complete, and when in any

---

11. Allan Nevins, *Henry White*, p. 305; T.R. to Lodge, Nov. 27, 1918, T. Roosevelt pa., L.C. Lansing desk diary, Nov. 28, 1918.

12. Auchincloss diary, Aug. 3, 1919. Dr. Cary T. Grayson wrote (in *Woodrow Wilson: An Intimate Memoir*, p. 58) that Wilson had complete faith in White's "unselfish and non-partisan patriotism."

13. House to Seymour, Seymour pa., box 52, f. 252, Mar. 17, 1920, Y.H.C.

14. *I.P., 4*, p. 224. The decision to appoint no senator was a departure from the policy of President McKinley, which was criticized for the reason that now moved Wilson, Henry M. Wriston, "The Special Envoy," *Foreign Affairs*, 38 (January 1960), 229–30.

15. House diary, May 17, 1918.

critical matter it is completed the government is virtually committed. Whatever its disinclination, the Senate may feel itself committed also."[16] Seeing no practical prospect of dealing effectively with the membership of the upper chamber as it would be composed in 1919, Wilson felt justified in negotiating a treaty without the Senate's advice and in seeking consent to it as a fait accompli. He could not conceive that the senators would dare to defeat a treaty of peace after victory in the First World War. He was so confident of his mandate, despite the outcome of the congressional elections, that he remarked to the French ambassador that "the Senate must take its medicine."[17]

However, the Senate at the end of World War I was in a mood to rebel against a presidential leadership that had drawn strength from the martial emergency.[18] Republican dissenters took courage from the results of the Congressional election. Lodge did not believe that the vague provision of the Constitution or the precedents of history limited the function of the Senate to that of "consent." The senators, he had written in 1902, "stand on a perfect equality with the President in the making of treaties. They have an undoubted right to recommend either that a negotiation be entered upon or that it be not undertaken. . . . The right of the Senate to share in the treaty-making at any stage has always been fully recognized both by the Senate and the Executive."[19] Lodge felt that Wilson's tactics were unfair to the Senate as well as to the Republican party. But political realism restrained him. "When a political situation is entirely favorable it is not wise to meddle with it," he wrote on December 9 to Roosevelt; and the latter, cautioning his friends not to reveal their true feelings to the public, warned Lodge against making the mistake of overplaying their hand and causing a reaction of public sympathy.

Lodge did not take issue publicly with the president's decision to attend the peace conference, or with his choice of commissioners. Freely admitting that both his own opinions and his relations with

---

16. Woodrow Wilson, *Constitutional Government in the U.S.* (New York, 1908), pp. 77–78, 138–41; Harley Notter, *The Origins of the Foreign Policy of Woodrow Wilson*, pp. 145–46.

17. Nicholas Murray Butler, *Across the Busy Years*, 2, 201.

18. See John McC. Roots, "The Treaty of Versailles in the U.S. Senate," unpublished ms., Harvard University Archives, p. 25. A resolution introduced by Senator Knox on December 3 provided "that the extraordinary powers conferred upon the President for the prosecution of the war should be withdrawn and the country restored to a normal condition of peace with the greatest possible celerity consistent with the national interest." *Congressional Record,* 65th Congress, 3rd Session, Senate resolution no. 361.

19. Henry Cabot Lodge, "The Treaty Making Powers of the Senate," *Scribner's* (January 1902), cited by Kurt Wimer in "The League of Nations: A Victim of Executive-Legislative Rivalry," *The Lockhaven Bulletin,* ser. I, no. 2, 1960.

Wilson disqualified him from holding a position at Paris, the senator nevertheless gave notice to British diplomats that the Republican party would not give a free hand to a president who was ambitious to dictate the terms of peace.[20]

When Colonel House heard of the appointment of White, whom Wilson had not mentioned to him as a possibility, he feared that this was not a happy choice. Then, remembering that White was a friend of Lodge, he whistled and said: "Perhaps White is an olive branch."[21]

Lodge also conceived that White might be useful. After conferring with White at the bedside of Roosevelt, who was dying, he gave the Republican peace commissioner a memorandum that set forth his own ideas in detail, advocating terms that would render Germany impotent and would commit the United States to specific guarantees of certain European boundaries.[22] The document warned that any attempt to weave provisions for a league of nations into a peace treaty would make Senate ratification of the treaty extremely doubtful. Lodge asked that White show this paper in strict confidence to Balfour and Clemenceau, hoping that it would help "in strengthening their position" at the expense of that of the president.[23]

Theodore Roosevelt had insisted on "nationalism as against internationalism," and conceived of an international body as a concert of the powers victorious in the war and "as an *addition to,* but not as a *substitute for,* our preparing our own strength in our own defense." He would adopt "merely a platonic expression" in regard to the prevention of future wars, as a political expedient to please Taft and his pro-league following and also to forestall any accusation that the Republicans were "merely Prussian militarists."[24] Roosevelt and his

---

20. Barclay to Balfour, Nov. 21, 1918, Balfour pa., 49748, British Museum. In a letter to Balfour, in which he professed to present not a "party line" but actually "the weight of American opinion," Lodge set down Wilson's proposals as "almost hopelessly impractical" in many respects, and warned that to attach an arrangement for a league to the treaty would be "most unfortunate" and "might lead to great and most undesirable delays and possible amendments to the treaty of peace." Lodge to Balfour, Nov. 25, 1918, Balfour pa., 49742.

21. Typescript, "Nov. 30th," Bonsal pa., box 17.
House seized an opportunity to attempt to mollify Lodge by cabling to Polk on November 22, 1918: "Grew is very anxious to have Lieutenant G.W. Minot detailed to him and sent over at once. Minot is a grandson of Senator Lodge and for obvious reasons it would seem wise to grant Grew's request." Y.H.C.

22. Lodge was willing to underwrite the creation of independent Slav states in Central Europe, the neutralization of Constantinople, and the establishment of several republics in the Baltic area. Later Lodge was willing to guarantee France against German attack. John A. Garraty, *Henry Cabot Lodge,* pp. 347–49.

23. Nevins, p. 369. See below, p. 254.

24. T.R. to Beveridge, Oct. 15, 1918; T.R. to Leonard Wood, Nov. 2, 1918, Roosevelt papers.

followers thought of provisos and safeguards that could assure their country's security and freedom of action. Indignant at what he considered Wilson's arrogance in trying to dictate peace terms, he wrote to English friends to advocate that the British Empire and the United States "agree henceforth to arbitrate everything without any reservation." He urged that they look to the Congress and not the president as the genuine policy-maker in the United States.[25] He informed Lloyd George that the Republican party did not agree with Wilson's policies and, above all, felt that at the peace conference America should act, not as an umpire between "our allies and our enemies," but as one of the allies bound to come to an agreement with them, and then to impose this common agreement upon vanquished enemies. The "prime duty" of America, he wrote, was that "of standing by England and France."[26]

The president took no cognizance of the feelings of his adversaries. He did however remain in Washington long enough to continue his practice of appearing in person before the Congress to deliver his annual message. It dealt almost entirely with domestic matters. He expressed appreciation of the nation's "unity of purpose" during the war, and only at the end did he briefly speak of his mission abroad:

> The allied governments have accepted the bases of peace which I outlined to the Congress on the eighth of January last, as the Central Empires also have, and very reasonably desire my personal counsel in their interpretation and application, and it is highly desirable that I should give it in order that the sincere desire of our

In public Taft took a broadminded position, writing to the *Public Ledger* on December 4 that the president's plan to go to Paris was entirely proper, as was his aspiration to be president of a league of nations. Though Taft noted that Wilson's persistent ignoring of the Senate created resentment, he held that such feeling should be shown only in a political campaign. Taft commended the Republican leader in the House, James R. Mann, for his statement that there would be no concerted effort by the Republicans in the House to embarrass the president in any way while he was abroad.

Privately, however, Taft was severely critical. He wrote to Bryce: "If there was anything left undone by him [Wilson] to make his going [to Paris] unpopular in Congress, I don't know what it was. . . . [He] is likely to encounter . . . the charge that he went abroad for a junket. He named a commission which is as colorless as can be, utterly subservient to his dictation." House was set down as "a very pleasant gentleman but quite superficial." Letter, Dec. 5, 1918, Bryce pa., Bodleian Library, Oxford University, *10*, pp. 207 ff.

25. T.R. to J. Murray Clark of the Royal Canadian Institute, Dec. 15, 1918, copy in Borden pa., *8*, (1), doc. 87024, Public Archives of Canada; T.R. to Bryce, Nov. 19, Bryce pa., *9*, 254; T.R. to the Australian Press Association, n.d., Roosevelt pa.; William H. Harbaugh, *Lawyer's Lawyer*, p. 518; T.R. to Arthur Lee, Nov. 19, 1918, copy in Lloyd George pa., F/31/2/24, Beaverbrook.

26. Roosevelt to Lloyd George, Dec. 10, 1918, Lloyd George pa., F/24/3/81; David Lloyd George, *The Truth about the Peace Treaties*, p. 233.

Government to contribute without selfish purpose of any kind to settlements that will be of common benefit to all the nations concerned may be made fully manifest. The peace settlements which are now to be agreed upon are of transcendent importance both to us and to the rest of the world, and I know of no business or interest which should take precedence of them. The gallant men of our armed forces on land and sea have consciously fought for the ideals which they knew to be the ideals of their country; I have sought to express those ideals; they have accepted my statements of them as the substance of their own thought and purpose, as the associated Governments have accepted them; I owe it to them to see to it, so far as in me lies, that no false or mistaken interpretation is put upon them, and no possible effort omitted to realize them. It is now my duty to play my full part in making good what they offered their life's blood to obtain. I can think of no call to service which could transcend this.

I shall be in close touch with you and with affairs on this side the water, and you will know all that I do. . . .

May I not hope, gentlemen of the Congress, that in the delicate tasks I shall have to perform on the other side of the sea, in my efforts truly and faithfully to interpret the principles and purposes of the country we love, I may have the encouragement and the added strength of your united support? I realize the magnitude and difficulty of the duty I am undertaking; I am poignantly aware of its grave responsibilities. I am the servant of the Nation. I can have no private thought or purpose of my own in performing such an errand. . . .

And so the president left Washington without explaining just how he would apply his precepts to the peacemaking. The senators were filled with doubts and suspicions and within two days were engaged in a bitter debate of Wilson's policy. Just before he departed, on December 2, the president called a few of them to the White House, preached zealously about the duty of the United States to the people of Europe, and showed little interest in their reactions.[27] It seemed to the senators that they would be asked to approve a treaty about which they had had nothing to say. They thought the president was giving way to undigested idealism and had no considered plan. They resented the appointments to the peace delegation that were not subject to the Senate's confirmation. The Democratic majority in the Senate Foreign Relations Committee managed to kill a resolution calling for the inclusion of eight senators; but the tenor of the opposition did not augur well for the eventual reception of the treaty.

27. Sewell Thomas, *Silhouettes of Charles S. Thomas* (Caldwell, Idaho, 1959), pp. 194–96.

"The shadow of an impending Republican Congress hangs over Washington," Sir Arthur Murray reported to the British Foreign Office.[28]

The chilly political atmosphere made the president the more determined to pursue the course that he thought right. He was ready to exercise not only the peacemaking power conferred by the American Constitution, but also a voluntary initiative in world affairs that was contrary to the tradition of a century of isolation. Public opinion, at one extreme, regarded him as an arrant meddler and political adventurer. The opposite view saw him as one who, in taking upon himself the responsibility of an arbiter of the world's destiny, showed "that audacity which is the gift of the truly great."[29]

On December 3—a day on which the leaders of the Allies were in London, conferring tentatively about peacemaking[30]—Woodrow Wilson embarked on the *George Washington* for France. The list of 113 passengers included the experts of The Inquiry, technical advisers to the armed services, and State Department personnel responsible for publicity and printing, political and economic intelligence, counterespionage, finance, protocol, and general liaison.

New York gave the president a noisy send-off as the vessel, a German ship that had been converted into an American transport, put out from Hoboken. People crowded the docks in cheering throngs; and along the waterfront workers in the high buildings threw open windows and tossed torn paper to the breezes.

The morning papers set forth the popular expectations. An editorial in the *Times* recalled Horace's ode to the ship that bore Virgil to Athens; and the editor who wrote this told his friends at the Century

---

28. Murray to Reading, Wiseman, and Tyrrell, Nov. 22, Dec. 5, 1918, Wiseman pa., Y.H.C.

Frederick Cunliffe-Owen wrote to Wiseman on Dec. 2, 1918: "In all my experience in the United States, extending over a period of forty years, I have never known such bitter and savage resentment against a President of the opposition party as prevails at the present moment among the Republicans of every class against Woodrow Wilson. . . . This opposition to the President is rendered all the more obstructive to his policies by the fact that the big business interests of the Democratic Party in the South, in the Middle West, and West, have turned against him on economic grounds." Wiseman pa., Y. H. C.

The virulence of the opposition is indicated by an entry in Secretary Lansing's notebook: "Today the voice of the American people is . . . relentless as that of the ancient Romans when they fiercely cried out that Carthage must be utterly destroyed. . . . On the crest of this wave of passion . . . rides the malignant Roosevelt, the partisan Lodge . . . and all the lesser enemies of the Administration who have [been] seeking for a chance to bite." Private memoranda, Oct. 12, 1918, L.C.

29. R.S. Baker's notebook, Oct. 15, 1918, Baker pa., L.C.

30. See above pp. 102 ff.

Association that it was well that the president was to take a personal part in the peacemaking, but actually his entourage, without outstanding Republicans like Root and Taft, was "a right smart, colorful, weak group."[31] In his journal Frank I. Cobb set down the plenipotentiaries as "a purely personal commission of excellent gentlemen who . . . have no political standing."[32] Cunliffe-Owen of the *Tribune* wrote skeptically to Wiseman, rather regretting "the boat-load of Yale and Harvard professors of international law" whom the president was taking with him as experts, and predicting that they were "sure to make trouble."[33]

The president looked worn and weary and he had a cold and a cough. Admiral Cary T. Grayson, the doctor who had become his personal friend and constant attendant, was at hand to supervise his diet and exercise. This was the first long respite from the White House since the United States entered the war, and the *George Washington* took an extreme southerly course for Wilson's benefit. In a comfortable suite he enjoyed the relaxation that he always found in a sea voyage. He rose a little before noon, ate with Mrs. Wilson in their rooms, walked much on deck, and went early to bed. He made sparing use of the eye that had not been afflicted by arteriosclerosis. After two days at sea he seemed to his secretary "very genial and brisk," and handled "quite a batch of stuff."[34]

Most of the members of The Inquiry and others of his entourage lived a different life. They were served plain fare in the main dining room, and were crowded into dingy cabins that had hardly been altered since the vessel served as a troop-carrying transport. The president's personal staff noted that the State Department, having made hasty and inadequate provision for the "temporary gentlemen," assigned to itself the best staterooms and a bar and a dining salon where thirty officials of the department and military intelligence were served by a staff from a New York hotel. Admiral Grayson wrote: "They have adopted a very ultra-superior attitude towards our humble party . . . the President is much displeased."[35]

Meanwhile the men of The Inquiry, uncomfortable in crowded quarters on "D" deck, speculated as to the use that would be made

31. F. Fraser Bond, *Mr. Miller of "The Times"* (New York, 1931), p. 153.

32. Entry of Nov. 30, 1918, Cobb journal, L.C.

33. Cunliffe-Owen to Wiseman, Dec. 2, 1918, Wiseman pa., Y.H.C.

34. Gilbert Close's letters home of Dec. 7, 8, 10, 1918, Closs pa., Princeton University Library.

35. Grayson to Tumulty, Dec. 12, Tumulty pa., box 5, L.C.; Auchincloss to Polk, Dec. 15, 1918, Y.H.C. "There is . . . a certain amount of social segregation, which is keenly felt by the more aristocratic of The Inquiry." Charles Seymour, *Letters from the Paris Peace Conference*, p. 6.

of their accumulation of knowledge.[36] At first there was a tentative plan for a series of conferences of the whole delegation, but the scholars were deterred by the danger that remarks that would have been appropriate for academic utterance might now be thought indiscreet.[37] There was little contact with the peace commissioners. Henry White was the most approachable of the three who were aboard. Invited to tea by four of the scholars, White brought in Secretary Lansing, who seemed reluctant to come but became interested in the conversation and took part in it.[38] The president talked only once with the secretary of state, and it was evident that the State Department, which was concerned with the conditions under which the American Commission would work, was to have little to do with the actual negotiations at Paris.[39]

The scholars were given an insight into the thinking of the president only because William Bullitt, acting in liaison between the State Department and The Inquiry, directed his attention to the fact that his advisers felt entirely left out and were in a skeptical, cynical mood.[40] Wilson brought them together very casually, failing to notify some, and talked for more than an hour about the task ahead. Speaking with warmth, wit, and frankness, he proclaimed that the new order must neither perpetuate the system of a balance of powers, which in his view had failed because of its essential nature rather than because of faulty management, nor set up a concert of great

---

36. Bowman diary, Dec. 3, 1918, Johns Hopkins University Library. Bowman and Professor Haskins were given a better stateroom on "the second day out."

37. Ibid., Dec. 9, 1918.

38. Present at this conference, in Bowman's cabin, were Professors Bowman, Day, Haskins, and Young. Clive Day's diary letter mailed Feb. 14, 1914, Y.H.C. According to Shotwell, Lansing "thawed out and became cordial" when he saw that The Inquiry could be useful. James T. Shotwell, *At the Paris Peace Conference*, p. 76. Lansing talked with White and with Ambassador John W. Davis, who was en route to London to replace Walter Hines Page, and they agreed that the president should not sit at the peace table as a delegate. Lansing diary, appendix, entries of Dec. 4, 5, 17, 1918.

39. Lansing, private memoranda, appendix, box 1, Dec. 8, 17, 1918.

"Officers of the Military Intelligence Division under General Marlborough Churchill . . . had secured control of the large forward salon on the upper deck of the ship and transformed it into a handsome and impressive map room; they obviously took it for granted that they would be the technical advisers of the president and commissioners on all territorial aspects of the settlement. Secretary of State Lansing was not happy over the prospect; he regarded the M.I.D. with even more suspicion than he did The Inquiry. President Wilson visited the map room more than once, but it was reasonably clear that he did not intend that the M.I.D. should exert serious influence then or later." Seymour, *Letters*, pp. xxx–xxxi. The scholars of The Inquiry were not greatly impressed by the room of the M.I.D. and relied on the maps of Mark Jefferson, an able cartographer brought into service by Bowman. See Geoffrey J. Martin, *Mark Jefferson;* Shotwell, pp. 67–68.

40. Seymour, *Letters*, p. 21; Bullitt to the writer, April 2, 1951.

powers like that of 1815, which he regarded as repressive rather than stabilizing.

Except for a discussion with Lansing and Ambassador Davis, which raised doubts in the mind of the secretary of state,[41] the president had taken no one but House into his confidence with respect of a constitution for a league of nations.[42] He now told his advisers of his hope that a league would provide both security and elasticity by guaranteeing the political independence and territorial integrity of nations and at the same time by providing for later alteration of terms and boundaries if it could be shown that injustice had been done or that conditions had changed. He doubted that at Paris they could work out plans for an international court or an international police force. Machinery such as that proposed by the League to Enforce Peace would break down in a day, he thought. Better to work out covenants in general form, and trust to experience and necessity to guide future action. This was the Anglo-Saxon way of building law. A council of ambassadors might meet at Berne or The Hague to give full publicity to war-breeding issues that would be referred to it, and perhaps to apply an economic boycott against aggressive nations. He suggested that a league might derive stability from the assumption of a definite responsibility, such as that for the administration of former German colonies under trusteeships to be exercised by small powers. It was his hope that a league would do for the world what the Monroe Doctrine had done for the Western Hemisphere.

Much of his talk was boastful. He took an attitude without diplomatic precedent when he arrogated to himself a higher authority than that of the duly accredited statesmen with whom he must negotiate.[43] He declared that Great Britain and France had put in writing that they would have had to quit if the United States had not entered the war. His nation was the only disinterested one, he said, and was under a moral compulsion to exert every effort to secure "justice," even in boundary settlements in which it had no interest. At the same time the prophet who had only a dubious political mandate from his own people dared to assert that the statesmen of the Allies did not truly represent the temper of their peoples, and were "too weather-wise to see the weather." Unfortunately, some of the men of

41. Lansing desk diary, Dec. 8, 1918.

42. See above, p. 13.

43. "Neither before nor since has a national leader approached a conference with his national opposite numbers in such a frame of mind." H.G. Nicholas in J. Joseph Huthmacher and Warren I. Susman, *Wilson's Diplomacy*, p. 89.

The Inquiry, when they reached Paris, talked and acted in a way that reflected the moral arrogance of their chief.[44]

The president raised the spirits of the scholars by appealing to their emotional commitment to democracy. He reminded them that "only that government is free whose people regard themselves as free." He hoped that, in contributing to world government some of the genius that went into the building of their own federal union, Americans might regenerate their own enthusiasm for freedom. By proving themselves fair, he said, as they had in advocating an "open door" in China, they could become trusted by the rest of the world as umpires and thus help to counter "the curious poison of Bolshevism," which was being swallowed by some in protest against the status quo. In a talk with Raymond B. Fosdick, who had been his pupil at Princeton, Wilson showed himself a liberal not only out of conviction but because he thought this faith was the only thing that could save civilization from a flood of radicalism that would swamp the world.[45]

Wilson regarded the scholars as men of his own kind, disinterested thinkers who considered the questions of the peacemaking in terms of both facts and solutions.[46] He asked them to work through the other peace commissioners but to feel free to come straight to him with any vital facts that affected critical decisions. "Tell me what's right and I'll fight for it," he said. "Give me a guaranteed position!"[47]

After the talk he consulted some of the men individually about their specialties. They were impressed by his general knowledge and thought he was preserving a scholarly openness of mind.[48] Some wished for more explicit satisfaction of their curiosity. At least one felt that it was dangerous for the president to commit himself. "It would be extremely mortifying," George Louis Beer wrote prophe-

---

44. See below, p. 139 and note.
45. Raymond B. Fosdick diary letter, Dec. 11, 1918, Wilson pa., 14.
46. Bowman to T.A. Bailey, July 24, 25, Aug. 8, 1918, Geoffrey J. Martin's copy.
47. The substance of Wilson's talk has been taken from the contemporary notes of Seymour, *Letters*, pp. 21–24; from those of Isaiah Bowman (*I.P., 4*, pp. 280–83); from the diaries of George Louis Beer and William L. Westermann in the Butler Library, Columbia University, and the diary of William C. Bullitt, and from Shotwell, pp. 75–78.
48. "The president showed good general information and asked good questions. He showed what seemed to me to be in general sound ideas. He suggested a plan of procedure which might shorten the period of deliberation and which we are going to study. He wants matters put at first in certain broad lines, and does not wish to be bothered by details, He is interested in simplifying everything as far as possible." Seymour, *Letters*, pp. 28–30; Clive Day diary letter, Dec. 14, 1918, Y.H.C.

tically in his diary, "if the Senate rejected a league plan that he had induced Europe to accept."[49]

Thus Wilson cheered the scholars by holding out a prospect that they could be useful. His words were those of a great leader of men, but hardly those of an effective diplomat.

In remarks to the three journalists aboard the ship Wilson lowered his tone. Though he had been the first president to hold regular press conferences he had given up the practice in 1915, complaining that the men were interested in "the personal and the trivial rather than in principles and policies."[50] He was well aware of the importance of good relations with newsmen, however, and in the comparative leisure of the ocean voyage he talked frankly with them in the language of a political campaigner. Much perturbed to learn that the peace conference could not begin for a month, he asked the journalists to send home dispatches that would counteract any impression that he was going on a junket.[51] Revealing prejudices that were hazards to good diplomacy, he spoke cynically of the motives of the statesmen of the Allied governments. He said: "They are evidently planning to take what they can get frankly as a matter of spoils, regardless of either the ethics or the practical aspects of the proceedings." (After he reached Paris Wilson continued, in the privacy of the family, to indulge in petty criticism of the Allies.)[52]

Putting Great Britain in a baleful light, he suggested that there was turpitude in the very act of colonial administration—which his own nation had practiced with the justification of "manifest destiny." He no longer expressed the tolerant view of the British Navy that he had taken in an interview with Wiseman before the armistice; and he threatened to upset the delicate and tentative understanding that House had reached on the incendiary issue of freedom of the seas. Reacting to a public declaration of Winston Churchill against any budgetary restrictions that would prevent the British Navy from maintaining its supremacy,[53] he reminded those around him that it was American ships and troops that turned the tide of battle. He confirmed an impression he had left in a talk with Sir Arthur Mur-

---

49. Beer diary, Dec. 10, 1918, Butler Library, Columbia University; Shotwell, p. 75.

50. Baker, *4*, p. 232.

51. Benham diary letter, Dec. 11, 1918, Helm pa., box 1.

52. Benham diary letter, Jan. 10, 1919, Helm pa. The above quotation and the following remarks of Wilson to newsmen are taken from the unpublished book ms. of Charles Swem, which is based on Swem's stenographic notes of the president's remarks, Princeton University Library.

53. The ship's newspaper, *The Hatchet,* quoted Churchill to this effect on Dec. 6. Benham diary letter, Dec. 5, 1918, Helm pa.

ray: that he intended to use American naval estimates as a lever to force his program upon the peace conference.[54] At least one of his academic advisers was alarmed.[55] Wilson said that if he found any Americans serving in the peace delegation who failed to put America first, he would send them home; and he complained that it seemed impossible to appoint an envoy to London who did not take the English point of view. He had told Ambassador Davis—in jest, he said—that he would be recalled if he ceased to represent the United States.[56]

The president again was revealing a moral outlook that the diplomats of Europe found arrogant. Repeating the threat that House had made in the pre-armistice meetings, he said that, if opposed, he would "be compelled to withdraw. . . . and return home and in due course take up the details of a separate peace." "Of course," he said, "I don't believe that that will come to pass. I think that once we get together, they will learn that the American delegates have not come to bargain, but will stand firmly by the principles that we have set forth; and once they learn that that is our purpose I believe we shall come to an early agreement."

He gave notice that he would use his arbitrage to establish a "peace without victory." He warned that it must be a peace of justice to the defeated nations or it would be fatal to all the nations in the end. Asked to speak especially about a league of nations, Wilson indicated to the newsmen that he would be as uncompromising toward the political ambition of Republicans as to the demands of European statesmen. He said that he would take pains to follow precisely the course against which Senator Lodge had warned him and would "insist that the league be brought out as part and parcel of the treaty itself."

The president's understanding of history was too acute to permit him to be as confident of success as his facile words suggested.

---

54. Telegram, Murray to Wiseman and Reading, Dec. 5, 1918, Wiseman pa. Murray questioned whether a Republican Congress would agree to a naval building competition with Great Britain. On December 9 the London press printed dispatches from American correspondents about a determination of the United States to lay two keels to every one laid by Great Britain. The American Embassy in London reported that such articles were "in the highest degree mischievous" and stirred feeling on a subject that did not need to be controversial. Laughlin to Polk, Dec. 12; J.W. Davis to Polk, Dec. 19, 1918, *F.R., PPC, 1,* pp. 413–14.

55. Charles Seymour wrote on December 5: "What I fear is that Wilson will go to Lloyd George holding an American greater navy and mercantile marine as a club to enforce his interpretations of the 'freedom of the seas.' Then if Lloyd George does not back down, and I don't think that he will, we shall be driven by the President to unlimited naval expansion." *Letters* p. 10.

56. Benham diary letter, Dec. 5, 10, 1918, Helm pa.

Thanking George Creel for publicizing his wartime addresses, Wilson said: "It is a great thing that you have done, but I am wondering if you have not unconsciously spun a net for me from which there is no escape. It is to America that the whole world turns today, not only with its wrongs, but with its hopes and grievances. . . . People will endure their tyrants for years but they tear their deliverers to pieces if a millennium is not created immediately."

Before leaving New York he had predicted that his trip would be "the greatest success or the supremest tragedy in all history," and he confessed that only belief in "a Divine Providence" kept him from insanity. It "frightened" him, he said now, to see what people expected of him. Yet, convinced that no peace could endure that was not based on "progressive" principles, he was eager to carry on his crusade.[57]

---

57. George Creel, *The World, the War and Woodrow Wilson*, p. 163; Joseph P. Tumulty, *W.W. as I Knew Him*, p. 335; Fosdick diary letter, Dec. 11, 1918, L.C.

☆IX☆

Wilson's Triumphal Entry

The people of France welcomed Woodrow Wilson in the same spirit in which Americans had cheered him off—as a leader who had struck a winning blow against evil and who aspired to make a just and secure peace. Landing at Brest on December 13, he exchanged greetings with the city's socialist mayor. The next day he arrived at Paris on a brilliant morning that broke the grayness of the season. Greeted at the station by the great men of France, he was driven through the Place de la Concorde, where captured German cannon were displayed wheel to wheel and the cheers of the populace mocked the motto that was engraved on the guns: *"ultima ratio regis."* People scurried and climbed, curious to see the illustrious American as he rode beside President Poincaré. Colonel House, watching from his room in the Crillon, flitted from one window to another to get the best view possible, eager that the demonstration should exceed that given the monarchs of the Allied nations.[1] Mrs. Wilson was entranced by the pageantry.[2] House, asked by the Quai d'Orsay whether an official reception should be given for the president alone or for Mr. and Mrs. Wilson, wrote in his diary: "Knowing Mrs. Wilson as I do, I advised the latter."[3]

In the intoxicating air of victory the moral commitments of the prophet from the New World did not weigh heavily. Wilson's broad smile and doffings of his tall hat persuaded the crowds that he was not the grim preacher that caricatures represented. Nevertheless the light-hearted reception deepened his commitment to his ideals. He

1. Dr. Albert Lamb's notes from his diary, Princeton University Library; Fosdick letter, Dec. 14, 1918, Wilson pa., 14, L.C.
2. Edith Bolling Wilson, *My Memoir,* pp. 177ff.
3. House diary, Dec. 4, 1918, Y.H.C.

thought he was "instructed by acclaim" to stand fast upon the principles and purposes that he had avowed.[4] He was the more convinced that these people would force their national leaders to accept his doctrine. To exert political pressure on any statesman who might offer opposition, the president would appeal directly to the constituency of the obstructor. (As early as July 6, 1918 he had said: "I am satisfied that if necessary I can reach the peoples of Europe over the heads of their rulers.") Secretary Lansing, noting the effect upon French officials of the ovation given to Wilson, reversed an earlier opinion and wrote: "There can be no doubt of the wisdom of his coming to Europe and of the effect it will have on the acceptance of our program."[5]

A strategy such as this, which was entirely consistent with Wilson's wooing of new constituencies in the past, was contrary to the code of the old diplomacy. Its success depended in large measure on the cooperation of the press.

The journalistic welcome to the president on his arrival at Paris reflected the social and economic predilections of the various editors. French papers of the labor and socialist groups were prolific of praise. The leftist press called attention to what it described as a "campaign on the sly" against Wilson. Lansing noted this and wrote to Polk on December 15: "The statesmen from the Allied countries are extremely jealous of the President, who has the absolute confidence of the mass of the people. They are beginning a sort of campaign to undermine his popularity. It is going on very cautiously since if the people suspect it, it will react on the authors."

Conservative journals, claiming that Wilson was in complete agreement with Clemenceau, publicized the political opposition to the president at Washington.[6]

A few of the papers, ignoring strict orders from the government censor, printed hostile speeches of Republican senators. Some reporters went so far as to spread scurrilous slander of Mrs. Wilson.[7]

---

4. W.W. to H.B. Brougham, Dec. 17, 1918, Wilson pa., 5B.

5. Oscar T. Crosby's record of interview, R.S. Baker pa., L.C.; Lansing to Edward N. Smith, Dec. 17, 1918, Lansing pa., box 3, Princeton University Library. Henry White believed that any European government suspected of being out of harmony with Wilson was likely to be overthrown. Allan Nevins, *Henry White*, p. 361. "Probably no other foreign statesman had ever been as popular in France as Wilson was in December of 1918." Jean-Baptiste Duroselle in J. Joseph Huthmacher and Warren I. Susman, *Wilson's Diplomacy;* p. 28.

6. Dispatch, Ambassador Sharp to Sec. State, Oct. 10, 1918, N.A., R.G. 59, 763.72119/2544.

7. George Bernard Noble, *Policies and Opinions at Paris* pp. 74–75, 82–83; *Écho de Paris,* Dec. 14, 18, 1918; report of a talk of Albert Thomas with House, Nov. 3, 1918,

House, who had already worked with some success to impress upon the French newsmen the fact that the permanence of Wilson's tenure in the presidency gave him a certain shield against political attack that the European premiers lacked[8] was distressed by the hazard to good diplomacy that the president had raised. House's task was complicated by the immoderate remarks that his chief had made on the *George Washington* without any attempt to have them held in confidence. It seemed as if they were a frontal attack upon the men with whom Wilson must negotiate. When Clemenceau asked whether the reports of the utterance were correct and whether Wilson actually was coming in a hostile spirit to make peace, House reassured him. Yet versions of the indiscretion, according to Bonsal, "were circulating like wildfire." The president took the aspect of a liberal crusader who was to be feared. To many European officials he had become an enemy against whom they must battle to preserve the vital interests of their nations.[9]

All sections of the French press except the extreme left joined in putting forward the national demands for security against future attack by Germany. To enlist Wilson's sympathy they sought to have him visit the areas that had been devastated by warfare. Only in this way, they thought, could the American leader appreciate the realities of France's suffering. Four days after his arrival Tardieu presented for his consideration a two-page "Projet de Voyage . . . pour Répondre a un Désir Exprimé par M. le Président." Actually Wilson had not expressed any such desire.[10]

President Poincaré had satisfied popular sentiment by going to Al-

---

Y.H.C.; Marcel Berger and Paul Allard, *Les Dessous du Traité de Versailles*, pp. 33–35, 37–41, 44, 50ff.

8. Bonsal diary, Dec. 6, 1918, L.C.

9. Bonsal wrote in his diary on December 18 of the publication of many unfriendly articles in the Paris press. "Some of these are positively villainous and all tend to belittle the President. . . . It is a thousand pities that the President disclosed his opinion of his fellow delegates before they had revealed their real attitudes. . . . It is charged that Dr. Bowman and his fellow members of The Inquiry have been most indiscreet—that they have unduly emphasized the President's challenging words. . . . Unfortunately they were urged to make the announcement of the President's opinion and they have made it in no uncertain terms." Bonsal pa., box 17, "Dec." folder. Bonsal wrote, further: "I recalled, for the benefit of House, a saying that fell from the lips of Grand Vizier Tewfik Pasha, one of the wise old Turks I knew in Constantinople: If you can't cut off your enemy's head don't scratch his face. The President has scratched many faces, . . . and a lot of people would like to see European affairs settled by Europeans. Above all else they would like to have Wilson go back to Washington and that of course is one of the reasons why the President means to stay here, for some weeks, at least."

10. Tardieu to General Harts, Dec. 18, 1918, Wilson pa., 5B; David Lawrence, *The True Story of Woodrow Wilson*, p. 259.

sace and Lorraine, accompanied by American generals and by Ambassador Sharp, and celebrating the prospect of the return of these provinces to France. Speaking at a luncheon to welcome Wilson, Poincaré reminded him that he too would be able to see the extent of German depredations; and the president responded with an expression of sympathy for French indignation at "the ruin wrought by the armies of Germany." But when French papers reported, inaccurately, that Wilson asked to be taken to the war-devastated regions, the president resisted their importunity. He explained that what was proposed would make him "see red." To a journalist[11] he said: "I was reared, as a boy, in a devastated region [after the Civil War.]" He had no wish to deal with matters of state in an angry mood. Actually, according to a member of the Wilson household, the pressure of French propaganda annoyed him so much that he almost gave up an intention to go eventually to the battlefields of his own volition.[12] It was not until January 26 that the Wilsons spent a day in Rheims and Soissons and at the battlefield where American troops had distinguished themselves near Château Thierry. The delay added to the disappointment of many who hoped to use his influence to promote their causes.

The Allied premiers had refused a request by a French congress of socialists for permission to present an appeal to Wilson; but they agreed at the London Conference that they would not intervene if the socialists addressed themselves directly to him.[13]

The French government was determined to thwart the designs of the leftists. Receiving petitions from several groups, officials required that the workers do no more than salute the American president in the streets. This edict brought pleaders for labor to House's door. They complained not only of the ban, but of the interdiction of publicity about it and the printing in French rightist journals of articles disparaging Wilson.[14] They divulged to House their plan for a parade of 150,000 workers. Auchincloss, by his own record, had been "egging the labor leaders . . . on to a gigantic demonstration for the President." ("They don't need much egging," he wrote. "They play our game absolutely and will make their governments sit up and take notice before they are through.")[15] André Tardieu called on House in behalf of Clemenceau to discuss the at-

11. Oliver Newman, *International Cosmopolitan,* Jan. 1930.

12. Benham diary letter, Jan. 20, 1918, Helm pa., L.C.

13. French procès-verbal, Dec. 3, 1918, F.C.

14. House diary, Dec. 8, 1918; Noble, p. 76; Auchincloss diary, Dec. 10, 1918, Y.H.C.

15. Dispatch, Auchincloss to Polk, Dec. 5, Y.H.C.; House diary, Dec. 7, 8; Auchincloss diary, Dec. 5, 10, 1918.

tempt of the Socialists to take Wilson under their wings.[16] Ambassador Sharp, aware that Clemenceau would be uncompromising in his opposition to Socialist attempts to gain control of government anywhere in Europe, let alone at Paris, came to take counsel with the colonel.[17] Despite their knowledge of the disapproval of the French authorities, they agreed that subject to further talk between Sharp and Clemenceau, the president should be responsive.

When House informed Wilson by radiogram that the parade would "probably take place," Wilson, who had no sympathy for any popular outburst that might disrupt civil order,[18] replied from mid-Atlantic asking that the demonstration be avoided, and saying, "The President fears embarrassment from any seeming identification with any single element." Nevertheless, on the afternoon of his arrival at Paris a small group of militants displayed a red banner extolling "la paix Wilson" and paraded until they were dispersed by the police; and afterwards the president received eight labor delegates in accordance with arrangements made by House.[19] This recognition was interpreted by the American Embassy as "no espousal of socialist policies," but rather as symbolic of Wilson's love for the French people.[20]

Although Wilson doubtless still wished to believe that he could reach the peoples of Europe over the heads of their rulers, he moved with caution, perhaps remembering the counsel that House had given to the effect that the support of labor was "uncertain and erratic"and that it was with the statesmen of the Allies that he would have to reckon at the peace conference.

On the day of his arrival at Paris the president made it clear to House that he depended on him not only to manage his public relations but to organize the American peace delegation as well.[21] Thus, he removed a misapprehension that had been in House's mind since Lansing's revision of the elaborate plans of Mezes.[22] Just before leav-

---

16. House diary, Dec. 7, 1918. After talking with Cachin, the Socialist leader, R.S. Baker wrote in his journal on Dec. 23: "wholly for the Wilson program . . . also a party politician and is no doubt using Wilson's immense popularity as a stick to beat Clemenceau with." Ms. for *American Chronicle, 53,* 9, Baker pa.

17. Sharp to Sec. State, Oct. 10, 1918, N.A., R.G. 59, doc. 763.72119/2544.

18. R.S. Baker, Paris Notebook XIX, p. 112, R.S. Baker pa., L.C.

19. Four represented the Parti Socialiste, and four the C.G.T. Report of House's conversation of November 16 with Cachin and Longuet, and statement dated Nov. 27, 1918, Y.H.C. See Arno J. Mayer, pp. 170–76.

20. William G. Sharp, *The War Memoirs of William Graves Sharp,* p. 394.

21. "I found him in an ugly mood towards Lansing," House wrote in his diary after their talk. The colonel had no wish to intercede in behalf of the secretary of state, though appreciative of the fact that Lansing was playing his minor part without complaint. House diary, Dec. 14, 1918.

22. See above, p. 81. According to an entry of Dec. 14, 1918 in House's diary, Wilson said that he had not empowered the secretary of state to organize the Ameri-

ing Washington, House had assured Wilson that there would be at Paris "ample trustworthy people to do the coding, stenographic and other special work."[23] However, a message from Lansing had informed him on November 13 that the president felt they must economize in the matter of clerical force and expected to draw largely from the army supply base at Paris. House concluded that the State Department had in hand the organization of a clerical force. "He has never cabled me that he was relying upon me to look out for him while here," House recorded. "I offered to do so in a cable. Not having heard from him I presumed he was bringing organized help himself."

In his first talk with Wilson House expressed surprise that the president's staff was so small.[24] He noted that the secretaries lacked a command of foreign languages and in other respects were inadequate to handle the president's correspondence. He arranged to have Wilson's office work done competently. "It leaves me practically without a staff," House wrote, "but I can readily build another. . . . I shall give his matters my personal attention."

Now that his chief was on hand House could feel less insecure in his position of influence. He acted immediately to embellish the public image of the president, which in England was losing some of the luster cast upon it in the hour of victory. Sir William Wiseman, continuing to serve in liaison at Paris as he had in New York, was pleased to find his friend and confidant effectively in charge of the American peace delegation. "House is in his best form," he reported to the Foreign Office on December 12, "and the President appears to be leaving everything in his hands. Whole situation is more favorable than I supposed."[25] Wiseman spoke to House of the unfortunate impressions created by Wilson's indiscreet remarks on the *George Washington* and other statements that were attributed by the press to American officials.[26]

Wiseman suggested that Wilson give an interview to *The Times* of London that would express appreciation of Great Britain. In carrying out this plan House found a useful ally in Lord Northcliffe, the

can Commission to Negotiate Peace, but had assumed that House would do this and would have full authority over the personnel.

23. House diary, Oct. 16, 1918.

24. House diary, Dec. 14, 1918. The writer has found no evidence to support Floto's statement that House "would try to get Wilson to limit his staff so that he would have to use that of House." Inga Floto, *Colonel House in Paris*, p. 67.

25. Dispatch in Wiseman pa., Y.H.C. "I am in constant touch with Sir William Wiseman who is working earnestly and intelligently for the best interest of all," House wrote in his diary on the seventeenth.

26. David Lawrence, p. 249.

British press magnate who was in charge of propaganda in the United States. Northcliffe had discovered that he could not dictate to his satisfaction to Lloyd George. Resentful when the prime minister refused to give him a prominent place in the British delegation at Paris, he offered assistance to House, with whom he had collaborated to strengthen the war effort of Americans and for whom he had developed a genuine respect. "Lloyd George hates Northcliffe," Auchincloss informed Polk, "can't get rid of him, and Northcliffe takes fiendish pleasure in cracking the whip."[27]

Three days after Wilson's arrival House committed Northcliffe to the president's plan to give priority to the framing of a constitution for a league of nations and to make it an integral part of the treaty of peace. "I made him admit," House recorded in his diary on December 17, "that the Entente Governments as now constituted could not interpret the aspirations of the peoples of their respective countries and that Wilson was the only statesman who could do so." Northcliffe, impressed by the ovation that the Parisians gave to the president, promised to use his press to stir the statesmen of England to action. He opened the columns of *The Times* to an interview with Wilson[28] that paid tribute to the wartime achievement of the British fleet and recognized "Britain's peculiar position as an island empire." The president now revealed himself as a man who would be an appreciative visitor in England though no supporter of imperialism. He did not refrain, however, from including a sentence that was not in the tradition of good diplomacy. He said that he had come to Europe so that he could "in some measure assist" in the solution of issues before the peace conference. Many Europeans felt that American assistance in their political affairs was not called for.[29]

Northcliffe reciprocated by giving a statement to *The New York Times.* Unfortunately, Auchincloss added a page in praise of his father-in-law, thus sullying the image of self-effacement that House

---

27. Sir Arthur Willert, *The Road to Safety,* p. 162; memorandum, Paris, Dec. 15, Wiseman pa; Auchincloss to Polk, Dec. 20, 1918, Y.H.C. In the view of Nicolson, "the figure of Northcliffe brooded over the [Peace] Conference as a miasma." Harold Nicolson, *Peacemaking,* pp. 60–61.

28. Edward Bell of the American embassy at London, to whom Northcliffe fervently praised Wilson's program, suspected that Northcliffe would play up the president's popularity as a means of inducing Lloyd George to support social reforms advocated by Northcliffe. Bell to Harrison, Dec. 24, 1918, N.A., R.G. 256.012/13.

The interview drafted by Auchincloss and Wiseman and given journalistic trimmings by Adam of *The Times* was read by Wilson, who changed a few phrases. House diary, Dec. 17, 18, 1918.

29. Bonsal diary, Dec. 22, 1918. It was thought wise to explain in *The Times* on December 21 that the words "in some measure" were "not a vain or camouflaged expression of [Wilson's] real desire to help."

had taken pains to create. Probably Wilson was not pleased. On the day of the publication of Northcliffe's interview the president wrote to a New York publisher who asked permission to promote a biography of House: "Frankly, I do not think this is the time to advertise Colonel House, and I am sure I am speaking as he would in advising that the book be let rest for the present."[30]

Simultaneously with House's effort to woo the British people through Northcliffe the colonel sent a personal note to Foreign Secretary Balfour, expressing the hope that they might "keep in very close touch throughout the whole of the negotiations." House wished to negotiate through Wiseman with Balfour and his secretary, Sir Eric Drummond, and to avoid distasteful legal arguments with Reading.

Balfour, whose career went back to 1871, foresaw that the coming peace conference would be a rough-and-tumble affair. The foreign secretary—"a supremely well informed, brilliantly dialectical, open-minded conservative, perfectly poised between the past and the future" [31]—reciprocated the confidence that House put in him. Revealing his hope for a real and full intercommunication of ideas, Balfour confessed to amazement "at the crop of ambitions, fears, dislikes, and even hatreds which so plentifully spring up in the sunshine of approaching peace." Ready to go far to foster Anglo-American friendship, and rising above the suspicion and jealousy with which Lloyd George regarded Wilson and his ideals, he expressed a fear that neither he nor House would be able to escape the embarrassments that sinister forces must inevitably produce.[32]

House marveled at the power of Balfour's broad and perceptive mind—"perhaps the best," he thought, that he had ever encountered—but he lamented a lack in the foreign secretary of those dynamic qualities that had made Lloyd George, who was fourteen years younger, the political leader of Great Britain.

House had proposed, the day after the signing of the armistice, that informal talks commence on December 16. At the conference of the Allied premiers at London on the second it was understood that they would respect the wish of Wilson as to the date of their meeting with him. The president now hoped that it might begin the seventeenth, three days after his arrival. On the fifteenth he had his first

---

30. House diary, Dec. 17, 18, 1918; Baker, p. 546.
31. J.M. Keynes, *Collected Writings* (London, 1972), *10*, 43.
32. Balfour to House, Dec. 17, 1918, Y.H.C.; Willert, *Road to Safety*, p. 162. Premier Borden of Canada advised Lloyd George to "set Balfour on Wilson, as they got on well together"; and when the prime minister protested that the foreign secretary was too much inclined to agree with the president, Borden replied: "Instruct him how far he can go." R.L. Borden, *Robert Land Borden, His Memoirs*, p. 872.

conversation with Clemenceau. Both were devoted to the establishment of a just peace and to the practice of democracy, but each had firm convictions that he would not yield easily. Clemenceau resented Wilson's delay of almost three years in joining the war against the common enemy, but appreciated the vigor with which he had pursued the fight once he had joined it.[33]

In the first conversation and in another three days later, the strong wills did not clash. House, who had been asked by Wilson to be present, took pains to go to the president's residence fifteen minutes before Clemenceau was to arrive, to suggest an easy conversational approach to the topic nearest Wilson's heart—the creation of a league of nations. He proposed that the president talk first about freedom of the seas, a subject on which French and American views harmonized and opposed Great Britain's. Wilson did this; in fact, when he ventured to say that the American people were anti-British and could easily be persuaded to build a navy larger than that of Great Britain, House thought that he overdid it. But the outcome was happy.[34] Wilson said that he wished to sit in the peace conference as the executive head of the American government, and would like to have his wish made known to the public. He expressed willingness that Clemenceau preside. Afterwards the premier told the British ambassador of his satisfaction with the talk, reporting that the president seemed very amiable, although shockingly ignorant of the European situation, and not likely to give much trouble. Clemenceau expressed the opinion that, although House said he "had talked the President out of sitting in," it would be ungracious to oppose Wilson's desire to participate.[35] When Derby immediately notified House that the British government would be delighted if the president chose to be a member of the peace conference, House, who still thought it unwise for Wilson to take part in the negotiating sessions, feigned satisfaction.[36]

Clemenceau's skepticism about the practicality of a league of na-

---

33. See Jean-Baptiste Duroselle, "Wilson et Clemenceau," *Centenaire Woodrow Wilson,* pp. 75–94, and in J. Joseph Huthmacher and Warren I. Susman, *Wilson's Diplomacy,* p. 28.

34. House diary, Dec. 15, 18, 19, 1918.

35. Derby to Balfour, Dec. 16, 1918, copy in Y.H.C. House diary, Dec. 16, 1918.

Possible reasons for Clemenceau's change of mind are given in *I.P., 4,* p. 216. President Poincaré, who was shocked by the prospect of the head of a foreign state sitting in a conference on French soil, attributed Clemenceau's acquiescence to a desire to preside over Wilson. Raymond Poincaré, *Au Service de la France, 10,* entries of Nov. 17, 28, Dec. 6, 18, 1918. Years later House accepted Clemenceau's explanation that he changed his mind because of a desire of American support against British opposition, House diary, June 10, 1922; House to Seymour, July 3, 1922, Y.H.C.

36. Derby to House, Dec. 16 Y.H.C.; House diary, Dec. 21, 1918.

tions was not overcome, though he agreed that the experiment should be tried. He showed no desire for haste. "It would be absurd," he said to House, "to make hard and fast arrangements with governments as shaky as those of Lenin and Ebert." But the Americans suspected that the Europeans had another, hidden motive. It seemed to some that Clemenceau and Lloyd George were procrastinating in the hope of shortening Wilson's participation in the peace talks.[37] They knew that he must return to Washington in February.

Wilson held to the opinion he had expressed to Wiseman before the armistice: that to enter into any formal peace conference without German participation would be to create the impression that the Great Powers were dividing the spoils in advance without giving Germany a chance to state its case. He desired to confine the first informal conversations to delegates of the United States and the three chief allies, and to call in smaller allies from time to time.[38] He did not wish to hold conferences at London with the British leaders, for he felt that this would commit him to similar discussions at Rome and at Brussels. He instructed House to insist that the British statesmen come to Paris to confer before Christmas.

House therefore suggested to Wiseman that Lloyd George carry out an expressed intention[39] to visit Paris during the week before Christmas.[40] But the returns from the general election were not yet in, and the prime minister told the cabinet petulantly on the twentieth that they must have time to discuss the questions of peacemaking before meeting with Wilson.[41]

House thought it best to arrange a presidential trip to England.[42] If Wilson could get from the English people an endorsement as con-

37. *I.P., 4*, p. 208; Bonsal diary, Dec. 19, 1918. *See* above, pp. 102, 115.

38. House to Sec. State, Dec. 6, 1918, endorsed "Repeated to the *George Washington*, Dec. 7, 11 A.M., 1918," N.A., R.G. 59, doc. 763.72119/3221/1/2; W.W. to Lansing, Dec. 7, 1918, Wilson pa., 5B; Wilton B. Fowler, *British-American Relations*, pp. 289–90.

39. B. Wright to Wiseman, Dec. 10, transmitting message from House, Lloyd George pa., F/3/3/48, Beaverbrook Library, London; telegram, Dec. 11, 1918, Wiseman to House, Y.H.C.

40. Balfour commended House's plan as "clearly the best. Otherwise Wilson may be thrown into the arms of French and Italian representatives for some important days before he sees a single Englishman." Balfour to P.M., Lloyd George to Balfour, Dec. 10, 1918, Lloyd George pa., E/3/3/48. A letter of December 13 from Balfour to House and messages from Wiseman and Drummond made it appear that Lloyd George and Balfour would go to Paris on the twenty-first at the latest. Docs. in Y.H.C. This was the intention of the prime minister on the seventeenth, according to Hankey's diary record of that date. Stephen Roskill, *Hankey, 2*, p. 36.

41. Minutes of the I.W.C., Dec. 20; telegrams Wiseman (at London) to House, Dec. 11, Drummond to Wiseman (at Paris) Dec. 16, 1918, Y.H.C.; Auchincloss diary, Dec. 19, 1918.

42. House diary, Dec. 19, 1918.

vincing as that accorded by the French left, House reasoned, Lloyd George would not dare to oppose American policies at the peace conference. He felt that British-American relations, none too friendly, would benefit if the president could be feted in England and speak as the only guest of the government. He therefore persuaded Northcliffe to send a letter by special bearer to Balfour, proposing that the British receive the president by the end of the year. Moreover, Ambassador Derby informed Balfour that Wilson would like to visit England without Clemenceau and Orlando present. House, suspecting that Lloyd George was trying to persuade the French and Italian premiers to come to London, cabled to Polk: "George has a passion for staging conferences in London where he can preside."[43]

The British officials had been warned of the president's desire to use the political power of "the laboring masses on both sides of the Atlantic" in support of his ideals. However, determined that Wilson should not go to Italy first, they accepted the proposal of a visit to London on December 26 despite a desire on their part to enjoy a holiday on Boxing Day. And Wilson, although disinclined to visit England, consented without argument to carry out House's plan.[44]

Auchincloss went to London with Wiseman the day before Christmas to prepare the way for the president. The British Foreign Office had invited House; in fact they had almost insisted, over the

---

43. Auchincloss diary, Dec. 19, 1918.

44. Cable, Murray to Reading, et al., Nov. 25, 1918, Wiseman pa.; Roskill, *2*, 36; Northcliffe to Balfour, Dec. 17, Balfour to Northcliffe, Dec. 18, 1918, Balfour pa., 49748, British Museum; minutes of the I.W.C., Dec. 18, 1918; "Secret conversation with Northcliffe," Memo. in Minutes of the ACTNP, Jan. 3, 1918, Grew pa., Houghton Library, Harvard University.

House thought it important that the president go to England at once (diary, Dec. 17, 1918). The British government had officially invited Wilson to England (Derby to House, Nov. 12, 1918, Y.H.C.), and he was asked to deliver an academic lecture and to receive a degree. House had advised him (cable of Nov. 11, 1918) that it was "essential" that he land in England. Baker, pp. 579–82. However, two days later, when Willard Straight declared that the president "must not take anything from anyone," not even an academic degree, House "agreed but didn't know that he could do anything." Straight diary, Nov. 13, 1918, microfilm. Apparently he did not confess that a week earlier he had cabled to Wilson that a presidential landing in England was "an essential part" of Houses campaign to "win a people's victory." House to W.W., Nov. 5, 1918, Y.H.C.

Jusserand had discouraged such a "detour," warning that American public opinion would resent such an unnecessary extension of his absence. The ambassador reported to Paris that the president seemed impressed by this advice. Jusserand to M.A.E., Archives du M.A.E., Nov. 5, 1918, À paix, A 1000.1, f.30.

In a meeting of the Imperial War Cabinet on November 26 Sir Robert Borden had remarked that it was unfortunate that Wilson would not visit England before France. Lloyd George agreed that it was indeed a pity, that a visit to London might improve the President's attitude, or his tone. Minutes of the I.W.C.

telephone to Wiseman. His son-in-law wired from London to beg him to come, reporting that Lloyd George, Balfour, and especially Lord Robert Cecil relied on him for help, and warning that if he lost touch now it would make their work much more difficult. But House remained at Paris and offered advice by long-distance telephone. He noted that Ambassador Derby was "in a perfect funk," thinking that the president ought not to go alone and make mistakes and enemies; but House, according to his diary, assured him that Wilson was "fully able to take care of himself" and though saying "some foolish things," righted himself quickly.[45]

Whatever the reason for House's decision to remain in Paris,[46] the result was that though Wilson still received counsel from him, it came through Auchincloss, a young man who did not give it in the tactful and persuasive manner of House. The president's personal staff found Auchincloss brash and officious and communicated their feeling to Wilson.[47]

Woodrow Wilson's visit to England was a return to the homeland from which his Woodrow grandparents had come. As a boy he had admired the British Navy and drawn pictures of its ships. In his writings he had striven to emulate the best models offered by English men of letters, even adopting their spelling of such words as "honour" and "programme." During his academic years he had revered the great Liberals of the nineteenth century. In several pilgrimages to literary and religious shrines in what he once called "the old country," he found solace for body and soul. Nevertheless, he distrusted British conservatives and imperialists, made fun of ineffective aristocrats, and once went so far as to characterize Balfour, when he was prime minister, as "a philosophical dreamer."[48]

---

45. House diary, Dec. 19, 24, 1918. House and Wiseman talked with Wilson on December 20 and found him looking forward to long, informal talks at London without any necessity for an interpreter. The president was determined not to take along Secretary Lansing, who bored him. Wiseman to Drummond, Dec. 20, 1918, Balfour pa., 49741.

46. Auchincloss recorded that House stayed at Paris because he chose to and not because he had a cold (diary, Dec. 24, 1918). House was not unmoved by a desire to give his son-in-law a position of prominence and influence (diary, Dec. 27, 1918).

Frank L. Warrin, Jr., Miller's assistant, felt that House was apprehensive that if he went to London British leaders might show their preference for dealing with the colonel, and thus hurt Wilson's feelings. F.L. Warrin, Jr., to the writer, Nov. 1, 1962.

These considerations seem more credible than another motive that has been ascribed to House—a fear of "losing his grip" on the American delegation. Floto, p. 85. During Wilson's five-day absence from Paris there were no crises of procedure or organization that required the presence of House, and he could well have entrusted his office to his able staff.

47. Gilbert Close to the writer; I.H. Hoover diary, Hoover pa., L.C. The antipathy was mutual. Auchincloss diary, Dec. 27, 1918.

48. See Patrick Devlin, *Too Proud to Fight*, pp. 10, 26–29.

There were large elements of the British people that looked to Wilson for leadership in giving effect to the moving words that he had uttered during the war. Indeed, the prestige of the president raised political difficulties for the prime minister. The votes cast in the national election were still being counted. Lloyd George had appealed to the voters in order to strengthen his position. He had campaigned vigorously on a platform calculated to satisfy the resentment felt by the British people against Germany. But at the same time he had spoken publicly of a league of nations as "an absolute essential to permanent peace" and he had advocated reduction of armaments and the abolition of conscription.

When the president came to London on the day after Christmas, Lloyd George had the opportunity that he was seeking to probe his thought. The prime minister regarded his visitor respectfully, but with a measure of suspicion and apprehension. He invited Wiseman to lunch and quizzed him for an hour about Wilson.[49] Though attracted by what he called the president's "stern and dauntless radicalism" he thought the American leader hesitant, even timorous.[50]

Auchincloss, under instructions from the absent House, undertook to play the same role that his father-in-law had taken with respect of Clemenceau. He talked with both Lloyd George and Wilson to prepare them for the meeting, their first face to face. The prime minister promised not to leave the peace conference until an effective league of nations had been created; and Auchincloss concluded that British public opinion, influenced "remarkably" by the speeches of Wilson, would support his program. Reporting Lloyd George's views to the president, he advised that Wilson had best press for a league and nothing more, and be noncommittal about British aims.

Wilson said that he would follow this suggestion, and did so when he conferred with Lloyd George and Balfour. At the very beginning of the talk the president gave the impression that the creation of a league was the only thing that he cared much about. Open-minded as to powers and machinery, he was eager to make it the first matter of business at the peace conference.[51] Wilson asked for a definite

---

49. *I.P.,* pp. *4,* 261.

50. David Lloyd George, *The Truth about the Peace Treaties,* pp. 227–28. Lloyd George gave the impression, when Frank I. Cobb interviewed him in November of 1918, of being reluctant to oppose the president on any issue except one of major importance. Cobb to House, Nov. 11, 1918, Y.H.C.

51. Wiseman, memo, Dec. 15, 1918, Wiseman pa. According to a report made by Lloyd George to the Imperial War Cabinet, he and Balfour were inclined to agree in regarding a league of nations as an aid in disposing of troublesome questions. Lloyd George, *Truth about . . . Treaties,* p. 185; minutes of the I.W.C., Dec. 20, 1918; Auchincloss diary, Dec. 26, 27, 30, 1918, Jan. 2, 1919; Lansing desk diary, Dec. 31, 1918, L.C. Talking with both parties afterwards, Auchincloss concluded that "no points

decision on disarmament before a league began to function, but he could get the British spokesmen to agree only that the peace conference must limit armaments in the vanquished nations and forbid conscription there. It was their hope that France would have to disarm correspondingly. In pleading the first of his points, however, the president apparently made progress. Lloyd George was almost convinced that no strict censorship should be applied to the proceedings of the peace conference. Wilson disappointed the prime minister's hope of enlisting his support for a reparations settlement that would reimburse Great Britain for more than actual damages to property.

The Imperial War Cabinet had indicated eagerness to induce the United States to assume a mandate for the rule of German colonies that had not been occupied by the Dominions.[52] The president now promised nothing, but suggested that the German possessions be put under league of nations trusteeships, and that Constantinople be mandated to a small power. Wilson's preference for small nations as trustees apparently had not been shaken by an effort at Paris on the part of Lord Derby to convince him that experience had shown that small nations were not the best colonial administrators and the British Empire could do better. During the week following Derby's attempt House had not persuaded Wilson to change his views with regard to the colonies. However, the colonel assured the ambassador he could do so whenever necessary.[53]

The prime minister gave a stag dinner party in London for his American guest. During the evening reports came in indicating that Lloyd George had received a popular vote more overwhelming than any yet recorded in English history.[54] Telegrams of congratulations arrived and the guests shook his hand; but Wilson remained aloof, perhaps embarrassed by recollection of the unfavorable outcome of the American election in November. Yet in a tête-à-tête Lloyd George found him "extremely pleasant," without any of the "professional condescension" that gossip had led the prime minister to expect.

were definitely settled but in general the conferees found themselves in accord." Wilson wanted no record kept of his conversation with Lloyd George. Roskill, 2, 39.

52. Lloyd George, *Truth about . . . Treaties*, pp. 39, 66–67.

53. Ibid., p. 190; Howard I. Elcock, *Portrait of a Decision*, p. 55.

54. Charles Seymour, *Letters from the Paris Peace Conference*, p. 4. Bryce thought this election "an unqualified misfortune," resulting in what was said to be "the poorest House of Commons . . . in many years." Bryce to Charles Eliot, March 20, 1919, Bryce pa., 2, p. 185, Bodleian Library, Oxford University. Lloyd George was to have many difficulties in handling the diverse elements of the coalition that won about 80 percent of the seats.

King George V entertained the Americans at Buckingham Palace and thought the president quite easy to get along with.[55] However when, speaking in a pastoral sense and in measured tones that evoked no glow of friendship,[56] Wilson alluded to the American people as "my people," diplomats thought him imperious and a change was made in the text released. When Mrs. Wilson made herself at home in the palace and chatted in a democratic way with the servants, she seemed to the French ambassador to be ill bred.[57]

Given the freedom of the City of London at the Guild Hall, Wilson made an eloquent plea for a peace that would result not in "one powerful group of nations set off against another, but a single overwhelming powerful group of nations who shall be the trustee of the peace of the world." Yet this and other utterances left the auditors cool. "Blue-water" Englishmen resented Wilson's advocacy of his government's naval program and his failure to speak appreciatively of British protection of American shipping. Unwilling to accept a large American navy as a partner in policing the seas under a league of nations, they asked themselves whether the Yankees would replace the Germans as maritime rivals in the future.[58]

The president neglected, until he was prompted,[59] to pay tribute to the military and naval contributions made by Great Britain to the common victory. In his annual message to the Congress on December 2 he had not only failed to give credit to the British Navy but had impugned its effectiveness. Aware that Churchill was saying openly that the United States owed everything to the British Navy and that a league of nations would be no substitute for the supremacy of the British fleet, Wilson said at Buckingham Palace: "Well, Mr. Churchill, and how is the Navy?" Churchill flushed and made no reply.[60]

In the Midlands the president felt at home. Paying tribute to the "great forward-looking sentiments" of Gladstone and his other heroes of the nineteenth century, he spoke warmly of the ties of kinship to audiences that shared his devotion to the ideal of a

---

55. Lloyd George, *Truth about . . . Treaties*, pp. 140–44, 184; Harold Nicolson, *King George V*, p. 328.
56. J.W. Davis to Julia Davis, Feb. 1, 1919, J.W. Davis pa., Y.H.C.; William H. Harbaugh, *Lawyer's Lawyer*, p. 138.
57. Poincaré, *11*, 32. "Wilson was not at his best during this visit to Buckingham Palace." D.H. Elletson, *Roosevelt and Wilson* (London, 1965), pp. 159–61.
58. Derby to Balfour, Dec. 24, 1918, Balfour pa., add'l. mss., 49744; Miller *My Diary, 1*, entry of Dec. 3, 1918; Cobb to House, Nov. 29, 1918.
59. Bell to Harrison, Jan. 6, 1919, L. Harrison pa., L.C., box 103.
60. Benham diary letter, Jan. 27, 1919, Helm pa.

league.[61] He proclaimed the importance of good will to trade and the value of trade—"that great amicable instrument of the world"— to an understanding of "international processes." His trip to this region was in response to suggestions made by Northcliffe and House that he go to Carlisle to visit the church where his grandfather Woodrow had been the pastor. His direct appeal to British subjects, undertaken without any invitation from the British government, was in violation of accepted practice. It was resented by the prime minister and by some of his colleagues.[62] Nevertheless it served to embellish Wilson's public image.

"There is only one thing that can bind peoples together," Wilson declared at Manchester, "and that is a common devotion to right. . . . The United States will join no combination of power which is not the combination of all of us. She is not interested merely in the peace of Europe, but in the peace of the world." In an interview with C.P. Scott, of *The Manchester Guardian,* the president was told that the outcome of the British election was not a vote against the creation of a league. Scott assured him that all the better and deeper feeling of the nation would support him if he appealed to it, and advised that if he was vigilant he would be able to influence Lloyd George, who was impulsive and inconsistent. Wilson replied—"with a twinkle," according to Scott—that though he liked Lloyd George very much, if the obstacles at Paris became unsuperable he would state his own position, politely and clearly, and appeal to the public opinion of the world.[63] The president told Scott that the November election in the United States had been in no degree a demonstration against his own policy.

Wilson had other assurances of support from the peoples of Great Britain and the empire. A letter signed by 903 prominent Englishmen expressed the hope that Wilsonian doctrine might prevail at Paris against the sort of thing that had "already led Europe to the

---

61. Oswald Garrison Villard of *The Nation* recorded that he had "never attended a meeting so moving and reverential" as that addressed by Wilson in the Free Trade Hall at Manchester. *The Fighting Years,* p. 380.

62. When Wilson took leave of Lloyd George at the station in London, he explained that he would congratulate the prime minister on his recent victory were it not that he might seem to interfere in English politics. Lloyd George laughed and recalled that a British ambassador once had been recalled from Washington for seeming to interfere in American politics. Benham diary letter, Jan. 2, 1919, Helm pa.

The French ambassador, though Wilson seemed to him more *souple* than expected, criticized his dogmatic and theoretical approach to the question of a league of nations. Poincaré, *11,* 32.

63. C.P. Scott's account of his interview with Wilson, R.S. Baker series B, folder "H- general" under "Hammond," L.C.; J.L.L. Hammond, *C.P. Scott,* pp. 249–50; Trevor Wilson (ed.) *The Political Diaries of C.P. Scott,* pp. 366–67.

verge of ruin, and must, if persisted in, destroy civilization."[64] British Labour was sympathetic and offered its allegiance.[65] The newspapers of Northcliffe continued to aid.[66] However, the Imperial War Cabinet were questioning many of the president's ideas.

Pleased and somewhat surprised by the frank and forthcoming responses of the British prime minister, Wilson was uncertain as to the permanence of Lloyd George's views. He remarked to Ambassador Davis that Lloyd George was "a second-rate politician." Yet if only he could trust "the little man," he told House, he could get along with him more easily than the urbane Balfour.[67]

The visit to England had given assurance to Wilson of his eminence as a leader of liberal opinion there. On the day of his arrival the children of Dover had strewn flowers in his path. The people of the Midlands appeared to worship him. If not acclaimed a king, the American Prophet was without question the prince of peace. Yet the responsible officials of His Majesty's Government entertained reservations.

On the last day of the year Paris became again the center of the stage. The French leaders were preoccupied by the necessity of satisfying the elemental passions that were still supreme among the people. Clemenceau had just won a parliamentary victory that boded ill for the American cause. In a tempestuous session of the Chamber on December 29 radical deputies marched out in a body and forced

---

64. Letter in Wilson pa., 5B.

65. Villard, p. 378; Villard to Mrs. Villard, Jan. 8, 1919, copy attached to letter, Bell to Harrison, Villard folder, Harrison papers, box 104. The Labour party, breaking away from the coalition which the exigencies of war had held together, now constituted His Majesty's Opposition in the British Parliament and demanded an international understanding that would guarantee the rights to organize and strike and would outlaw inhumane conditions of work everywhere. Immediately after Wilson's visit to England the party and the Trades Union Congress sponsored popular demonstrations and passed resolutions for a "Wilson peace." See Carl F. Brand, "The Attitude of British Labour toward President Wilson during the Peace Conference," *American Historical Review 42* (1937): 244–45; *British Labour's Rise to Power* (Stanford, 1941), pp. 121–49. Resolutions sent to Wilson are in the Wilson papers, 5B.

66. Northcliffe interceded in Wilson's behalf with Balfour, explaining that the American newsmen insisted that the president must return to his people with a league of nations in hand, lest credence be given to the canard that England and France were secretly conspiring against the Americans at Paris. Memorandum, Malcolm to Balfour, Dec. 24, 1919, P.R.O., FO/800/211. Northcliffe said he had assured Wilson of "considerable" support for a league from all sections of "political society," while warning that the British people would not permit any interference with their command of the sea.

67. House diary, Dec. 31, 1918; J.W. Davis diary, Dec. 31, 1918, Y.H.C. Hankey, the secretary of the cabinet, noted that Lloyd George, once his position was made secure by the election victory, showed "a sort of lust for power" and an almost disdainful disregard for the opinions of his colleagues. Roskill, *2, 39.*

the premier to defend his peace program. He did not go to the
tribune nor raise his voice despite fierce interruptions from the
left.[68] He spoke with all due regard for solid frontiers well defended, armaments, and the balance of power. He said that if in
1914, France, Great Britain, Italy, and the United States had made it
clear that whoever attacked one of them attacked the world, there
would have been no war. He conceived that strategic security could
serve as a base for collective security, that there need be no conflict
between the two. "If France is allowed to establish its own defense,"
he said, "I for my part accept with joy every addition of supplementary guarantee which may be offered to us." He explained that his
"chief preoccupation" was to avoid raising too many hopes and thus
avert the shock of too many disappointments. "I am not disposed to
tell you of my demands," he said, "because there are some I may
have to sacrifice to superior interest." Speaking thus with candor and
precision he won the support of the Chamber by a vote of more than
four to one.

In relegating the league of nations to the place of a secondary
guarantee Clemenceau directly challenged Wilson's intention to give
priority to the adoption of a covenant for a world body. To the deputies the premier spoke openly of differences of opinion:

> I should lie if I said that I was immediately in agreement with him
> on all points. America is far distant from the frontiers of Germany,
> as I remarked a little while ago. I have, perhaps, preoccupations
> which I would not say are foreign to him, but which do not touch
> him so vitally as they touch the man who has seen his country
> devastated during four years by an enemy who was within several
> days of Paris. . . . Mr. Wilson . . . has a broad mind, open and
> elevated. He is a man who inspires respect by the simplicity of his
> words and the *noble candeur* of his spirit.[69]

Clemenceau used *"noble candeur"* not in the French sense of "well-in-
tentioned simplicity," he assured House, but in the sense of "noble
candidness." Actually, the bilingual premier had cleverly chosen
words that Americans would find flattering and the French would
understand as traducing.[70]

---

68. Letter, Clive Day to Mrs. Day, Dec. 29, 1918, Y.H.C.; Seymour, *Letters,* pp.
84–85.
69. *Annales de al Chambre,* Dec. 29, 1918, p. 3352, cited in Noble, p. 89; also clip-
ping from *Journal Officiel,* Dec. 31, and translation, enclosed with letter, R.W. Bliss to
Sec. State, Jan. 8, 1919, N.A., R.G. 59, 763.72119/3829.
70. J-B. Duroselle, *La Politique Extérieure de la France de 1914 à 1945,* Les Cours
de la Sorbonne, Paris, *I,* 129–30; Stephen Bonsal, *Suitors and Suppliants,* 211.

Taking note of this speech, House wrote in his diary on December 30: "The situation strategically could not be worse." He felt that the president's only hope lay in holding the Allies stringently to the terms of the pre-armistice agreement. Obviously the thought of the French people, after their war sacrifices to preserve their freedom, was centered upon guarantees of their security in the future.

Upon his return to Paris Wilson showed displeasure at Clemenceau's speech and reasserted the prime importance of a league of nations. He accepted House's suggestion that it would be necessary to work with the British rather than the French to achieve American aims.[71] The president continued to frown upon the convoking of a formal conference at any given date. He felt that the informal talks already undertaken should continue and be extended by calling in the lesser allies from time to time.[72] Secretary Lansing thought his chief had become "very buoyant and cocksure," and, believing that the considerateness of Clemenceau and Lloyd George was "feeding the President's vanity," he was sure that the Europeans were "laying a trap" for Wilson.[73]

---

71. House Diary, Jan. 4, 1919.
72. Auchincloss diary, Dec. 30, 1918.
73. Lansing, private memoranda, January 1, 1919, L.C.

☆ Y ☆

Italian Irredentism

Stimulated by his contacts with the British and the French, the president responded at the first of the New Year to suggestions that he carry his mission to the people of Italy, millions of whose kindred were residents of the United States.

Before the pre-armistice meetings, Thomas Nelson Page, the Virginia man of letters whom Wilson had appointed ambassador at Rome, had urged House to visit Italy, a country that he described as a "whole complex combination of sentiments, principles, and purposes," but "governed by sentiment." Page explained that by and large the Italians worshiped Wilson and felt neglected; and he feared that House, at Paris, would be influenced by French opinion that was unfavorable to Italy. He reported the existence of "a certain element composed of very diverse classes" that was perhaps more friendly even then to the Central Empires than to France. "One cannot be too certain what will happen," he wrote to House. "The final success of Mr. Wilson's plans may hinge on your coming here and feeling out the situation for yourself." One might as well hope to understand the Negro question without going to the South, Page told the Texas colonel.[1] On October 28th House accepted Page's invitation "with the greatest pleasure"[2] and recorded in his diary that he would go to Italy "under certain conditions," but in the end he did not. As in the case of the London Conference a month later, he seems to have been wary of pressure for commitments in the name of the president.

---

1. Page sent a copy of this letter of October 22 to the State Department for the president and wrote other long reports to House and Wilson on the situation in Italy. *F.R., Lansing Pa., 2,* p. 163ff.; G.C. Speranza, *Gino Speranza's Diary,* entry of Nov. 9, 1918; Réné Albrecht-Carrié, *Italy at the Paris Peace Conference,* p. 67.

2. House to Page, Oct. 28, 1918, Y.H.C.

In dealing with the French leaders House encountered a consistency on which he could depend. Clemenceau and Foch spoke for France with both authority and precision, the one on affairs of state, the other on military matters. However, the Americans found themselves in treacherous political waters when it became necessary to negotiate with the Italian government. At the time of its entry into the war in 1915 Italy had been promised certain lands of the enemy by the secret Treaty of London. With the signing of the Armistice of Villa Giusti on November 3, 1918, however, Austria-Hungary had ceased to exist, and opportunity beckoned Italians to move even beyond the provisions of the London pact in order to gain strategic security on the eastern coast of the Adriatic. The people of Italy had lived for centuries in fear of attack from the well-protected ports and there was danger now that a new Slav state would take the place of the Hapsburg empire as a menace in the east.[3]

In the summer of 1918 Major Douglas Johnson,[4] visiting Italy and talking with political officials and military officers, came away with the impression that it was generally understood that the city of Fiume (now Rijeka) would go to a new Slav state, and that Italian security required only an island off the Dalmatian coast on which a central naval base could be constructed.[5] Nevertheless, Italian statesmen took alarm when Wilson, in replying to the Austrian peace note of October 19, 1918, recognized the justice of Slav aspirations "in the fullest manner." As the military resistance of the enemy collapsed and the army of Italy crushed the Austrians at Vittorio Veneto, the war-weariness of the Italians gave way suddenly to assertiveness. There was no clear consensus in the parliament at Rome. In the view of many ardent patriots the eastern boundary of Italy that had been defined in the Treaty of London became a minimum rather than a maximum demand.[6]

The Italian spokesmen at Paris were not in an enviable position. Aware both of the appetite of their people for power and glory and of the low opinion in which Italy's military and political strength

---

3. See David Hunter Miller, "The Adriatic Negotiations at Paris," *Atlantic Monthly* (Aug. 1921), p. 267ff.; also Charles Seymour, "The Struggle for the Adriatic," *Yale Review*, 9: 3 (April 1920); Phillips to Sec. State, Nov. 26, 1918, N.A., R.G. 59, 765.72/12663.

4. See above, pp. 78–79.

5. Sir Arthur Evans drew a boundary line that was published in *The New Europe* of October 11, 1917, giving only the Lussin Islands and Lissa to Italy. This solution "was almost identical with that later proposed independently by American experts, at the peace conference of 1919." Major Douglas Johnson, "Resumé of Negotiations in re Adriatic Problem," clipped to letter, Johnson to Bliss, July 16, 1919, Bliss pa., box 6, L.C.

6. See Pierre Renouvin, *Le Traité de Versailles*, p. 17; John Wells Gould, "Italy and the U.S., 1914–1918," pp. 174, 266–69.

were held by its Allies, and conscious of the inconsistency of their aims with Wilson's purposes, they temporized and maneuvered, with both subtlety and consistency.[7]

The pre-armistice negotiations glossed over and confused the fundamental issue. On October 30 Foreign Minister Sonnino read a vague and general reservation to Wilson's Point Nine,[8] which called for a "readjustment of frontiers . . . along clearly recognizable lines of nationality." This point would give to Italy less territory than that granted by the Treaty of London and would deny certain boundaries that the Italians thought essential to their security. Making no reference to that pact, the Italian foreign minister advocated a frontier that would guarantee military security and peace, "taking account of geographic and historic considerations." This reservation was brushed aside as irrelevant to the question of an armistice with Germany.[9] Despite the efforts of Sonnino and Orlando to register a reservation Italy, in the opinion of House's legal adviser, accepted Point Nine by agreeing to the German armistice.[10]

Clemenceau, who had won acceptance of French occupation of the Rhineland by promising that territory would be evacuated just as soon as Germany fulfilled the conditions of the treaty of peace, advised Orlando to try to persuade Colonel House. Thereupon the Italian premier, by his own record, induced House to accept the line proposed by the military advisers, which allowed Italy to occupy the lands that were promised by the Treaty of London. At the same time House exacted Orlando's assent to the exlusion from the Austrian armistice of any mention of the Treaty of London.[11]

House shared the desire of Clemenceau and Lloyd George to put an end quickly to the resistance of Austria. In keeping with Wilson's hesitation to discuss territorial settlements at the risk of unanimity, he wished to avoid the complications that would be introduced if the conflicting claims of Italy and the South Slavs were considered while the fighting was going on. He disregarded the great advantage that would accrue to Italy by the occupation of lands of which the ownership was in dispute. He reported to Wilson: "It is my opinion that the submission of terms of armistice to Austria under the circum-

---

7. See Harold Nicolson, *Peacemaking,* pp. 166–67.

8. See above, p. 69 and note.

9. French procès-verbal, Oct. 30, 1918, B.D.I.C.; Charles Seymour, *American Diplomacy during the World War,* p. 392.

10. *F.R., PPC 1,* pp. 359, 463.

11. Gould, pp. 184–85. There is no record that House exacted at this time the "explicit promise," similar to that given by Clemenceau with respect of the Rhineland, that he later assured Wilson he had obtained in the pre-armistice negotiations (*I.P., 4,* p. 233), but of which there is no clear record.

stances and without any express qualification, may be construed as acceptance on the part of the Allies of the president's proposals." [12]

Actually, House's acceptance of military terms that permitted Italian occupation of enemy lands up to the line drawn in the Treaty of London was given to Orlando in such a way as to lead him to hope for American acquiescence at the peace conference in Italian claims for which Wilson could have no sympathy. After an emotional outburst in which both celebrated the acceptance of the armistice by the Austrians, House went so far as to say that Wilson's silence with respect to Italian claims resulted from a lack of information, and that the president would consider the question in the most sympathetic spirit. It is quite possible that House overestimated Orlando's tractability because of a remark attributed to Orlando by Steed at this time.[13] There is no record that House uttered the "word of caution" which, as he informed Wilson a week later,[14] the British and French could not speak because of their commitment to the Treaty of London. (Actually, Lloyd George had confided to Cobb that he and Clemenceau were counting on Wilson to dispute the Italian claims.)[15] At the cost of imprecision that avoided immediate controversy House succeeded in meeting the necessity of the moment, the quick ending of hostilities with Austria-Hungary. But this imprecision was to become exceedingly embarrassing during the peace conference.

In an interview with Sonnino on November 15 House, indulging his sense of humor, suggested that the Italian foreign minister with-

---

12. Auchincloss diary, Oct. 31, 1918, Y.H.C. Because of the garbling of this message we cannot be certain that it was reassuring to Wilson. His transcription may have conveyed an opposite meaning to the president. It reads: "It is not [?] very probable that the submission of terms of armistice to Austria under the circumstances and without any express qualifications may be construed as acceptance on the part of the Allies of the President's proposals." *F.R., 1918, I, 1,* p. 431. It is possible that Wilson read House's mind well enough to substitute "now" for "not."

13. House-Orlando conversation, Nov. 3, House's conversation with Amendola, Nov. 6, 1918, Y.H.C. According to Steed, Orlando said to House: "If I could only return to Italy with the certainty that we shall get the Evans line [see above, p. 157n.] I should be able to tranquilize the whole country and to bring about an agreement with the Yugoslavs."

14. Cable, House to W.W., Nov. 11, 1918, Y.H.C.

15. Gould, pp. 195–97;; Cobb to House, Nov. 19, Y.H.C.

General Bliss refused to sign the report of the military advisers on the Austrian armistice because he saw its political implications. However, neither Secretary Baker nor Secretary Lansing, to whom House cabled the terms for Austria on October 31, alerted Wilson to the danger. See Gould, pp. 186–88.

House explained to newsmen that he did not object to the line of occupation as a military expedient and did not think its acceptance could be construed as a recognition of the Treaty of London or the frontier it prescribed. Charles T. Thompson, *The Peace Conference Day by Day,* pp. 77–78.

hold his plea for execution of the Treaty of London until Clemenceau and Lloyd George had attempted to justify the special demands of their governments. House recorded that he made his suggestion in "a spirit of sheer deviltry" and looked forward to a good chuckle if the spokesmen for France and the British Empire, who had their own claims to territory but were embarrassed by those of Italy under the Treaty of London, were faced with such a challenge to their consistency.[16]

Unwilling to take the risk of starting an argument, House did not draw the question of a league of nations into the talk at this time. He went only so far as to ask Sonnino whether it would not be sufficient if the powers guaranteed the territorial arrangements that were to be made by the peace treaty. This question brought the reply that "somebody else's guarantee was not enough to ensure safety and security," as the violation of Belgium's neutrality in 1914 had proved. Sonnino recorded afterwards that House "strongly agreed" with the geographical and historical arguments in support of the Italian demand for security. Doubtless the foreign minister drew the inference that the United States government was at least not unalterably opposed to what he sought.[17]

At the same time Wilson, well aware of the thorny nature of the Adriatic question,[18] was talking in Washington with Count di Cellere, the ambassador of Italy, in a vein that was both conciliatory and noncommital. Among the president's national constituency were some three million people of Italian blood as well as more than a million Slavs,[19] and any careless show of partiality might be dangerous to his leadership at home as well as to his position as arbiter abroad. He had explained to di Cellere in January of 1918 that the league of nations that he proposed would do away with the importance of strategic frontiers because it would guarantee the territorial integrity of its members. He granted that if the league should fail the question of Italy's boundaries would have to be considered in a different light. Wilson took pains to visit the Italian embassy at the

---

16. House diary, Nov. 15, Y.H.C.; Sidney Sonnino, *Diario*, *3*, 314–5. Sonnino remarked that "the historic reason appealed to by France concerning Alsace-Lorraine could not be valid only insofar as she was concerned." Sonnino recorded House's suggestion with no sign of appreciation of the humor of its author. Nor does his record indicate the "delight" that House ascribed to him.

17. Sonnino, *3*, 314.

18. Jusserand to M.A.E., Nov. 5, 1918. "The President is counting on strong Italian claims," Tardieu reported to Clemenceau. Dispatch of Nov. 11, 1918, Archives du M.A.E., À paix, A1025.1. Wilson had told House on January 31 that Italy had entered the war "on cold-blooded calculation" to get what it wanted, Baker, *7*, 513.

19. See Joseph P. O'Grady (ed.), *The Immigrants' Influence on Wilson's Peace Policies*, pp. 111–39, 173–203.

end of November and to assure the ambassador of his desire to regard Italy's case with a sympathetic and open mind. He made no specific promises. However it was not until December 12, en route to Paris, that he intimated to di Cellere that Italy would be expected to make some slight sacrifices in the Adriatic that would be in its own interest and in harmony with his hope of preserving the peace of Europe.

Di Cellere was so impressed by the president's cordiality toward Italy and by his expressions of mistrust of France, Italy's natural rival, that he reported to Rome: "Wilson stands with Italy, and wants to support that country." His dispatches in November were on the whole optimistic and suggested that Wilson would accept the claims of the Italians in exchange for their support of a league of nations. However, di Cellere transmitted on November 24 a warning of the State Department against any premature action by Italy that might seem to invade the domain of the peace conference.[20] The reports of the envoy, as well as House's advice to Sonnino, gave inadequate guidance to the Italian government. At Rome there was political uncertainty arising from intemperate popular expressions of irredentism and from strife in the cabinet between Bissolati, liberal leader and advocate of Wilsonian ideals, and Sonnino, who had directed Italy's foreign office during the war with the expectation of giving his country defensible boundaries and sharing in the territorial expansion of victorious powers.[21]

Although Italian liberals were disposed to cooperate with the Yugoslav movement there was concern in Italy when, on December 1, the prince regent of Serbia proclaimed the formation of a "kingdom of the Serbs, Croats, and Slovenes." The pendulum of sentiment, nudged by elemental fear for the nation's security, was swinging toward a strong and aggressive policy in the Adriatic region. Premier Orlando, in an address to the legislature on November 27,

20. Justus, V. *Macchi di Cellere all' ambasciata di Washington, memorie e testimonianze* (Florence, 1920); a review of this work by G.A. Andriulli, *Il Secolo*, (Milan, Nov. 30, 1920), translation in *The Living Age*, 8th series, *xxi* (1st quarter, 1921), 266–70; telegrams, di Cellere to Sonnino, Nov. 14, 24, 26, 30, 1918, *I Documenti Diplomatici Italiani*, 6th series, *1*, docs. 159, 318, 349, 406.

21. For brief expositions of the political situation in Italy in November and December, 1918, see Albrecht-Carrié, pp. 66–71, 89, and Roberto Vivarelli, *Il Dopoguerra in Italia é L'Avvento del Fascismo (1918–1922)* (Naples, 1967), *2*, 195–218.

According to the observation of Ambassador Thomas Nelson Page, Sonnino, inclined to secrecy and silence and not appreciative of democracy, would have favored siding with the Allies in 1915 even without the Treaty of London; but having exacted its benefits he felt entitled now to ask that they be delivered to Italy, which had fulfilled its part of the agreement. He was determined not to allow the French government to force concessions from Italy in the Balkans that would redound to the credit of France. Page to House, Oct. 29, 1918, Y.H.C. "The Italian feeling towards France may perhaps best be described as one of hypersensitivity." Albrecht-Carrié, p. 67.

embraced Wilson's principles but at the same time promised that he would go to the peace conference with an Italian, not an ecumenical, mind.[22]

During the pre-armistice meetings a naval crisis had arisen in the Adriatic when warships of Austria-Hungary were surrendered at Pola to a local government of Croats and Slovenes that had not been recognized. Trumbić, the president of the Yugoslav Committee at London, told the Americans at Paris that the new crews of the ships, more hostile to Italy than to Austria, would turn the vessels over only to the American navy. President Wilson was invited to send a naval unit of the United States or of any disinterested Allied power to Pola to receive a salute "as an ally and friend."[23]

The Italians, who had hoped to acquire these ships, were incensed. Their naval commander made it clear that he did not welcome the presence of French or American warships, operating independently of his command, in the upper Adriatic. His attitude brought an emphatic protest from Admiral Benson, and House had to get from the Italian ambassador at Paris a statement of policy that would reassure his American colleagues and also Clemenceau.[24]

When the question was discussed in the pre-armistice meetings, House said little. However at the London Conference at the beginning of December the matter was considered serious and a commission of four admirals was proposed, to inquire and report on the Adriatic situation and to recommend pacifying measures. House, having a message from Wiseman warning of an immediate clash, asked Benson to name an American commissioner.[25] Admiral Bullard was chosen, and he and the admirals of France and Great Britain were unanimous in making certain proposals that were rejected by the Italian admiral.

In mid-November a crisis in the city of Fiume required House to make a decision that ran counter to the intention of the War Depart-

---

22. Albrecht-Carrié, p. 77; Vivarelli, p. 197.

23. Dispatch, Sharp to Sec. State, Nov. 1, 1918, N.A., R.G. 59, 763.72/12038, 12044; Page to Lansing, Nov. 2, 1918, *F.R., 1918, I, 1,* p. 862f.; Ivo J. Lederer, *Yugoslavia at the Paris Peace Conference,* pp. 54–56.

24. Gould, pp. 200–202; *F.R., PPC, 2,* pp. 301–2; House diary, Nov. 12, 1918. The Italian ambassador explained that American warships were rejected along with the French in order to mitigate the offense to France.

The Supreme War Council was unsuccessful in persuading the Yugoslavs to turn the vessels over to a French admiral at Corfu, and a compromise was arranged whereby both Yugoslavia and Italy retained Austrian ships in their hands pending a ruling by the Peace Conference. Victor S. Mamatey, *The United States and East Central Europe, 1914–1918,* pp. 365–7; Lederer, p. 59. Eventually the fleet was divided among the Allies.

25. "Joint Proposals," doc. in Bliss pa., box 69, "Lansing" folder; *F.R., PPC, 4,* p. 259.

ment to bring home American troops rapidly. Italian armed forces, taking advantage of the terms of the Austrian armistice to occupy parts of Dalmatia that were assigned to them by the Treaty of London, behaved as if these lands were already a part of Italy.[26] The city of Fiume and the adjoining port of Susak, the outlet for lands populated by Croats, had not been promised to Italy, and House's interpretation of Point Nine required the creation of a free port. Nevertheless Italian residents, who were a majority in the city proper, had set up a national council.[27] Invoking the support of the United States—"the mother of liberty and universal democracy"[28]—they proclaimed annexation to Italy on October 30. Orlando responded promptly to their plea for protection by ordering troops to occupy the city.[29]

The Supreme War Council had given some justification for this act in its pre-armistice meeting of October 31, when it included among the terms for Austria-Hungary a provision permitting occupation of enemy lands for the purpose of preserving order. This concession was granted to satisfy the desire of Serbia, seconded by Lloyd George, to go into Bosnia-Herzegovina; and it contravened an opinion expressed by Colonel House, who, instructed by Wilson to keep hands off the pieces of Austria-Hungary, spoke in favor of limiting occupation to that required for military purposes.[30] Orlando argued that the occupation of Fiume was necessary for the purpose of maintaining public order. He said that American and English citizens had reported hostile acts by Slavs in Fiume, and in any event the occupation was a fait accompli.[31] In spite of the adverse decision of the Supreme War Council on the thirty-first, House reported to Wilson the next day that he had been able "to prevent discussion of political questions."[32]

---

26. R.W. Seton-Watson, *Italy from Liberalism to Fascism 1870–1925* (London, 1967), pp. 506–7.

27. A census of the city of Fiume proper, taken in December 1918, showed 19,684 Italians out of a total of 31,094 inhabitants. Speranza, Feb. 21, 1919. A memorandum in Wiseman's papers set the population of Fiume, including the port of Susak, at 25,781 Italians and 26,602 Yugoslavs. Y.H.C.

28. Vivarelli, p. 196.

29. Luigi Aldrovandi-Marescotti, *Guerra Diplomatica,* pp. 100, 207.

30. According to the French procès-verbal of October 31, 1918, House said: "If you try to assure order in all Austro-Hungarian territory you will have to occupy the whole monarchy. I believe it is better to take a military point of view exclusively."

31. House to State Dept., Nov. 21, 1918, Auchincloss diary. Sonnino, according to his record (*3*, p. 314) said to House: "The principle of self-determination should not be translated into a reward for long-standing [Slavic] persecutions aiming at denationalizing a territory."

32. Actually the Treaty of London was excluded as a consideration with respect of the occupation.

The troops of Italy moved into Fiume on November 18, to remain. In the eyes of emotional Italians the fate of the city became an issue that tested Wilsonian "justice." Orlando informed the French ambassador that although the other Allied Powers had the right to send armed forces into every zone of occupation, the Italian government would regard such action as "distinctly unfriendly."[33] Nevertheless French troops entered Fiume with the intention of establishing a base for France's Army of the East; and they were joined by a small British force. Also taking part was an American battalion[34] that belonged to a regiment which House decided to leave at the disposal of Italy. He did this at the request of both Orlando and Yugoslav spokesmen, after a plea from the British cabinet and a warning from Ambassador Page of bolshevism among the Croats, and with Wilson's cabled assent.[35]

The decision to use American troops was contrary to the judgment of Secretary of War Baker, who feared entry into the Adriatic controversy "by the back door" and ordered Pershing to withdraw

House said: "From the American point of view it is preferable to take the necessary guarantees without invoking this Treaty."

Clemenceau: "That is understood. We'll only mention the territories to be evacuated. That will not prejudge their future according to the terms of peace."

Orlando: "There is, besides, German territory that we propose to occupy during the Armistice without having any intention of annexing it in the peace." French procès-verbal, Oct. 31, 1918.

33. Lederer, pp. 62–66; Mamatey, p. 356; Gould, 223–24. Sonnino, at Paris, warned Orlando, at Rome, that it would be dangerous to enter discussions at this time of any Italian aspirations that went beyond the terms of the Treaty of London. Telegram, Nov. 14, 1918, *I Documenti Diplomatici Italiani, 1,* p. 154.

34. Admiral Bullard, the American naval commander in the Adriatic, reported that Fiume "had every appearance of being occupied by the Italians and not by the Allies." Bullard to Benson, Dec. 15, 1918, Bliss pa., box 227. He observed that the Italian occupation appeared to be permanent and went further than required by the necessity of preserving order or by the terms of the armistice with Austria. Bliss to War Dept., Nov. 26, 1918, Wilson pa., 2, L.C.

35. House to Derby and to Pichon, Nov. 21, Auchincloss diary; cable, W.W. to House, Nov. 18, 1918, Wilson pa., 5C. The British cabinet instructed its ambassador at Paris to tell House that it would be of the greatest possible value to have an American force accompany Italian troops that occupied, or intended to occupy, any part of Austria-Hungary. Minutes of the B.W.C., Nov. 22, 1918. Ambassador Derby conveyed the message to House. Letter, Nov. 22, 1918, Y.H.C. "American troops would be everywhere welcomed," Yugoslav nationalists at London notified the State Department on Nov. 1, 1918. N.A., R.G. 59, 763.72/12007½. A request came to House from the Italian government for one or two regiments of Americans in addition to the small contingent that had been in Italy to fight against Austria. Bonin to House, Nov. 7, 1918, Orlando-House corres., Y.H.C.

On October 19 the president had received from Lansing a dispatch from Ambassador Page that recommended the sending of more American troops. N.A., R.G. 59, 763.72119/2223. Page thought the presence of a single regiment was not "politically adequate." Page to State Dept., Oct. 31, N.A., R.G. 59, 033.1140/3, Nov. 1, 3, 1918, N.A., R.G. 59, 763.72/12104, 12263, 12283.

the men.[36] However the president was persuaded by House to allow
the regiment to remain. "I am still of the opinion," the colonel cabled to Wilson on December 2, "that they should be retained there
for some little time longer both for the purpose indicated [preserv-
ing order] . . . and also because their withdrawal at this particular
time might create an unfortunate impression in Italy. The numbers
involved are very small and the Italian Government has made few
demands." House thought that the Adriatic situation, "always tense,"
might lead to serious differences between Italy and Yugoslavia, to
say nothing of differences between Italy and France.[37]

Thus House, who had accepted the armistice with Austria-
Hungary allowing Italy to occupy the lands promised by the Treaty
of London, now gave American military support to the presence of
Italian troops in a city that was beyond the limits drawn in the treaty
and that until very recently the irredentists in Italy had not hoped to
acquire. This concession, unlike the one in the pre-armistice meetings, was not made under compulsion to end warfare quickly. House
thought the issue too unimportant to justify noncooperation with the
interested parties. Thus he provided a "neutral gloss"[38] on Italian
designs in the Adriatic. General Bliss reported to Wilson that an
American officer sent to Fiume to observe had found that American
troops were being used to further a policy of penetration of Slav territory that was unjustifiable. Moreover, there had been an incident
that very nearly brought American and Allied troops into conflict
with Italians. Nevertheless Bliss recommended that the regiment not
be withdrawn "at this late stage," because it had been merged with
certain units of Allied forces.[39] The president agreed.

On January 10, meeting with the other American commissioners,
Wilson shared the opinion that the Italians were entirely wrong in
what appeared to be efforts to influence the decisions of the peace
conference by using force, without authorization from Paris, to establish themselves in territory that they desired. At Bliss's suggestion
the president directed that the American regiment be allowed to

36. Baker to Bliss, Dec. 2, 3, 1918, Bliss pa., box 75.

37. House diary, Dec. 4; cables, House to W.W., Nov. 18, 19, 22, Dec. 2, W.W. to
House, Nov. 19, House to Sec. State, Nov. 18, 20, 24, *F.R., PPC, 2,* pp. 297, 301, 310,
311; House to Derby, Nov. 21, 1918; House to Pershing, Nov. 28, copies in Pershing-
House correspondence, Y.H.C.; N.D. Baker to Bliss, Dec. 23, 1918, Bliss to Baker,
Jan. 11, 1919, N.D. Baker pa., box 9, L.C.; Frazier to Page, Nov. 29, Dec. 3, 1918,
House-Page correspondence, Y.H.C.

38. The circumstances attending this concession by House are described by
Gould, pp. 204–8.

39. Bliss to W.W., Dec. 23, *F.R., PPC, 2,* p. 337f, with notation "approved Woodrow Wilson"; Bliss to N.D. Baker, Dec. 18, 24, Baker pa., box 5, L.C.; Bliss diary, Dec.
23, 1918.

function only under certain general rules that would preserve its national identity and limit its operations within the line set by the Austrian armistice.[40] It was not until March 22, 1919 that Bliss asked for
and received Wilson's approval for the withdrawal of the regiment
that served Italian purposes.[41]

By the military concession to Italy, House compounded the misapprehension that he allowed the Italian statesmen to entertain. In his
desire to avoid friction that he thought unnecessary, he deferred a
confrontation that, because of increasing pressure from irredentists
in Italy, was more violent when it was finally forced by the president
four months later.[42] Thus the colonel allowed his chief to drift toward an impasse.

And so the question of Italy's reward under the terms of the
Treaty of London was unresolved and becoming critical when Wilson set out for Rome to persuade the Italian people to put their faith
in a league of nations rather than in immediate measures that would
provoke Slav resentment.

The president decided to spend the first week of January wooing
the Italians. American officials at Rome had reported a tempest of
emotion. Gusts of opinion blew in many directions. Ambassador
Page warned that neglect of Italy might result in its realignment with
Germany. He reported that the Italian press—"certainly reflecting
general opinion"—bluntly asked whether the United States would
accept Italy's claims under the Treaty of London. Page hoped that
the president by his prestige and moving oratory would give pause
to passions of class strife and patriotism. On the day of Wilson's em-
barkation at New York, Page telegraphed from Rome: "For God's
sake don't go home without visiting Italy."[43]

In the eyes of some Italians the president bore a mystic halo. A
congress favoring a league of nations was meeting at Milan.[44] How-

40. Bliss diary, Jan. 10; telegram, Bliss to Pershing, Jan. 16, 1919, Bliss pa., box
202.

41. Bliss to W.W., W.W. to Bliss, March 22, 1919, Bliss pa., box 7. Bliss forwarded the president's authorization to Pershing.

42. Sonnino warned House on November 15 (*3*, p. 314) that if the peace treaty
was not made in less than four months, there would be "time for new questions,
complications, and groupings to arise." Four months later Orlando expressed regret
that the Adriatic boundaries were not settled soon after the armistice, before the question of Fiume became insoluble. *I.P., 4*, p. 441.

43. Page to Sec. State, Dec. 3, 1918, N.A., R.G. 59, 033.1140/3; Albrecht-Carrié,
p. 85. Page informed Wilson that English propagandists in Italy were busy destroying
American prestige in that country. Baker, p. 580.

44. On December 24 Page wrote urgently to the president: "The Italian people,
whatever their faults, are singularly idealistic and every word that you have uttered
has found its way to their heart. You have become to them something which I scarcely

ever, Ray Stannard Baker, a liberal journalist who had been observing public opinion in Italy, reported to the State Department that the upper class thought the league idea "moonshine," and felt that Italy must compete with France and Great Britain in empire-building. At the same time he found that Wilson's popularity with labor and socialist groups was greater in Italy than in France or England. He suggested that by manipulating the supply of food, which was scarce, the United States might tone down Italian demands.[45]

Aboard the *George Washington* Wilson had anticipated a visit to Rome.[46] An admirer of Garibaldi, he had never been in Italy. Italian rights under the Treaty of London was one of the few questions to which he gave serious study during December.[47] When Fiume was occupied and Orlando and Sonnino asserted their nation's claims in talks with the Americans at Paris, Wilson fell into a mood that Lloyd George described as "distinctly anti-Italian."[48]

In mid-December Ambassador Page came from Rome to reinforce his plea, the king of Italy called upon Wilson, and Sonnino insisted that it would be well for the president to visit Italy.[49] Ambassador di Cellere collaborated with House in making plans for a tour.[50] Wilson quickly approved them. Indeed, House's diary records that at the year's end the president was signing all papers that the colonel vouched for, disposing of a vast accumulation of business in a few hours.[51]

On New Year's Day the president and Mrs. Wilson set off with their personal staff. House and Auchincloss remained at Paris. The president asked Lansing to accompany him, but the secretary of state, after learning that House thought it both unwise and unneces-

---

know how to express." T.N. Page to W.W., Dec. 24, 1918, Wilson pa., 5B; Auchincloss diary, Dec. 9, 1918; Speranza, Dec. 14, 16, p. 226.

45. Memorandum, Dec. 18, 1918, Wilson pa., 5B.

46. Charles Seymour, *Letters from the Paris Peace Conference*, pp. 28–29; Swem book ms., Princeton University Library; Auchincloss diary, Dec. 18, 1918.

47. Auchincloss diary, Dec. 18; A.A. Young to president, Dec. 13, 1918, with documents attached, Wilson pa., 5B; Lawrence E. Gelfand, *The Inquiry*, p. 223. Isaiah Bowman drafted, for the president, suggestions for a compromise of Italian and Yugoslav claims. Bowman diary, Dec. 15, 1918, Bowman pa., file 1, drawer 1, Eisenhower Library, Johns Hopkins University.

48. David Lloyd George, *The Truth about the Peace Treaties, 1,* 193. C.P. Scott recorded that Wilson told him he found the Italians particularly difficult and Orlando and Sonnino obsessed by their ideas about the eastern Adriatic. J.L.L. Hammond, *C.P. Scott of the Manchester Guardian,* p. 249.

49. House diary, Dec. 4, 14, 15, 1918; Sonnino, *3,* pp. 313, 314.

50. Telegram, House to W.W., Dec. 25, 1918, Y.H.C. House pointed out that it was essential that Wilson go to Milan and Turin, where his "greatest strength" lay, even though Orlando and Sonnino did not urge him to visit these cities.

51. Auchincloss recorded that the president was angry when other men than House made plans for him. Diary, Dec. 15, 1918.

sary for him to go, decided against it. Lansing explained that he "begged off" because it was a tiring trip and would be a useless drain upon his strength. He thought that since the president had played "a lone hand" without the secretary of state in England, he could do the same in Italy.[52]

The Romans welcomed the American with an enthusiasm that they thought was due to this man of the hour, honoring him by sprinkling yellow sands in his path.[53] The press displayed extravagant headlines. Responding boldly when the Italian Chamber invited him to be the first foreigner to address them from the floor, the president solicited sympathy for the Balkan states that "must now be independent" under governments of their own choosing. He also made the overoptimistic suggestion that if small states were to replace great empires, there would be less "secret influence" and "intrigue" in the Balkans.

Gino Speranza, a political observer at the American Embassy, insisted that Wilson meet representative Italians outside of official and social circles.[54]. A talk was arranged with Bissolati.[55] This socialist leader, who had just resigned from the cabinet and who disapproved of extravagant claims in the Adriatic, gave assurance that the Italian people were at one with the president in their desire to prevent future wars and to establish frontiers that would make war impossible. Bissolati proposed that Fiume be a free city under Italian protection and Susak a free port under that of Yugoslavia, and he suggested a boundary line not much different from that drawn by Wilson's advisers of The Inquiry. He insisted on the abandonment of all Italian pretensions to Dalmatia. These opinions were pleasant for Wilson to hear, and of a nature to make him the more determined to resist extreme Italian claims; but they came from a man whose political influ-

52. Lansing desk diary, Dec. 31, 1918, Jan. 1, 1919, L.C.; Eleanor Lansing to W.W., Jan. 1, 1919, Wilson pa., 5B; Lansing to J.W. Davis, Jan. 4, 1919, Davis pa., Y.H.C.

53. According to a French diplomat the crowd on the sidewalks was somewhat restrained and only appropriately demonstrative. François Charles-Roux, *Souvenirs Diplomatique*, p. 360. However, Dr. Grayson thought the reception at Rome "the greatest the President . . . ever received anywhere." Grayson to Tumulty, Jan. 7, 1919, Wilson pa., 5B.

54. "I fear," Lansing reported to William Phillips of the State Department on Feb. 13, 1919, "that [First Secretary] Jay and some others bored the life out of the President when he was in Italy by telling him how to act like a gentleman. At any rate the Embassy did not please him." Letter in Lansing pa., box 3, folder VII, Princeton University Library.

55. Ambassador Page told the French ambassador, Barrère, that the talk with Bissolati was arranged at the president's initiative. Dispatch, Barrère to M.A.E., Jan. 6, 1919, Archives du M.A.E. À Paix, A 1154.1, f.154–55.

ence was on the wane,[56] and the talk did little or nothing to strengthen the president's position. Premier Orlando and Foreign Minister Sonnino were the men who would have to be dealt with. Apparently under the delusion that Orlando, the political leader who appealed to the principle of self-determination to justify the seizure of Fiume, would be less demanding than Sonnino, the professional diplomat, the president was disappointed when he found it impossible to talk with Orlando without Sonnino present.[57]

The king and queen departed from tradition so far as to go to the American Embassy for lunch with the president, and then they entertained him at the Villa Savoia. Wilson visited the Vatican despite the protests of Protestant clergymen in the United States, and Pope Benedict greeted him warmly and commended his advocacy of a league of nations.[58]

Wilson was not satisfied by the privilege of addressing the chamber. He yearned to speak to the populace as he had spoken to the English in the Midlands, and to win their allegiance. Plans were made at Rome for an address to a huge gathering in the Piazza Venezia. But the government did not permit this. The official press explained plausibly that the people might get out of hand and it was unnecessary for the American to address them, that in fact he had no intention of doing so; and rumors circulated that he had a phobia for crowds, that it was feared someone might throw a bomb. Afterwards, according to Mrs. Wilson, her husband was "fairly blazing with anger" in his frustration and expressed himself in no uncertain terms to the press and to the officials.[59]

The president's greatest support lay in the north, an industrial

---

56. Speranza, Dec. 29, 1918, Jan. 17, 22, 24, 1919. A digest of Bissolati's conversation with Wilson may be found in Page to Wilson, Jan. 7, 1919, Wilson pa., 5B. It is printed in part in Inga Floto, *Colonel House in Paris,* pp. 91–92.

57. Dispatch, Polk from Auchincloss, Jan. 9, 1919, Y.H.C. If Sonnino had a definite program, based on an exact execution of the Treaty of London, Orlando had not; his main concern was to avoid the difficult and seek what was politically feasible. Albrecht-Carrié, pp. 71–72, 85. "The President said the King of Italy was very alive to that ['the rights of the masses,'] but Sonnino not, and from Orlando they got no original expression." Benham diary letter, Jan. 2, 1919, Helm pa., L.C.

58. Auchincloss diary, Dec. 28, 1918; Cardinal Gibbons to W.W., Nov. 27, 1918, Wilson pa., file 2; Benham diary letter, Jan. 2, 1919, Helm pa.; E.B. Wilson, *My Memoir,* p. 217; Norval Richardson, *My Diplomatic Education,* (New York, 1923), p. 190. Urging his chief to go to the Vatican, Tumulty alluded to the influence the pope could wield in favor of Wilson's ideals among the free peoples of all countries. Cable Tumulty to W.W., Dec. 17, 1918, Wilson pa., 5B. The president insisted upon calling on the same day at the vestry of the American Episcopal Church, where an old friend was in charge.

59. E.B. Wilson, p. 217; Speranza, Jan. 17, 1919; George Creel, *Rebel at Large,* p. 207; *The World, the War, and Wilson,* p. 168–71; Benham diary letter, Jan. 6, 9, 1919, Helm pa. See Arno J. Mayer, *Politics and Diplomacy,* pp. 212–15, Gould, pp. 348–55.

region to which the Italian government did not urge him to go. At Milan—where placards announced "Italy demands only the frontiers marked out by God"—Wilson made six short speeches. Crowds filled the streets as far as the eye could see.[60] He appealed directly to these people for a new world order.

Wilson's visit to Italy aggravated his differences with its government. By refraining from precise support of Italian aspirations, by meeting with Bissolati, and by insistence on addressing the public in defiance of the wish of the constituted authorities, he sowed seeds of mistrust. He was misled by the popular acclaim in northern Italy. The moderates and middle classes were not convinced. They were reluctant to accept an experiment like a league of nations as the principal guarantee of their national security. The permanent officials of the foreign office, lacking Wilson's enthusiasm for constitution-making, looked forward to the settlement of pending matters of difference and sought practical assistance from the Americans. Wilson's ideas seemed both too glamorous and too simple—put forward to charm leftists rather than to meet the fundamental desires of a victorious people.[61]

Popular clamor for annexation of Fiume mounted. Within a fortnight after the president's departure from Rome, Ambassador Page wrote that the Italian liberals, who valued the new Slav state as a check upon German aggression in the future,[62] were losing ground and the moderates were tending to join in the national indignation at the position of the Yugoslavs. At the same time Page reported an effort on his part to induce Sonnino to give up the claims to Dalmatia and concentrate on making Montenegro independent of Yugoslavia, an objective close to the heart of the Italian foreign minister. "I felt he was ready last night to yield more than before," the ambassador wrote, suggesting that the change might be due to the fact that Wilson had proposed to Sonnino that Yugoslavia be forbidden to have a navy or to fortify any Dalmatian islands that were awarded to it.

Bissolati, who favored the renunciation of claims under the Treaty of London to nonItalian regions and proposed that Fiume become a free city under Italian protection, appealed to the nation at Milan on January 11, but he was silenced by a demonstration led by Mussolini and other violent nationalists.[63]

60. G. Close's letter of Jan. 9, 1919, Close pa., Princeton University Library.

61. See Sir Alfred Zimmern, *The American Road to World Peace*, pp. 62–63.

62. Page to House, Nov. 29, 1918, Y.H.C.

63. T.N. Page to W.W., Jan. 7, Page to Ammission, Jan, 12, 1919, Wilson pa., 5B; Leo Valiani, *The End of Austria-Hungary* (London, 1973), p. 294; T.N. Page, *Italy and the World War*, pp. 395–96.

Although Wilson had failed in this test of his power to move governments by appealing to liberal elements of the populace, the president returned to France on January 7 in a mood of overconfidence. He persuaded himself that his genius for leading a moral crusade was still alive, and might yet succeed in bringing the people of Europe to accept a new order in international affairs. He had inflated his own hopes for an enduring peace even as he allowed his audiences to put unwarranted faith in his sympathy for their national aims.

Diplomats of the Old World, however, looked behind what seemed to them a façade of faith and eloquence. They deplored the delay that resulted from the public triumphs and speechmaking of the political leaders. Ambassador Paul Cambon, observing the desire of Wilson and the kings of Belgium, Greece, and Italy to be received in Paris, wrote on December 4: "This itching to be acclaimed is assuming unhealthy proportions."[64] Men who had long lived close to European politics and statecraft, which for a century before 1914 had succeeded in avoiding a general war, were not prepared to kneel before the American prophet.

---

64. P. Cambon, *Correspondance, 3,* 291.

☆XI☆

Self-Determination in Fallen Empires

The collapse of four empires at the end of the war left many peoples without the essentials of civilized living, and with no faith in the royal regimes under which they had suffered the misery of defeat and impoverishment. In all the vast heartland, from the Rhine to Vladivostok and from the White Sea to the Indian Ocean, hardly a government could be accounted stable and secure. Political chaos led to economic dislocation. National minorities, heretofore kept loyal by force, by token recognition, and by adroit politics, now asserted themselves. The components of Austria-Hungary that had been held in uneasy federation were set free by a manifesto of the premier shortly before the armistices. In Vienna and Budapest, as well as in Warsaw, Prague, and Belgrade, citizens were attempting to set up new and independent regimes.

The doctrine of Woodrow Wilson made a timely appeal to the peoples who, released from imperial rule against which they revolted, were groping for a way out of the dismal aftermath of defeat. Native minorities seized upon the principle of "self-determination" as a means of furthering their national aspirations. At the same time their hopes were lifted by a prospect of relief by the United States from the shortages of food and supplies they were suffering.[1]

During the last months of 1918 the American government had not escaped a measure of involvement, as the peoples of the Hapsburg domain formed national councils and the Balkan states resumed controversies that had provoked violence in the past. Racial minorities within the United States did not fail to remind American officials of the claims and aspirations of their kinsmen in Europe, and rep-

---

1. See below, ch. XIII.

resentatives of the various peoples met in Washington in October to define and reconcile claims to be made after the war's end.[2]

A year earlier a report of The Inquiry, recognizing the economic benefits of a unifying political order, had stated: "We are strongly of the opinion . . . that a settlement which insures economic prosperity is most likely to be a lasting one. . . . Our policy must . . . consist first in a stirring up of nationalist discontent and then in refusing to accept the extreme logic of this discontent which would be the dismemberment of Austria-Hungary." The United States would thus enter upon the dangerous course of arousing popular expectations that it would later try to control.

The American people were sensitive to the challenge that came from regions of Europe whence many of them had emigrated. They feared the importation of revolutionary ideas into their republic; and at the same time they were moved by the appeal to their charitable impulses. They expected their leaders to meet the danger with firmness and the appeal with indulgence. Many had a naïve faith that democracy could be dispensed as easily as arms and machines. Hardly aware how deep-rooted were the ways of life of the peoples of Europe, how enduring and diverse their heritage, the Americans did not take account of the absence in many countries of those established and other-than-political centers of social organization that Lord Acton deemed essential to the preservation of liberty in a democracy. Indeed the spirit of the times, which was about to force a sumptuary law into the Constitution in the hope of promoting sobriety, did not move the Americans to give adequate consideration to the power of use and wont even at home, to say nothing of the compulsion of ancient and customary ways abroad. They encouraged nascent minorities to arrive by their own efforts at the particular kind of self-government that the United States practiced with success.[3]

---

2. See Joseph P. O'Grady (ed.), *The Immigrants' Influence on Wilson's Peace Policies.* "An organization called 'The Conference of Oppressed Nationalities' is meeting in Washington under the auspices of the U.S. G[overnment]. The object is to arrive at an understanding between the peoples now oppressed by the Central Empires. It is hope[d] to include representatives of the Poles, Czechs, Jugo-Slavs, Ruthenians, Finns, Lithuanians, and Estonians, as well as some unofficial Italian representative. They will endeavour to adjust their various claims, both political and economic, so that they can come to the Peace Conference each supporting the demands of the others. They are working closely with House's Bureau [The Inquiry] and House himself is encouraging the scheme in every way." Dispatch for Reading from Wiseman, Oct. 3, 1918, Y.H.C.

3. American thinking tended to ignore the vast difference between the conditions obtaining in the British colonies of North America when they rebelled in 1776 and those that prevailed in central and eastern Europe in 1919. Carl N. Degler, "An Unsuspected Obstacle in Foreign Affairs," *The American Scholar,* [Spring 1963], *32,* 192–200.

Wilson's capacity for sympathy with revolution against repressive rule was great. However on election day, appealing to "peoples of the constituent nations of Austria-Hungary," he wrote:

> It is the earnest hope and expectation of all friends of freedom everywhere and particularly of those whose present and immediate task it is to assist the liberated peoples of the world to establish themselves in genuine freedom, that both the leaders and the peoples of the countries recently set free shall see to it that the momentous changes now being brought about are carried through with order, with moderation, with mercy as well as firmness, and that violence and cruelty of every kind are checked and prevented. . . .[4]

The president wanted to help other peoples to develop responsible governments. At the same time he continued to be cautious about interference with the exercise of their political rights.[5] Intervention in Caribbean states, resulting in frustration and in military action, had suggested that any intrusion by one government in the domain of another, no matter how worthy the motive, might have embarrassing consequences not easily foreseen. Before he arrived at Paris he had made no effort to delineate boundaries or to arbitrate among aspiring political factions in Europe. Responding to a report from House that the pre-armistice conference was to discuss steps to be taken if disorder in Austria-Hungary made policing necessary, the president instructed him to keep "hands off the pieces of Austria-Hungary," where local control would be "infinitely better" than foreign control. "The peace of Europe pivots there," he said.[6]

Wilson was now ready to accept the democratic states that were in the making, for it was plain that the Hapsburg regime was doomed and certain native promoters of independent nations made a strong appeal to American sentiment. Stimulated by mounting political pressures from organizations of Slavs within the United States,[7] the president on September 2 recognized the Czechoslovak National Council at Paris as a de facto belligerent government. The question of a loan came up, and the State Department sought "authentic

---

4. Message sent through the U.S. Legation in Switzerland, *F.R., 1918, I, 1,* p. 470. Cf. above, pp. 28–29.

5. Wilson remarked to a group of foreign news correspondents on April 8, 1918: "There isn't any one kind of government which we have the right to impose upon any nations. So that I am not fighting for democracy except for the peoples that want democracy. . . . the people have the right to any kind of government they please." Swem ms. notes, Princeton University Library.

6. Cables of Nov. 1, 1918, Baker, 541–42.

7. See O'Grady, pp. 204ff., 224ff., and 250ff., and Charles Pergler, *America in the Struggle for Czechoslovak Independence* (Philadelphia, 1926).

data" as to the extent to which the national council actually had the approval of the people it claimed to represent, elements of whom were scattered in the United States, England, France, and Siberia. Reassured by reports received from Paris, Secretary Lansing notified the Treasury that credits might be advanced.[8]

A revolutionary assembly met at Prague on November 14 under a constitution framed by the national council and elected Thomas G. Masaryk to the presidency of the new nation; and the next day Wilson received this pioneering statesman and fellow professor and gave him his blessing. Soon afterwards Masaryk went to Paris.

Calling on Colonel House on December 10 he said that he saw little difference between the Prussians, who had sought empire, and the new government of Germany, which sought new and exclusive markets. Fearing that the Germans in the Sudeten would resist the rule of a Czechoslovak state, he was disinclined to let them move to Germany, for they were efficient workmen who were essential to the revival of industry. Actually a plea came at this time from the new minister of foreign affairs at Vienna, asking for a plebiscite in the Sudeten region and for arbitration of the German desires there. On the other hand Benes, the Czech foreign minister, argued heatedly that the restoration of law and order in Central Europe required a prompt recognition of historic boundaries.[9] In December Masaryk departed hastily for Prague in order to deal with threats there to what he called "an American solution" of the nation's problems.[10]

Another ancient people who aspired to independence were the Poles. During the war Polish patriots at home and abroad had worked for freedom. When Poland was granted independence by Russia after the March Revolution of 1917, Poles had formed an army on French soil. Ignace Jan Paderewski represented a national committee of his people at Paris that advocated the cause of a new Polish state.

The political sympathies of the Poles in the United States, and also of those in Poland, reflected a diversity of religious faith as well as the partitions of the eighteenth century that had divided their

---

8. L. Woolsey to Miles, Oct. 23, Woolsey to Masaryk, Nov. 6, 1918, Woolsey pa., box 2, L.C.

9. Typescript, Dec. 15, 1918, Bonsal pa., box 17, L.C..

10. Stephen Bonsal, *Unfinished Business,* pp. 83–84, Masaryk had misgivings about the future of Silesia. Bonsal was impressed by his observation that the Hapsburg government had "favored, perhaps pampered" the Germans in Bohemia for political reasons and left them expectant of similar treatment from the Czechoslovak state, which they would not get. *Suitors and Suppliants,* pp. 146–51; record of a conference of House with Masaryk, Dec. 10, 1918, at the Meurice, Bonsal pa., box 15.

country among Austria, Prussia, and Russia.[11] Paderewski, who was better known to Americans as a distinguished pianist than as a political leader, was associated with the Russian element of his people. His great charm and childlike naïveté and his tale of the woes of Poland captivated Colonel House, whom Paderewski called "a providential man." House accepted him as the spokesman for all American voters of Polish blood and commended him to Wilson, who received him the day before the 1916 election and heard his impassioned plea for aid.[12]

In the "peace without victory" address of January 22, 1917 the president gave the support that Paderewski sought. "Statesmen everywhere," he said, "are agreed that there should be a united, independent, and autonomous Poland."[13] A year later in Point Thirteen he reaffirmed this position.

Having drawn Wilson's interest to Poland's cause, House sought to enlist Balfour also. In a conversation in April of 1917 he had advocated a restored and rejuvenated Poland, large and powerful enough to serve as a buffer state between Germany and Russia. However, Balfour took a different view. He objected that a Polish state, cutting off Russia from Germany, might hurt France more than Germany because it would prevent Russia from coming to France's aid in the event of an attack by Germany. He argued for a Poland "autonomous under the Russians." But House thought they had to take into consideration the Russia of fifty years in the future.[14]

The British government, hoping to check pro-German intrigue in Poland, joined with the French in proposing that the Polish National Committee in Paris be recognized as official experts on Polish questions and unofficial representatives of the Polish nation. On November 10, 1917, three days after the Bolshevik revolution, the United States accepted the Paris committee as an official organization. Recognition of it as the supreme Polish political authority did not come until late in 1918—by France and Italy in October and by

11. See Louis L. Gerson, *Woodrow Wilson and the Rebirth of Poland*, pp. 14–15, 46–48, 50–54.

12. House diary, Sept. 22, 1917, Y.H.C. "It was solely through Paderewski," House later confessed, "that I became so deeply interested in the cause of Poland, and pressed upon the President Paderewski's views which I had made my own. . . . His views regarding Europe were clear, ennobling and free from undue prejudice." House to Orlowski, Jan. 15, 1931, Y.H.C.; Gerson, pp. 48, 60–71. Mrs. Wilson was deeply moved by Paderewski's pleading. E.B. Wilson, *My Memoir*, p. 113.

13. Commenting on the drafting of this address, House wrote: "We thought that since Germany and Russia had agreed to free Poland that should be put in." Diary, Jan. 3, 1917; Gerson, pp. 22–23.

14. *I.P., 3*, pp. 43–46; *F.R., Lansing pa., 2*, p. 28.

the United States in November. Poland did not receive de jure recognition from the United States until January 22, 1919, from Great Britain until February 26.[15]

During 1918 Paderewski pressed vigorously for American favors. But Wilson, feeling that Poland was as yet unorganized, resisted his efforts to negotiate a loan; and attempts to get the Congress to act were blocked by both the president and by American Poles who disliked Paderewski. At the same time Roman Dmowski, a pronounced conservative and the chairman of the Paris committee, came to the United States. Joining forces with Paderewski, he succeeded in winning the support of American Poles and started a campaign to educate Americans on Polish territorial claims. It seemed to Dmowski that the armistice terms exposed Poland to a "Bolshevik flood," and that the only legislator who understood what was going on was "an old Senator of the Republican Party, Lodge."[16]

Calling at the White House to say farewell on Armistice Day, Dmowski found the president somewhat cold toward the Polish cause. He therefore played his last trump. Believing that Wilson would not have been re-elected in 1916 without the Polish vote, he hinted at the loss of this support if the Poles were not satisfied at the peace conference. Under this pressure Wilson responded politely but without any commitment. A month later, according to the record of Charles Seymour, he "showed much dry humor" in telling of the demands of the Poles.[17]

When the war ended the Polish people, remote from the national committee at Paris, were without effective native leadership. In the north the Bolsheviks held Vilna and the Germans remained in Posen. Eastern Galicia was in the hands of Ukrainians; western Galicia under the authority of a Polish Committee. A Socialist republic took shape at Lublin.

Order began to emerge when General Joseph Pilsudski, released from a German prison, made a triumphal return to Warsaw. Granted full military power by the regency council that had ruled during the German occupation, he directed campaigns to bring Galicia and Poznania within the Polish state despite their large proportion of alien peoples. Pilsudski had many adherents among American Poles but powerful enemies both within Poland and without.

---

15. *F.R., 1918, I, 1*, pp. 878–81, *PPC, 2*, pp. 412, 432; *1919, 2*, 741; Gerson, pp. 81, 93.

16. Roman Dmowski, *Polityka Polska* (Warsaw, 1925), pp. 389–92, 400–402, cited in Gerson, pp. 95–96, 98–99. Dmowski talked with House and submitted to the president, at his invitation, a map and memorandum defining Poland's aspirations.

17. Dmowski, pp. 401–2, in Gerson, p. 99; Charles Seymour, *Letters*, p. 30.

Dmowski thought him pro-Austrian as well as pro-Bolshevik, and at first would not recognize him.[18]

Hugh Gibson, diplomatic representative at Warsaw and destined to be the first United States minister to Poland,[19] had a long talk with Pilsudski and advised him to collaborate with Paderewski in a new government. In a letter to a secretary of the American Commission to Negotiate Peace, Gibson wrote: "Pilsudski has been getting on a high horse and trying to take things into his own hands. . . . The scheme is to have socialistic governments in Poland, the Baltic Provinces, White Russia, and the Ukraine, all of them joined in a strong confederation held together by the iron hand of Pilsudski as the socialist military dictator dominating the whole of Europe. . . . They are trying to put this scheme in effect through the use of the old methods of the Czar. . . . I like the old gentleman very much . . . but I am afraid there may be complications. . . . Even with a little lunacy the two men [Pilsudski and Paderewski] at the head of the government form a splendid combination and ought to be kept there."[20]

When Dmowski returned to Paris from the United States, House urged him to base his diplomacy on the possible and to settle on a coalition.[21] The Department of State hesitated to respond favorably to a French plea for recognition of Poland until the differences were settled between its leaders.[22] Paderewski went to Warsaw, arriving on New Year's Day and claiming the support of four million American Poles. The populace welcomed him tumultuously, as they had welcomed Pilsudski two months before. But the first encounter between the proud patriots did not give promise of cooperation. Paderewski objected to the cabinet then in office and complained that it was under German influence. He charged that Bolsheviks lurked behind Pilsudski's throne.

Paderewski sent alarming messages to House, urging that the Allies and the United States give protection to Poland to save it from anarchy.[23] Complaining that Pilsudski's government was weak and

18. *F.R., PPC, 2*, p. 422.
19. Hoover asked House to send Gibson to Prague, where the French had an envoy and the Americans, in Hoover's opinion, had been caught napping. According to Hoover, Gibson "was a trained diplomat and knew something about food," and few others did. Bonsal recorded that Lansing did not want to send a career man to Prague. Typescript, Dec. 17, 1918, Bonsal pa., box 17.
20. Gibson to Leland Harrison, Dec. 8, 1918, L. Harrison pa., Box 107, L.C.
21. House diary, Dec. 4, 1918.
22. *F.R., PPC, 2*, pp. 412, 422.
23. *I.P., 4*, p. 262. Picturing Poland as a country put upon by its neighbors, Paderewski pleaded for military aid, otherwise the war might "only result in the establishment of barbarism all over Europe."

"almost exclusively radical-socialist," he wrote: "I have been asked to form a new cabinet, but what could I do with the moral support of the country alone, without the material assistance of the Allies and the United States?" His position was already buttressed by assurance from an American food mission at Warsaw that relief supplies would come to Poland only if Paderewski was in charge of the government. With such practical benefits in prospect Pilsudski soon overcame his aversion and accepted the purveyor of Western aid as prime minister. When American relief was terminated late in 1919 Paderewski lost his position and voluntarily exiled himself from the country.[24]

As the American delegates prepared for the peacemaking they were committed to play a part in the settlement of the Polish question, which had long perplexed the diplomats of Europe and in which the United States had little more than a sentimental interest. Already the American government had received protests against Polish aggression.[25] When Paderewski asked that Americans of Polish blood be assigned to a legion to serve in defending the frontiers of Poland "against the Russians and several other peoples who are menacing it," Wilson heeded Secretary of War Baker's warning that the situation in Europe would be complicated by the creation of any sort of foreign force that might pursue nationalistic objectives of any kind pending the determinations of the peace conference. Moreover, the American government must free its soldiers for industrial pursuits at home.[26]

On January 4th a Polish delegation arrived at Paris to get recognition for Pilsudski. In fact in the first week of the new year the Crillon was overrun with Poles who aspired to speak for their people. It was apparent that unless unity of action was attained the peace con-

---

24. Gerson, pp. 105–10.

25. For example: a warning from Lithuanians that they could defend themselves without Polish help (*F.R., PPC, 2*, p. 416) and a protest from the Western Ukrainian Republic against the dispatch by the Warsaw government of "troops in large number" to eastern Galicia (ibid., 420).

26. N.D. Baker to W.W., Nov. 23, W.W. to Baker, Nov. 25, 1918, Wilson pa., 2. Beginning in October of 1917 American Poles not subject to the draft had been allowed to volunteer for service with Polish units that, by arrangement with the French government, were fighting under their own colors against Germany. However, on January 2, 1919 the president asked Lansing to have a "frank talk" with the Polish committee at Paris. "It is clearly out of the question," Wilson wrote, "to allow Poles to be enlisted in the United States to fight against peoples with whom the United States is at peace and whose affairs the United States is trying to compose." Polk to Ammission, Jan. 3, 1919, Wilson pa., 5B; *F.R., PPC, 2*, 424–26, 430–34.

On December 11 Major Julian L. Coolidge reported to the headquarters of the A.E.F. that Pilsudski's request for military assistance in restoring order was in response to the Soviet policy of spreading propaganda and the German practice of sending many penniless and half-starving Polish and Russian prisoners to shift for themselves in Poland. N.A., R.G. 120, series 7, box 1280, docs. 17488 F and N.

ference might deem Poland incapable of self-government and might
be little disposed to give assistance.

House, determined not to indulge the policy of *liberum veto* that
had contributed to the downfall of the old Polish state, instructed
Bonsal to summon all the delegates to a room in the Crillon and say
that Poland was to have only two spokesmen at the peace conference
and they must decide who they would be; else their country could
not be represented. Bonsal delivered the ultimatum and retired,
closing the door. After three hours, when the babel of voices had
subsided, he went in and was told that Paderewski and Dmowski had
been chosen.[27]

A third nation that was coming into being at the time of the armistice, but with no ancient tradition of statehood, was Yugoslavia. In
the birth of this country Americans had little share. The Yugoslavs
in the United States were fewer in number and of less influence than
the Czechs and the Poles; and their native leaders showed less genius
in winning American hearts than Masaryk and Paderewski. Their
cause was represented only by unofficial emissaries and by blood
brothers who raised volunteers for the Serbian army and funds for a
Yugoslav committee that functioned at London. Wilson and Lansing
persisted in rebuffing pleas in their behalf, being aware of the jealousy of Italy and the desire of Serbia to absorb its neighbors rather
than to become federated with them.

In mid-September the Congress of Oppressed Nationalities came
together at Paris. At the first meeting of congress, held at Rome in
April, the nascent peoples had pleaded for self-determination and
had denounced the Hapsburg monarchy; and the Allied governments, eager to subvert the unity of the enemy, had listened with
sympathy. Now, at the session in Paris, the United States was represented by Bonsal, then a major in military intelligence.[28] Bonsal read
to the insurgent delegates the statement of September 2 by which
the United States recognized the belligerency of the Czechoslovak
National Council. "The delegates went wild with enthusiasm," Bonsal recorded. "It seemed to them that we . . . had thrown ourselves
without reservations of any kind into the traditional cockpit of
Southeast Europe and had pledged ourselves to an adjustment and a

27. Bonsal, *Suitors and Suppliants,* pp. 120–21. Twenty years later Bonsal received
a letter from his colleague Frazier that said: "When one thinks of Dmowski and the
other Poles with whom we used to discuss the future of Poland I could tear my hair."
Sept. 22, 1939, Bonsal pa., box 2.

28. Bonsal, *Suitors and Suppliants,* p. 2.

settlement of all their difficulties, of course in strict accord with the Fourteen Points."

When several hands went up for recognition, the French chairman, who had advocated his government's policy of developing a chain of anti-German nations from the Baltic to the Adriatic, foresaw the danger of free discussion of contentious issues. He quickly declared the session adjourned. A few days later a call went out for another meeting on November 15, but with the conclusion of the armistices this plan was given up.

The ardent spokesmen of the several incipient nations, and of factions of those nations, sought sympathy and favors from the Crillon. Upon Bonsal, who had been a journalist in the Balkans for three years and knew something of the ways and languages of the peoples of southeastern Europe, devolved the responsibility of dealing with what he called "the ethnic factors." He had to cope with lively antipathies among the Serbs, Croats, and Slovenes. "I confer with them," he wrote, "and haul them over the coals—separately." It was apparent to him that "in view of the stiffening attitude . . . apparent in every quarter" the conciliatory resolutions that had been adopted by the Congress at Rome in April were now "simply literature." After House's arrival at the end of October an Italian spokesman came to advise him that Italy would not sit at the peace table if a chair was given to the Croats, Italy's enemy.[29] DiMartino, the permanent undersecretary of the Italian Foreign Office, brushed aside the Fourteen Points as "mere literature," and predicted that the inevitable result of the application of self-determination on Italy's frontiers would be that "over the weak rampart of Yugoslavia the Germans would reach the Brenner and the Adriatic." Then Italy would be "face to face with a Germany stronger and better equipped for battle than she was . . . in 1915."[30]

On November 8 Colonel House forwarded appeals of factions of South Slavs and, aware of the vital interest of Italy, he advised Wilson to reassure the Yugoslavs with caution.[31] On the thirtieth the president let them know that he had their case on the docket, and considered the question one of the most important to be considered at the peace conference.[32]

On December 1 Alexander, the prince regent of Serbia, pro-

---

29. Ibid., pp. 96–98, and a ms. on which this was based, and a three-page typescript, "Nov. 8," concerning the "Ethnic Factors." Bonsal pa., box 24.
   30. Ibid., p. 98.
   31. *F.R., Lansing pa., 2,* p. 140; *F.R. PPC, 2,* p. 287.
   32. W.W. to Phillips, Nov. 30, 1918, N.A., R.G. 59, 763.72/12413.

claimed "the Kingdom of the Serbs, Croats, and Slovenes"; and on
the eighth he announced the first coalition government. Ambassador
Jusserand notified Secretary Lansing that France was ready to recognize the new state if the United States and Great Britain also would
do so. He added that the British and Italian governments preferred
that the question be settled by the peace conference and France had
no objection. It was not until February 7, 1919, that the United
States granted its recognition,[33] with the proviso that "the final settlement of territorial frontiers must be left to the peace conference
for determination according to the desires of the peoples concerned."

And so the American delegates went to the peace table with the
relationship of their government to the Yugoslav state undefined.
Some of its people were technically still regarded as citizens of Austria-Hungary, an enemy state no longer in existence; others—the
Serbs and Montenegrins—were Allies in the war and so entitled to
representation at the peace conference.

The emergence of three new states from the realms of the monarchs in east Central Europe raised perplexities enough; but beyond
these the statesmen at Paris inherited the responsibility for coping
with chronic confrontations among the Balkan nations. The collapse
of the empires that had dictated relationships removed traditional
restraints upon governments that were not accustomed to treat peace-
fully among themselves. A prophecy made just before the armistice by Ambassador Thomas Nelson Page was being fulfilled all too
rapidly. "Balkan peoples hostile to each other as ever," Page cabled
to Washington from Rome on November 8, "and likely to be at each
other as soon as active hostilities cease and military authority retired."[34] By the time the peace conference assembled the various nationalities were advancing claims that clashed and precipitated local
conflicts.[35] Page advised House that the arranging of Balkan frontiers would be "the most difficult, complex, and indeed perilous part
of the work of the peace conference" and required "persons as free
from any excessive predilection as possible." Warning against inter-
Balkan feuds, he thought "outside power" essential to the keeping of
peace.[36] Secretary Lansing had concluded that the differences

---

33. Victor S. Mametey, *The United States and East Central Europe*, pp. 374–75; *F.R.*,
PPC, 2, p. 346; Ammission to Polk, Feb. 6, 1919, *F.R., 1919, 2*, 892–99.
34. Dispatch, N.A., R.G. 59, 763.72/12201.
35. "Conversation with Secretary Lansing, Dec. 9, 1918," Bowman pa., file 1,
drawer 1, "Inquiry" folder, Eisenhower Library, Johns Hopkins University.
36. Page to House, Nov. 15, 22, 1918, Y.H.C.

among the little nations were irreconcilable. He suggested, in a letter to the president on September 30 that the United States ought to insist that consideration of the whole Balkan question be postponed until the peace conference. Lansing feared a renewal of "the old political game" and a premature treaty between the Allies and Bulgaria.

Woodrow Wilson, who a year earlier had been advised by The Inquiry that it would be unwise at that time to try to draw Balkan boundaries,[37] was now willing, in his zeal to create a peaceful world, to grapple even with the complex politics of the region known as "the tinderbox of Europe." The sympathy of Americans toward Christians in the Turkish Empire and in Bulgaria and their horror of the Bolshevist terror gave moral sanction to intervention in southeastern Europe.

At the end of September the Allies concluded an armistice with Bulgaria, a nation to which American educators had contributed much and with which the United States was not at war. Its government had asked Wilson to exert friendly influence upon the Allies and had used the services of American diplomats in seeking a truce. However, the armistice that was signed did not mention Wilson's program. House's interpretation of Point XI proposed frontiers for Bulgaria that took account of that nation's legitimate interests.

On October 1 the president gave the secretary of state his statement of policy for the Balkans:

> Government of the United States cannot be [*sic.*] regard every question that concerns any one of the Balkan States as an essential part of the general peace settlement, inasmuch as there is no part of Europe that is more likely to be a seed-bed of war than the Balkans. . . . It would be very hazardous to treat separately any part of the whole.

From the British government came assurance that it would respect this principle, and Ambassador Jusserand apprised the State Department that France believed that the difficult settlement of the Balkan question should await the peace conference.[38] The European diplomats had lived with the problem for generations without solving it with any degree of permanence. But British scholars, preparing a handbook on the Eastern question for the Foreign Office, hopefully outlined a basis for solutions:

> Any permanent pacification and reconciliation of the Balkan peoples must depend on how far it is possible to meet and satisfy their

---

37. *I.P.*, *3*, 333–34.
38. *F.R.*, *Lansing pa.*, *2*, pp. 157–58; *ibid.*, *1918*, *I, 1*, p. 174.

various national sentiments and aspirations, or, where these are mutually incompatible, to effect a reasonable compromise between them. Only in this way is it possible to avoid a sense of bitterness and injustice, which is sure to lead to further trouble in the near future; and it is to be hoped that a broad sense of justice and expediency, rather than any desire to reward friends and punish enemies, will be the guiding spirit. . . . There appear to be three main considerations affecting any permanent settlement of Balkan affairs— nationality and popular sentiment; economic conditions, especially access to the sea and to important routes of international commerce; and scientific frontiers, from the military and naval point of view.[39]

The American advisers were less precise. A French observer perceived that some of them dreamed of a Balkan federation to which the United States would give economic aid.[40] House believed the Balkan nations should become strong barriers against both bolshevism and German expansion. The sixty-three reports of The Inquiry that dealt with this region, written for the most part by scholars not familiar with Balkan politics or languages, failed to deal with the situation as a whole and lacked both objectivity and conclusiveness.[41] There was a tendency to give more weight to economic factors than to ethnic affiliations. The detailed recommendations did not consistently follow the Cobb-Lippmann interpretation of the president's Points Nine through Eleven.[42]

The State Department stood aloof from affairs in the southern Balkan states. It was reluctant to interfere with the volcanic politics of Albania, which had remained neutral but now faced a threat of partition.[43] American experts doubted that Albania's qualification as a nation entitled it to admission to the peace conference, and they

---

39. F.O. Handbook No. 15, *History of the Eastern Question,* pp. 49–50.

40. *Note sur les Travaux de l'Inquiry et sur les solutions de Paix Américaines,"* 11 Dec. 1918, signed "L. A[ubert]," Archives Diplomatiques du M.A.É., À paix, vol. 161. Aubert, a member of Tardieu's "High Commission" to the United States, warned against the "tenacious Bulgarophilia of a group of Americans [educational missionaries] who lack precise understanding of Serbia's thesis."

41. Lawrence E. Gelfand, *The Inquiry,* pp. 216ff. This scholar cites Robert J. Kerner's report on Yugoslavia and William S. Ferguson's on "The Greek Case" as exceptionally valuable (pp. 218–29).

42. See ibid., pp. 144–45, 216ff.

43. Although Albania seemed about to fall apart a national assembly convened on December 25, 1918, and elected a president. On November 27 the State Department learned through its London Embassy that the British Foreign Office favored a large Albania "to block Serbian and Greek advance," and though preferring an American protectorate, was "willing Italy should act" (*F.R., PPC, 1,* 409). Italy had occupied southern districts and proclaimed under the terms of the Treaty of London a "protectorate" which disregarded the territorial limits prescribed by that treaty. Harold Nicolson, *Peacemaking,* pp. 174–75.

were willing to have it partitioned.[44] Neither Wilson nor House took a direct interest in the fate of the little country.

Unlike Albania, Greece was fortunate in having a diplomat who knew how to appeal to American sentiment. Not content to rest upon the certainty of British support, Premier Veniselos saw the wisdom of establishing rapport with Washington. Though Greece had doubled in size as a result of the Balkan wars of 1912–13 it still included only about half of the Greeks resident in the Levant. A desire to "liberate" the rest, as well as a wish to recapture some of the nation's ancient glory, inspired Greek policy. Greeks in northern Epirus had set up an autonomous provisional government and carried on propaganda for independence. Greece, according to Veniselos, claimed the Dodecanese Islands and lands in Thrace, Macedonia, and Asia Minor.[45]

In November the State Department received two communications from Athens that pleaded for mutual effort in the peacemaking, not primarily to secure Greece's national war aims, but rather to realize the international vision of Woodrow Wilson.[46] It was refreshing to the American leaders to have at this time, when many politicians of eastern Europe seemed preoccupied by local and limited purposes, the Greek protestation of the primacy of the common good. Americans educated in the classical tradition welcomed this avowal. Their peace delegates, like the English, saw in the new Greece a cause that stirred the same emotion that was kindled by the concepts of the new Czechoslovakia and the new Poland. Such a cause—in the words of Nicolson—"made hearts sing at heaven's gate."[47] Veniselos arrived at Paris before the signing of the armistices and established an office that poured out propaganda. He called on the president in December and won his heart. The Greek government could look forward confidently to a seat of honor at the peace table and to a sympathetic hearing of its claims by the English-speaking delegates.[48] At least one Allied official in the Balkans did not think the Greeks innocent of intrigue. A French commander, investigating a

---

44. *F.R., PPC, 1,* 311, 361, *2,* pp. 373–74.

45. F.O. Handbook No. 15, pp. 46, 50.

46. *F.R., PPC, 1,* pp. 3–6. See E.K. Veniselos, *Greece Before the Peace Congress* (New York, 1919).

47. Nicolson, *Peacemaking,* p. 33.

48. Only two days after reaching Paris Wilson asked Professor Day of The Inquiry to see Veniselos. Bowman diary, Dec. 16, 1918.

Wilson informed Lansing that he was committed to "as full a discussion of all the questions which affect Greece as it is possible for us to undertake." However, the secretary of state did not surrender to the charm of the Greek premier, and mistrusted his diplomacy. W.W. to Lansing, Dec. 20, 1918, Wilson pa., 5B; Robert Lansing, *The Big Four and Others of the Peace Conference,* p. 158; House diary, Oct. 27, 1918; Joseph C. Grew, *Turbulent Era, 1,* 343.

Greek-Bulgar border squabble, suspected that the Greeks were eager to provoke strife with a view to exhibiting the Bulgars at the peace conference as troublemakers. The American chargé at Sofia thought this suspicion perhaps justified.[49]

The kingdom of Rumania had a complicated account to settle with the Allies, who had offered, as an inducement to enter the war on their side, the acquisition of that part of Hungary which was predominantly Rumanian in race and language. When Rumania made peace with the enemy in May of 1918 its claims became questionable. In June representatives of the Rumanians of Hungary took matters into their own hands and at Paris organized a national committee of Rumanians of unredeemed territories.[50] In the United States a Rumanian National League came into existence. Its president was assiduous in keeping his country's cause before American officials in Washington. Rumanians came to regard the United States as their court of last appeal.[51]

On November 5 the State Department issued a declaration of policy that was approved by the president. This expressed deep sympathy with "the spirit of national unity of the Rumanians everywhere" and promised that the United States would not neglect at the proper time to exert its influence that the just political and territorial rights of the Rumanian people might be obtained and made secure from all foreign aggression. For this assurance Queen Marie cabled her "heartfelt thanks" to Wilson, and personally thanked the American minister to Rumania. She added that she anxiously awaited the delivery of food and other supplies to her people by the Red Cross. The president promised "friendly assistance."[52]

The Rumanian army was mobilized and began ridding the country of Germans. On December 14 Bratianu, the pro-Allied leader of the Liberal party who was to represent the nation at the peace conference, returned to the premiership. Already Rumanian troops had entered Bukovina to fight the Ukrainians; and now

---

49. Dispatch from Sofia forwarded by Polk to Ammission, Jan. 3, 1919, Wilson pa., 5B.

50. In September of 1918 the national committee at Paris became the National Council of Rumanian Unity under the presidency of Take Jonescu, who worked in November for an agreement among four Balkan states. Nicolson, *Peacemaking*, p. 136. "Jonescu appealed to me as much as any man I have met here," House wrote in his diary on Nov. 11, 1918. On December 23 House commended him to the president as a man worth talking with—"intelligent, broad minded and unprejudiced." Memorandum, Dec. 23, 1918, Wilson pa., 5B. Jonescu, according to Nicolson, was "rubicund, dapper, and continental," and was bitter about his treatment by Premier Bratianu, and vengeful. *Peacemaking*, pp. 223–25.

51. Mamatey, p. 376.

52. *F.R., PPC, 2*, pp. 386–87, 390, 395.

others went into Transylvania and also the Banat, where Serbians put up strong resistance in behalf of kinsmen who inhabited part of that district. The American minister notified the State Department that Bratianu was trying to force the Allies to give to Rumania not only everything promised "but a great deal more."[53]

But Western statesmen dared not be too peremptory with Bratianu. He was flourishing the magic key that the leaders in eastern Europe found effective in unlocking the hearts of Western officials and the purses of Western governments. Early in January the premier talked much about famine and economic distress and the consequent vulnerability of his people to Bolshevist doctrine.[54] A strong Rumanian state could be of some value as a bulwark against bolshevism and also as a guarantee of free navigation on the Danube; and no one could be sure that if Bratianu resigned another man could form a stable government at Bucharest. The premier felt that he could safely become more assertive, and he protested repeatedly that Rumania was "treated like a poor wretch deserving pity" and not like an ally who had a right to "justice."

The American government did not undertake at this juncture to argue with this aggressive nationalist. It recognized Rumania as a belligerent and joined with the Allies in giving approval to the seating of two delegates at the peace conference, where the problem of Rumania's boundaries would be thrashed out.[55]

American concern for peoples liberated from imperial rule extended beyond the Balkans to the Ottoman Empire. The United States, which had gone only so far as to break diplomatic relations with Turkey, followed a policy that stemmed from sentiment as well as from practical interest. The American Board of Commissioners for Foreign Missions could count on the sympathy of the president because of his friendship with its patron, Cleveland H. Dodge. Wilson's compassion for persecuted Christians in Armenia was particularly deep. In response to Armenian claims for independence he described his interest as "profound" and his sympathy as "really poignant."[56]

---

53. *F.R., PPC, 2*, pp. 394–403. The ministers of the Allies questioned the validity of some of the premier's claims and tried to guard against injustice to other peoples, deciding that French troops should occupy the Dobrudja and protect Bulgars there until the peace conference could adjudicate.

54. Telegram from the Allied Ministers, Jan. 7, 1919, *F.R., PPC, I*, pp. 265–66.

55. Lansing to Polk, Jan. 16, 1919, *F.R., PPC, 2*, pp. 721–22.

56. *F.R., 1919, 2*, pp. 817–24. Wilson received a long, undated memorandum from Dodge and two officers of the American Board, dealing with the situation in Turkey, and especially in Armenia. Doc. in Wilson pa., 5A, microfilm pp. 1426–33.

Even before the United States entered the war the president and House had agreed that the Ottoman Empire should cease to exist.[57] The great Allied Powers had made secret agreements early in the war that provided for a division of Turkish territories among them.[58] Realizing that it could expect little mercy the Ottoman government, when ready to request an armistice, asked Wilson to take upon himself the task of the reestablishment of peace on the basis of his proclaimed principles; and at the end of October an intimation reached Washington that the Turkish government was very desirous of renewing diplomatic relations with the United States.[59] A month later the State Department responded not by reopening its embassy at Constantinople but by sending a commissioner to observe conditions and report. Americans were the object of trust and good will.[60] A Wilson League, which an American attaché reported to be capable of forming a strong political party, took shape with the support of a dozen of the city's newspapers. It proposed to invite the United States to send advisers and to administer the empire for fifteen to twenty-five years under eight conditions. An international guarantee of neutrality was suggested.[61]

The Allies, whose warships were anchored off Constantinople and who on December 8 set up a military control in that city, consulted the American government regarding the execution of the provisions of their armistice with Turkey. Clemenceau and Balfour expressed willingness, at the London Conference of December 3, that the United States should have a mandate to govern Constantinople in the unlikely event that the American government would consent. The United States stationed a naval vessel at Constantinople at the suggestion of the American minister at Athens, who had been receiving innumerable Greek petitions for the security of their countrymen at Smyrna. In a report of December 4 he prophesied: "For some years we shall have the worst passions let loose in Asia Minor

57. House diary, Jan. 3, 1917.
58. See Laurence Evans, *U.S. Policy and the Partition of Turkey*, pp. 56–57, 109–13.
59. U.S. Chargé in the Netherlands Bliss to Sec. State, Oct. 29, 1918. *F.R., 1918, I, 1,* p. 416. See above, p. 20 and note.
60. *F.R., 1919, 2,* p. 810. Later, on May 3, 1919, the State Department ordered Ravndal to Constantinople to replace Commissioner Heck and to open a consulate general, but not to resume diplomatic relations. Ibid., 811–12. Heck reported that the financial situation was becoming more and more critical, and the Turks found hope only in Wilson's principles. Heck to American Embassy, Paris, Jan. 4, 1919, *F.R., PPC, 2,* pp. 280–82; U.S. Consul, Salonika, to State Dept., Dec. 15, 1918, N.A., R.G. 59, 763.72119/3007.
61. Brief no. 77, doc. 867.00/6, "Turkish Wilsonian League," Bowman pa., file 1, drawer 3, "unclassified" folder.

unless we settle [the] question with a single eye to [the] resident population." Moslem fanatics were sullen, resenting the joy with which Christians celebrated the end of the war, and were contemplating violent reprisals.[62]

The State Department, receiving appeals from Allied governments for American action in behalf of their particular interests, refrained from committing the United States on the ground that it was not a party to the Armistice of Mudros. American diplomats were able to dodge many vexing problems in this way. But Greece and the great powers entertained ambitions that challenged the president's principles and that the American commissioners would have to deal with one day in the peacemaking. Moreover, the concern of the Navy Department for an "open door" to the oil deposits of the Middle East gave the United States Government a particular interest in the politics of the region.[63] This practical consideration received little attention in the 220 reports of The Inquiry that pertained to the area. Indeed, the studies were not well directed to the questions that would be faced in the peacemaking. As in the case of the Balkans the participating scholars were not adequately trained and qualified. "Missionaries, lawyers, and ancient historians took up the cudgels"[64] and produced papers that were often not relevant.[65] The Cobb-Lippmann commentary on Point Twelve suggested that Constantinople and the Straits should come under the control of a league of nations, and Wilson conceived that a mandate might be given to a small power.[66]

The concern of the United States for the peace and welfare of the nascent peoples of fallen empires, with whom millions of Americans had ties of kinship and whose political independence Wilson had encouraged, created a desire on the part of the peace commission at Paris for reliable intelligence. In order to deal with requests that came from pleaders for food and arms and for credits for their purchase, there was a sudden and unprecedented need for precise information about political and economic conditions. American dip-

---

62. *F.R., PPC, 2*, pp. 275–77.
63. Gelfand, pp. 250–52.
64. Ibid., p. 227.
65. Ibid., pp. 240–50. A notable exception was a paper by William L. Westermann entitled "Report on Just and Practical Boundaries for the Turkish Empire." George Louis Beer had suggested a British mandate for Mesopotamia and at the request of the State Department Captain Alfred L.P. Dennis had made definite recommendations on "the Syrian Question." Ibid., pp. 233–34, 250–51.
66. Lloyd George, *The Truth about the Peace Treaties*, p. 189.

lomatic posts in enemy territory had ceased to function. A central source of information was lacking.[67]

Before the armistices Colonel House had cabled to Wilson:

> We are getting a mass of misinformation respecting conditions in Austria, Bohemia, and the Ukraine. . . . We have no American source of information. The reports received . . . are often colored by the self-interest of the persons who furnish them. I regard it as exceedingly important that we send at once to those countries agents who will be in a position to furnish us with accurate and unbiased information respecting conditions.

House proposed that these observers take with them a staff that included military and naval officers who would be a part of a political intelligence section of the peace mission. A man would be sent to each of several key cities, with a small staff and courier service. They would not be accredited to the governments of the various countries, but the governments would be asked to facilitate their work. Their reports would clear through a central office to be set up at some point in the Balkans, and then through the political intelligence section of the American Commission at Paris. The whole operation was to be coordinated with American agencies for relief work. These proposals were made to the president in a cable of November 12.[68]

Secretary Lansing asked House on the fifteenth to have Military Intelligence arrange to send secret agents into Poland, Bohemia, the Ukraine, Austria, Hungary, and even Russia, and also through Italy into Yugoslavia and from Rumania into Bulgaria and Turkey.[69] House consulted Hugh Gibson, representing Herbert Hoover, as well as General Nolan, chief of Military Intelligence in Europe; and a plan was drafted on which all could agree.[70] It provided for a choice of "trained men of known ability," from the diplomatic service and the army, to be accredited as members of an American

---

67. Intelligence had been collected during the war by the Committee on Public Information, the War Trade Board, and The Inquiry; and in 1916 a new bureau of secret information had developed in the State Department and the legations at Berne, Copenhagen, and Stockholm became the main channels through which intelligence came from the enemy countries. Professor Shotwell thought the British secret service "far ahead" of American intelligence. "They knew the inside of Europe and the inside of other countries much better than Americans did." Shotwell record in OHRO, Low Library, Columbia University, p. 95.

68. House diary, Nov. 20, 21; *I.P., 4*, 232–33; *F.R., PPC, 1,* 194–96; Grew, 1, 355–56; Auchincloss diary, Nov. 14, 1918, Y.H.C.

69. Dispatch in Auchincloss diary, Nov. 16, 1918.

70. Auchincloss diary, Nov. 20, 21, 1918. House explained his plan to Lansing in a cable of Nov. 21, 1918, Wilson pa., 5C.

relief organization. Thus it was hoped to allay Allied suspicions of political and commercial implications.

Meanwhile the State Department instructed its diplomatic missions abroad to provide the American Commission to Negotiate Peace with copies of their dispatches; and a liaison officer of the commission undertook to keep in touch with all important political and diplomatic offices at Paris.[71] Arrangements were made for communications with whatever special missions might be sent out, for the preparation of daily summaries on the basis of intelligence received, and for evaluations by specialists.[72]

It was some time, however, before a formula was found under which special agents could operate without too great risk of political complications. At the end of December Secretary Lansing proposed that the men should function as representatives of the American commission, without diplomatic status. When he suggested that the attached army officers should wear civilian clothes General Bliss warned that they might be treated as spies; but the commissioners decided that this danger could be met by obtaining permission through military channels. They agreed to put the question of the status of the agents before the president, and they prepared a public statement identifying the men as "observers" and not propagandists.[73] Missions went into Germany and Austria without presidential direction but using funds under his control, and without precise understandings with the foreign offices of the Allies.

With respect to Austria-Hungary, House concurred with the French Foreign Ministry in feeling that the establishment of an Allied commission at Vienna to supervise the carrying out of the armistice terms would be unnecessary and unwise. Such a commission was proposed by the Italian Supreme Command and suggested to the State Department by the Italian chargé at Washington. However, House feared that a body of this sort could not function without armed detachments that would "create military and political complications."[74]

Although House had allowed an American regiment to remain and support Italian designs east of the Adriatic,[75] the American gov-

---

71. *F.R., PPC, 1*, pp. 202, 206–7.

72. Ibid., p. 208. A confidential intelligence bulletin, prepared under the direction of William C. Bullitt, was soon discontinued because it was found preferable to convey intelligence to the peace commissioners by word of mouth. Ibid., p. 210.

73. Lansing to Acting Sec. of State, Dec. 30, 1918, N.A., R.G. 256, 184.01/3A and 4–6; Minutes of the ACTNP, Dec. 24, 30, 1918, Grew pa., Houghton Library, Harvard University; Grew, *1*, pp. 369–70.

74. Dispatches in *F.R., PPC, 1919, 2*, pp. 198–200.

75. See above, pp. 164–65.

ernment resisted several pleas for the use of its armed forces in southeastern Europe. The consul at Sofia, reporting German looting and sporadic fighting between factions of Bulgars, begged that troops be sent: "They will be royally welcomed by the people—and their coming will mean that American influence in the Balkans will be permanent."[76] He also requested "a large Red Cross contingent . . . with ample supplies" to alleviate widespread suffering. But the officials at Washington were not moved to rush to the assistance of Germany's quondam ally. Nor did they accede to a request from the new government at Vienna that a company of United States troops go to Klagenfurt and another to Villech, which Yugoslav armed forces were said to intend to occupy.[77] They also acted negatively upon a French request for two or three companies of American engineers to repair the railway from Western Europe to Constantinople.[78] The most persistent opponents of military involvement abroad were the high officials of the War Department. Secretary Baker perceived that the United States, which had responded ebulliently to the German challenge to battle, would not willingly maintain troops overseas for purposes ill defined.[79]

The establishment of intelligence units without close supervision, no less than the dispatch of troops or the distribution of relief without rigid controls, could be a hazard to the foreign relations of the United States. The danger was highlighted by incidents in Carinthia and Teschen that embarrassed the peace commissioners at Paris. From a headquarters in the old American consulate at Vienna, Archibald Cary Coolidge, a distinguished historian who had once served in the embassy at Vienna, sent observers into Central Europe and the Balkans and forwarded their reports to Paris. Acting on his own initiative in an effort to prevent bloodshed, he sent American conciliators into the Klagenfurt basin to try to settle a violent boundary quarrel between German Austrians and Slovenes. However, he was reminded by the American plenipotentiaries at Paris that this matter was "entirely outside the competence of any single person or of the American Commission." Having made no commitment, he was able to withdraw his men from the controversy.[80]

76. Murphy (Sofia) to Sec. State, *F.R., 1918, I, 1,* p. 479. This dispatch called attention to a quotation from Will S. Monroe's *Bulgaria and Her People* (Boston, 1914); "Bulgaria is the only country in Europe in which the United States has played an important role in the development of a state."

77. Memorandum, Swedish Legation to State Department, Dec. 7, forwarding message from German-Austrian government, State Dept. to House mission, Dec. 10, 1918, N.A., R.G. 59, 163.72/12517 and 12560.

78. Memorandum of Jan. 17, 1919, sent through House to Wilson, Wilson, pa., 5B.

79. N.D. Baker to W.W., Nov. 23, 1918, Wilson pa., 2.

80. H.J. Coolidge and Robert H. Lord, *Archibald Cary Coolidge,* pp. 204–7.

The American commissioners found it necessary also to issue a warning that officers of the United States Army who were at Teschen and who reported to Coolidge must not take part in the dissemination of propaganda by George Creel of the Committee on Public Information. On January 30 the commissioners considered the advisability of recalling an agent who acted indiscreetly at Teschen during a Czech-Pole confrontation.[81] The conduct of some of the American officers and newsmen who visited Vienna moved one of Coolidge's men to write: "We have our own peculiar Prussians."[82]

Twenty-four American intelligence missions went out from Paris. Nine of them were sponsored jointly with the Allies: one, to Montenegro, with the British government. The proliferation of American "observers" seemed to be limited only by funds available for their expenses.[83] The extent of the network of intelligence that was in existence early in January is revealed by a report of an army officer who made a trip through east Central Europe at that time and found that courier service to Paris was required by (1) representatives of the political intelligence section of the American commission, (2) representatives of the Inter-Allied Economic Commission and such organizations as they might set up with respect of the United States Food Administration, (3) naval representatives at Fiume, Constantinople, and other points, (4) liaison officers with the Czechoslovak army and any who might be sent to the Polish and Yugoslav forces, and (5) American troops who were or might be stationed in Central Europe.

The missions were given clearance by the various governments, and were received as deputations from the all-powerful President Wilson. They were sought out by officials of new governments and emigrés from the old. Their work inevitably became quasi-diplomatic as well as quasi-military. They exerted influence on the ruling authorities, and if they were not practitioners of "secret diplomacy," they at least constituted channels through which diplomacy could function secretly.[84] They supplied much current information that influenced American policy at the peace conference.[85]

"Those American officials," Arno J. Mayer has observed, "did not

---

81. Minutes of the ACTNP, Grew papers, Houghton Library, Harvard University.

82. W.G. Davis to Allen W. Dulles, Feb. 12, 1919, Davis pa., Y.H.C.

83. Grew to Coolidge, Feb. 24, 1919, N.A., R.G. 256, 184.011/90. See *F.R., PPC, 12.* The missions are listed and briefly described in N.A., R.G. 256, 184.01/39.

84. Of the American intelligence agents Arno J. Mayer has written: "Since they requested advance clearance, their hosts considered them as informal diplomatic missions. . . . National and local authorities were very sensitive to intimations and suggestions emanating directly or indirectly from the American missions." *Politics and Diplomacy of Peacemaking,* p. 370.

85. Mezes, memo. of Jan. 21, 1919, Bliss pa., box 69, "Lansing" folder, L.C.

have concise and informed notions of bolshevism, but on the contrary, quite vague and confused ones. For almost all of them bolshevism was a dictatorial form of government thriving on political rivalries, famine, economic chaos, and national disillusionment, and almost all of them believed in a combination of economic aid, Wilsonian peace, and democratic rule as the only effective prophylaxis."[86]

---

86. Mayer, *Politics and Diplomacy of Peacemaking,* p. 370.

☆XII☆

Russia: Friend or Foe?

No American mission was sent from Paris to the central regions of Russia. There a new and strange regime, emerging from an ordeal of war and revolution, was without diplomatic relations with Western governments.

Formal ties between the United States and Russia, continuous for a hundred years, had ceased after the Bolshevik revolution of November 1917. Following the first upheaval of March 1917 the United States had recognized Kerensky's provisional government. Its ambassador, Boris A. Bakhmeteff, remained at Washington. There he continued to give advice on Russian affairs and to attempt to honor arrangements made in the name of his defunct government. He encouraged American hopes that another constitutional government might come out of the chaos that prevailed.

Point Six presented the president's policy for dealing with Russia:[1]

> The evacuation of all Russian territory and such a settlement of all questions affecting Russia as will secure the best and freest cooperation of the other nations of the world in obtaining for her an unhampered and unembarrassed opportunity for the independent determination of her own political development and national policy. . . . The treatment accorded Russia by her sister nations in the months to come will be the acid test of their good will, of their comprehension of her needs as distinguished from their own interests, and of their intelligent and unselfish sympathy.

Wilson said in May of 1918 that he would "stand by Russia," but he thought the Bolsheviks who had seized power at Moscow not yet

---

1. See Appendix, p. 277. George F. Kennan has cited (*in Russia Leaves the War*, pp. 255–57) respects in which Wilson's eloquent passage on Russia was "inaccurate and unrealistic."

worthy of recognition as the rulers of the nation. He had predicted, in a talk with Colonel House in 1915, that eventually there might be just two great nations in the world, the United States and Russia;[2] and it was his hope that they would be friends.

The Allies, resentful because Russia had forsaken the common crusade against Germany, sent armed forces to Murmansk in June of 1918 to protect war materiel that had been shipped there and to encourage resistance to the German armies that then occupied a large area. Six months earlier the British and French governments had agreed secretly to devise economic and military methods to stimulate resistance to Germany in certain parts of Russia. France undertook responsibility for Bessarabia, the Crimea, and the Ukraine, and Great Britain for Armenia, the Caucasus, Georgia, and Kurdistan. The proclamation of Point Six by Wilson did not check the operations of the Allies in these regions. Gradually their purpose became the overthrow of the Soviet regime.[3]

In July House wrote to urge Wilson that "something must be done immediately about Russia"; otherwise it would become the prey of Germany.[4] After adroit persuasion by Wiseman, the receipt of a letter from Marshal Foch, and pressure from a special French delegation, Wilson was brought to consider a qualified participation.[5] In cooperating with the Allies on military grounds he could avoid a direct confrontation with either of the political pressures that were strong in the United States, for and against tolerance toward the Soviet regime. The president feared that any intervention would be controlled by reactionaries and would intefere with the right of the Russian people to choose their own form of government. He saw danger that the United States might appear in the eyes of the Russians as an ally in aggression. But he yielded so far as to send American armed forces to North Russia and to Siberia. A small unit of marines, followed in September by three battalions, went to Archangel, and about eight thousand troops to Vladivostok. At the same time he repeated the pledge he had given in his Point Six against any interference with Russia's sovereignty or internal affairs.

In consenting to the dispatch of American soldiers to Siberia the

---

2. House diary, August 30, 1914, Y.H.C. House suggested that there would be a third, China.

3. Louis Fischer, *The Soviets in World Affairs*, (New York, 1930), 2 vols., 2, 836; Richard H. Ullman, *Britain and the Russian Civil War*, p. 9; A. Kerensky, *Russia and History's Turning Point* (New York, 1965), pp. 503–4, 507; G.F. Kennan, *Russia and the West*, pp. 46–47. See G.R.I. Reading, *Rufus Isaacs, 1st Marquess of Reading*, 2, 118–20.

4. House to W.W., July 21, 1918, Wilson, pa., 2, L.C.

5. See Wilton B. Fowler, *British-American Relations, 1917–1918*, p. 172ff.

president cited three purposes: to safeguard Czech prisoners-of-war who were fighting their way eastward out of Russia; to protect American engineers who, by arrangement with the defunct provisional government, were operating the trans-Siberian railway; and to guard military supplies. The president did not object to Japanese participation in the Siberian venture provided it was kept within reasonable bounds and did not result in exploitation.[6]

The president was more interested in economic assistance than in military expeditions. He approved plans for aid under the direction of the War Trade Board. A Russian Bureau was set up and its representatives at Vladivostok made use of existing Russian cooperative organizations.[7] In an aide-mémoire addressed to the Allies on October 10 the State Department protested that the United States desired only to "relieve the immediate economic necessities of the Russian people," and intended "to permit its merchants to trade with Russia only under such direction on its part as would insure to the Russian people absolute fair dealing and complete protection against exploitation and profiteering."[8]

Despite all precautions, however, there ensued friction with the Allied governments and resentment in Russia. The economic measures taken by the United States could easily be interpreted as serv-

---

6. Wilson was informed by House that Ambassador Ishii thought it intolerable that Japanese be excluded from Siberia while other Asiatics were admitted. "Unless Japan [is] treated with more consideration," House wrote to Wilson on July 6, "she would have to be reckoned with—and rightly so."

Wilson's willingness to permit Japan to undertake operations in Siberia reflected the counsel both of The Inquiry and of naval advisers, as well as American concern for Japanese observance of an "open door" policy in China. Cf. Levin, *Woodrow Wilson and World Politics*, pp. 112–19. The experts of The Inquiry, considering Siberia to be a field where Japanese expansion would be less objectionable than in China and the Pacific isles, had suggested that Russia be asked to sell to Japan certain eastern provinces and also its half of the island of Sakhalin. Lawrence E. Gelfand, *The Inquiry*, pp. 214–15, 268–70. Secretary Lansing thought that Manchuria and Mongolia were a proper field for the expansion to which Japan was being driven by overpopulation. "Conversation with Sec. Lansing, Dec. 6, 1918," Bowman pa., file 1, drawer 1, "Inquiry" folder, Eisenhower Library, Johns Hopkins University. A paper prepared by the General Board of the Navy advised that the present opportunity be taken the better to secure America's strategic position in the Pacific, and that it was "of vital interest to the United States to turn Japan towards the continent of Asia." Doc. enclosed with letter, J. Daniels to W.W., Dec. 3. In acknowledging this report Wilson wrote: "I am mighty glad to get it." W.W. to Daniels, Dec. 7, 1918, Wilson pa., 5B, L.C.

7. Wilson gave authority in this matter to Vance McCormick, chairman of the War Trade Board. Polk to W.W., Sept. 9, Y.H.C.; B. Long's diary, Sept. 8, Oct. 3 L.C.; House diary, Sept. 19, 24, 1918. See Fowler, p. 194, n. 86. The Russian Bureau was never very active and in June 1919 it was dissolved. John M. Thompson, *Russia, Bolshevism, and the Versailles Peace*, p. 36.

8. *F. R., 1918, Russia, 3*, pp. 147–50.

ing the expansion of the nation's trade. Cooperation became very difficult. Lloyd George thought the smallness of the American military contribution "really preposterous."[9] The Foreign Office endeavored through Wiseman and House to arrive at a common policy. Lord Reading explained, in a letter of September 19 to Wiseman, that the British government had no desire to control the government of the Russian people and was doing the utmost to act in accordance with President Wilson's views. He went on: "The difficulty we are in is that in both East and West in Russia we must be to some extent in the hands of the military authority on the spot but we are unfailing in our efforts to preserve civilian control."[10] On October 20 Ambassador Francis reported that he had learned that a large Russo-British corporation was being organized to trade with northern Russia. Russian authorities at Archangel objected that this would result in "exploitation," and so did Francis.[11]

Contrary to orders from Washington that all military efforts in northern Russia be given up except those necessary to guard the ports, American troops were assigned a part in movements toward union with anti-Bolshevik forces in Siberia.[12] When this became known at Washington and it was reported that the soldiers were suffering casualties and the British commander was dealing tactlessly with the local government in Archangel, the president protested vigorously.[13] The Allied governments were notified that Wilson had no interest in creating an eastern front against the Bolsheviks, that no more American troops would be sent to north Russia, and that all military effort there would be given up except that essential to the security of the occupied ports.[14]

At the same time American relations with Japan were disturbed by the joint intervention in Siberia. The United States government was shocked when it learned that Japan, which had agreed to send no more soldiers than were needed to protect the Czech legions, actu-

9. Richard H. Ullman, *Intervention and the War*, pp. 215–27.

10. Wiseman-Reading corres., Wiseman pa., Y.H.C.

11. David Francis to Sec. State., Oct. 20, 1918, *F.R. 1918, Russia, 2*, 560–61; Poole to Sec. State, ibid., 567.

12. Francis to Sec. State, Oct. 25, 1918, *F.R., 1918, Russia, 2*, 503.

13. D. Francis, *Russia from the American Embassy* (New York, 1922), pp. 266–67; B. Long to the writer, April 1, 1953; British embassy (Washington) to Foreign Office, Sept. 9, 1918, Wiseman pa., "Russia" folder; Sec. State to Page (London), Sept. 12, 1918, *F.R., 1918, Russia, 2*, pp. 533–34 and see ibid., pp. 551, 563; Lansing desk diary, Sept. 9, 12, 1918, L.C. See E.M. Halliday, *The Ignorant Armies* (New York, 1960), pp. 46–48, and Kennan, *Russia and the West*, pp. 77–78.

14. Telegrams, Sec. State to ambassadors to Allies, Sept. 26, *F.R., 1918, Russia, 2*, pp. 394–95, 546; cable Wiseman to Reading, Sept. 21, 1918, Wiseman pa. See Fowler, pp. 193–95; Betty M. Unterberger, *America's Siberian Expedition*, pp. 100–101; and Ullman, *Intervention*, pp. 243–45, 251.

ally dispatched many more men than were at first proposed. As Wilson had feared, the presence of American military units might be taken to give sanction to what appeared to be a Japanese occupation. General Graves, the American commander in Siberia, adhered so faithfully to his orders prohibiting political interference that he appeared to the Allies to be favoring the forces of disorder and yet became in Soviet mythology a hostile and imperialistic invader.[15] On November 27 Secretary Baker advised the president that the American forces in Siberia should be brought home "by the first boat."[16]

As Wilson had foreseen, the wound to national pride that was inflicted by the penetration of Russian territory against the expressed wishes of the principal de facto government grew deeper and festered. Early in 1918, before making peace at Brest-Litovsk, the Soviet government had supported the Allied project at Murmansk as an anti-German measure,[17] but on August 5 Chicherin, commissar for foreign affairs, protested to American representatives that the occupation of Archangel and the killing of Bolshevik party members without a declaration of war was a breach of the most elementary principles of international usage. Moreover, since a state of war existed de facto, British and French civilians were being arrested and interned and the Soviet government could not be responsible for their lives. It did not desire to break diplomatic relations, according to Chicherin, and it intended to take measures of war only in response to acts perpetrated against it.[18]

The incursions into the territory of Russia had given to the insecure new rulers a rallying cry that they exploited to the limit.[19] After an attempt to assassinate Lenin failed the Cheka perpetrated a series of mass executions. On August 31 a mob stormed the British embassy and in an exchange of fire the naval attaché was shot dead. Hundreds of foreigners were arrested without due cause. Foreign Secretary Balfour, declaring in an election speech that Russia was in a condition of "septic dissolution," [20] announced that unless full rep-

---

15. See George Stewart, *The White Armies of Russia* (New York, 1933), pp. 266–79; Unterberger, p. 125; and John A. White, *The Siberian Intervention,* (Princeton, 1950).
16. Letter in Wilson pa., 5B.
17. Brenda Kurtz Shelton, *President Wilson and the Russian Revolution,* p. 121; John Silverlight, *The Victor's Dilemma* (London, 1970), pp. 26, 32.
18. Memorandum (by Consul DeWitt Poole?), Aug. 5, 1918, N.A., R.G.59, 861.00/3025.
19. "I think it may well be questioned," Kennan has written, "whether bolshevism would ever have prevailed throughout Russia had the Western governments not aided its progress to power by ill-conceived interference." (*Russia and the West,* p. 117). See Kennan, "Soviet Historiography and America's Role in the Intervention," *American Historical Review, 65* (Jan. 1960): 302–22; and Silverlight, p. 2.
20. Kenneth Young, *A.J. Balfour* (London, 1963), p. 405.

aration was made the British government would hold Soviet officials individually responsible and would "make every effort to secure that they shall be treated as outlaws by the governments of all civilized nations." [21] By the end of 1918 none of the major governments had official representation at Moscow.

The surge of terror in Russia, as well as the continuing threat posed to Western society by Bolshevik propaganda,[22] severely tried the hopeful patience with which Wilson had regarded the Soviet regime. Without seeking the advice of the State Department or of the Allied governments he permitted George Creel of the Committee on Public Information to publish, on September 15, a file of Russian documents that the committee's agent in Moscow had discovered and that seemed to impugn the integrity of the Soviet leaders in their dealing with the German government. The dossier, known as the Sisson papers, was thought by the State Department and the British Foreign Office to be largely spurious, an opinion shared by experts of the present day.[23] The accused Russians, resentful of the affront, poured out propaganda at home and abroad that spun a legend of imperialistic exploitation and economic slavery.

In August Wilson acquiesced when the secretary of state classified the Soviet government as a belligerent on the side of the Allies;[24] but after the release of the Sisson papers the president, asked by House whether this act did not in effect amount to a virtual declaration of war upon the Bolshevik government, agreed that it did.[25]

---

21. Ullman, *Intervention,* p. 290.

22. See above, pp. 2, 35.

23. *F.R., Lansing pa., 2,* pp. 384–85; Lansing desk diary, Sept. 13, 14, 20, 1918; Drummond to Willert, Oct. 9, 1918, Willert pa., Y.H.C.; Willert to *The Times,* Sept. 21, Wiseman from Drummond, Oct. 3, Drummond from Wiseman, Oct, 5, Wiseman pa.; Drummond from Wiseman, Oct. 16, 1918, Balfour pa., Vol. 49687, British Museum. Upon the publication of the Sisson papers the State Department ordered its representative in Moscow, Consul DeWitt Poole, to leave immediately and take with him as many Americans as possible. Long diary, Sept. 15, 1918, L.C.

Kennan has written of the Sisson papers: "The essential reality behind the entire controversy is that even if as the documents do not wholly prove but as is wholly possible the Bolsheviks received financial support from official German sources prior to the revolution, there is no evidence that they considered themselves by consequence under any moral or political obligation to the Germans in the period following their own seizure of power or that the Germans had any illusions of this nature. In fact, there is powerful evidence of the contrary." "The Sisson Documents," *Journal of Modern History,* 28:2 (June 1956).

Also, see the records of Consul DeWitt Poole and John W. Davis, OHRO., Butler Library, Columbia University; Kennan, *Russia Leaves the War,* pp. 413–20, 441–54; Edgar Sisson, *One Hundred Red Days* (New Haven, 1931); James R. Mock and Cedric Larson, *Words that Won the War* (Princeton, 1939), p. 314ff.

24. Baker, p. 338.

25. House Diary, Sept. 24, 1918.

The signing of the armistices did not entirely remove the prime motive for Allied action in Russia; the fear of German influence there. Military measures for meeting the menace of pan-Germanism had been discussed in the pre-armistice meetings at Paris. The Supreme War Council had decided that the peace treaties that Germany had dictated to Russia and to Rumania were to be annulled. Moreover the Allies were to have complete control of the Baltic and the Black Sea, as well as free access to the eastern territories evacuated by the Germans in order to convey supplies to the populations "or for the purpose of maintaining order." Marshal Foch, commissioned to draft terms for the eastern front, asked the council whether it would take over territories as the Germans evacuated them, or would abandon them to whatever their fate might be. To this question House, recognizing the possibility that a Bolshevist regime might fill any vacuum that the German armies left, replied that the question was "very delicate." The council, accepting the actual limit of its powers, agreed on a vague formula requiring all German forces in the East to withdraw within the frontiers of 1914. They were to draw back according to no time schedule but as soon as the Allies thought it wise under the prevailing conditions.[26] This inconclusive prescription provided no definite assurance that Germany would not fill vacuums in the Baltic states, and no safeguard against such a combination of German and Russian might as that which later developed at the beginning of World War II.[27]

The best hope for building an enduring political barrier between Germany and Russia seemed to lie in the development of the nascent nations of Eastern Europe. Immediately after the Bolshevik revolution, The Inquiry had advised that the border provinces might develop economic and political stability as independent states.[28] But the United States government, warned by both Ambassador Bakhmeteff and the Soviet government against supporting buffer states, was reluctant to take a position.[29] General Bliss refused

---

26. Procès-verbal, meeting of S.W.C., Nov. 1 at 3:00 P.M., Y.H.C. The German armistice negotiators boasted that they "succeeded in establishing a common ground with the enemy" under article 12, which delayed the evacuation. Arno J. Mayer, *Politics and Diplomacy*, p. 95.

27. "On August 27 [1918] a secret agreement laid the bases of military cooperation between the Germans and the Bolshevik Government." Réné Albrecht-Carrié, *Diplomatic History of Europe* (New York, 1958), p. 359. The text may be found with a dispatch, Sharp to Sec. State, March 7, 1919, N.A., R.G.59, 763.72119/3451.

28. Gelfand, p. 215.

29. On October 3 and November 3 the Soviet commissar for foreign affairs sent messages to Wilson that chided him for helping the Czechs and other counterrevolutionaries and asked why he did not demand freedom for Ireland, Egypt, India, and the Philippines. *F.R., Lansing pa., 2,* 435–37, p. 449ff.

to accede to French suggestions that American forces be used in the Ukraine. The State Department declined to intervene in Estonia, Latvia, and Lithuania, where Soviet armies were advancing, German forces were trying to protect the estates of "Balts" of Teutonic blood, and native factions were attempting to establish independent states under popular rule. Lansing explained to the British government that the United States was restrained from taking any "premature action" by its various declarations of friendship to Russia and the Russian people.[30]

After the November armistice the Soviet leaders lived in constant fear that the power of the victors would be directed immediately and conclusively against them. Unable to control the liberated Russian bear, the Allies had irritated it by ineffective goads. The United States government, participating in intervention side by side with the Allies, though not always in step with them, exposed itself to a share of the vitriol that Soviet spokesmen sprayed at all intruders.

A large body of conservative opinion in the West would have welcomed the fall of the radicals at Moscow. American idealists were disappointed because the constitutional regime that they had encouraged in 1917 had been thwarted by a dictatorship that was more in keeping with Russian tradition. Men who held religion and private property sacred resented violence to both.[31] Many Americans, like their president, sympathized with the Russian people and still hoped for a counterrevolution that would restore constitutional processes. Despairing of any turn toward democracy by any faction at Moscow, Americans cherished a wish that an effective leader might appear among the czarist generals who still commanded large armies.

There was no response from the West when the Soviet govern-

On November 2 Ambassador Bakhmeteff said to Assistant Secretary Phillips at the State Department that it would be a mistake to consider the apparent claims of border states to independence, and pointed out that their claims originated in Germany. Polk and Phillips agreed. Bakhmeteff to Sec. State, Oct. 31, Polk to Ammission, Dec. 13, Phillips to Polk, Nov. 2, 1918, N.A. R.G.59, 763.72119/2442-3. Bakhmeteff expressed to Lansing the fear that Russians would be policed by German troops, and urged that the Germans in Eastern Europe be expelled as soon as possible and replaced quickly by Allied garrisons. Bakhmeteff to Lansing, Nov. 14, Lansing to Bakhmeteff, Nov. 18, Lansing to Embassy, Paris, and House, Nov. 16, 1918, N.A. R.G.59, 763.72119/3089.

30. *F.R., 1918, Russia, 2,* pp. 839–42, 851–52, 856–61; J.W. Davis (London) to Sec. State, Dec. 19, 1918, N.A., R.G.59, 763.72119/3046.

31. Secretary Lansing burned with righteous wrath, setting down bolshevism as "the most hideous and monstrous thing that the human mind has ever conceived," an "orgy of blood and raping and cruelty" that, spreading westward, made the Terror of 1793 in France seem "gentle and colorless" and appealed to the basest passions of "the criminals, the depraved, and the mentally unfit." Private memoranda, Oct. 26, 1918, L.C. microfilm.

ment, temporarily adopting a conciliatory tone, sent word to the State Department early in November that it would negotiate with the United States and the Allies on a liquidation of hostilities. To various overtures that might have led to a settlement of the issue of Russian debts[32] and might have brought Russia to the peace table, the Western governments made no reply. "My mind is not clear as to what is the proper immediate course in Russia" Wilson wrote to a friend[33] on November 27. "There are many more elements at work there than I conjecture you are aware of, and it is harder to get out than it was to go in."

Wilson consulted Lansing at this time and the secretary of state replied that it was clear to him, perplexed as he was by the many complications, that if the associated governments at Paris undertook to settle Russia's affairs and judge the interests of its people, their responsibility would be heavy.

Lansing proposed elements of a definite policy. Hoping to prevent confusion at the peace conference, he made three suggestions: first, that they propose to the Associated Powers that Russia's interests be safeguarded and her problems considered as parts of a whole and not as separate difficulties resulting from what might prove, for the most part, temporary disintegration; second, that the peacemakers state that they would admit, as signatories to the treaty, "only delegates from a constitutional assembly or from some general government of Russia based on democratic principles," though they could welcome the appearance of "representatives from existing elements of order in Russia" and hear them on "questions relating to their affairs"; and third, that they exclude only representatives of elements that were "definitely undemocratic and unrepresentative of the majority will." He thought it vital to offer economic aid wherever it was possible "to come in contact with elements desiring to maintain democratic principles." He wrote: "while we must set our faces sternly against anarchy and the class tyranny and terror of Bolshevism, we must at the same time cut to the root of the sore and relieve the misery and exhaustion which form such a fertile soil for its rapid growth." [34]

---

32. Dispatches in *F.R., 1919, Russia, 1,* pp. 3, 8–9. At the end of 1918 credits of the United States government to the Russian provisional government amounted to $325,000,000 and cash advances to about $188,000,000. Crosby to W.W., Dec. 31, 1918, Wilson pa., 5B. Lloyd George told the Imperial War Cabinet on December 23 that the Soviet government was willing to recognize the debts of preceding Russian governments. I.W.C. Minutes.

33. Grenville S. MacFarland, Wilson pa., 3.

34. W.W. to Lansing, Nov. 20, Lansing to W.W., Nov. 26, 1918, *F.R. 1918, Russia, 2,* pp. 268–71.

In proposing that Russia must have a constitutional government in order to come into the world family of nations, the secretary of state showed himself a naïve doctrinaire. The president was less unrealistic. Recognizing Lansing's solution as the ideal one, from the American point of view, he was not at all sure that it was possible in Russia. He could not forget that for centuries the Russian people had known no other national government than one of despotic authority. To one of his colleagues[35] at Princeton he had explained that Russian peasants were like birds in a cage, unconscious that they were unfree because they had never known freedom. Now they had peace and a promise of land; and it seemed most unlikely that they would show the same ardor for political representation that had animated the American and French revolutions.

During the last months of 1918 Wilson continued to temporize. Marxist philosophy was distasteful to him. He was out of sympathy with the concept of government that was based on an economic theory and managed by leaders who did not get the explicit consent of the governed. "I believe in letting them work out their own salvation," he said to Wiseman on October 16, "even though they wallow in anarchy for a while . . . a lot of impossible folk, fighting among themselves. You cannot do business with them, so you shut them all up in a room and lock the door and tell them that when they have settled matters among themselves you will unlock the door and do business." He thought it impossible to eradicate German influence in Russia and wished to bring the whole question, which was giving him great anxiety, to the peace table.[36] He assured the president of the provisional government in north Russia that in any negotiations with Germany the interests of Russia would be carefully safeguarded.[37] He continued to entertain the possibility of giving support to one of what he called "the nuclei of self-governing authority" that had appeared in Siberia.[38]

At the end of 1918 Wilson saw nothing that he could do but await the appearance of responsible government in Russia itself and in the border states, use the opportunity that the peace conference would

---

35. Professor Edward Elliott, Elliott pa., Princeton University Library; Arthur Walworth, *Woodrow Wilson*, 2, p. 93.

36. Fowler, p. 288. Wilson gave evidence of his anxiety about Russia when, during a visit to the quarters of The Inquiry in New York on October 12, he showed an intense interest in Professor Young's studies of the resources and ethnography of Soviet Russia. Bowman to Miss Wrigley, Oct. 9, 1939, Bowman pa., file 1, drawer 1.

37. President to State Dept., Oct. 21, 1918, N.A., R.G. 59, 763.72119/2291.

38. On April 18, 1918 Wilson had asked Lansing for "all we know about these several nuclei," writing: "It would afford me a great deal of satisfaction to get behind the most representative of them if it can indeed draw leadership and control to itself," *F.R., Lansing pa., 2,* p. 360.

give to discuss the matter with leaders of Western Europe,[39] and try to save Russia from exploitation. When he visited London in December he did not take time to receive Ambassador Francis, who in a report to Lansing painted a black picture and recommended drastic action.[40] Nor did he respond to voices in the United States that advocated recognition and guidance by the American government of the new de facto regime at Moscow.[41]

Both in Western Europe and in the United States there was strong pressure from representatives of Russian factions who wanted to speak for their nation at the peace conference. "White" émigrés converged on Paris, seeking a chance to plead their country's cause as well as an opportunity to get Western sympathy for any action that might unseat the "Red" Bolsheviks. An organization formed at New York by Russians of all shades of moderate opinion—the Interparty League for the Restoration of Free Russia—asked the president to recognize the Whites as the first step in establishing an orderly free government that could claim representation at Paris. At Washington, Ambassador Bakhmeteff asserted his country's right to "a full and equal participation" in the settling of questions that concerned it.[42] In the anomalous position of an envoy accredited by a government no longer in existence, Bakhmeteff, with the cooperation of the American government, had preserved embassy funds against the demands of American creditors and had used them to finance shipments of arms to White enemies of the Bolsheviks. Persisting in the hope that the Soviet regime would fall, he put faith in Kolchak when in November this ex-admiral of the Tsar's navy overthrew an all-Russian directory at Omsk that included members of the provisional government. Bakhmeteff sought a loan for Kolchak, in whom Lansing and other Americans saw a possibility of strong liberal leadership for Russia.[43]

39. Polk to Lansing, Jan. 6, 1919, *F.R., 1919, Russia,* p. 3; J.W. Davis diary, Dec. 1918, p. 6, Y.H.C.

40. Francis to W.W., W.W. to Francis, Dec. 27, 1918, Wilson pa., 5B.

To give the Russian people a chance to choose a government without domination by either Bolsheviks or Germans, Francis advocated that the Western powers send a force to occupy the embassies at Petrograd and supply relief for starving people. Francis to Lansing, Jan. 1, 1919, Lansing pa., box 40, L.C. It was not until Wilson's return voyage on the *George Washington* in February that he conferred with Francis and rejected his proposal to send 50,000 American volunteers to Russia. Francis, p. 310.

41. Christopher Lash, *The American Liberals and the Russian Revolution* (New York, 1962), pp. 77–96.

42. *F.R., PPC, I,* pp. 267–68. Bakhmeteff suggested that the Omsk and Archangel governments might authorize him and colleagues at Paris to choose Russian peace delegates. Polk diary, Nov. 20, 1918, Y.H.C.

43. R.J. Maddox, "Woodrow Wilson, the Russian Embassy and Siberian Intervention," *Pacific Historical Review* (Nov. 1967), p. 437ff.

Most of the ministers of the Allies, meeting at London on December 3, were of the opinion that Russia could not be officially represented at Paris.[44] However, on the same day Basil Miles, the chief of the Far Eastern Division of the State Department, suggested to Secretary Lansing that all factions should be heard, and he warned that unless the question of representation was solved the decisions of the peace conference were likely to be repudiated by future governments of Russia.

When Bakhmeteff set off from Washington for Paris on December 5 there was no assurance that Russians could take part in the peacemaking. He had urged the United States government to insist upon the treatment of Russia as an entity that might later be subjected to a test of self-determination.[45] He petitioned the secretary of state for a "proper representation," explaining that Russian émigrés at Paris were engaged in a preliminary study of the questions of peace and that to exclude them from the conference would be to provoke ill-will.[46] Bakhmeteff became spokesman for an organization of ambassadors and other distinguished officials of pre-Soviet regimes.[47] In their behalf he sought recognition of the reactionary government at Omsk and, pending that, participation in the peace conference by Russians of moderate views.

At Paris, particularly among the French officials, there persisted a general belief in military measures as a cure for bolshevism.[48] The fear of anarchy in Eastern Europe was accompanied by a dread of German domination in that region. It was foreseen that at the end of a generation Germany might hurl armies toward the East and protect itself there so that it could then turn upon the Western Powers.

44. At this conference Clemenceau, Lloyd George, and Balfour spoke bitterly of the Russian defection in the war. Balfour observed that a state of war with the Soviet government existed; Clemenceau said "let them cook in their own juice"; but Lloyd George remarked that the new regime had endured for a year and could last much longer. French procès-verbal, Dec. 3, 11:15 A.M., F.C.

45. Phillips to Polk, Nov. 2, 1918, N.A., R.G. 763.72119/2442–3.

46. Aide-mémoire sent by Bakhmeteff to Sec. State, Nov. 20, 1918, Jan. 10, 1919, *F.R., PPC, 1*, pp. 267–68.

47. For a discussion of the Russian Political Conference, composed of émigrés at Paris and financed by Russian funds held in the United States Treasury, and of British and French policy with respect of Russian representation at the Peace conference, see J.M. Thompson, pp. 66–81. Also see Mayer, *Politics and Diplomacy*, pp. 180–2.

Stephen Bonsal, who assisted the American commissioners in making contact with the Russian spokesmen, distrusted all except Prince Lvov. Bonsal wrote in his diary on April 20, 1919: "They came [to the Crillon] from the beginning, in droves (now they are fighting among themselves and come singly)." *Suitors and Suppliants*, p. 27.

48. "Almost everyone here believes in military resistance to down the Bolsheviks," General Bliss wrote in his diary on Dec. 29. Bliss pa., L.C.

As a precaution it seemed necessary to French officers to strengthen the White Russians and, as a condition of economic aid, to require that they stand resolutely against Bolshevik success.[49]

At the same time the officials of the Soviet government were asking to be let alone. To this plea the Americans were not insensitive.[50] Wilson made it clear to Lloyd George at London late in December that he wished to withdraw American forces from north Russia,[51] House elicited from both Clemenceau and Orlando admissions that effective military intervention was impossible,[52] and the War Department continued to question its wisdom.

Pressed by public opinion that he described as "extremely restive,"[53] Polk notified the American Commission at Paris that the armed units would be withdrawn from Siberia at the earliest moment possible unless the president gave directions to the contrary. However, when Wilson received this message he immediately gave instructions to refrain from recalling the troops until he was consulted further. He suggested that Polk use regular diplomatic channels to present urgent questions to the governments concerned. He thought it best to make no change in the status quo, since the matter was one of the first to be considered at the peace conference.[54]

Polk was beset at Washington by questions from the Congress, which was sensitive both to public denunciation of the Bolsheviks

---

49. Statement by Capt. Henri Lorin, head of the Bureau of Economic Studies of the Presidency of the French Council, in *La Democratie Nouvelle,* Dec. 25, 1918.

50. "The only demand that Soviet Russia has put to the Allies," Litvinov wrote on January 10, 1919, "is that they should discontinue all direct or indirect military operations against Soviet Russia, all direct or indirect material assistance to Russian or other forces operating against the Soviet government, and also every kind of economic warfare and boycott." C. K. Cumming and Walter W. Pettit (eds.), *Russian-American Relations; March, 1917–March, 1920; Documents and Papers* (New York, 1920), p. 276.

51. Hankey observed that Wilson was "very much opposed to armed intervention." *The Supreme Control,* p. 16.

52. House diary, Jan. 8, 1919. Actually House recorded a belief on his part that intervention by a small force well equipped with artillery and tanks could succeed. But no government felt able to supply the necessary resources. "There is not a western country that could safely send troops into Russia without creating labor troubles at home," House wrote.

53. Polk cabled to Lansing on January 2: "The reports we receive . . . show the growing menace of bolshevism outside of Russia. I believe no one can take the lead so well as the President in defining the attitude of the Associated Governments on this question and would be glad to know what steps, if any, in that direction have been taken." *F.R., 1919, Russia,* p. 3. Lansing explained that he was without a policy with respect of Russia and was handicapped by the absence of the president, who was touring Italy. Lansing to Polk, Jan. 2, 1919, Y.H.C.

54. Polk to Ammission, Jan. 7, Wilson pa., 5B; Minutes of the ACTNP, Jan. 9, 11; Lansing to Polk, Jan. 10, 1919, Y.H.C. In proposing withdrawal from Siberia, Polk warned that some understanding must be reached with the Soviet government to protect those Russians who collaborated with the Americans. Dispatch, Polk to Lansing, Jan. 11, 1919, Wilson pa., 5B.

and to criticism of retention of American troops in Russia. Stories were circulating about the plight of the soldiers at Archangel.[55] Polk reported that the Foreign Relations Committee intended to interrogate him and that he was inclined to respond frankly if the president did not object. In a "very confidential" dispatch Wilson replied that he wished to make the experiment of taking members of Congressional committees into his confidence and that to this end Polk should, in strictest secrecy, make known the government's policy.[56] Polk was instructed to stress the importance of the Siberian railway as a means of access to and from the Russian people and of economic aid to Czechoslovaks and other anti-Bolsheviks.[57] Funds for the railway were needed; but Polk finally reported that the Congress was in no mood to make appropriations for any purpose in Russia, and the president was compelled to withdraw a request for funds.

For a time during 1918 the president had not been willing to eliminate the possibility that the Soviet government might come to satisfy the needs of the Russian people. By the end of the year, however, he appears to have shared the common opinion of the American peacemakers that they must look elsewhere for the constitutional order that they envisioned for Russia. Wilson would recognize neither Soviet rule nor that of the reactionary generals who had British and French support; and he still hoped that the various elements might come together on middle and moderate ground.[58] He was impressed by an appeal addressed to him by Maxim Litvinov, who undertook to negotiate an understanding; and he put the Russian's proposals, which were moderate and expressed with sensitivity toward Wilson's prejudices and ideals, before his fellow commissioners at Paris. It was agreed that William H. Buckler should go to Stockholm to hear what this Soviet diplomat had to say.

The policy of military intervention still was thought unwise by Wilson and the War Department. House, who had at first advocated it, now felt obliged to apologize for the situation that had resulted. On December 26, when the French foreign minister announced that the only concern of France was the rooting out of bolshevism, the colonel said to the press: "The United States is not at war with Russia. It

55. N.D. Baker to W.W., Jan. 1, 1919, Wilson pa., 5B.

56. Polk to Sec. State, Dec. 31, 1918, *F.R., PPC, 2,* p. 483; Lansing to Acting Sec. State, Jan. 11, 1919, Wilson pa., 5B.

57. *F.R., 1919 Russia,* pp. 248–51. Secretary of War Baker and Polk conferred and arranged to make "harmonious answers" to inquiries from the Congress. Gilbert Hitchcock, chairman of the Committee on Foreign Relations, defended the policy toward Russia in the Senate by characterizing the intervention as "defensive and friendly." Dispatches, N.D. Baker to W.W., Jan. 1; Polk to Ammission, Jan. 6, Wilson pa., 5B; Jan. 11, 1919, N.A., R.G. 256, 763.72119/3384a.

58. See Levin, pp. 197–202.

is inconceivable that it would ever take part in a war against that nation."[59] Yet American troops remained for eight months in northern Russia,[60] and in Siberia until April of 1920.

The defining of a consistent joint policy with respect of Russia—a country without a government that could be clearly accounted either a friend or a foe—presented a major challenge to the peacemakers at Paris. Their prime duty in the light of the subsequent history of the century was to attempt to establish some sort of understanding with the distrusted and unrecognized regime at Moscow. The largest country in Europe stood in isolation and in fear of dismemberment by arrangements to be made at Paris in which its public men would have no authentic voice. And in the absence of diplomatic relations between Moscow and the Western capitals, vituperative propaganda flourished and made it difficult for any minister of state in the West to take any initiative toward an understanding without serious risk to his own political position.

---

59. Marcel Berger and Paul Allard, *Les Dessous du Traité de Versailles,* p. 56.

60. N.D. Baker to F. Palmer, Dec. 24, 1930, N.D. Baker pa., L.C.; report of Sir Henry Wilson to the Secretary of the War Cabinet, Dec. 31, 1919, Foster pa., box 81, National Archives of Canada.

☆ XIII ☆

The American Plan of Relief

The intelligence missions that were sent out by the Americans at Paris became entwined with efforts to provide material aid to peoples whose plight aroused fears of proletarian revolts.

The new ministry at Berlin lost no time in making the most of the prevailing fear that Germany was about to fall apart. The Foreign Office appealed to Wilson to use his influence to modify those armistice terms that would continue the wartime blockade, cause starvation, and "produce among the German people feelings contrary to those on which alone the reconstruction of the community of nations" could rest.[1] The American peace mission, as it crossed the Atlantic, read reports of rioting and bloodshed in the streets of Berlin, where radicals seized this hour of uncertainty to strike for a proletarian dictatorship. On December 9 Foreign Minister Solf urged House to supply American troops to police Berlin and Munich.[2]

Before taking any action House thought it wise to send an unofficial mission to investigate the possibility of the emergence of an orderly government that would sign a treaty of peace. Ellis Dresel, who

---

1. Notes of Nov. 10, 12, 16, 28, Dec. 4, 1918. The State Department responded noncommittally on Nov. 15 and Dec. 7. *F.R., PPC, 2*, pp. 17–19, 34–36, 43–45.

2. House diary, Dec. 9, 1918, Y.H.C. "Dr. Solf, in a private conversation with me, painted the situation as extremely grave. . . . At the conclusion of our talk Dr. Solf broke down and wept, finally exclaiming: 'Tell Colonel House for God's sake to send American troops into Germany. Only American food or American troops can save us, and I'm afraid the food will come too late.' " Memorandum for Col. House from Lincoln Eyre, an American journalist, Wilson pa., 5B, L.C. See above, p. 94 and note.

Solf had been advised by Count von Bernstorff that Wilson was an uncertain factor and much depended on House, "the most honorable and upright proponent of a Wilson peace." Dispatch, Bernstorff to the German Foreign Office, Oct. 20, 1918, cited in Ludwig Schaefer, "German Peace Strategy in 1918–1919."

had served in the embassy in Berlin just before the United States entered the war, went to Germany and interviewed twenty-three journalists and public officials. He found that President Wilson was "everywhere spoken of with great respect" and his program was entirely acceptable. The Germans fully realized, he reported, that they had lost the war. The general sentiment was of utter depression. At the same time the old habits of order and discipline had not been superseded. Any return to military activity was looked upon with the utmost aversion. German society was suffering from a lack of food and raw materials, as well as from inflation of the currency. The men with whom Dresel talked saw no acute danger of a turn to bolshevism, and said that if the levies upon Germany could be lightened the people would be the more able to rehabilitate their economic system. They were counting on the United States to take the lead in bringing this about.[3] They showed an embarrassing fondness for the Western land to which many of their compatriots had emigrated, and they wanted to establish relations immediately.

The German leaders assumed that the conditions of peace would be negotiated between their delegates and those of the victors, and that there would be an opportunity fully to explain the German position. They hoped that Germany's reliance on the Fourteen Points would be sustained. They asked Dresel whether Count von Bernstorff would be acceptable as a delegate to the peace conference and were told that this would be a mistake because Americans regarded the ex-ambassador to Washington as the chief of the German system of propaganda and espionage in the United States during the war.[4]

Dresel made four recommendations: (1) organization of a political commission of objective and impartial observers and the exclusion of American newsmen from Germany;[5] (2) the dispatch of a commission to study the economic and food situation, possibly in combina-

---

3. Holborn has written that in this respect Dresel observed "quite correctly." Gordon Craig and Felix Gilbert (eds.), *The Diplomats, 1919–1939*, p. 131.

4. On February 13, 1919, the German foreign ministry was warned by Henry White, through his daughter in Germany, that in view of American animosity toward von Bernstorff, it seemed impossible he could be a peace delegate. Memo in White pa., Ac. 9376, box 3, folder "331—Germany," L.C.

5. Dresel's first recommendation led to the dispatch from Paris to Berlin at the end of January of Captain Gherardi with a staff of eleven men and of Dr. H.H. Field to Munich. On January 22 Dresel wrote to the State Department: "I do not think the humanitarian point of view the important one to consider at all, and no doubt the Germans have put themselves so much outside the pale that ordinary standards should not be applied to them." Letter to William Phillips, Dresel pa., Houghton Library, Harvard University. On April 16, 1919 Dresel headed a small civilian mission to Berlin, remaining only three weeks and leaving a press bureau to supply information. N.A., R.G. 256, 184.012/20 and 184.0131/34.

tion with the political commission; (3) an immediate investigation of the coal situation, to alleviate "the very serious conditions" in Bavaria and elsewhere; and (4) the issuance "at the very earliest possible moment" of an official statement making it clear that unless there was a stable government elected by the people and capable of giving the proper guarantees, the commodities needed would not be supplied.[6]

In addition to the Dresel report the American peace mission had British intelligence. Ambassador John W. Davis transmitted to Secretary Lansing, on January 6, 1918, a Foreign Office memorandum on "Prospects of Order and Ordered Government in Berlin." This paper pointed out that the political situation hinged upon the economic, which at the moment was very menacing.[7]

Article 26 of the German armistice called for continuance of the wartime blockade of Germany; but it also stated that the victors contemplated "the provisioning of Germany during the Armistice as shall be found necessary." Balfour regarded this as "almost a promise." Lloyd George told his Cabinet that it should take a large view and, having beaten the Germans, should help them to maintain orderly government.[8] Although officials of the Allied governments wished to continue the blockade against Austria-Hungary as well as Germany they accepted a proposal of Wilson, presented by House and seconded by Balfour, to make a supplementary statement that the victorious Powers would do all they could to respond to any appeals for relief that came from the peoples of Austria-Hungary, Bulgaria, or Turkey.[9]

On November 8, when it seemed clear that Germany would sign the armistice, House had proposed to the president a plan for the relief of civilians. This seemed to him the most pressing challenge that the end of fighting would bring. Against the menace of bolshevism House advocated the building of a barrier of self-respect in Central Europe. He predicted that the work of succor and reconstruction would "have to be done almost entirely through American

---

6. *F.R., PPC, 2*, pp. 130–72.
7. Ibid., 125–29. W.H. Buckler sent from London to House's office voluminous reports on the German food situation that were compiled for the *Cambridge Review*. W.H. Buckler to Frazier, Dec. 27, 1918, Y. H. C. See Thomas T. Helde, "The Blockade of Germany, Nov. 1918–July 1919," p. 95.
8. Cobb to House, Nov. 11, 1918, citing testimony of Lord Milner, Y.H.C.
9. James A. Huston, "The Allied Blockade of Germany," *Journal of Central European Affairs*, 145, 150; *F.R., PPC, 2*, 6. Hoover recorded that he "obtained" the modifying sentence "through the President." Herbert Hoover, *The Ordeal of Woodrow Wilson*, p. 151; *F.R., PPC, 4*, p. 281.

effort, and with the use of American food, raw materials, and finished products." He also foresaw that difficult questions of priority and allocation of shipping would arise.

House suggested that the president propose an "international relief organization" under Herbert C. Hoover, in which France, Great Britain, Italy, and Germany would each have two seats. Hoover had served effectively as food administrator in Washington during the war. Moreover, by virtue of his direction of a program of relief for Belgian civilians he had become, in the eyes of many Europeans, the incarnation of all that was at once idealistic and effective in their picture of America.

The proposed body would have the duty of procuring supplies and allocating them. It was House's hope that, with joint action of this sort, adequate relief could flow without provoking controversy between governments whose citizens could be expected to seek favorable conditions for trade. House suggested that Germany's merchant ships be put at the disposal of the new organization rather than placed under the direction of the Allied Maritime Transport Council, as Balfour proposed in a pre-armistice meeting. House's project did not differ fundamentally from the plan finally adopted.[10] It was the subject of a sharp and persistent difference of opinion between the Americans and the Allies.

Before receiving House's recommendation the president had already made arrangements with Hoover for independent American action. They had discussed in Washington the questions raised by the relatively large food surplus of the United States and the possibility of using it to combat revolution. They had also considered the difficulties of shipping and finance and the share that the Allies might have in the enterprise. Many of the needy nations had no means to pay for imports, the American Congress had appropriated no funds, and both ship and rail transport would be hard to find. Hoover proposed that since American resources were "dominant," the United States should "maintain a complete independence" and use its economic power "to confer favors" and even "to restore government and order in Russia."[11] He thought the United States should provide the necessary credits for the program. "Let it have our brand," he said.[12] On the seventh he was asked by Wilson to

---

10. House wrote that Balfour's proposal presented "obvious objections." *I.P., 4,* pp. 230–32; *F.R., PPC, 2,* p. 628; Herbert Hoover, *Memoirs, 1,* 278–79, 336; S.L. Bane and R.H. Lutz (eds), *The Organization of American Relief in Europe, 1918–1919,* p. 3.

11. Bane and Lutz (eds.), *Organization of American Relief,* pp. 26–27.

12. Josephus Daniels, *The Cabinet Diaries of Josephus Daniels,* ed. by E. David Cronon, pp. 342, 347.

transform the American Food Administration into a new agency for relief and reconstruction in Europe.[13] The President notified House that Hoover was going to Paris immediately "to discuss the matter and propose one method of handling it."[14]

The president, addressing the Congress on Armistice Day, called attention to Article 26 and announced that steps were being taken, with "humane temper and intention," to organize relief. He spoke frankly of the great political purpose that moved him. "Hunger does not breed reform," he said; "it breeds madness and all the ugly distempers that make an ordered life impossible." Alluding to the "excesses" in "unhappy Russia," he said: "I am confident that the nations that have learned the discipline of freedom and that have settled with self-possession to its ordered practice are now about to make conquest of the world by the sheer power of example and of friendly helpfulness."

Secretary Lansing replied favorably the next day to a request from Berlin that the United States "promise foodstuffs only if public order was maintained and an equitable distribution was guaranteed." To carry the food the use of the idle tonnage of the Central Empires was suggested. On November 24 Wilson responded similarly to notes from a provisional government at Vienna. By making the maintenance of order a condition of relief he exerted a powerful force in Central Europe, where to many people food was of more immediate consequence than the precise nature of the new governments. Lenin's response was to charge that with "a simple weapon—the noose of famine," Wilson's agents were "throttling revolution."[15]

Hoover, ardent to use food to combat the growth of what he called "a communist tyranny with aggression in its soul," had made an estimate of the needs of Europe and of the supplies available. The American surplus was found to be about three times the amount exported in an average year before the war. Using Belgian Relief and Army stocks, he arranged for the concentration of large stores and many vessels at eastern seaports of the United States, and for the shipment of more than a quarter-million tons of foodstuffs to neutral ports in Europe, to be transported and financed by the

---

13. *F.R., PPC, 2,* p. 627; H. Hoover, *Memoirs, 1,* pp. 278–79, 336; Arno J. Mayer, *Politics and Diplomacy,* pp. 266–67, 272. On November 4 the president wrote to Hoover: "I have learned to value your judgment and have the greatest trust in all your moral reactions."

14. *I.P., 4,* pp. 231–32. Sending a copy of Hoover's suggestions for control of food and shipping to the State Department on November 8, Wilson approved them. N.A., R.G. 59, 103.97/837. The official statement of relief policy, sent by Hoover with the president's approval to American officials in Europe on November 14, is in *F.R., PPC, 1919, 2,* p. 632.

15. *F.R., PPC, 2,* pp. 629–30; Mayer, *Politics and Diplomacy,* pp. 260–66.

War Department and the Food Administration.[16] The new venture could be expected to bolster the prices of American products by reducing the surpluses.

When Hoover reached Europe, accompanied by Edward N. Hurley of the United States Shipping Board and by Norman H. Davis of the Treasury, and undertook the relief of what seemed to him "the greatest famine since the Thirty Years War," his ardor struck an iceberg. The British would not permit any breach of the wartime blockade, even for the provisioning of the enemy peoples after the armistice. In England it was a shibboleth of patriotism, a weapon of warfare created by genius.

The German people were bitterly resentful. They regarded the blockade as a savage penal measure, designed to keep them prostrate, delay peace, and permit the victors to seize the world's markets and dictate their own terms.

Americans abhorred the use of this instrument to withhold food from people who were in danger of starving. But it was very difficult to dissociate a mission of mercy from national political and commercial ambitions. The Italians wished to administer relief to Yugoslavia and Austria, the French wished to administer it in Rumania, Poland, etc., and they could not quite understand how the United States could wish to handle the matter in the common interest, without any demand for special advantage.[17]

The British government felt that its people, having borne the brunt of the war, should have prior claim to shipping and to supplies for their own recovery. The provisioning of the enemy was looked upon as only a part of more far-reaching arrangements. As the only Allied state that had a surplus of ships at the beginning of hostilities, Great Britain had exercised the ultimate power of decision in matters of transport.[18] Two days after the armistice the British government suggested that the wartime Allied Maritime Transport Council now serve as an authority to coordinate mutual enterprises of trade and relief in the future, and that a joint control of raw materials function in the common interest.[19] Sir Maurice Hankey, secretary of the British cabinet, wanted to use the Allied machinery for food and shipping as the beginning of a league of nations, Lloyd George agreed with Clemenceau that it was essential

16. Frank M. Surface, *American Food in the World War and Reconstruction Period* (Stanford, 1931), p. 23.

17. N.H. Davis to R.S. Baker, July 26, 1922, Davis pa., box 3, L.C. See H. Hoover, *Memoirs, 1,* p. 287ff.

18. J. Arthur Salter, *Slave of the Lamp* (London, 1967), p. 83.

19. Stephen Roskill, *Hankey, 2,* p. 26.

that German ships be used for revictualing, and the Admiralty ordered the German government to prepare the merchant vessels for sea. The prime minister took steps to have plans made by Allied councils for the provisioning of nations that needed supplies.[20]

Hoover talked the hard language of business. Reports of Allied arrangements to distribute food through agencies already existing drew from him, on November 7, an assertion of American interests and rights that was so blunt that the State Department thought it unwise to communicate it to the Allies:

> This government will not agree to any programme that even looks like inter-Allied control of our economic resources after peace. After peace over one-half of the whole export food supplies of the world will come from the United States and for the buyers of these supplies to sit in majority in dictation to us as to prices and distribution is wholly inconceivable. The same applies to raw materials. Our only hope to securing justice in distribution, proper appreciation abroad of the effort we make to assist foreign nations, and proper return for the service that we will perform will revolve around complete independence of commitment to joint action on our part . . . the efficient thing is to organize a duplication of the Belgian Relief organization. . . . The representation of the Allies in such a commission could be proportional to the actual resources in food and money that they find for its support. Such a commission can cooperate with the Food Administration here directly in food purchases. . . . Thus the international disorganization . . . will be avoided and above all the extension of the functions and life of Inter-Allied Food and Maritime Councils either now or after peace will be prevented.[21]

Stopping in London for a day en route to Paris, Hoover advocated the sort of direct executive action in which he excelled. He regarded himself as a trustee of his country's surpluses, coaxed from the people by subsidies and wartime propaganda to meet the emergencies of war. The president supported him staunchly, as had been his custom in the war cabinet in Washington, giving him jurisdiction over the large surplus of army and navy supplies that had accumulated in Europe.[22]

20. Edward F. Willis, "Herbert Hoover and the Blockade of Germany," pp. 274–77; P.M. to Clemenceau, Nov. 20, 1918, P.R.O., FO/800/207; B.W.C. minutes, Nov. 18, 1918.

21. S.L. Bane and R.H. Lutz (eds.) *The Blockade of Germany after the Armistice*, pp. 10–11; *F.R., 1918, Suppl. 1, 1,* 616–7. Lansing transmitted the text to House and told him it had the approval of the State Department, but would "not be communicated" to the Allies. A copy went to Wilson on November 7.

22. Bane and Lutz, *Organization of American Relief*, pp. 32–33, 41; Cobb Journal, Nov. 26, 1918, R.S. Baker pa., L.C.; H. Hoover, *Memoirs, 1,* p. 278; W.W. to Sec. War, Dec. 16, 1918, *F.R., PPC, 2,* p. 670; Hoover to the writer.

When a suggestion came from Washington that Hoover travel to Berlin to investigate economic and political conditions, he found the British government opposed to any such mission in which they did not participate. Hoover informed House that he was "not disposed to abide by this domination." He proposed that the Foreign Office should be told that the United States was sending food experts into Germany. "Do nothing else," he advised House. "That is, simply inform them." He made the suggestion, he said, for the sake of amity. But his tone was not that of friendly collaboration.[23] He sent three investigators to Germany: two food experts, and a colonel whom he considered "a competent observer of public affairs." It was thought at Washington that the dispatch of these men, rather than of Hoover himself, would arouse less publicity and less British protest.[24] They reported the food shortage far worse after the armistice than before, and found rationing and transport was breaking down, industry was almost stopped by shortages of coal and raw materials, disease and crime were rampant, and unemployment great. They were impressed by the danger, on the one hand, of a military coup, and on the other, of a Communist revolution.[25]

German authorities who tried to reach Hoover through an agent in Brussels for discussion of the question of provisioning feared that an American relief commission would attempt to function at Berlin, and inevitably would exert political influence.[26]

With British officials questioning American motives as suspiciously as Hoover regarded British purposes, the strain upon diplomats was heavy. The State Department mistrusted Hoover's judgment in matters of diplomacy. It was felt that he was handicapped as a negotiator by his earnest Americanism. Polk talked with him before he left Washington and urged him not to cause unnecessary friction with the British authorities by attempting to take the lead and ignoring existing organization. To Hugh Gibson, who became Hoover's liaison officer with the State Department, Polk wrote: "Hoover has got a great job but he cannot play it alone. We have been rather prone making our own plans and telling the Allies where they could get on and off. That day is by." And Polk cabled to House: "The President confidentially thinks you will have to calm Hoover down a little."[27]

23. *F.R., PPC, 2,* pp. 104–5; Auchincloss diary, Nov. 28, 1918, Y.H.C.

24. Mayer, *Politics and Diplomacy* p. 262.

25. H. Hoover, *Memoirs, 1,* 337–38, *The Ordeal of Woodrow Wilson,* p. 152. An American business man in Berlin, Arthur E. Dunning, testified at Spa that the German food ministry expected a general famine within three or four months. Klaus Schwabe, *Deutsche Revolution und Wilson-Frieden,* pp. 266–67.

26. Schwabe, pp. 265–66.

27. Polk to Gibson, Nov. 15, 1918, Polk correspondence, Y.H.C.; Polk diary, Oct. 28, Nov. 14, 1918, Y.H.C.; Auchincloss from Polk, Nov. 13, 1918, Auchincloss diary.

Hoover had the counsel of Norman H. Davis, a patient negotiator who understood the need for cooperation with the Allies in working out complex details.[28]

Discouraged by talks with British officials while at London, Hoover went to Paris and on November 25 took his troubles to House, who was disposed to help the able administrator.[29] Together they sent a cable to the president proposing a program for submission to the Supreme War Council. The message explained that the American plan was formulated to provide "the most practicable means" of carrying out the pre-armistice resolution of the council to relieve civilian populations. "Owing to the political necessity of American control over American resources and the greater coordination and efficiency to be obtained thereby," the United States Food Administrator would be director general; but his policies would be determined by the Supreme War Council, to which he would report.

The cable went on: "The chief problem presented is the difficulty of devising a plan which will not antagonize the Allies and particularly Great Britain[30] and at the same time permit single American leadership. I am sure that you will agree that American leadership is essential, taking into account the fact that we are the most disinterested nation and the other Allies are affected by local political interests." Then the message mentioned the consideration that was peculiarly that of the United States: "Further, the supplies to be utilized for this purpose must in the main be obtained in the United States and will dominate American markets." House reported that French officials acquiesced, and he even went so far as to say, with charac-

---

28. Davis thought that Hoover, whom he considered "a very impulsive man," gave too little consideration to the ideas of others. H.B. Whiteman, Jr., "Norman H. Davis and the Search for International Peace and Security 1917–1944," pp. 67–71; Auchincloss diary, Jan. 4, 1919.

29. "Hoover is the kind of man I like to help push to the front," House wrote in his diary on Nov. 5, 1918. "He cannot fail to have much influence upon our public life. He has sense and a spirit of fairness that appeals to me." Auchincloss, impressed by Hoover's quick decisiveness, enjoyed working with him. Auchincloss diary, Nov. 10, 1918.

30. Wiseman had warned House of serious dangers of political complications that might result from Hoover's plan, and suggested that a committee representing the four powers should have the right to veto the recognition of de facto governments during relief operations. He expressed satisfaction with a proposal of Miller that the American draft of a relief plan should simply mention the difficulty. David Hunter Miller, *My Diary, 1,* Nov. 20, 1918. Auchincloss recorded after a talk with Hoover that the "crux of the matter" was the availability of German merchant ships. The American plan provided that these be placed not in an Allied pool, as Balfour had suggested in a pre-armistice meeting, but under the director general of relief. Auchincloss diary, Nov. 26, 1918.

teristic wishfulness, that the British with whom Hoover had talked at London, though showing a "desire to effectually dominate" and to operate the new organization under the wartime economic bodies that they controlled, indicated their "full approval" of the American program.[31]

On November 29 the president authorized House to propose the American plan to the Supreme War Council. The colonel had to take account of dissents by Edward N. Hurley of the United States Shipping Board, who was jealous of America's place in the world's markets.[32] Hurley had been a member of the little war cabinet at Washington and was vexed with his colleague Hoover for drafting a plan without consulting him about the shipping features. Before leaving Washington, Hurley had suggested to the president that Hoover must work with the Allies; and Wilson agreed, while warning against too much yielding to British influence.[33] House brought Hoover and Hurley together informally and they suggested that daily conferences be held.[34] Hoover apologized for neglecting to consult Hurley. House thereupon informed the president that Hurley approved the American relief plan but that it was agreed that all American passenger tonnage should be available for the transport of troops.

On December 1 House presented the American plan, slightly revised, in a long memorandum written in the name of the president and addressed directly to the prime ministers of the Allies. He thought that this course would be more likely to get favorable action

---

31. Cable, House to W.W., Nov. 27, 1918, Y.H.C. "The matters that Hoover and I have discussed will not permit of delay in reaching a decision," House said.

32. Hurley thought American ships should not be committed to relief cargoes to the extent of interfering with plans for using the shipping strength of the United States as a subtle bargaining counter at the peace conference. House diary, Dec. 11, 1918, Hurley to W.W., Dec. 20, 1918, Wilson pa., 5B. See Jeffrey J. Safford, "Edward Hurley and American Shipping Policy," *The Historian*, 570–74.

33. Letter, Auchincloss to Polk, Jan. 5, 1919, Y.H.C.; E.N. Hurley to Ray Stannard Baker, Sept. 2, 1926, Baker pa., L.C.; E.N. Hurley, *The Bridge to France*, pp. 264–68.

34. House to Sec. State, Nov. 30, 1919, Wilson pa., 5B; Safford, pp. 580–86. Auchincloss felt the full force of the friction between Hoover and Hurley as well as that between the American and British maritime interests. He thought Wiseman "unduly exercised" about the dangers in Hoover's plans. It seemed to him that Hurley, "pretty upset" by Hoover's disregard of him and "entirely ignorant of the present international situation," was trying to seize control of the economic office of the peace mission. Auchincloss diary, Nov. 27, 29, 30, Dec. 15, 1918. At the same time he wrote: "Hurley is going to play the game all right. He has got about as much use for the A.M.T.C. as the Devil for holy water." Auchincloss to McCormick, Nov. 28, 1918, Y.H.C. See also Helde, p. 64ff.

House was so distrustful of Hurley that he arranged to have Hurley's cables from London to Washington reported to him without Hurley's knowledge. Miller, *My Diary, 1*, Dec. 1 and 2, 1918.

than a formal approach to the Supreme War Council.[35] He advised Hoover to make no concessions before the president arrived in Europe. The food administrator agreed at this time to designate as relief workers any men whom House wished to send out as intelligence agents.[36]

At the beginning of December Hoover and Hurley, with their differences temporarily ended[37] and impatient to get on with the job, went to London, where the Allied premiers were conferring. There they found the atmosphere still unsympathetic to their program for independent control of relief. The torpedoing of vessels and the allocation of British tonnage to the transport of troops and munitions from overseas had left the island nation short of food as well as of ships with which to replenish exhausted stocks. Combined with a reluctance to allot their reduced shipping to carrying food to the enemy was some concern as to the possible long-range implications, both political and commercial, of the program of the Americans.

The Imperial War Cabinet had engaged in a full and frank discussion in a meeting of November 28. Lord Reading explained that the three major Allied powers were agreed that any meeting with the German delegates to discuss food shortages should be held in London. However Hoover, on his own responsibility, had already spoken to the press in favor of Brussels. Reading regarded this independent declaration as possibly a precursor of others like it, and felt that it would be very unfortunate if American officials made a practice of playing a lone hand. Lloyd George, who was in favor of doing what was necessary to help the German people to their feet[38] and hoped to do so through Allied wartime agencies centered at London, remarked that the independence of the Americans seemed a bad omen for a league of nations. When Reading warned that the Allies might cause a crisis by combining to outvote the United States, the prime minister asked whether it was not rather a case of the United States acting against the combined Allies. He was content to leave the prickly question in the hands of Reading, with no specific instructions.[39]

---

35. Hurley, pp. 164–68; Hurley to W.W., Nov. 28, W.W. to Hurley, House to Balfour, in Auchincloss diary, Dec. 1, 1918; House to W.W., Nov. 27, 30, 1918, Wilson pa., 5C Miller carried a copy of the American relief plan to Balfour. Miller, *My Diary, 1,* 23; Drummond to Davies, Nov. 28, 1918, Lloyd George pa., F/3/3/44, Beaverbrook Library, London.

36. *F.R., PPC, 1,* pp. 99–203; Auchincloss diary, Dec. 1, 1918. Cf. above, pp. 190–94.

37. House diary, Dec. 3, 1918; Miller to House, Dec. 6, 1918, Y.H.C.; Miller, *My Diary, 1,* pp. 36–37; H. Hoover, *Ordeal of Woodrow Wilson,* p. 99.

38. Winston Churchill, *The Aftermath,* p. 5; Frank I. Cobb's journal, entry of Nov. 11, 1918, L.C.; Chaim Weizmann, *Trial and Error* (New York, 1949), p. 298.

39. Minutes of the I.W.C., Nov. 28, Dec. 12, 1918, P.R.O., Cab/23/17. Reading, suffering from influenza, had to be persuaded to undertake this assignment, which

House wrote to Balfour in an effort to clear the air, denying ulterior motives on the part of the Americans.[40] Nevertheless Lloyd George apprehended that economic dictation by Hoover would give the United States great political power, and he suspected that this was its purpose. He feared that Hoover, a very strong personality who strove to be pre-eminently successful in whatever he undertook, would feed Germans and neutrals first and leave only remnants for the Allies. He presented these views at the conference of the premiers on December 3 at London, where no recommendations were made on the touchy question.[41] Instead the matter was referred to a committee for examination and report. Hoover and Hurley were designated to represent the United States.

The men nominated came together in London a week later. Reading argued that the American plan was not adequate and that the hand that fed Europe would control its destiny.[42] Hoover persisted in inquiring, specifically, what each of the Allies would contribute to relief operations, and in suggesting that they should take part in the management in proportion to their contributions. He demanded a considered reply to the American proposal of December 1. Estimating that the United States would supply 60 percent of the funds and 85 percent of the food, he thought that the director should be an American—perhaps General Harbord.[43]

When the committee at London failed to reach an understanding the British and French decided to submit their arguments in writing.

---

might stand in the way of his desire to return to Washington and complete his work there. Roskill, *2*, p. 26. He did not go to the United States until February.

40. Auchincloss diary, Nov. 30, 1918. Miller reported to House on December 4 that the letter to Balfour was "referred to a committee."

41. French procès-verbal, Dec. 3, 4 P.M., F.C.

42. Hurley reported Reading's argument, which he found tiresome, to Wilson. Letter of Dec. 23, 1918, Wilson pa., 5B.

43. H. Hoover, *Ordeal of Woodrow Wilson*, p. 94. According to Hoover, he told the president that he wished to resign as soon as relief work in Belgium and elsewhere was well provided for, but Wilson refused to permit him to leave. Reading told the British cabinet that he had asked Hoover whether he was prepared to direct American relief in Europe and Hoover said no, he had to go to Washington. I.W.C. minutes, Nov. 28, 1918.

Hoover reported to House that Reading stated that if an American was to be chairman of an inter-Allied committee to administer relief, he must not be an American official. "In other words they wish to insist [on] my resignation as food administrator," Hoover's message said. Telegram, Hoover to House, Dec. 9, 1918, Auchincloss diary.

Hoover wrote in an interoffice memorandum on November 15: "The food world today requires a commander-in-chief just as critically as it required Foch. He should be limited only by legislation from the Versailles conference, not from pinheads of bureaucratic Europe. This man should be an American—the disinterested nation; the nation having to furnish the bulk of the supplies; the nation that could increase its supplies by call from its own citizen as commander." Bane and Lutz (eds.), *Organization of American Relief*, p. 50.

Hoover despaired of immediate action of a joint nature; and his gloom deepened when, just as he returned to Paris, he received a report of the committee.

This paper, agreeing that neutral and even enemy peoples should not have to endure unnecessary privation and that cooperation with the United States was desirable, insisted that "certain general principles . . . must govern the supply of food." Relief operations should not reveal a disunity that the enemy might exploit or an appearance of monopoly by one nation that would put its associates at a disadvantage. The British wished to set up a council with power to determine, with advice from an inter-Allied staff, questions of both policy and general program. Existing inter-Allied organizations would have priorities and the Allied Blockade Council would make allocations to neutrals. Hoover was to act as "a mandatory" of the Powers in the administration of relief in accord with the new council's direction, and was to keep representatives of the Allies informed of the progressive execution of the relief program for each country.[44]

This report on the London talks came to Hoover through Clémentel, the French minister of commerce. Opinion in France showed scant sympathy for undernourished enemies who were held responsible for the millions of lives lost in the war and the wanton devastation of northeastern France. French journals, whose correspondents in Germany denied that there were serious food shortages there, suggested that the Germans were crying "Wolf!" and deserved no attention until they made restitution for damages done. French officials regarded food as an antidote to bolshevism that was less effective than military action.[45]

Clémentel suggested that American control of economic arrangements would jeopardize Wilson's ideal of a league that would order the economic affairs of the world, and that rather than upset plans for an effective league of nations they should await the president's imminent arrival. Hoover, perceiving that the French spokesman had been encouraged by Hurley to aim his argument at a sensitive spot in American sentiment,[46] gave Clémentel, to understand that

---

44. *F.R., PPC, 2,* pp. 654–58.

45. G.B. Noble, *Policies and Opinions at Paris,* pp. 166, 168–69. Ambassador Paul Cambon expressed to Balfour the opinion that any relief afforded to Germany should be limited to what was strictly necessary and, above all, should be contingent upon the cessation of propaganda promoting Bolshevist intrigues. Translation of a note of Dec. 6, 1918, Foster pa., file 82, Canadian National Archives.

46. Hoover to House, rec'd Dec. 11, 1918, Auchincloss diary. See Hurley, p. 269; also cable, Hurley to W.W., Dec. 12, 1918, *F.R., PPC, 2,* pp. 661–64. Auchincloss recorded that Hurley, by encouraging Clémentel to advocate for a league of nations economic features that Wilson opposed, was now ignorantly "messing things up nicely," and that by giving to the Allied statesmen the impression of a difference be-

his suggestion was not basically unacceptable.[47] However, indignant at Reading's insistence that "certain general principles . . . must govern the supply of food"[48] and by the suggestion that he, Hoover, should be merely a "mandatory," he pointed out that the proposal of the London committee could not be acted upon until the Supreme War Council—not then in session—held its next meeting. Meanwhile the Americans would act independently to deal with emergencies.[49]

Hoover and Davis noted that the plan of the Allies would make action impossible except by unanimous vote of a board that would have broader powers than ever had been granted to an inter-Allied body and would have in effect a total control of the markets of the world, including the United States. The board would assume executive functions that would stand in the way of the American ideal of the "single-handed administration" that would give efficiency in an emergency. The Americans pointed out that no definite proposal was made as to financing purchases for relief, and they inferred that the new council would not authorize the use of German ships and would not permit the enemy to exchange hard assets for supplies for fear of reducing their capacity to pay reparations to the Allies. It seemed doubtful that the American people would allow their markets and trade to come under "such a domination" as the European plan appeared to contemplate.[50]

Upon Wilson's arrival at Paris, Hoover took up the question with him. The food administrator was in a morass of gloom. He told Wilson that the air was "impregnated with currents of indescribable malignity," and the Europeans were accepting the United States as a "golden-egged goose whose life would be safe but whose eggs would not." He advised the president that the Allies had few resources

---

tween him and Hoover, Hurley encouraged them to delay in approving the American relief program. Auchincloss diary, Dec. 11, 12, 1918. The British ambassador at Paris talked with Hurley and reported to the Foreign Office that Hurley was "entirely opposed to Hoover's views." Telegram, Derby to F.O., Dec. 26, 1918, P.R.O., FO/800/201.

47. Etienne Clémentel, *La France et la Politique Economique Interallié*, p. 308; Helde, p. 71ff.; Memorandum by Clémentel for Clemenceau, Lloyd George, and Wilson, Jan. 17, 1919, D. H. Miller pa., box 89, IV, 21, L.C.

48. Reading felt that the Germans should be convinced that they were being fed by all the victors, and not by the United States alone. Wiseman explained to House that Reading, whose past record had been under attack in England, now felt it necessary to out-British the British. The Americans thought his arguments too sharp and limited. Probably not aware of the effort made by Reading to moderate anti-American feeling in cabinet meetings (see above, p. 220, and below, p. 238), House went so far as to hint to Balfour that Reading would not be persona grata at the peace conference. Auchincloss diary, Dec. 11, 15, 16, 27, 28, 30, 1918.

49. H. Hoover, *Memoirs, 1,* 293.

50. "Analysis and Comparison of the Plans of President Wilson and the Plans of the Allied Representatives," *F.R., PPC, 2,* p. 658ff.

other than the ships the British could contribute. "I advised him to go over the heads of the massed bureaucrats," Hoover recorded, "and insist upon his own plan."[51] He proposed to inform the Allies that because the situation was desperate the United States Food Administration would provide food and an organization to distribute it and would notify the Allies of its acts in detail so that they might plan their own efforts accordingly and protect their political interests among the populations to be relieved.

The president accepted this advice and asked House to send off a note, which Wilson modified by rewriting in the third person. In forwarding this communication House reminded the British government that the president was still expecting a reply to his proposal of December 1.[52] It was made clear that the Americans did not approve a British plan for the pooling of the merchant ships that Germany was to provide,[53] but insisted rather that they carry cargoes for relief or serve to transport American troops.

Actually the execution of Hoover's plan was but little delayed by the controversy. In fact the American food administrator regarded the talks at London and Paris as "considerably academic" and "more mental exercise than reality."[54] He was scornful of what he called "the second class minds and jealousies of the inter-Allied Councils." Without waiting for the negotiation of an understanding he proceeded to meet the emergency, with the approval of Wilson and the support of House.

Impatient with red tape and organizational charts, Hoover set to work. He found quarters for his men in fifty rooms of an apartment house.[55] He had brought civilians from the United States who worked with skill and devotion and without salary, and he recruited a staff of some fifteen hundred officers from the American armed forces. From Hoover's office relief administrators went into eighteen

---

51. H. Hoover, *Ordeal of Woodrow Wilson,* p. 100; in *Saturday Evening Post* (Nov. 1, 1941), p. 9.

52. House to Derby, Dec. 17, 1918, Y.H.C.; *F.R., PPC, 2,* pp. 664, 672; Auchincloss diary, Dec. 15; W.W. to House, Dec. 15, 1918, with tissue copy of the draft with Wilson's changes, Wilson pa., 5B.

53. See above, pp. 215–16.

54. Mayer, *Politics and Diplomacy,* p. 276; Bane and Lutz (eds.), *Organization of American Relief,* p. 50.

55. Hoover, like the other economic advisers, occupied rooms in the Hotel Crillon; but the American Peace Commissioners did not think it right for the economic advisers to ask for space in the Crillon for their whole staffs. They put their opinion in a letter to the president. Minutes, Dec. 31, 1918, Grew pa., Houghton Library, Harvard University; N.H. Davis to R.S. Baker, July 26, 1922, Davis pa., L.C., box 3. Grew recorded that Hoover wanted more than his thirteen rooms in the Crillon and threatened to leave Paris himself if any of the thirteen were taken away. Diary, Jan. 9, 1919.

"liberated" and enemy countries and six neutral nations, disclaiming political motives but at times exerting decisive political influence.[56] In general they sought, by serving as economic advisers to government departments, to assure equitable and adequate distribution of provisions and to secure payment from those who had the means to pay. The resources of the armed forces were put at their disposal and the Red Cross offered help in distributing supplies. Wartime restrictions were removed from trade in American foods as rapidly as Hoover thought possible without putting surpluses "at the mercy of the consolidated Allied buying agencies to manipulate."[57]

When Hoover and Davis came to House and complained that the British were blocking them at every turn, and that the population at Vienna must have supplies immediately, the colonel, convinced that the emergency was "a matter of hours," took the responsibility of telling them "to go ahead regardless of what the French and English Governments might think."[58] Believing that French and Italian officials were trying to control food distribution east of the Adriatic to advance their political purposes, Hoover sent cargoes of provisions to Trieste[59] and got the consent of the British and French governments to the use of American troops to protect trains carrying supplies to Vienna, where Hoover saw danger of mass starvation within ten days.[60] Austria got some relief, although little could be done for Germany while the blockade was in force. Such was the power of food at this juncture that Hoover recorded: "Never did we make a request that was not instantly law (except in some Balkan States)."[61]

56. Louis L. Gerson, *Woodrow Wilson and the Rebirth of Poland,* pp. 68, 108–10; Bane and Lutz, *Organization of American Relief,* p. 95ff.

57. Cable, Hoover to Food Administration, undated and filed under Jan. 9, 1919, Wilson pa., 5B.

58. House diary, Dec. 13, 1918. House, thinking that the Allies were "taking a perfectly impossible stand" (diary, Dec. 26, 1918), asked Frazier to notify the British and French governments of the American intention. *I.P., 4,* p. 240. A week later Hoover complained to General Bliss that arrangements approved by the Allied controllers for the export of certain products to neutrals, without restriction as to reexport, had been rejected by Great Britain because of objections by "high military authority." Bliss diary, Jan. 3, 17, 1919.

59. Palmer, *Bliss, Peacemaker,* p. 367. Miller recorded in his diary, on December 13, that Norman Davis told him that he had rejected efforts of the Italians to obtain control of relief as a means of coercing the Yugoslavs. Miller, *My Diary, 1,* p. 44. The Serbian legation at Washington protested against Italian interference with imports of food. Polk to House and Hoover, De. 7, 1918, N.A., R.G. 59, 763.72119/1958b.

60. Derby to House, Nov. 16, 1918, Y.H.C.; Polk diary, Dec. 17, 1918.

61. H. Hoover, *Memoirs, 1,* pp. 293–96; *I.P., 4,* p. 240. Capt. Walter G. Davis, attached to Coolidge's mission at Vienna, wrote in his diary on Jan. 3, 1919: "Coal has already begun to arrive in Vienna from Bohemia which is probably evidence of the power of H.C.H., who has indicated to the Czechs that food will not be forthcoming from the Entente if they do not reciprocate by supplying coal to other portions of the late Empire." Y.H.C.

Norman Davis saw the long-range implications. On January 3 he
wrote to the Treasury about his quandary:. "Hoover is, of course,
absorbed in this relief undertaking and is giving it a great deal of
publicity and prominence . . . to appeal to the imagination of the
public. . . . It is therefore difficult sometimes to draw the line between the requirements for relief and the requirements for an outlet
for the surplus stocks of food.

> There are many factions aspiring for control of government in
> enemy countries and in liberated territories in which new nations
> are being moulded, and the power to furnish food supplies to such
> peoples manifestly gives the power to decide what factions shall
> hold control of the government, because the crowd which can ob-
> tain food supplies for the people should be able to maintain them-
> selves in office. I have constantly expressed the opinion that it is
> very important for us to avoid pauperizing any sections of Europe
> and that the peoples must be told that whatever relief is supplied is
> only temporary to meet an emergency and to give them an oppor-
> tunity to take care of themselves. If this policy is not pursued, it will
> be difficult to withdraw our support (which of course cannot go on
> indefinitely) without turning a feeling of gratitude and good effect
> created by the assistance into one of criticism and ingratitude.[62]

Although House authorized independent action by Hoover in the
emergency at Vienna, negotiations with the Allied governments continued. During the last days of December they fell into what Davis
described as "a hopeless tangle," and the task of unraveling it fell
largely upon him and upon House.[63] Ambassador Derby assured
House that there would be no misunderstanding were it not that
Hoover wished to be food dictator and that the British and French
governments thought this unacceptable. At the same time the Americans understood that Lord Reading wished to serve as chairman of
the committee so that he could have a proper seat at the peace conference. Wilson was still waiting for a reply to his proposal of December 1;[64] and when the president visited England after Christmas

---

62. N.H. Davis to Rathbone, Jan. 3, 1919, Davis pa., box 11, "official and semi-
official 1918–22."
63. Vance McCormick, reaching Paris on January 11, 1919, recorded that
Hoover gave the impression of trying to "dominate everything" and seemed to be
making enemies. Auchincloss told McCormick that the situation had almost reached a
point of open break with the British. McCormick diary, Jan. 11, 13, 1919, Y.H.C.
Wiseman had recommended that the British government use the good offices of
House, who seemed to take a more reasonable view of the British case. Memorandum
Dec. 15, 1918, Wiseman pa., Y.H.C.
64. Davis to Rathbone, Jan. 3, 1919, copy in Davis pa., box 11, House to Balfour,
Dec. 16, Balfour to House, Dec. 19, 1918, *F.R., PPC, 2,* pp. 672, 678. Of Lord Derby's
assertion that Hoover wished to be a food dictator House wrote in his diary on

he seemed inclined to take responsibility for relief of Germany into American hands.[65]

In order to justify his position in the eyes of the American public Hoover authorized a release to the press from his Washington office, asserting his belief that "no one has the right to hand the control of American producer and manufacturer and national resources to anybody not responsible to the United States Congress or the American people, no matter how praiseworthy the object may be."[66] By this public appeal to national sentiment and journalistic exploiters of it he risked causing further embarrassment. Two days before Hoover sent the message House talked with him and asked questions about his political affiliation and ambition. The administrator declared himself ready to support either party that had "a progressive program." He said he did not desire the presidency. But House commented in his diary: "In my opinion he is mistaken in believing he would not like to be President." The colonel thought that he detected in Hoover's action a political pattern that he had seen woven many times by public men in the United States, and he recorded in his diary the annoyance that the self-seeking politician often caused to those more disinterested.[67]

In the latter part of December the governments of France, Great Britain, and the United States arrived at an informal understanding. The American plan had proposed that the director general of relief report to the Supreme War Council; but when Ambassador Derby pointed out that this would be impractical because there were no food experts in the Council, House suggested in a letter to the foreign ministers of the Allies that a small board be set up to deal with questions of relief. On December 19 Balfour took up this idea.[68] "I think that the best plan," he wrote to House, "will be to set up this council at once, without giving any special directions." He envisioned that the body would deal with all questions, including the extent of its own powers, within the general limits prescribed by the joint committee that had met already at London.

December 27: "I take it there is some reason in his assertion, for that is Hoover's besetting fault." Cf. J.M. Keynes, *Two Memoirs*, p. 23.

65. Trevor Wilson (ed.), *The Political Diaries of C.P. Scott*, p. 366.

66. Hoover to Rickard, Dec. 21, 1918, *F.R., PPC, 2*, p. 682.

67. "I am weary of the ordinary politician and his methods," House wrote. "Everything is done to glorify himself and to make his opponents seem less important. The result is the people get a totally erroneous idea of public situations. I have in mind now senators and congressmen at home who are drooling about international politics and the international situation as it relates to the United States. They are as ignorant as the constituency that credit their statements." Diary, Dec. 19, 23, 1918.

68. House diary, Dec. 5, 1918; Bane and Lutz (eds.) *Organization of American Relief*, pp. 92–96, 104.

The French government took action on December 23 after Norman Davis sought its help.[69] In a note addressed to House and replying to Wilson's proposal of December 1, it agreed that the United States should manage the relief administration. At the same time the French insisted on coordination with the operations of the joint wartime organizations. It was proposed that the work of relief be overseen by a new, specialized council comprised of two representatives each from the United States, Great Britain, France, and Italy.[70]

The British Foreign Office accepted the French proposal on January 1; and the president asked Hoover, as "director general of relief," to call a meeting of the new council as soon as possible. It was agreed that tentatively there should be no chairman of the board, but that if the board should have a chairman the French would support the appointment of Hoover.[71]

Denied the title of chairman, Hoover acted as an executive secretary. On January 11 the Inter-Allied Council for Supply and Relief held its first session at Paris. The body was ineffective and short-lived—"a futile chatterbox," in Hoover's opinion. It gave way early in February to a Supreme Economic Council, a loose organization for which Hoover drafted a constitution. The chairmanship was to rotate. The new body gradually took over the work of the wartime councils. A food and relief section took shape and drew food and funds chiefly from the United States, although Great Britain's contributions were considerable.[72]

---

69. *F.R., PPC, 2*, p. 678. "I finally took the matter up with the French government and they finally wrote a letter." Davis to Rathbone, Jan. 3, 1919, Treasury Dept., Bureau of Accounts, "Peace Commission" file. Davis worked to induce Hoover to approve a joint board, as well as to persuade Allied diplomats that Hoover did not wish to be a dictator for the sake of wielding power. Whiteman, pp. 72–73; *F.R., PPC, 2*, pp. 684–85.

70. Bane and Lutz (eds.), *Organizational Relief*, pp. 115–56, 138.

The French position was further elucidated in a memorandum approved by the French Cabinet and sent by Tardieu on December 24 to Wilson through House. Conceding that the wartime organizations must be modified, the document urged that American representation be continued and that the old councils not be suppressed before opportune new steps could be worked out.

71. *F.R., PPC, 2*, pp. 689–91; Davis to Rathbone, Jan. 3, 1919, Treasury Dept., Bureau of Accounts, "Peace Commission" file.

On January 4 House sent a note to Derby agreeing that the director general of relief should "in practice act on behalf of the Council" *F.R., PPC, 2*, p. 699. House expressed regret that Reading and Sir John Beale were to be the British representatives since both were adversaries of Hoover. Minutes of ACTNP, Jan 10, 1919.

72. H. Hoover, *Memoirs, 1*, p. 298, *Ordeal of Woodrow Wilson*, pp. 86–87; R.S. Baker, *Woodrow Wilson and World Settlement, 2*, pp. 322, 341–42; *F.R., PPC, 2*, p. 718, *3*, pp. 934–35.

Hoover's American associates on the council were Davis, Baruch, McCormick, and Robinson of the shipping board.

At the beginning of the New Year Hoover was still irritating the British government as well as his colleague Hurley by his independence.[73] Moreover he offended French opinion by an ill-considered public statement that appeared in the French press and was interpreted to mean that the United States government was undertaking charity in the liberated areas.[74]

As the peace conference was about to open Wilson was of the opinion that food relief was not only "the real thing to stop bolshevism" and a "means of stemming the tide of anarchism," but actually "the key to the whole European situation and to the solution of peace."[75] In a meeting of the American commission on January 3 it was the opinion of those present that to counteract the spread of bolshevism everything possible should be done to provide food and improve the enemy's economic situation. In acting to relieve people in want the Americans continued to be moved by the menace of violent revolution and by the necessity of liquidating American surpluses as well as by humane good will.[76]

The administration of relief was directed by a public servant of

73. On Jan. 5, 1919, Auchincloss wrote thus to Polk: "Hoover gets into one row after another with the British and he does not represent the situation in an entirely fair way because he colors everything by his own personal troubles." Letter in Y.H.C.

74. Clémentel made it clear to Hoover that the public regarded his statement as "a clear proof of the inability of the French Government" to deal with its own problems; and he released a bulletin attributing the offending announcement to American sources, Clémentel to Hoover, Jan. 4, 1919, and enclosure, *F.R., PPC, 2,* pp. 701–2. Auchincloss commented: "Hoover's statement caused some trouble over here. . . . We did not see Hoover's statement before it was given out." Auchincloss diary, Jan. 9, 11, 1919.

75. W.W. to Lansing, Jan. 10; cable, W.W. to Tumulty, Jan. 10, 1919, Wilson pa., 5B.

76. The mixture of motive appears in a letter written by Hoover to Rickard on Jan. 5, 1919, N.A., R.G. 256, 103.97/88: "While it is urgently necessary to dispose of our surplus foods in order to relieve congestion and protect producers from disaster and consequent chaotic results, it is most fortunate for the saving human lives [*sic.*] that we have this surplus."

The relief program of the American government was to be supplemented by the work of the American Red Cross, whose council was willing that the organization might help in the distribution of supplies. Polk to Ammission, Jan. 2, 1919, Wilson pa., 5B.

After Wilson brought his persuasive talent to bear (S. Axson to W.W., Dec. 3, 1918, Wilson pa., 5B) Henry P. Davison, the chairman, considered with House and Hoover the possibility of enlarging the scope of Red Cross work in order to give certain services to the needy in time of peace. *I.P., 4,* pp. 257–59; Davison to Hoover, Jan. 2, 1919, Wilson pa., 5B. House took up the matter with Clemenceau and Lloyd George, and in May of 1919 an International Red Cross, composed of thirty-two national societies, with the Germans excluded by the wish of France and Great Britain, was formed at Paris and coordinated with the League of Nations. *I.P., 4,* pp. 259–61; "Memorandum for the President" from G.F. Close, March 25, W.W. to H.P. Davison, March 26, 1919, Y.H.C.

great energy, ability, and integrity. In arranging for the distribution of rations Hoover and his staff sought channels that were free from graft and incompetence, and so inevitably they influenced political affairs in the interest of honesty and efficiency. However, this unprecedented enterprise, undertaking a prudent distribution of food as a preventive of bolshevism, aroused suspicions on the part of some who resented the injection of American influence into the political and economic affairs of Europe. Moral and material support was to go to governments that resembled those of the Western democracies, and would be witheld from peoples who having thrown off the rule of monarchs, might submit to the sway of minority parties that would abrogate constitutional rights.

Partisans of the Soviet order, ready to take advantage of the desperation of impoverished peoples and of native resentment of military invasions by neighbors, lacked material resources to satisfy the necessity for sustenance and could not contribute materially to the armies of the new regimes. The Western powers, however, although exhausted after achieving the military victory that made it possible for the various peoples to realize long-cherished aspirations, were able to help, thanks largely to the unexhausted wealth of the United States.

☆XIV☆

"Economic Men"
and "Outside Activities"

The American delegates at Paris at the end of 1918, taking ad hoc measures to relieve economic distress and induce orderly government in Eastern and Central Europe, were challenged to develop a precise policy for the regulation of postwar trade among nations. At the end of hostilities the United States held the finances of the world in its hands, had ships on all seas, and was manufacturing goods at a rate undreamed of before the war. Business executives conceived that the prosperity might be sustained in the future by a system of international commerce under which American entrepreneurs could freely make use of their talents and their capital. Competition for markets threatened to disrupt the economic collaboration that had been enforced by the exigencies of war. The political leaders could not be insensitive to the commercial ambitions of their peoples; and the rivalry that resulted was a hazard to the making and the keeping of peace.[1]

Herbert Hoover, in administering a constructive enterprise that appealed to humanitarian sentiment everywhere, took the center of the stage while European ministers of commerce found themselves little more than spectators of his extraordinary performance. His zeal for immediate and independent action raised practical aspects of certain large questions of international trade that Wilson spoke of only in generalities. It was asked whether it would be possible to revive and give validity to the complex and sensitive system of national loans, balances, and tariffs that existed before the war. Or might the financial and commercial transactions of all men be

---

1. Carl P. Parrini, *Heir to Empire,* pp. 1–2, 37–8; J.J. Safford, "Edward Hurley and American Shipping Policy," *The Historian,* 568ff.

brought within a single economy that would command universal confidence and would provide equal opportunity for men and nations everywhere? Moscow sought a world state to which individuals would surrender their freedom, economic as well as social and political. This was a challenge to diplomats of the western world who wished to preserve free competition and at the same time keep economic strife among nations from erupting into violence.

In each of the Western democracies there were those who hoped that positive action would be taken to apply Wilson's Point Three: "The removal, so far as possible, of all economic barriers and the establishment of an equality of trade conditions among all the nations consenting to the peace and associating themselves for its maintenance." Indeed the governments of the Allies were ready to transform the joint wartime agencies that had regulated economic matters in the common interest into continuing commissions that would manage postwar affairs so that the necessities of each nation might be met. The emergency had forced economic cooperation upon the enemies of the Central Powers. Even before the United States entered the war an American, E.R. Stettinius, directed huge British procurements through the office of J.P. Morgan in New York. At the end of 1917 the United States stimulated the formation of joint councils, at the same time putting limits on its own participation in their work.[2] Subsequently inter-Allied agencies managed the supply of munitions, food, petroleum, and shipping, and an understanding was reached on ways and means of enforcing the blockade against Germany. The aims of the joint councils transcended national interests and contributed vitally to the outcome of the war. Their members, including "associated" Americans, felt that they were in a strategic position to consolidate the gains of victory in the common interest.[3]

---

2. The United States was represented on the Inter-Allied Council on War Purchases and Finance, organized in London in December 1917. Oscar T. Crosby served as president and Paul Cravath as advisory counsel. This council's recommendations of priorities went to the secretary of the treasury at Washington for final decisions there. *The Times History of the War, 21*, pp. 74, 85.

3. Sheldon, representing the War Trade Board at London, reported to his chief, Vance McCormick, on November 15 that he had found "almost universal consensus of opinion" among Americans in charge of government work in England that the associated governments should maintain existing controls at least long enought to direct the transition from war to peace. *F.R., PPC, 2*, p. 732ff.; Harold Nicolson, *Dwight Morrow* (New York, 1935), p. 223. Willard Straight recorded that McFadden and Crosby, American representatives on inter-Allied boards at London, were "keen for the retention of their connections," and thought that Hoover and Hurley were "trying to play the thing selfishly for the United States." Diary, Nov. 12, 1938.

Lord Eustace Percy, who at the British Embassy in Washington during the war made social contacts with Americans that gave him a position of "precocious author-

During the last months of the war there was evidence that efforts to promote national trade might lead, with the coming of peace, to a departure from cooperative action and a reversion to bitter competition. House foresaw that the United States might replace Germany in a commercial rivalry with England that would inspire jealousy, fear, and hatred.[4] He conferred with Reading late in July about this danger and they agreed to attempt to control overaggressive promoters of commerce in both nations.[5] The president, however, constantly mistrustful of British motives, had challenged a recommendation of Ambassador Page that an American delegation be sent to an Allied meeting on commercial matters in the summer of 1918. "These are dangerous conferences," Wilson wrote, "because the nations engaged in them have some purposes which are in no respect our own." A month later he denied that Americans were, "like the English . . . planning to dominate everything and to oust everybody" they could.[6] In September he warned Wiseman against any international combination that would discriminate against German trade. Wiseman wrote to the Foreign Office on September 14, 1918:

> The President seems to think that the Allies, particularly England, want to form an economic alliance against Germany after the war. The thing has evidently been put to him in quite the wrong way and he thinks that we want to smash German trade permanently. He is determined that America shall be no party to this policy. . . .
>
> At the same time he is quite willing that economic pressure be used, if necessary, to force Germany to live up to the terms of the Treaty of Peace.[7]

ity," observed that the United States had "tied itself" to Great Britain in the inter-Allied executive authorities in "a way far more drastic than any contingent promises to enforce awards of a league of nations." Sir Arthur Willert, *Washington and Other Memories*, p. 47; letter, Percy to Wiseman, Sept. 3, 1918, Wiseman pa., Y.H.C.

4. See Ross J.S. Hoffman, *Great Britain and the German Trade Rivalry* (Philadelphia, 1933).

5. House diary, July 28, 1918, Y.H.C. Cf. above, p. 14 and note. In August The Inquiry took note of a report of a British Committee on Commerical and Industrial Policy after the War, which alluded to "the great importance of maintaining British export trade in neutral markets" and pointed out that economic self-sufficiency was very closely associated with union among the parts of the empire. Auchincloss to Barclay, Aug. 21, 1918, correspondence of The Inquiry, Y.H.C.; official bulletin of the Foreign Office, June 11, 1918.

6. W.W. to Secretary Redfield, July 30, 1918, Baker, 7, p. 306; W.W. to Hurley, Aug. 29, 1918, ibid., p. 365. Parrini wrote (pp. 1–2) that actually American businessmen, thinking foreign markets essential to full employment in the United States, hoped to replace British interests as managing components of the world's economy.

7. Copy of letter in Wiseman pa. One of those who saw the situation in what Wiseman regarded as "quite the wrong way" was the journalist Frank I. Cobb, who wrote on November 30: "The British plan to retard peace talks seems to be dictated wholly by trade considerations. The moment peace is signed the blockade ends and

When American officials in Europe criticized their British associates for manipulating the blockade of the enemy in ways that
seemed advantageous to British trade, House enlisted the aid of
Wiseman. Asked by the president to take up with Loyd George the
desirability of framing a common policy on postwar commerce, and
warned by House that any future statements of aggressive or vindic-
tive economic aims by the Allies might lead Wilson publicly to dissociate his nation from such purposes, Wiseman set forth his ideals to
Reading:

> We should explain our policy and program without reserve, and in
> our dealings avoid any suggestion of bargaining for our own trade
> advantage after the war . . . we should bear in mind that the dig-
> nity and traditions of the British Empire demand that we should be
> patient rather than quick to resent, sympathetic and helpful to the
> American administration in their many difficulties, ready to give
> way to American opinion in everything excepting questions of vital
> importance and principle. . . . While we should be most careful
> not to overdo, either by propaganda or celebrations, the outward
> signs of Anglo-American friendship, we should always have faith in
> the real tie which binds us together—that of our common tradi-
> tions, ideals, and our sense of what is fair.[8]

The Labour party was apprehensive and issued a manifesto demanding economic cooperation; and officials in London prepared
memoranda as a basis for an understanding with Washington. The
British government suggested, two days after the Armistice, that a
joint control of raw materials function in the common interest.[9]

Nevertheless the prospect of British-American rivalry grew. Efforts to enter into any formal discussion of postwar economic policy
were not encouraged by the White House.[10] Moreover, at the pre-armistice meetings House had evaded any definition of the precise
meaning of Point Three.[11] Afterwards he sent a message to the president saying:

> Among the important questions which will arise not only at the
> Peace Conference but probably also at the preliminary inter-Allied

German competition must be met." Memorandum in Cobb pa., [Nov. 17, 1918] Wilson pa., 14, L.C.

8. Cables, Reading from Wiseman, Aug. 31, Sept. 5, 17, 1918; letter, Murray to
Wiseman, August 13, 1918; Wiseman memorandum, "Attitude of the U.S. and of
President Wilson towards the Peace Conference," Wiseman pa.

9. Eustace Percy, *Some Memories,* p. 70.

10. Polk diary, Oct. 9, 1919, Y.H.C.

11. See above, p. 67.

> Conferences will be those pertaining particularly to finance, com-
> merce and the use of our raw materials and food. The whole world
> is vitally interested in what manner we propose to use our great
> strength in finance and in raw materials. England, France, and Italy
> [are perhaps more interested] in these questions than in almost any
> others.[12]

Wilson hoped to persuade the Congress to give him power to control American exports for a time after the war, and it was clear that
authority of this sort could be a formidable weapon at the peace conference.[13] He was willing to use economic pressure, if necessary, to
compel Germany to adhere to the peace treaty. However, he would
not support any desire of the Allies to deny to Germany the commercial rights it had enjoyed before the war under prewar treaties.
He had been disturbed by a speech made by Loyd George on July
31, which seemed to suggest a crushing of German trade when
peace came.[14]

Relatively self-sufficient and wealthy, the United States could afford better than its European associates to take a broad view of the
general economic welfare, the "common good" of which its president had spoken often and eloquently. But after the armistice the
merchants in the United States, like those abroad, began to urge
their government to further their special interests. It was argued
that they would not be served by supplying Germany with food and
raw materials so that Germans might again compete in the world's
markets. The United States Chamber of Commerce, meeting in New
York in the first week of December, considered resolutions favoring
a new protective tariff and legislation that would facilitate the combining of American business men against foreigners in export operations. The Department of Commerce, with the president's approval,
arranged to send more experts to aid the commercial attachés at European posts in promoting trade. An intelligence section was set up
in the office of the foreign trade adviser in the State Department, to
constitute an economic general staff for the government.[15] A French

---

12. The words in brackets were garbled in the transcription in Wilson's file,
cable, House to W.W., Nov. 22, 1918, Y.H.C. and Wilson pa., 5B.

13. Wiseman to Reading, Aug. 20, 1918, reporting views on economic policy that
Wilson asked Wiseman to transmit to London, Y.H.C. See Wilton B. Fowler, *British-
American Relations, 1917–1918*, pp. 213, 257.

14. See S.J. Kernek, *Distractions of Peace during War*, pp. 93–94.

15. Cable, Tumulty for Redfield to W.W., Dec. 15, 1918, Wilson pa., 5B; address
by Breckenridge Long, an assistant secretary of State, to the American Manufac-
turers' Association, U.S. Official Bulletin, Jan. 31, 1919. "I wonder if we will forget
that we have seen the world," Long said in conclusion.

"There will be very keen competition in both France and Belgium," Sir Robert

official in New York reported to Clemenceau that Americans did not want to be outdistanced in commercial rivalry with England, and wished to continue to develop their merchant marine and to trade directly, and not through England, with consuming countries.[16]

The War Trade Board, pressed by Americans who wished to move commodities, tried to accommodate them without losing touch with the British and abandoning the blockade.[17] The board notified its representatives at London immediately after the armistice that it was now possible to relax many of the export regulations, but that such action should not be construed by British officials as indicative of a desire to gain trade advantages. The board insisted that although there should be no "breakdown of the spirit and practice of inter-allied cooperation" or abandonment of the blockade, the war-time organizations should not be allowed to grow or to become permanent.[18] By mid-December European neutrals making purchases in the United States were no longer required to get licenses from the War Trade Board,[19] and Great Britain and France had materially modified their restrictions on commerce with neutrals. With respect of trade with the enemy some restrictions were lifted in December, with the assent of the Allies.[20]

Borden wrote in a memorandum of Jan. 6, 1919. "The United States has been by no means backward in placing advance agents on the ground in both countries." Secret memorandum, Borden pa., file OCAY 198, doc. 81553, National Archives of Canada, Ottawa. Sir Arthur Murray reported from Washington to the Foreign Office on "the almost frenzied eagerness of the American commercial world to get back to business as usual." Telegram, Dec. 5, 1918, P.R.O., FO/800/US/105.

16. Dispatch, de Billy to Présidence du Conseil, Dec. 20, 1918, Archives du M.A.E., "L'Amérique 1918–1928," f.168.

17. Relaxation of restrictions on trade was the subject of many exchanges between the State Department and the London Embassy. *F.R., PPC, 2*, pp. 729–95. Ambassador John W. Davis feared that the Americans might withdraw from the joint agencies too soon, inviting friction with the British and giving to the embassy a responsibility that it lacked knowledge to carry. Diary, Jan. 4, 1919, Y.H.C.

18. Dispatch for Sheldon prepared for the War Trade Board by J.F. Dulles, Nov. 20, 1918, D.H. Miller, *My Diary, 2*, 43–44; War Trade Board to Sheldon, Nov. 16, 1918, *F.R., PPC, 2*, p. 710.

19. Sheldon from War Trade Board, Dec. 13, War Trade Board from Sheldon, Dec. 13, 20, 1918, *F.R., PPC, 2*, pp. 754, 768. The board insisted that the trade permitted with neutrals must not be used as a channel for feeding the enemy. W.T.B. to Sheldon, forwarded to Hoover, Jan. 3, 1919. Hoover thought that the War Trade Board was unwittingly playing into the hands of those who were trying to break the market for American surpluses. Food Administration from Hoover, Jan. 4, 1919, *F.R., PPC, 2*, pp. 782, 789–90).

20. Sheldon from War Trade Board, Dec. 10. 1918, *F.R., PPC, 2*, p. 751; Auchincloss diary, Dec. 18, 1918, Y.H.C.

McCormick recommeded to the president that war censorship of communications with enemy countries—"one of the recognized measures of blockade"—should continue until the peace delegates reached a common understanding on the matter. Without censorship, McCormick pointed out, America's Trading with the Enemy Act

Just before leaving Washington the president addressed the Congress on this point. "The moment we knew the Armistice to have been signed," he said, "we took the harness off. Raw materials upon which the government had kept its hand . . . have been released and put into the general market again. Great industrial plants . . . have been set free to return to the uses to which they were put before the war. It has not been possible to remove so quickly the control of foodstuffs and of shipping . . . but even these restraints are being relaxed as much as possible and more and more as the weeks go by." At the beginning of January Wilson approved a memorandum from Hoover that advocated a modification of the blockade that would allow "a partial revival of the ordinary activities of life within enemy territories."[21]

Wilson recognized the importance of providing markets for his country's products. His government wished to permit the export and import of fixed tonnages of certain commodities under agreements as to credits and transport. Merchants were to play a role in America's mission to the world. To a group of businessmen he had once said: "With the inspiration of the thought that you are Americans and are meant to carry liberty and justice and the principles of humanity wherever you go, go out and sell goods that will make the world more comfortable and more happy, and convert them to the principles of America."[22] He had spoken at Manchester of international trade as "that great amicable instrument." Ideally, the Open Door was to serve to promote exchanges of goods that would aid, not exploit, peoples who wanted to share the benefits of twentieth-century civilization. "I do not recall," Link has written, "a single instance when Wilson and his subordinates ever sought to obtain for any American citizen monopolistic concessions or preferential treatment in investment and trade."[23]

---

could not be enforced and the alien property custodian would be deprived of a valuable source of information. Moreover, the Allies might interpret an American move to end censorship as an effort to secure an advantage in trade with the enemy, and as a strategem calculated to place the onus of responsibility for the blockade on the Allies. The next day Wilson assured McCormick that "the censorship should be carefully maintained so far as it constitutes a trade blockade against the Central Empires." Cable from McComick for the president, received at House's office about Dec. 16 and forwarded by Auchincloss to the president, Dec. 18; Close to Auchincloss, Dec. 18, 1918, copy in Wilson pa., 5B; cable for McCormick from the president, Dec. 19, 1918, Auchincloss diary. Cf. above, p. 86 and note.

21. Seven-point statement "approved by the President." Auchincloss diary, Jan. 3, 1919.

22. See Bradford Perkins, "What's Good for the U.S. Is Good for the World, and Vice Versa," SHAFR *Newsletter*, 6: 1 (March 1975).

23. Arthur S. Link, in J.J. Huthmacher and W.I. Susman (eds.), *Wilson's Diplomacy: an International Symposium*.

In January the president took cognizance of certain pleas from American producers. To members of his cabinet he cabled: "I fully appreciate the importance of providing markets for our products." He promised to do everything possible to this end, so far as was consistent with the military situation, peace objectives and the maintenance of accord with the associated governments.[24]

Hoover reported to Wilson on February 24, 1919 that by the end of that month control of all but four or five commodities would end, and that to abolish all controls would cause large losses by individuals whom it would be hard to compensate.

In France and Great Britain the officials responsible for economic policy tried to reconcile the special needs of their war-shattered economies with the necessity of doing business with the United States. In December the Imperial War Cabinet took steps to protect the commerce of the empire against the threat of competition. On the nineteenth it approved a policy of licensing shipping in order to get back as quickly as possible some of the enormous commerce that had been lost during the war. Foreign competition was said to be already pushing into all trades.[25] Reading explained on the thirtieth that though Wilson wanted the United States to be capable of independent action, the president opposed the desire of many Americans to rush into trade and make huge profits by forcing up prices in Great Britain. But Lloyd George declared that Wilson "meant nothing particular" by his advocacy of equality of trading opportunity. It was announced that the Raw Materials Board had decided unanimously to remove restrictions at the earliest moment possible, and that commerce within the empire would get priority.[26]

France had less to fear than England from American competition. However, like Italy it was largely dependent on the United States for raw materials and funds with which to purchase them.[27] In a letter of September 17 to Clemenceau and Wilson, Clémentel, the minister of commerce, had defined the French policy as one designed "to protect the interests of its production; to preserve, during a period of reorganization, the inter-Allied bodies in order to return

24. Lane, Redfield, and W.B. Wilson to W.W., Jan. 23, W.W. to L., R., and W.B.W., Jan, 31, 1919, N.A., R.G. 59, 033.1140/2160.

25. Minutes of the I.W.C. and memoranda of Ministry of Shipping, G.T. 6472 and 6482 P.R.O.; letter Maclay to Lloyd George, Dec. 18, 1918, Lloyd George pa., F/35/2/89, Beaverbrook Library, London.

26. Minutes of the I.W.C., Dec. 30, 1918. Clémentel recorded that the British government seemed disposed to end wartime controls gradually and with protection of the essential needs of France and Italy. *La France et la Politique Économique Interallié*, pp. 310–13.

27. War Trade Board from McFadden, Nov. 9, 1919, *F.R., PPC, 2*, p. 729.

smoothly and by degrees to a freedom of trade as large as possible; in fine, to stimulate production by the use of all its national resources and by the creation of new industries, with a view to meet, by the increase in output, the debts left by the war."[28] Jean Monnet, Clémentel's assistant, let it be known that any development of American trade before France had an opportunity to prepare for its postwar commerce would make the United States, as well as a league of nations, unpopular.[29] American officials felt that some French spokesmen, in asking for economic help from the United States, presumed too much upon the war sacrifices of France.[30]

Thus, a few weeks after the armistice, the governments that were most desirous of establishing a league of nations found it difficult to determine what the general interest in economic matters might be. This distressed officials in the British Foreign Office who had schooled themselves in precision. Lord Eustace Percy gave expression to his uneasiness in a letter on November 24 to Hoover: "Just now vagueness rules supreme everywhere—on not one of the urgent points of international policy which I am keen on can I get anything approaching to an answer from Washington—and in this atmosphere of vagueness, sentiment here has been deteriorating in the last fortnight more rapidly than at any period in the nine years during which I have watched Anglo-American relations."[31]

---

28. Clémentel pp. 337–48.

29. Miller to House, Dec. 3, 1918, Miller, *My Diary, 1,* 25–26. Auchincloss recorded that Monnet was exceedingly clever, spoke English perfectly, and had the "entire confidence" of the American delegates. Auchincloss to Polk, Dec. 20, 1918, Polk-Auchincloss correspondence, Y.H.C.

30. Auchincloss diary, Nov. 21, 1918. Setting down Clemenceau's speech of December 29 to the French Chamber (see above, p. 154) as a great diplomatic blunder, House wrote in his diary on Jan. 1, 1919: "It may have the effect of cooling our ardor and it may cost France many millions that she might otherwise have had from us."

Tardieu explained (in *France and America,* pp. 80–243) that Secretary of the Treasury McAdoo offered, in November 1918, to get credits from the Congress for French reconstruction, that the French government did not desire credits for purchases of manufactured goods in the United States because it wanted orders for French factories, and that when American leaders of industry came to Paris early in 1919 and offered credits they met polite but firm refusals.

Wiseman reported to Balfour that with respect of contracts having to do with war matériel and French railways hard trading by the French was creating surprising bitterness between them and the Americans, and that Tardieu was rapidly making matters worse by antagonizing the Americans.. Wiseman to Drummond, Nov. 22, 1918, Balfour pa., 49741, British Museum. American representatives, meeting with committees set up at French suggestion to regulate the trade of occupied areas of Germany, objected strenuously to efforts to discriminate against German industries that needed raw materials in order to resume production. Cables in *F.R., PPC, 2,* pp. 759–61, 763–64, 779–80.

31. Percy to Hoover, Nov. 24, 1918, in S.L. Bane and R.H. Lutz (eds.), *Organization of American Relief,* p. 57; Percy, pp. 71–72. Percy wrote: "A needless disintegration

The American apprehension of a British monopoly of trade endured through subsequent months.[32] A crisis developed when, on the last day of 1918, the Allied Blockade Council forbade the sale to neutrals of pork and certain manufactures, and at the same time arranged for the cancellation of their usual monthly orders for pork for their own peoples.[33] This was not surprising, since many commodities could now be bought at lower costs from distant countries where they had accumulated during the war as a result of a lack of shipping. But immediately the American Food Administration was embarrassed by an oversupply. The surplus of pork and its products reached four hundred million pounds. Hoover, learning that orders had been canceled with the purpose of reducing world food prices,[34] protested vigorously to Wilson. Hoover predicted a panic in the United States if the surplus pork was not sold.[35] He got the president's approval of a letter to the foreign secretaries and food controllers in Allied nations explaining that the United States had accumulated perishable surpluses in order to stimulate production for the common cause during the war. The note appealed to the Allies to indicate quantities that they would need, and to allow shipments to neutrals and to enemy peoples.[36]

The British could not be induced either to reinstate their order for January or to accept a plan for using the surplus to feed Germans.[37] However the food controllers in France and Italy, threat-

---

of agreements and controls, such as began almost immediately after the Armistice, must tend to restore, not freedom of trade, but irresponsible action by individual governments."

32. When Wilson's economic advisers later considered the possibility that British controls in Europe might "make it rather nasty for a time on food," Hoover remarked that he had "foiled them" in December of 1918 by turning in a lot of shipping, establishing warehouses in Europe, and selling food direct. Memorandum, "At the President's House, Paris," June 13, 1919, Lamont pa., 165, pp. 10, 18, Baker Library, Harvard University.

33. F.M. Surface, *American Pork Production in the World War* (London, 1926), p. 83ff.

34. Herbert Hoover, *The Ordeal of Woodrow Wilson*, p. 156.

35. Some British officials thought Hoover was bluffing. Beer diary, Jan. 10, 1919, Butler Library, Columbia University. Auchincloss wrote to Polk on Jan. 16: "Hoover has undoubtedly been a little too rough with the British and French and has not told them the whole story and has been too anxious to sell pork at any cost. At the same time, his roughness has done some good." Y.H.C.

36. Draft of letter in Auchincloss diary, Jan. 3, 1919; cable, Snyder to Hoover, Jan. 7, 1919, copy in Wilson pa., 5B. House told Hoover on December 28 that he would attempt to get constructive action from the Allies "in a day or two." Bernard M. Baruch, when he arrived at Paris, tried to comfort Hoover by reminding him of the natural eventual correction of the maladjustment by the law of supply and demand, and advised that nothing could be accomplished by immediate efforts to promote sales at American prices. House diary, Dec. 28, 1918; Baruch to the writer, May 31, 1961.

37. Surface, pp. 89–94.

ened by Hoover with cancellation of the United States Treasury's advances for purchases, gave assurance of continuing orders.[38] Hoover increased shipments to Belgium and neutral destinations, where they were delivered in disregard of the blockade. An agreement was reached with the Allies for the distribution of pork, the most perishable of the large food surpluses.[39]

The successful execution of Hoover's program of relief depended on the availability of cargo ships. Sentiment at London was chronically sensitive about competition on the seas; and Americans were suspicious of any move that might augment the fleets of British traders.[40] In finding tonnage Hoover was dependent to some degree upon the British government, which was loath to transport or finance relief cargoes without a voice in the management of the enterprise.[41] Tonnage for use in unregulated trade was scarce and the Allied Maritime Transport Council was slow to relax its wartime hold upon shipping. As for American ships at the disposal of the Allies, the United States government ruled that they should be used first to meet military needs and provide essential imports, and for purposes of relief second.[42]

In furthering the ambition of members of the cabinet and the Shipping Board to increase the size of the national merchant

38. A letter sent by Hoover to the food ministers of Great Britain, France, and Italy, January 2, 1919, explained that if the blockade continued to back up American surplus products, there might be financial troubles in the United States that would injure the hope of continued economic aid to the Allies for a long time to come. *F.R., PPC, 2,* p. 695. House sent a copy of Hoover's letter to Balfour and, asking him to put it before Lloyd George, appealed to the foreign secretary for the removal of remaining restrictions on trade with neutrals, a lifting of the blockade of both direct and indirect shipments to the enemy, and the encouragement, as rapid as possible, of private trading that would relieve shortages of food. House to Balfour, Jan. 3, 1919 with enclosure, P.R.O., FO/800/215.

Secretary Glass, who in view of a Senate investigation of pork prices was as eager to bring them down as Hoover was to maintain them, cabled to Norman Davis on January 9 that the treasury was "unwilling to agree to extend further credits to the British as an inducement to them to purchase pork they do not need, and thus prevent a reduction of domestic prices." Wilson pa., 5B.

39. H. Hoover, *Memoirs, 1,* 331–33, *Ordeal of Woodrow Wilson,* p. 156. Oscar T. Crosby commented, in a letter of Feb. 1, 1919 to Senator Henry F. Hollis, that it was rather awkward, after asking the Allies to diminish their purchases during the war, to urge them now to take more than they wanted and to propose lending them money if they would. Crosby pa., box 1, L.C. Also see Auchincloss diary, Jan. 14; Beer diary, Jan. 10, 1919. By May of 1919 Hoover rejoiced that overstocks of pork, as well as of cereal flour, rye, and wheat, would soon be "cleaned up . . . beautifully." Bane and Lutz (eds.), *Organization of American Relief,* pp. 470–71.

40. Letter, J.W. Davis to Polk, Jan. 4, 1919, Y.H.C.

41. J.F. Dulles to Gay, Jan. 2, 1919, Dulles pa., II corres, 1919, Princeton University Library.

42. Lansing to all American Missions and Consulates, Nov. 21, War Trade Board to Sheldon, Dec. 14, 1918, *F.R., PPC, 2,* pp. 738–58.

marine, the president expressed to the Shipping Board, soon after the armistice, a desire that it "buy everything there is to be bought."[43] However, officials at both London and Washington were distressed by a possibility that the United States government would feel forced to purchase stock in the International Mercantile Marine, a private American corporation that financed certain trans-Atlantic lines under an agreement of 1902 that kept many of the vessels under British registry. The British shipping controller, not consulted, denounced such a move as a "wantonly provocative step," feared the removal of 800,000 tons of passenger ships from British registry, and foresaw difficulty in taxing the profits and controlling the movements of a fleet owned principally by the American government. He advised Lloyd George that the plan should be "resisted to the last."[44]

Polk feared that to challenge the British position would lead to "tremendous irritation," and asked House to intercede with Wilson without letting the latter know that Polk had raised the question. House, who also had advice in the same vein from Attorney General Gregory, replied on January 6 that he entirely agreed that it would be most unwise to press the matter at that time, and that he had not been consulted but would take up the question immediately with the president.[45]

Hurley had plans for the abolition of the Allied Maritime Transport Council and the resumption of control of American shipping by the United States. He envisioned the building of a huge modern merchant fleet for his country and fully realized that this ambition was "of great concern" to British interests. Reminding Wilson that American law required that shipbuilding contracts with foreigners must have the approval of the United States government, Hurley recommended to the president that they should keep American shipyards busy in a way that would meet French and Italian needs and thus win their support for "the larger project," Wilson's league of nations. Hurley was determined to come to no agreement with the Allies with respect to shipping until there was an understanding about a league.[46]

43. W.W. to Colby of the Shipping Board, Nov. 11, 25, 1918, Wilson pa., 2; Daniels diary, Nov. 21, 1918, L.C. See Safford, p. 575 and sources cited.

44. Letters, Maclay to P.M., Dec. 27, 1918, Jan. 3, 1919, and enclosed copy of telegram to Hurley, Jan. 3, 1919. Lloyd George replied on January 5 that he "fully" approved. Lloyd George pa., F/35/2/94 and F/35/3/1, 2.

45. Polk to House, Dec. 21, 1918, House to Polk, Jan. 7, 1919, report by Buckler of talk on Dec. 2 with " a prominent representative of British Shipping Interests." Y.H.C.

46. Baruch to W.W., Nov. 12, 1918, enclosing two dispatches to the Department of State from Summers at London, W.W. to Colby, Nov. 11, 1918, Wilson

Liberals in the United States and England were hopeful that House and Wilson would include some economic provisions in the constitution of a league of nations that would be truly effective in the common interest of trade and peace. However, Wilson showed little interest in specifications of a new international economic order, either within the compass of a league of nations or otherwise.

The last of the four "particulars" that the president proclaimed on September 27 suggested that a league should use economic power only "as a means of discipline and control," and should not tolerate "special economic combinations that a stern moral sense might consider to be selfish." Wilson adhered to his resolve that sovereign nations should be subject to restrictions only insofar as was necessary to prevent discrimination.[47] The settlements at the peace conference, he explained, would be political, geographical, and racial. "Distinct economic problems," he wrote, "if worked out by international conferences at all, will necessarily be worked out by special bodies to whom the peace conference will delegate their consideration."[48] Secretary Lansing told the American Commission that the United States could not be bound under a league of nations to suspend commerce with offending states because the Constitution vested power to regulate commerce in the Congress.[49]

The Americans fell back upon the laissez-faire practice of prewar days. The president did not respond when British and French and even American sources suggested that a league of nations might serve to legitimize the economic aims of the victors. It was clear to Wilson that a continuance of wartime cooperation under the aegis of a league would jeopardize acceptance of the league itself by a Senate suspicious of arrangements that might strengthen foreign interests

---

pa., 2; telegrams in *F.R., PPC, 2,* p. 745ff., Polk diary, Nov. 19, Auchincloss diary, Nov. 27, 1918; Hurley to W.W., Dec. 20, 1918, Wilson pa., 5A; Miller, *My Diary, 1,* 24; Safford, p. 575. Reading and British shipping officials told Hurley that they planned to turn British ships back to their owners at the earliest date possible, and they sought assurance from Hurley that the United States would do likewise. "I felt," Hurley wrote to Wilson, "that it might be well for them to entertain their fears until you find it advantageous to state your position." Hurley to W.W., Dec. 12, 1918, *F.R., PPC, 2,* 662. A report by W.H. Buckler to House, Dec. 2, 1918, of a talk with "a prominent representative of British shipping interests," told of "great uneasiness" in British shipping circles as to the policy of the United States, and stated that Hurley was regarded as a man "prepared to push American trade by ruthless and perhaps unscrupulous methods." Y.H.C.

47. See William Diamond, *The Economic Thought of Woodrow Wilson,* pp. 182–84.

48. W.W. to Charles C. McCord, Nov. 22, 1918, Wilson pa., letterpress book.

49. Bliss diary, Dec. 21, 1918, L.C. The American interpretation of "Equality of Trade Conditions" under a league of nations was provided by The Inquiry in a paper that said: "The degree of equality . . . is limited by a nation's rights to give its traders preference in its own markets, by means of tariffs and other devices." Miller, *My Diary, 1,* 41, and *2,* doc. 55.

at the expense of American taxpayers. The Congress was jealous, he said, of being forestalled in commitments on such matters.[50] The president shared the opinion of his advisers that if the nations could agree to cooperate in political action a solution of economic questions might come gradually after more enlightenment.[51] In accepting the status quo he disappointed liberals who had been led by his leadership in economic reform at Washington to hope for regulation of the world's trade under a league of nations.[52]

Having no precise plan for economic action under a league, the president did not resist American influences that impelled him to take practical measures in the interests of his nation's commerce. During the voyage to France he had told his advisers that he was not much interested in the economic subjects to be discussed at Paris. However, his complacency was jolted by the obstacles that beset the American relief program and the determination of American officials to safeguard the national advantage in commerce that the United States enjoyed at the end of the war.

Hoover, determined to protect the prices of surpluses of products that Americans had created to meet wartime necessities, insisted on making sales to needy peoples under his own direction. Bernard M. Baruch of the War Industries Board sought markets for the raw materials and manufactures of his country. Members of the Shipping Board hoped to create a merchant fleet second to none. The American admirals planned to lay enough keels to challenge the traditional supremacy of the British battle fleet. There was no disposition on the part of these men to relinquish any of the material power that had accrued to their country during the war.

Moreover Carter Glass, who succeeded McAdoo as secretary of the Treasury, acted quietly to constrict the flow of credit, which had risen to an unprecedented height. Mindful of the Congress he forbade any discussion at Paris of a revision of Europe's financial obligations to the United States. When in a few cases European countries found themselves in desperate need the Treasury provided credits to purchase supplies, with the proviso that they be bought in the United States. The resulting financial pressure on the debtor governments of the Allies could not fail to stimulate the popular demand for the payment of huge reparations by the enemy.

The policy of the Treasury was of prime importance to the gov-

50. Minutes of the Council of Ten, Jan. 27, 1919; Davis to Baker, July 6, 1922, copy in N.H. Davis pa., L.C.; *F.R., PPC, 3*, p. 731.

51. Hoover to Rickard, Jan. 8, 1919, *F.R., PPC, 2*, p. 110; letter, N.H. Davis to R.S. Baker, July 26, 1922, N.H. Davis pa., box 3.

52. H.G. Nicholas, in Huthmacher and Susman (eds.), *Wilson's Diplomacy*, p. 97.

ernments that were its debtors. In mid-November 3.9 billion dollars were owed by Great Britain, 2.5 billions by France, 1.2 billions by Italy, and many millions by Russia, Belgium, Greece, and Serbia.[53] The funding of these debts and the financing of postwar necessities were of great consequence and required solutions that would neither precipitate financial disaster in Europe nor increase the burden upon the American Treasury beyond reason. Immediately after the armistices British officials suggested that the obligations of the European governments be reduced so that reconstruction and a return to normal trade might be possible.[54] William G. McAdoo proposed at the beginning of December that the Congress authorize the use, for purposes growing out of the war, of credits awarded to the Allies for purchases made in the United States.[55]

On November 25 the new secretary of the Treasury, Carter Glass, sent to the president a summary of the credits authorized and established in favor of foreign governments. (See Appendix B.) At the same time he asked Wilson's approval for additional advances of 600 millions to Great Britain, 300 each to France and Italy, 50 each to Belgium and Serbia, 25 to Greece, and 10 to Czechoslovakia. There was a sufficient residue from the 10 billions already voted by the Congress for war purposes to cover these sums.[56] Receiving the president's consent two days later, the Treasury proceeded in December to provide special credits to Great Britain up to a quarter billion dollars in the expectation that these would suffice to meet outstanding British commitments in the United States and also additional purchases to be made before "the normal channels of finance" would be open. "The meeting of our own large war expenditures," the Treasury explained, "imposes a burden . . . which cannot be ex-

---

53. Letters, O.T. Crosby to W.W., Dec. 23, with enclosure, Dec. 31, 1918, Wilson pa., 5B. Smaller amounts had been borrowed privately in the United States. O.T. Crosby to Lansing, Dec. 27, 1918, L. Harrison pa., box 114, "memoranda re post-war Europe" folder, L.C.

54. A tentative statement from the British Ministry of Munitions, given to House and forwarded to the secretary of war on November 11 and sent to the president, postulated as the first condition of sound economic organization after the war the cancellation by the United States and Great Britain of the debts owed them by France and Italy, as well as the cancellation by the United States of "at least a large part" of the British debt. Cable, Stettinius to Sec. of War, Nov. 13, 1918, Wilson pa., 2. The press reported movements within the British and French governments toward a pooling of war expenditures. Dispatch, president from Glass, Dec. 20, 1918, Wilson pa., 5B. On December 24 French officials suggested to House that an international bank be set up to guarantee the debts of the Allied powers. Bliss diary, Dec. 25, 1918.

55. Polk to Auchincloss, Dec. 12, 1918, Auchincloss diary, Y.H.C..

56. Glass to Mr. President, Nov. 25, 1918, with Wilson's endorsement: "Approved: 27 November, 1918," enclosing the summary presented in Appendix B, p. 285. N.A., R.G. 39, box 220.

tended." It was suggested that the Exchequer secure loans in the American private market to meet obligations maturing on February 1. However, the Exchequer, unable to get assurance of payment of loans made to continental Allies, was certain that additional advances from Washington would be needed during the period of transition.[57]

The American Treasury was authorized to lend to foreign governments only for national defense and prosecution of the war. The legislators in Washington were in no mood to allow concessions[58] that in their view might result in further burdens on American taxpayers and in the restoration of London as the money market of the world.[59] Secretary Glass, fearful that embarrassing concessions might be made by the American plenipotentiaries at Paris, notified the President on December 20 that any default of foreign obligations might lead the Congress to refuse to authorize further loans that were needed and sought.[60] Wilson immediately referred this message to House for advice and two days later replied to Glass: "I am trying to keep close watch on the various plans and movements about the loans to which you refer. . . . There can be no proper basis for a discussion of our foreign loans in connection with the Peace Conference. At the same time it will be very serviceable to have some one in whom you have the utmost confidence sent over here to represent you."[61] Norman H. Davis, who accompanied Hoover to Europe, was the sole financial adviser of the American commission until the appointment early in January of Thomas W. Lamont, a Republican, who as a partner of J.P. Morgan commanded the confidence of financiers and as the owner of the New York *Evening Post* was able to influence public opinion.[62]

On December 27 the secretary of the Treasury outlined for the

---

57. Rathbone to Sir Hardman Lever, Decc. 18, 31 1918; Lever to Rathbone, Dec. 18, 1918, Jan. 2, 1919, N.A., R.G. 39, box 119.

58. Lucien Petit, *Histoire des Finances Extérieures de la France Pendant la Guerre (1914–1919)* (Paris, 1929), pp. 531–32; dispatch, Polk to Auchincloss, Auchincloss diary, Dec. 12, 1918; Parrini, pp. 47–50. *Congressional Record,* 65th Congress, 3rd Session, p. 796.

59. In forwarding to Polk a document from the British Foreign Office that proposed a release of indebtedness, Auchincloss wrote: "[This] would simply result in putting London back as the money market of the world, a position which it would seem to me we should not give up without a struggle." Dispatch, Auchincloss to Polk, Nov. 15, 1918, Y.H.C.

60. Dispatch, Glass to W.W., Dec. 20, Close to House, Dec. 21.

61. W.W. to Tumulty for Glass, Dec. 23, 1918, Wilson pa., 5B; W.W. to Davis, Jan. 7, 1919, Auchincloss diary.

62. Carter Glass to House, Jan. 9, N.H. Davis pa.; Glass to W.W., Jan. 6, 1919, Wilson pa., 5B. In the latter communication Glass said: "Assume you will agree that so far as peace commissioners or Hoover or others are in need of financial advice they should get it from an organization under my general direction and responsible to me."

Allied governments the policy that the United States would follow with respect of loans. It was not disposed to establish further credits for purchases by the Allies outside the United States. Moreover, contrary to the desire of Hoover to sell American surpluses abroad and that of Baruch to increase American exports, the Treasury looked for an early curtailment of credit for foreign purchases in the United States. Giving assurance that existing contracts that could not be canceled would be covered by loans, Glass suggested that borrowing governments use private financing as far as possible. He gave notice that he considered all loans made after September 24, 1918 as "demand obligations, technically and in fact," subject to funding at his discretion, and not transferable into time obligations at the option of the finance ministers of France and Great Britain, as the latter had indicated.[63] This very definite withdrawal from financial responsibility for the reconstruction of Europe, dictated by the conservatism of the Congress and the secretary of the Treasury, made it difficult for the Americans at Paris who were attempting to negotiate provisions for Europe's economic welfare.

Advised by some of his advisers to trade economic concessions to further his political cause,[64] Wilson was well aware that the fortunate position of the United States provided a formidable weapon that could be used to good effect in dealing with Germany at the peace table. He had confided to his cabinet: "I want to go into the Peace Conference armed with as many weapons as my pockets will hold so as to compel justice." Told that France wanted steel and Great Britain many things, he remarked that the British were selfish and he would be cold and firm.[65] This combativeness presaged conflict when he entered negotiations with diplomats who would plead national necessities that were more urgent than any felt by the American "economic men" and that must be accommodated in the interest of the economic well-being of Western Europe.

63. O.T. Crosby to Lansing, Dec. 27, 1918, enclosing confidential papers. L. Harrison pa., box 114, "memoranda re post-war Europe 1918–21" folder; Crosby to W.W., Dec. 25, 1918, and enclosure, Wilson pa., 5B.

64. As early as November 14, Frank I. Cobb reported to House that food and raw materials were the only levers that would move the British government. Cobb to House, letter, Nov. 14, 1918, Y.H.C. General Bliss, noting that Italy was requesting large loans, recorded in his diary on December 23 that in a conference with Crosby, Hurley, and Norman Davis, the question came up of using various American agencies in Europe to strengthen the president's hand in realizing American peace aims. Bliss feared that if the economic demands of the Allies were granted without reference to the peace conference, the Allies might then feel that they could put off discussion of a league of nations.

65. J. Daniels, *The Cabinet Diaries of Josephus Daniels,* ed. by E. David Cronon, pp. 342, 347.

The president had indicated, both in public and in private, that he would not hesitate to use the potential of his nation as a means toward political leadership in the twentieth-century world. And at the same time he intended that the peace settlement should not restrict the development of American trade and industry. Wilson demanded freedom for his people to explore markets everywhere in competition with the industries of countries which, deeply involved in the war, had suffered damage, had not been able to develop new products and new methods of production, and had fallen into a weak competitive position.[66]

Thus the United States, eager above all to get back to "business as usual" and feeling strong enough to survive in a world of laissez-faire—provided only that doors were kept open and trading conditions were equal for all nations—pursued an economic policy that served the national interest. Committed to an immediate program of disposing of American surpluses and at the same time providing relief in Central Europe to prevent anarchy there, the Americans had no precise or far-reaching plan for the world's economy either under a league of nations or under a continuance of regulation by wartime councils. The American people and their Congress, living in comparative isolation for more than a century and conscious of a lack of sophistication in world affairs, were far from certain that their interests would be adequately protected if economic authority were to be shared with war-ravaged Europeans.

---

66. J. Svennilson, *Growth and Stagnation in the European Economy* (Geneva, 1954), p. 20.

☆ XV ☆

The Americans Shake Down

As the weeks passed and the nations looked to their own interests Wilson could no longer count upon the popular revulsion against war to give adequate support to his leadership, even in his own nation. Henry Cabot Lodge, who had warned both British and French leaders[1] against Wilson's program and who was to be chairman of the Committee on Foreign Relations in the new Senate, made a speech on December 21 in which he reminded that body that its right to advise was "a solemn, an imperative duty." Proposing specific terms for peace, he insisted that it was most important that the opinion of the Senate be known at Paris. He criticized the American naval building program, saying that he had never advocated a fleet as large as Great Britain's, and pointed to the obvious inconsistency with the ideal of disarmament. He called for "the most precise definitions" of what was intended in the way of a league of nations. The matter of national sovereignty—"the heart of the whole question"—

---

1. See above, p. 126 and note. Lodge informed Viscount Bryce on December 14 that the president's decision to go to Europe was "very unpopular" in the United States, that the other American plenipotentiaries, except White, would be mere mouthpieces of Wilson, and that the "general outside questions" on which the president's mind was fixed might lead to controversy that should be avoided until peace was made with Germany. Lodge to Bryce, letter in Bryce pa., vol. 7, Bodleian Library, Oxford University.

According to the record of André Chéradame, Lodge charged this French journalist to tell President Poincaré and Premier Clemenceau that the treaty of peace would not be approved by the Senate if it included provisions for a league of nations, and Chéradame delivered this message to Poincaré on January 10, to an assistant to Clemenceau on January 13, and to various foreign diplomats at Paris. French censorship prevented general publication of Lodge's warning, but Chéradame was given space in *La Democratie Nouvelle* on February 11 and March 11 and 23, 1919. Unpublished ms. by Chéradame, "Histoire des deux Interventions des États-Unis en Europe," B.D.I.C., Nanterre, p. 226.

must be squarely faced. Was the United States ready to abandon the Monroe Doctrine and control of immigration and the tariff? In Lodge's view, "to sign a treaty and then evade or disregard its provisions" was "the surest breeder of wars." It seemed to the senator that the victorious powers already constituted a league of nations that should be preserved. He gave an ominous warning: "I can conceive of extraneous provisions . . . being unwisely added . . . which would surely be stricken out or amended, no matter how many signatures might be appended to the treaty."[2]

In view of the strength of the opposition at Washington it became the more important that the president command the respect and loyalty of the American delegates at Paris. Four days after his arrival there, when he and House realized that they lacked adequate advice from men of affairs, they sent for two stalwarts who as members of Wilson's little war cabinet had served him with devotion and competence. He already had Hoover and Hurley at his side. Just before leaving Washington he had told Bernard M. Baruch, head of the War Industries Board, and Vance McCormick, chairman of the War Trade Board and of the Democratic National Committee, that he might need them at Paris at any moment, that he feared trouble with other governments over the control of raw materials.[3] On December 18 he agreed with House[4] that Baruch and McCormick should come over, without staffs.[5]

The work of Baruch as head of the War Industries Board had led the president to write to him: "I hope you have felt how entirely you have won my confidence not only, but my affection. . . . You have made yourself indispensable."[6] This forceful administrator volunteered a statement of American policy in a letter to Wilson:

---

2. *Congressional Record, XVII,* part 1, 724–28. Lodge explained to Theodore Roosevelt in a letter of December 13 that he had made a speech "intended chiefly for the benefit of the Allies." Breckenridge Long, an assistant secretary of state, recorded that Lodge, "ranting," was playing into England's hands and that British propaganda carried the speeches of Lodge and Senator Knox all over England, France, and Italy. Diary, Dec. 21, 1918, L.C.

Lodge's address evoked from his friend Henry White a letter giving assurance that Wilson would not assent to any league constitution whereby the American army and navy would be placed under any orders except those of the American government. Allan Nevins, *Henry White,* p. 362.

3. Benham diary letter, Dec. 3, 1918, Helm pa., L.C..

4. As early as October 22 House had suggested that the president bring to Paris a small body of economic advisers, or have them ready to come at short notice. House to W.W., Oct. 22, 1918, Wilson pa., 2, L.C. After avoiding controversy in the pre-armistice meetings with respect of the application of Point Three, House had reported to the State Department that the American officials at Paris were "more or less in a haze" about economic affairs. Auchincloss to Polk, Nov. 15, 1918. Y.H.C.

5. Auchincloss diary, Dec. 18, 1918, Y.H.C. They sailed for France on January 2, 1919.

6. W.W. to Baruch, Dec. 7, 1918, Wilson pa., 5B., L.C.

A just and continuing peace should include a just and equal access to the raw materials and manufacturing facilities of the world, thus eliminating preferential tariffs. No nation, including neutrals, should be permitted to enter into economic alliance, to the detriment of any other nations. . . . This will not prevent the making of tariffs so long as the tariff affects the export to or import from other nations equally. . . . The individual within each nation will thus have an opportunity through ingenuity and application to work out his own salvation.[7]

When Baruch arrived in Europe it became clear that his manners were not those of a diplomat. He did not endear himself when he boasted of his services as dictator of American industry during the war. "The capacity of Americans for uttering platitudes," Lord Robert Cecil wrote, "is really unlimited, charming as they are in many respects."[8] At the same time he was pleased by McCormick. In the midst of the jealousies and controversies that arose between various war boards McCormick had a reputation for selfless work. Polk and House agreed that he would be "most valuable" as head of what diplomats characterized as "outside activities"—that is, economic negotiations.[9]

It became very clear that the task of peacemaking included not only international agreements, but conciliation among the American delegates as well. House had soothed friction between Hoover and Hurley; and now two groups of experts vied for the privilege of supplying economic intelligence.

Before leaving Washington Wilson had agreed that the Central Bureau of Research and Statistics, which had advised the various war boards, should serve the State Department as the official source of economic data at the Peace Conference.[10] Professor Allyn Young, in charge of the economic studies of The Inquiry, heard of this and went to the president to ascertain his responsibilities in relation to those of the Central Bureau. He had arranged with Edwin F. Gay,

---

7. Baruch to W.W., Dec. 3, 1918, Wilson pa., 5B.

8. Diary, Jan. 14, 16, 1919, Cecil pa., 51131, British Museum. Lord Robert Cecil had resigned as "nominal minister of Blockade" and assistant foreign secretary (Lord Robert Cecil to Balfour, July 17, 1918, Balfour pa., 49738, British Museum), but continued to serve his government in special assignments. Auchincloss wrote in his diary on December 28: "We are making every effort to get Cecil placed at the head of the British group."

9. Bernard M. Baruch, *The Public Years*, pp. 94–95; W.W. to Baruch, Nov. 27, 1918, Wilson pa., letterpress book; Polk to Ammission, Dec. 19, W.W. to Polk for McCormick, Dec. 21, Tumulty to W.W., Dec. 26, 1918, Wilson pa., 5B; Polk to Lansing, Dec. 20, 1918, Y.H.C.; Auchincloss diary, Nov. 19, 20, 27, Dec. 18, 19, 1918.

10. Memorandum of Dec. 12, 1918, to Edwin F. Gay, chief of the Central Bureau of Research and Statistics, Gay mss., Huntington Library, cited by Lawrence E. Gelfand, *The Inquiry*, 166–67.

chief of the bureau, for such contributions as might be useful at Paris, and he learned that Gay was sending data on the next steamer with John Foster Dulles, a nephew of Secretary Lansing's wife.[11] When Young asked the president whether Gay had spoken to him about providing economic advice for the peace mission, Wilson, apparently forgetting the commission that he had already given to Gay, made a negative reply and asked Young to continue his responsibility for economic counsel.

However word came to House from Polk, at Washington, that Gay thought his bureau was to be the official agency for confidential economic information. "Gay wants it understood," one of Polk's messages said, "that this is no attempt to oust Young but rather work with him." House and Lansing thought that Young should continue to undertake the work alone. Young informed Gay in a letter of January 15 that the situation had been explained at Paris to Dulles; but this zealous young man, then only twenty-eight years old, professed shock at the "confusion, jealousy, wire pulling, and lack of accomplishment." He reported to Gay that The Inquiry was "very much in the saddle" that there was "a very distinct atmosphere of hostility" on the part of Young; and yet he had managed to negotiate an arrangement for the work of the economic advisers, with whom he met every few days.

Dulles offered to put his staff at the service of the American Commission to Negotiate Peace on two conditions: that their special qualifications and connections with the War Board at Washington be recognized; and that he, Dulles, be the recognized channel of communication with Gay and serve informally in liaison between the president's economic advisers and Young's office. According to Dulles, an understanding on this basis cleared the atmosphere and made it possible for him to arrange the technical work of the economic section.[12]

---

11. Young wrote to Gay on Dec. 19, 1918: "The prospects for a centralized control of information on economic matters is brighter than when I last saw you . . . we have been able to get a central office of economics and statistics, which will be under the charge of myself as economist and Colonel Ayres as statistician." Letter in Dulles pa., II, Correspondence 1919, Princeton University Library.

12. J.F. Dulles to Gay, Jan. 19, 24, 1919, J.F. Dulles to Janet Dulles, Jan. 5, 9, 14, 19, 1919, Dulles pa.; House to Mezes, Dec. 31, 1918, Inquiry correspondence, Y.H.C.; cables, Polk to Auchincloss, Dec. 19, 20, Auchincloss to Sec. State, Dec. 31, 1918, N.A., R.G. 256, 184.83/10; Polk diary, Dec. 18, 1918, Y.H.C.; Mezes to Grew, Jan. 2, N.A., R.G. 256, 184.83/11; Head of Central Economic Section of the Inquiry to Gay, Jan. 15, 1919, *F.R., PPC, 11,* p. 485; Gelfand, pp. 177–78; James T. Shotwell, *At the Paris Peace Conference,* pp. 91, 118.

Recording a conference with Gay and McCormick about the sending of experts to Paris, Polk wrote in his diary on Dec. 18, 1918: "Apparently Baruch wanted to keep control of the experts Gay was sending over. Suggested we could avoid difficulty by having them attached to the peace mission."

American diplomats could no longer afford to regard economic negotiations as "outside activities." There was an obvious need for a strong and consistent national policy. As emergencies arose, the "economic man" tended to do business less in formal councils and more in direct communication with the president. Eventually he came to rely on them for advice not only on economic and financial matters that were accumulating and awaiting decision but for counsel on other questions as well.[13]

As the hour for negotiations approached, three of the five American plenipotentiaries found themselves largely left aside and almost ignored by the president. General Bliss, disquieted by the "hazy and vague" ideas of Wilson and by the secretiveness of House,[14] tried to restrain himself from giving way to forebodings.[15] His independent and searching mind sought relevant information from the scholars of The Inquiry on questions other than military; and they learned to respect his driving conscience and the intelligence of his staff.[16] Bliss wrote to Lansing to urge a prompt determination of the extent to which they were to be guided by abstract principles and the degree to which principles might yield to expediency.[17] He warned that any American participation in a guarantee of independence and territorial integrity must be subject to the will of the Congress.[18]

Failing to get through to the president, Bliss felt that the knowledge and experience that he had acquired were not used. As the United States military representative, Bliss was the only American peace commissioner who had been directly in touch with the Allied councils during the war. Possessed of an abiding faith in the inher-

---

13. McCormick diary, Jan. 21, 19, 30, 1919 and passim, Y.H.C.

14. Bliss to Mrs. Bliss, Dec. 18, 1918, Bliss pa., L.C. Bliss complained to the War Department of House's secretiveness. Inga Floto, *Colonel House in Paris*, pp. 73–74, 95–97.

15. Bliss diary, Jan. 1, 1919; Frederick Palmer, *Bliss, Peacemaker*, pp. 360, 363. "It will be well," Bliss wrote in his diary on January 1, "to keep in mind not to give way too much to the spirit of criticism, complaint and faultfinding with what has been done and is being done—though, God knows, there is enough occasion for it." Bliss pa., box 65.

16. Charles Seymour, *Letters from the Paris Peace Conference*, pp. 56, 62, 78. Bowman statement, "Peace Conference," Bowman pa., file 1, drawer 1, "Miscellaneous Notes" folder, Eisenhower Library, Johns Hopkins University. Professor Westermann wrote of Bliss: "This is one Commissioner who will really study . . . hard, to make himself acquainted with what he must know. There is not another one in the bunch unless it be Colonel House. . . . [Bliss] is so honest-to-God American!" Westermann diary, Jan. 16, 1919, Low Library, Columbia University.

17. Bliss to Lansing, Dec. 15, 1918. On December 26, Bliss wrote to Lansing to ask what steps were being taken to concert American thinking. *F.R., PPC, 1*, pp. 297–98.

18. Bliss to Mezes, Dec. 26, 1918, Mezes pa., box 1, Butler Library, Columbia University.

ent virtue of American democracy and not versed in the ways of Old
World diplomacy, he expressed an opinion widespread among his
countrymen when he wrote to the Army's chief of staff, on November 30, that the president would find himself at Paris "con-
fronted by the wiliest and canniest diplomats in Europe"—men who
all their lives had been accustomed to barter principle for material
benefits and do it in such a way as to deceive anyone for a considerable time into the belief that they were actuated by the highest motives of honor and justice.[19]

Bliss's flinty concept of duty led him to think that the Americans
were at Paris not to negotiate as one among a number of free and
sovereign peoples, but to lay down certain fundamental principles at
the outset and thereafter to insist on their observance. He particularly sought to avoid involvement in the details of European and colonial settlements, except as far as necessary to prevent a violation of
principle.[20] Fully alive to the threat to human life that an armaments
race in the twentieth century would create, he read to his associates a
letter from Secretary of War Baker that reported the making of an
aerial bomb, with two hundred pounds of high explosive, that would
deviate less than one-eighth of one percent at a range of fifty
miles.[21] To Bliss this was an argument for a league of nations that
would effectively limit national armaments. He accepted the inevitability of conflict between Wilsonism and bolshevism.[22]

Like Bliss, Henry White was disturbed because there appeared to
be no plan for negotiating with the Europeans. Two days after his
arrival at Paris with the president's party, House talked with him at
some length and found him happy at the prospect of service—"a
well-meaning, accomplished old gentleman,"[23] receptive to the idea
of putting prime emphasis on the forming of a league of nations.
From him House learned the views of Republican leaders at home.
White had a letter giving the dissenting opinions of his friend Henry
Cabot Lodge, who asked that it be shown to Balfour and Clemenceau. But White had kept the message discreetly to himself.

In a conversation with Republican Senator Wadsworth, White
went so far as to say: "I have no knowledge whatsoever of his [Wil-

---

19. Bliss to March, Nov. 30, 1918, Bliss pa., Box 75.
20. Beer diary, Jan. 15, 1919, Butler Library, Columbia University. See
above, p. 45.
21. Seymour, *Letters from the Paris Peace Conference*, p. 54; N.D. Baker to Bliss,
Dec. 3, 1918, Bliss pa., box 75. Bliss to White, Dec. 16, 1918, box 61. On December 18
Bliss wrote to Baker to say that he had used Baker's letter as an argument of the futil-
ity of national frontiers. N.D. Baker pa., box 5, L.C.
22. R.S. Baker notebook, *XXII*, Baker pa., II, box 124, L.C.
23. House diary, Dec. 16, 1918, Jan. 3, 6; Bullitt diary, Jan. 1, 1919, Y.H.C.

son's] plans . . . not one of us knows what the President has in mind." When Wadsworth said he was astonished, White replied: "So am I. I wonder why I am here." Returning to Washington, Wadsworth reported this to his colleagues in the Senate and remarked: "President Wilson was totally unable to cooperate with people."[24]

Secretary Lansing's position was not very different. His work in the State Department was being carried on ably by Counselor Frank L. Polk.[25] The role that the secretary of state might normally expect to play at Paris was being filled by House, with whom European statesmen had become accustomed to deal in the pre-armistice negotiations. They respected his knowledge and his understanding, and could talk at their ease even when they did not agree with him.

House called on Lansing and on White and recorded that he found their offices "terribly vacant" in contrast with his own "busy shop." He was shocked by the secretary of state's ignorance of what was happening at Paris. "Lansing is a man that one cannot grow enthusiastic over," House wrote, "but I do think the President should treat him with more consideration." House listened patiently to Lansing's complaint that Wilson had talked with him only once on the *George Washington,* and explained that the president's coldness might well have its cause in ill health. When the secretary of state showed a desire to accompany the president to London, House promised to intercede. But Lansing was not invited to go to England, and then declined an invitation to visit Italy.[26]

The secretary of state hoped House would dissuade the president from sitting at the peace table and said that the Senate would never consent to the guarantee of territory that Wilson advocated.[27] On December 23 Lansing went so far as to warn Wilson in writing of the likelihood that the Senate would oppose such a positive commitment

24. Nevins, pp. 353–55, 361; record of James Wadsworth, pp. 236 ff., OHRO, Butler Library, Columbia University.

25. "We miss you terribly every day," Auchincloss wrote to Polk, "and your services could be used in this work better than those of practically any man we have here." Letter, Jan. 5, 1919, Y.H.C.

26. See above, pp. 148n. and 167–68. Aware of Lansing's frustration, House wrote in his diary: "Sometime ago I determined to let Lansing carry his own fortunes without help or hindrance from me. He had not been entirely considerate, after what I have done for him. On the other hand, I always appreciate the fact that I have been . . . 'super-secretary of State' and Lansing has played a minor part and done it without complaint." House diary, Dec. 14, 16, 18, 1919.

27. *F.R., PPC, 1,* pp. 515–16. In spite of their long and close association House thought that in the circumstances he could not press his friend too hard and thus risk restricting his own usefulness in the presence of the strain that the president's casualness was placing upon American relations with the governments of western Europe. Lansing wrote: "In such matters House is not courageous." Dec. 17, 1918, Lansing pa., "Appendix to Diary," microfilm 3, L.C.

as the president had in mind. In its stead he proposed an article in
the covenant of a league of nations that would bind member nations
not to undertake aggression or violate maritime rights, with expul-
sion from the league as the penalty for a breach.

Upon arriving at Paris, Lansing wrote to Wilson to ask just what
was expected of the secretary of state by the president. To this Wilson directed his clerk to reply that there was nothing in sight that
would warrant asking Lansing to hold his own engagements in
abeyance.[28] Indeed the president, aware that Lansing had a faculty
for irritating newsmen,[29] tried to persuade him not to give interviews. By January 6 Lansing evidently accepted the inevitability of
his position; for on that day House, embarrassed by the receipt of
messages that under normal procedure would have been brought to
the secretary of state, laid one of them before Lansing and was "astonished and pleased" at his matter-of-fact acceptance of the situation.[30]

House undertook to assuage the wounded egos of his three fellow
commissioners, whose uncertainty about Wilson's intentions he
shared to some extent. Trying to avoid personal publicity and to
play down the importance of the role that the president gave to him
but did not define precisely, he applied his energy and his patience
to the coordinating of the work.[31] Three days after the president's
arrival he met with the commissioners; and finding them "pretty
much at sea" as to what was expected of them, he arranged for Wilson to join them at the Crillon and for their pictures to be taken.
The talk was of other matters than the business at hand. Continuing
his efforts to maintain friendly relations[32] House invited General
Bliss to a family Christmas dinner.[33] To soothe Lansing, who objected to the use of House's office for the first meetings, the colonel
arranged to hold others in the quarters of the commissioners in rota-
tion. The president was usually absent, but attended a session on
New Year's Day and spoke in generalities. It was clear now that

28. Lansing's secretary to I.H. Hoover, Dec. 18, Close to Lansing, Dec. 18, 1918,
Wilson pa., 5B.
29. Swope of the *World* complained that Lansing would tell him a little and say
he could not tell more and then the English press would reveal the whole story.
Benham diary letter, Jan. 11, 1919.
30. House diary, Jan. 6, 1919.
31. "House has made a fine impression over here, although he has succeeded in
staying so far in the background even lately that the French people hardly know him."
Letter of Dec. 18, 1918, Seymour, *Letters from the Paris Peace Conference*, p. 51.
32. House diary, Dec. 17, 1918. Cf. Floto, p. 95. Not until four months later did
House finally give up trying to keep in touch with all of his fellow commissioners.
Diary, April 5, 1919.
33. Bliss diary, Dec. 25, 1918.

House, whose quarters eventually occupied twice as many rooms as those of Lansing, Bliss, and White combined, had a position of great responsibility, as well as one of such power that the jealousies that he dreaded were aroused.[34]

The president at first paid little attention to contacts with members of the American peace delegation or to any definition of their duties. The hundreds of delegates gathered in separate camps. There were the president and his small personal staff; commissioners Lansing, Bliss, and White; the State Department staff supervised by Grew; House's group, including The Inquiry; the economic advisers living at the Ritz or on the Avenue du Bois; and the military intelligence contingent under General Churchill.[35] These groups were not free from divisive ambitions.

In the absence of the stabilizing influence of a tradition of professional diplomacy, conflicts of authority were to impair the effectiveness of the delegates despite the intent of many to give disinterested service to the cause of peace. Few understood the difficulties of negotiating and drafting a treaty. Others were to learn in the hard school of experience. They looked to the president for guidance, and he was content to depend upon House.

Ill in his room in the Crillon, Jules Cambon, who was one of the French plenipotentiaries, was threatened with eviction in the American takeover of the hotel, which was a favorite hostelry of many influential people. His brother, the ambassador at London, was so dismayed by the invasion of his beloved Paris by foreigners that he wrote to his son on December 29th: "[They are] filling the hotels on the pretext of working at the conference. They are going to turn Paris into a bawdy-house. . . . What a mess they make and what future wars they will prepare!"[36]

Assisted by a staff of competent men who were in daily contact with him, respected him, and worked for him loyally, House was intent on serving the president as a catalyst. He was not qualified to

---

34. American delegates later began to speak of House's quarters in the Crillon as "the third floor front" and "upstairs." See Floto, pp. 97–98. Vance McCormick, reaching Paris on January 11, recorded that House was the "active man" of the delegation despite the fact that the colonel was at that moment ill. Diary, Jan. 11, 13, 1919.

35. See Floto, pp. 96–98. Approximately thirteen hundred people served the American Commission to Negotiate Peace (Seymour, *Letters from the Paris P.C.*, p. viii).

36. P. Cambon, *Correspondance 3*, p. 293; William A. Sharp, *War Memoirs*, p. 390.

The American peace commissioners, fearful that the continuing presence of Cambon in the Crillon might arouse British suspicions of a separate French-American understanding, decided that Henry White should see what he could do, in a friendly and informal way, to persuade Cambon to leave. Minutes of ACTNP, Jan. 10, 1919, Grew pa., Houghton Library, Harvard University.

originate policy, but he could facilitate its execution. Out of discord of interest he was able to produce some harmony of operation.[37]

Having no liking for administrative responsibility,[38] House entrusted the direction of the American delegation to Joseph C. Grew, who worked with Isaiah Bowman to solve some of the difficulties. The principal change was the absorption of the political intelligence group of the State Department by a Political, Territorial and Economic Intelligence Section, of which Bowman became chief. The Inquiry formed the nucleus of this section, losing its separate identity. On December 22, rejoicing in his power to choose men for their scholarly ability rather than for their rank or connection, Bowman wrote: "The day of great storm . . . threw out desks and men everywhere and got all rearranged so that we could get to work."[39]

"We should be lost if it were not for Bowman," Professor Clive Day wrote. ". . . A host of military men were detailed to the conference who are perfectly useless (and some are positively harmful), and these have got to be cleared out. . . . Some are first class—particularly those surrounding General Bliss. . . . Bowman called us together to say that the State and War Departments had practically

---

37. "This manifestation of the characteristics of the finished diplomatist is attested by those European leaders with whom he dealt." Charles Seymour, "The Role of Colonel House," E.H. Buehrig (ed.), *Wilson's Foreign Policy in Perspective,* p. 33. The writer's interviews with European participants in the peace conference confirm this opinion of House.

In a diary that was to be sealed for thirty years House revealed intense pride in the role of deus ex machina and also an exaggerated notion of his importance in the eyes of the American public: "I told him [Clemenceau] something of my career and expressed the intention of retiring after the President's term was ended. I thought if I went into another campaign and was defeated, I would be put out without having had the privilege of getting out voluntarily, and that it would be my first political defeat. On the other hand if I won, I did not believe the American people would look kindly upon another four or eight years of my influence." Diary, Dec. 21, 1918.

38. Auchincloss to Polk, Nov. 21, 1918, Y.H.C.

39. Isaiah Bowman's diary, Bowman pa., file 1, drawer 1; memorandum, Bowman to L. Harrison, Dec. 18, 1918, N.A., R.G. 256, 184/57. The reorganization was recommended in a memorandum sent to Grew on Dec. 12, 1918 by the Political Intelligence Department, the temporary chief of which was Charles Moorfield Storey. Storey felt that he was "very much in the fog." C.M. Storey to John W. Davis, Dec. 19, 1919, Y.H.C. His memorandum proposed that the military intelligence unit that General Churchill brought from Washington and which was judged to have "failed to provide for the requisite give and take" should be placed under the control of Mezes and Bowman. "Otherwise," the memorandum predicted, "there would be something nearly approaching chaos and at the end of a few weeks the complete refusal of either of the two to cooperate with the other." "Memo for Mr. Grew," Dec. 12, 1918, N.A., R.G. 256, 184/48; Shotwell, pp. 14–19; Seymour, *Letters from the Paris Peace Conference,* p. 48. Storey's recommendation resulted in his own removal from the position to which he had been tentatively assigned by Leland Harrison of the State Department. Bowman took his place. Memorandum, "Peace Conference of Paris, 1919," signed "I.B.," Bowman pa., file 1, drawer 1.

capitulated to The Inquiry."[40] General Churchill was ignored by
Bliss, who depended on direct contact with the scholars. Churchill
grew irritable and eventually fell ill.[41]

One of the officers for whom no place was found was Captain
Walter Lippmann, who had been of assistance to Colonel House as
draftsman of the commentary on the Fourteen Points. Bowman
thought that the brilliant journalist had contributed little to the essential scholarly work of The Inquiry, complained of his "cavalier attitude," refused his request for "a desk in a corner," and told Mezes
that he did not want to work with Lippmann.[42] In January an Army
order recalled Lippmann to the United States for discharge from
the service.[43] With the departure of Lippmann and that of Frank I.
Cobb[44] liberal opinion in the American delegation became less vocal,
although a *jeunesse radicale* led by William Bullitt remained to embarrass the peace commissioners by reminders of deviations from Wilsonian doctrine.

The upheaval was disconcerting to men of the State Department.
Leland Harrison, the assistant secretary of the American Commission, complained to Polk: "Mezes and his group [are] a kind of *im-
perium in imperio*. Having as they did an inside approach [they] got
everything in sight. It upset everything that had been done and
threw us all out of stride for three weeks."[45] Harrison asked Bowman to send all reports to the peace commission through Secretary
Lansing. Bowman, however, aware of Lansing's skepticism about
Wilson's program and fearing that the secretary of state would be

---

40. Day diary, Dec. 21, 1918, Y.H.C.

41. "Bowman, Peace Conference," statement of Oct. 7, 1939, Bowman pa., file 1,
drawer 1, "Miscellaneous Notes" folder.

42. Statement by Bowman filed with his diary, Oct. 5, 1939, Bowman pa., file 1,
drawer 1. Frank L. Warrin, Jr., who with Miller worked in harmony with Bowman,
told the writer that Bowman was distressed by a lack of objectivity in Lippmann's
reporting of intelligence.

43. Ralph Hayes to N.D. Baker, Dec. 31, 1918, Baker pa., box 6. A copy of the
order for Captain Lippmann's transfer is in the Bliss pa. (Order No. 3 of General
Headquarters of the A.E.F., Jan. 3, 1919, signed by James W. McAndrew.) General
Churchill told Bowman that he had seen the order; but Bowman, according to his
record, did not believe that there was one and insisted to Lippmann that he had
nothing to do with such a thing. Two-page statement, "Peace Conference," Bowman
pa., file 1, drawer 1, "Miscellaneous Notes" folder; statement filed with the diary, Oct.
5, 1939.

44. See below, pp. 262–63 and notes.

45. Harrison to Polk, Feb. 9, 1919, Y.H.C. For the point of view of another official, see Patchin to Polk, Dec. 24, 1918, Y.H.C. For Lansing's opinion of the baleful
influence of House's organization, see Lansing desk diary, May 1, 1919, L.C. and
Lansing to Polk, July 26, 1919, Y.H.C. "We had all felt that when we arrived we were
looked on with some suspicion, possibly as a fad of Colonel House." Seymour, *Letters
from the Paris Peace Conference,* pp. 100, 229.

obstructive, agreed only to consult with Harrison at times when he thought it would be useful to the State Department men to know what was going on.[46]

The task of organizing the work of the various divisions of the American delegation was never mastered in a way satisfactory to all concerned. Auchincloss wrote to Polk on January 5: "Everyone is jealous of the next man, and they are all so scared that someone is going to get something away from them that you have to be patting them on the back every few minutes. . . . Grew is a perfect angel and has reconciled all kinds of differences but he is not rough enough with these fellows." (Actually House thought him "not the man for the place" but "a gentleman . . . honest and trustworthy.")[47] Grew found it necessary to get a ruling from the president on the assignment of office space to the "economic men," all of whom expected first-class accommodations. Young Adolph Berle thought Grew "the most powerful man" in the "motley crew" at the Crillon. "There are hosts of minor retainers," he wrote, "gold-plated secretaries swaggering in splendid and unused uniforms, chargés drawn in from our legations, State Department officials and the like. Many are intriguing for themselves, but most are endeavoring to find themselves in a rather inchoate mass. . . . The surroundings are luxurious."[48]

House kept in touch, usually through Mezes,[49] with the scholars of The Inquiry. These men were ready to contribute what an English historian has called "a bedrock of politically colourless fact which any man of good will must recognize as rising above the conflicting claims of national sentiment or military pride."[50] Four days after the experts reached Paris, House chatted with them and showed appreciation of their efforts. The scholars had no well-defined relation to any permanent department of the government, or with other "temporary gentlemen."[51] Much was demanded in the way of direction in

46. Eight-page "Peace Conference" statement, Bowman pa., file 1, drawer 1, "Miscellaneous Notes" folder. "Our value at Paris would have been stultified if we had agreed to Harrison's request," Bowman wrote.

47. Letter in Y.H.C.; House diary, Dec. 14, 1918.

48. Grew diary, Jan. 9, 1919, Houghton Library, Harvard University; Baruch to W.W., Feb. 4, W.W. to Baruch, Feb. 5, 1919, Wilson pa., 5B; B.B. Berle and T.B. Jacobs (eds.), *Navigating the Rapids, 1918–1971*, p. 8. Harrison felt that Grew "smoothed over" the jealousies and malcoordination. Harrison to Polk, Feb. 9, 1919, Y.H.C. See Waldo H. Heinrichs, *American Ambassador* (Boston 1966), pp. 36–37.

49. Eight-page "Peace Conference" statement, Bowman pa., file 1, drawer 1, "Miscellaneous Notes" folder.

50. H.G. Nicholas in J.J. Huthmacher and W.I. Susman (eds.), *Wilson's Diplomacy: an International Symposium,* p. 87.

51. The Inquiry was housed in the Hotel Coislin, 4 Place de la Concorde, at the corner of the Rue Royale, and in the upper floors of Maxim's restaurant, to which a

order to use their talents. On December 31 House asked the scholars, through Mezes, to submit advice on all important territorial questions that were likely to arise in the peacemaking.[52] This request led to the preparation of memoranda that were bound in a "Black Book," dated January 21, 1919, and later simplified, especially with respect of colonial matters, in a "Red Book."[53] But on January 3 Lansing, Bliss, and White, meeting without Wilson or House and apparently ignorant of the action taken by the colonel, asked for memoranda on seven specific topics and agreed that, when received, these reports would be discussed by the commission in due course.[54]

Wilson's emphasis on the idea of a league as a general safeguard of peace led some Europeans to assume that the American delegates were less well prepared than they were[55] to deal with the technical questions that would arise. Actually a large store of authoritative advice was at hand. Lacking professional diplomatists with obvious qualifications as plenipotentiaries, the American government met the task of peacemaking in the same way in which it had responded to the challenge of war. It called into service private citizens of proven ability in politics, journalism, education, business, and finance. These men, accustomed to freedom of action and to productive operations, were unrestrained by the traditional disciplines of European diplomacy. Individuals were zealous to serve, each in his own way, and not infrequently in a way that would increase his own influence and power. A firm coordinating hand at the top was direly needed. During the war the president had supplied this hand and had kept the respect of his war cabinet. Now, in the release from the tension of war, he was content to leave matters of organization to House. For a time the colonel was able to guide a process of improvisation in which the men of proven fitness survived. At the same time

door was cut in the wall for direct access from the Coislin. A large reference library, assembled by Keogh of the Yale University Library, was in the care of Shotwell, who had further arranged for access to the documentation of the Bibliothèque de la Guerre at Paris. Shotwell, pp. 88, 89; Day diary. Dec. 23, 1918.

52. House diary, Dec. 31, House to Mezes, Dec. 31, 1918, Inquiry pa., box 3; Beer diary, Jan. 1, 1919; Shotwell, pp. 101–2, 133–34.

53. Shotwell, p. 134; Beer diary, Jan. 1, 1919. Noting that House's request to The Inquiry seemed to have resulted from pressure from Bullitt, Beer wrote: "There is in my mind considerable doubt whether the President wants this memorandum or will ever read it." See Gelfand, pp. 182–83, 332.

54. Minutes of the ACTNP, Jan. 3, 1919, Grew pa. The creation of a league of nations was not one of Lansing's seven topics.

55. "The President had thought nothing out," Keynes wrote. *Essays in Biography,* p. 24. A misunderstanding persists even today in England. Elcock, writing of the "remarkably little" preparatory work of the American delegation, appears to ignore the contributions of House and The Inquiry. See *Portrait of a Decision,* pp. 54, 58, 61.

House managed to keep his chief satisfied and confident of his historic mission and the prospect of success.

Now that House was more constantly associated with Wilson than ever before, certain strains upon their friendship developed. The president had been reluctant to undertake the trip to England that House had planned; and when Auchincloss attempted to fill the role of his father-in-law at London, Wilson resented the young man's officiousness.[56]

Irwin H. Hoover, head usher of the White House, who was with the president at Paris, wrote that through guarded suggestion "it was made to appear that Colonel House had presumed much and had taken advantage of his association and the confidence of the President to make it a junketing trip for those in whom he was interested." According to Hoover, "this in the mind of the knowing was the first blow struck at Colonel House."[57]

In the matter of organization Wilson had vetoed the elaborate plans of Mezes for a very large Inquiry staff. He protested now against putting the direction of communications in the hands of a man who had been associated with the hostile New York *Sun*.[58] Wilson told House of his disappointment at the absence of Frank I. Cobb, whom they had counted upon to direct the American publicity at the Peace Conference.[59]

---

56. Bullitt wrote: "House [was] quite blind to the depth of the President's dislike of Auchincloss." *Thomas Woodrow Wilson,* p. 164. Bonsal and Frazier thought that the indiscretion of Auchincloss was the prime cause of Wilson's eventual loss of confidence in House. Lansing's Private Memoranda, Oct. 14, 1921, L.C.; Frazier to Bonsal, Feb. 3, 1939, Bonsal pa., box 2, L.C.

57. "Col. Edward M. House," box 2, I.H. Hoover papers, L.C. Irwin Hoover told House, seven years later, that Baruch and his friend Dr. Grayson were most active in an endeavor to separate the colonel from the president, and that their efforts in this direction began before December 3, 1918. House diary, Dec. 20, 1925. Baruch wrote: "When I got to Paris, where Colonel House was the major-domo of the American delegation, I was not one of his clique" (*Public Years,* p. 142). See Cary T. Grayson, "The Colonel's Folly and the President's Distress," *American Heritage, 15,* (Oct. 1964): 4–7.

58. House diary, Dec. 14, 16; Benham diary letter, Dec. 10, 1918. Lansing wrote to Polk on December 15 that Philip Patchin and Leland Harrison, whom Wilson disliked, were "just the men" the president needed. Letter in Lansing-Polk correspondence, Y.H.C. House persuaded Wilson to accept them.

59. In a list of personnel that House submitted to Wilson on October 22, 1918, Cobb was set down as "editorial director." It seemed absolutely necessary, the colonel wrote at that time, "to have a man of the dimensions of Cobb to interpret to the newspaper people." Wilson had counted definitely on this able editor to take charge of press contacts at the Peace Conference, but he had not made this clear to House. House to W.W., Oct. 22, 1918, Wilson pa., 2; W.W. to Cobb, July 12, 1919, Wilson pa., 3.

After Wilson expressed his feeling about Cobb's absence House immediately sent word of this to Cobb, explained that the president had not previously made his wish clear, thanked Cobb for his work in Europe, and encouraged him to support Wilson's cause in the United States. Telegram, House to Cobb, Dec. 16, 1918 Y.H.C. At the

Cobb, protesting against House's practice of using discretion in selecting information to be forwarded to the White House, had insisted he must talk to the president himself—before Wilson was "pressed by official attention" in Europe. He wished to repeat the criticism of the British statesmen that he had given to House, and to warn the president against participation in the peace conference.[60] House had checked Cobb's departure, telling him that he was "badly needed" at Paris and that his advice was being conveyed to the White House by cable. However, he did not convey Cobb's extravagant criticism of the British, and thus he avoided aggravation of Wilson's prejudice.[61] Cobb, blaming House for delaying him, arrived in the United States after Wilson had departed. His warning reached the president a few days after Wilson's arrival at Paris, probably through Baruch.[62]

On December 4 House wrote in his diary: "[Ambassador] Sharp told me he had resigned, the resignation to take place February 1st. . . . He alleged financial difficulties. I think the fact that he was not appointed a peace commissioner had to do with it." House strongly recommended his friend Hugh C. Wallace as Sharp's successor at the Paris embassy and the president made the appointment. "Wilson did not like him," House wrote later, "and my pushing of Wallace's claims came near to alienating the President's regard."[63]

In retrospect, House designated his questioning of the president's

---

same time, apparently apprehensive that Cobb might make immoderate charges, House instructed Polk to keep him informed if Cobb called at the State Department. Auchincloss diary, Dec. 15, 1918.

60. See above, pp. 116, 247n.

61. House to Cobb, Nov. 14, 16, 1918, Y.H.C.

62. A penciled transcription of a cable, Tumulty to W.W., Dec. 19, 1918, Wilson pa., 5B, reads: "A mutual Harney [*sic*] saw Cobb in New York. Cobb suggested that I get in touch with you and say it is his opinion that Clemenceau and Lloyd George are in strict agreement and that the cards are stacked against you." The typed transcription reads: "A mutual friend saw Cobb . . ." One wonders whether Tumulty's actual words were: "Our mutual friend Barney [Baruch] . . ." Baruch recorded (p. 142): Cobb "quit abruptly and angrily, convinced, as he told me, that House, under British pressure, was weakening and qualifying the basis of peace which Wilson had laid down." It is not improbable that Cobb suggested, as he did more than a year later to Homer Cummings, that House had a dream of making a great reputation for himself as a peacemaker and then succeeding Wilson in the presidency. Cobb diary, memo by Mrs. Frank I. Cobb, Nov. 9, 1937, Cobb to W.E. Dodd, May 26, 1921, Cobb pa., L.C., Wilson pa., 14; Cummings diary, May 2, 1920, R.S. Baker pa.,; McCormick diary, May 6, 1919. See Seymour, "The End of a Friendship," *American Heritage, XIV*, No. 5 (Aug. 1963) pp. 4ff.: Grayson, "The Colonel's Folly . . . ," *American Heritage*, XV, No. 6, pp. 4ff., and Floto, pp. 69–71. Mrs. Frank I. Cobb confirmed to the writer the testimony that Dr. Floto cites.

63. House to Seymour, March 30, 1918, Y.H.C. Sharp was absent from Paris in January because of the death of a brother in the United States. He was not supplanted by Wallace until April 1919. *War Memoirs*, p. 401.

participation in the peace conference as the "first flat and vital difference" with Wilson.[64] In endeavoring to temper the stern morality of Wilson's challenge to the European statesmen, and in attempting to present the American program with diplomatic finesse, House created an impression that opened him to accusations of softness. Other men close to the president whispered that he was too much the compromiser and the "trimmer." Although evidence is lacking of any effect of such insinuations on Wilson, who found it very difficult to believe ill of a man to whom he had given his heart as he had to House, it is quite possible that his faith in the colonel's discretion was already yielding to the strains put upon it.

No arrangement was made for the regular briefing of the president on matters to be considered, nor for getting from him specifications as to information that he needed from time to time. Wilson was almost entirely isolated from the other commissioners except Colonel House, who, conscious of his friend's limitations, sought to shield him from what he was sure Wilson would find irksome. Lodged by his doctor's order in the Murat Palace, more than a mile from the Hotel Crillon, the president was protected from the hubbub of the American headquarters and depended on the private wire from House's office to keep him in touch with official business. In an inner sanctum the colonel received men who sought an opportunity to talk with the president.[65] House and his small and independent staff devoted themselves to undertakings that they conceived would be of more practical use to the president than the perfunctory operations of the career diplomats and their secretaries. The colonel was surrounded by men who would be completely loyal to him: his wife's brother-in-law, Sidney Mezes; his son-in-law, Gordon Auchincloss; the latter's law partners, David Hunter Miller and Frank Lord Warrin, Jr; and the invaluable Stephen Bonsal.

House, noting that since the armistices French opinion seemed to have grown more imperialistic, self-satisfied, and assertive, felt that Wilson's position was closer to that of the British, who demanded little except indemnification for war costs and restoration of the prewar status of the empire on the seas and in the markets of the world.[66] He had frequent talks with Wickham Steed of the North-

64. Seymour interview, Jan. 5, 1938, *American Heritage*, XIV, no. 5 (Aug. 1963), 8–9. See above, p. 119.

65. House diary, Jan. 7, 1919. House wrote, alluding to his fellow plenipotentiaries and to the advisers: "There is a constant passage of notes and conversations between these people and myself, and through me with the President, and back again the same way." Ibid., Dec. 23, 1918.

66. House diary, Jan. 4, 1919.

cliffe press[67] and with Tardieu, on whom Clemenceau depended in matters of negotiation and publicity. On January 7, House contrived to bring Clemenceau and Lloyd Goerge to his office with Wilson. At the risk of giving offence to the president,[68] he talked aside for a half-hour with the French premier and thought that he convinced him that French security would be well served by a league of nations. While discussing practical matters of immediate importance with both American and European delegates he put prime emphasis on the creation of a·league.

At the end of the first week in January House was in despair. Appeals for his intercession with the president came not only from the American commissioners and European pleaders, but from officials in Washington who lacked direction from the chief.[69] "I do not know," he wrote in his diary, "how I am to go through the many weeks ahead if matters are crowded upon me as they have been during the past few days. The other commissioners are willing to help, but I am sorry to say they are in fact a hindrance. So much time is taken up with them of a perfectly useless nature. The President seems to have no intention of using them effectively. It is the story of Washington over again. We settle matters between the two of us and he seems to consider that sufficient without even notifying the others. I feel embarrassed every day when I am with him."

The colonel had never felt strong enough himself to bear the strain of public office, and his misgivings were now justified. On January 9, three days before the first meetings of the peace conference began, he fell ill.[70] At this critical time he was unable to attend some of the sessions of the American commission. His chief, remote from his own delegation and its factional strife, would have to meet with the spokesmen for the European democracies in a political confrontation without assurance of diplomatic intercession.

---

67. Lord Northcliffe informed Geoffrey Dawson, editor of *The Times,* that he had long talks with the Americans, who wanted to work closely with the English. "In that respect," Northcliffe wrote, "Steed has been most extraordinarily useful. They all praise his energy and his knowledge in regard to his bailiwick and clearly value his general advice." Letter of Jan. 8, 1919, Willert box, Printing House Sq. pa., London.

68. House, fearful of awakening jealousies, instructed Auchincloss to withhold publicity of the fact that he had been closeted with the chiefs of Allied delegations. House diary, Jan. 8, 1919.

69. For example, McAdoo informed House that he had received no reply to two telegrams addressed to the president about the appointment of a new director-general of the railroads. McAdoo to House, Jan. 7, 1919, Wilson pa., 5B.

70. House suffered "a painful attack of kidney trouble," he recorded, "just when the momentum was at its highest and the peace organization was being perfected." Diary, Jan. 21, 1918.

The President continued to confer with the stricken adviser, and showed no lessening of appreciation of his counsel. While his other American associates came to feel that unless Wilson asked for their advice he was often less eager for it than he had indicated on the *George Washington,* House still held his confidence as a political catalyst, a reliable source of information, and a stimulating comrade in a common cause.[71]

71. Edith Benham recorded that when House came to lunch with the Wilsons the conversation became more interesting. Benham diary letter, Jan. 2, 1919, Helm pa.

☆ XVI ☆

The Prospect: January 1919

Two months after the signing of the armistices the ideals that Woodrow Wilson championed and that served so well as war propaganda still evoked popular enthusiasm, though they lost some luster as the weeks passed and the horrors of war became less vivid in the minds of the plain people.

Woodrow Wilson was the most zealous among Western leaders in championing humanitarian ideals. His appeal to the age-old yearning of men for freedom and justice derived authority from the practice of democracy in his own land. The American president also had a currency that weighed far more heavily than democratic idealism in the scales of traditional diplomacy in Europe. He commanded an immense store of material power in an impoverished world. He intended to use that power, if necessary, to enforce American concepts of justice for all peoples, even the smallest and weakest; and he was not interested in contributing to the strength of nations, such as those of the British Empire, that might be rivals of the United States in sea power and trade.

The acclaim that Europeans had given Wilson as a symbol of the common victory[1] had nourished the dream that was dear to him. He had characterized the age as one in which "the principles of men who utter public opinion dominate the world,"[2] and he believed that

---

1. H.W. Steed, *Through Thirty Years, 1892–1922, 2*, p. 267. "For a time after the Armistice he [Wilson] held the leadership of the world in a way that perhaps no other man has ever done." Sir Arthur Willert, "Random Notes on Woodrow Wilson," n.d., Willert pa., "1918" folder, Y.H.C. "What a place the President held in the hearts and hopes of the world when he sailed to us in the *George Washington!* What a great man came to Europe in those early days of our victory." J.M. Keynes, *The Economic Consequences of the Peace*, p. 34.

2. *P.P., 3*, p. 205.

the validity of the league and the execution of the treaty would depend upon the consent of public opinion. "Just a little exposure will settle most questions," he said in a speech at Paris. "My conception of the league of nations is just this, that it shall operate as the organized moral force of men throughout the world, and that whenever or wherever wrong and aggression are planned or contemplated, this searching light of conscience will be turned upon them."[3]

The president would have his country take the lead in establishing the new order and controlling the conflicts of the powers.[4] He held that the United States could act politically with the rest of the world without surrendering control of its own military and economic resources. He aspired to satisfy those of his countrymen who coveted moral prestige for their nation as well as those who sought trade and those who demanded protection against a repetition of the aggression that had thrust them into a brutal war.

Eager to seize the moment of opportunity, Wilson stood by the commitments that he had made under the pressures of warfare and without precise thought as to their application to the keeping of peace. In the new order there were to be no more treaties kept secret. Great powers that undertook to rule alien peoples were to be held accountable to the best interests of those peoples and to the moral judgment of the world. The seas were to be free of the right of a belligerent to control the passage of contraband of war, since there were to be no more belligerents. The exchange of goods between states belonging to an international association was to be free of discriminatory barriers so that increasing trade across national frontiers might bring the interests of all countries into close relation. National armaments were to be controlled by international agreement. And over all, an all-embracing league of nations was to keep the peace and provide for the amicable settlement of questions of contention among its members. This was to be brought about with the high hope and purpose of doing away with war everywhere and for all time.

In order that the envisioned league should be truly universal Wilson insisted at first that the defeated powers be admitted. If they were not, he feared, it would be thought that the spoils were being divided without giving the enemy a fair chance to state its case.[5] However, after he reached Europe he accepted the French demand

---

3. *P.P., 5,* p. 330.
4. Cf. N.G. Levin, Jr., *Woodrow Wilson and World Politics,* pp. 9, 251.
5. Dispatch, Murray from Wiseman, Aug. 10, Reading from Wiseman, Aug. 16, 1918, Wiseman pa., Y.H.C.; record of interview of Aug. 16, 1918, Wiseman pa.

that Germany be excluded at least until it showed itself worthy of admission.[6]

During the weeks following the armistice, however, certain underlying doubts that Europeans harbored and suppressed out of deference to American power rose gradually toward the surface.

To be sure, Wilson had found much support in England. It came both from the ranks of Labour and from statesmen who regarded the new concept as a means of enlisting American cooperation in governing the world by an adaptation of the traditional practices of the British Empire. Lloyd George told the Imperial War Cabinet that any British government not in earnest about the creation of a league "would be sternly dealt with by the people, and sooner rather than later." The league ideal continued to shine in the British political spectrum, with the exception of the extremes of left and right.[7] For the most part the premiers of the Allied Powers were disinclined to challenge openly the Wilsonian creed, in which many of their constituents believed.

Nevertheless American assertions of economic independence were shaking Allied hopes for the building of a postwar society upon patterns of wartime cooperation. Lloyd George remarked that the dissent of the United States in this respect, as well as the American program for competitive naval building, did not appear to provide an impressive beginning for the creation of a league of nations. Campaigning to get a conclusive mandate at the polls, the prime minister had not undertaken to moderate the passion of the British electorate for domination of the seas. Moreover he was bound to support the dominions that desired to take responsibility for governing nearby German colonies without international supervision; and he mistakenly supposed that he might barter colonial interests with Wilson.[8] Like the premiers of the Continental Allies, Lloyd George

---

6. In a memorandum written at Paris on December 15, 1918, Wiseman recorded that Wilson would "even agree to the French proposal that Germans be excluded for a while." When the king of England queried him on this point, at London in December, the president replied that Germany should not be a member of the league at present and that its entry ultimately would depend on its behavior. Auchincloss diary, Dec. 27, 1918, Y.H.C.

7. George W. Egerton, "The Lloyd George Government and the Creation of the League of Nations," *American Historical Review*, 424–41, and Henry R. Winkler, "The Development of the League Idea in Great Britain," University of Chicago microfilm, 1947.

8. Hankey recorded on December 23 "[Lloyd George] has told me plainly that he means to try and get President Wilson into German East Africa in order to ride him off Palestine." Stephen Roskill, *Hankey, 2*, p. 38.

failed to check the extravagant expectations of his people for reparations far beyond the enemy's capacity to pay.[9]

Foreign Secretary Balfour expressed a wish that the Fourteen Points be referred to as little as possible, since they seemed to him "very abstract"[10] and not a good basis for peacemaking. The ministers were in agreement that they would formulate British peace aims without regard to the Fourteen Points. They thought they need not raise questions touching upon their differences with Wilson, but might engage in argument if and when the president suggested that their aims were not compatible with his.[11]

Even the leaders of the league of nations movement in England, after Wilson met with them in December, were dismayed by the president's determination to meet political opposition with a dictatorial use of executive power. They foresaw that an ideal league, striving to enforce "a collective regard for the common weal of mankind," would meet resistance from elements moved by the same national pride and power that had driven European governments to pursue nation-centered policies. Influential voices questioned whether a league with effective sanctions was practical. Through centuries of conflict Europeans had learned that wars were usually contrived with expectation of victory, and that such an expectation diminished when there was a balance of forces that made victory difficult, if not uncertain. Armaments, strategic frontiers, and alliances had a defensive value that could be computed with some precision, but the worth of "virtue" was speculative. Morality in politics seemed a matter of the present alone, whereas political arrangements were conditioned by the past, concluded in the present, and dealt with the future. Veteran diplomats would not easily give up their faith in a balance of power and a continuation of the habit of conferences that had evolved during the war.[12] General Bliss wrote in his diary on January 8: "No one but the English and Americans seem to think that [a] league of nations will be any guarantee against the occurrence of war."

On the summit of their common triumph the Allied leaders, al-

---

9. The prime minister's dereliction in this respect was not unqualified. Keynes has written: "[Lloyd George] never, at any time, entertained any illusion about Reparations or made any statement which did not, if read carefully, include a saving clause." *Collected Writings, 10,* p. 56. However, he did say in a speech at Bristol: "If Germany has a greater capacity [than that required to meet the damages as reckoned by the British financial advisers] she must pay to the very last penny." Peter Rowland, *David Lloyd George* (London, 1975). See Nicolson, *Peacemaking,* pp. 20–23.

10. Nicolson, *Peacemaking,* p. 39.

11. Minutes of the I.W.C., Nov. 26, Dec. 18, 20, 23, 24, 1918, P.R.O.

12. Harold Nicolson, *Peacemaking,* pp. 192.

though still united in a common dread of revolution and anarchy in Europe and a common fear of its effect upon the societies of their own countries, began to pursue divergent purposes. Many issues that had not been discussed during military crises for fear of creating rifts in the alliance came to the surface. Faced with the responsibility of making the first treaty of world peace that had ever been attempted by democratic governments, the peacemakers would have to deal not only with popular pressures growing out of barbaric warfare and social unrest, but also with national goals to which politicians were committed.

Allied generals were disarming the enemy and occupying territory in a way that in some cases would make it difficult to set permanent boundaries in accord with Wilson's principles. Italy, acting in the interest of national security and the repatriation of Italians, was sending troops into regions even beyond those promised by the secret Treaty of London. The French leaders, relying on American sympathy for the war suffering of France and hoping the extent of the damage might be impressed upon Wilson by a first-hand view of the devastated regions, were ready to challenge the United States to carry out its commitment to an international league in ways beneficial to the security of their nation.[13] The three Great Powers, as well as Greece, had designs upon the Turkish Empire that were sanctioned by the secret treaties. And the Balkan nations and new states of Eastern Europe were claiming boundaries for which they found justification sometimes in the principle of self-determination, sometimes in that of economic or territorial security. Pleaders for national interests were quick to choose from Wilson's principles those that served their causes.[14] They were ready to use every opportunity to take advantage of the reservations with which they had qualified their tentative acceptance of Wilson's program in the pre-armistice meetings.

---

13. Louis Aubert, secretary to Tardieu and serving with him on the French High Commission in the United States, observed that Wilson spoke on September 27 of the "price" that each nation would have to pay in order that a league of nations might come into existence. Aubert suggested that if the Allies were to give up the benefits of the secret treaties and of their economic alliance of 1916 the American government, having no desire for territory and possessing great economic power, ought to be willing to abandon its position of isolation and enter the common "pool" of sacrifices, limiting its armament and making its military and economic power available to a league of nations and for the protection of the exposed frontier of France. From such a commitment, Aubert wrote, France would have much to gain at slight cost. *"Note sur les Travaux de l'Inquiry et sur les Solutions de paix Américaines,"* Dec. 11, 1918, signed "L.A.," Archives du M.A.E., À paix, vol. 161.

14. See R.C. Binkley, "New Light on the Paris Peace Conference," *Political Science Quarterly*, 338.

The president himself, by appealing in war propaganda to the "imperative principle" of self-determination, had undermined the argument for an effective universal government. A league of nations, if it were democratic, would have to depend upon the submission by minorities to the will of the majority. Moreover the Continental Allies, in their resolve to get secure frontiers, were ready to disregard the native impulses of peoples who stood in their way.[15] Secretary Lansing perceived that the doctrine of self-determination, as well as the pledge to guarantee territorial integrity, were leading the president into deep waters, uncharted by lawyers.[16] Citing self-determination as an "element of falsity" in "the gospel of Woodrow Wilson," Nicolson has written: "The Anglo-Saxon is gifted with a limitless capacity for excluding his own practical requirements from the application of the idealistic theories which he seeks to impose on others. Not so the Latin. . . . They observed that the doctrine of self-determination had not been extended either to the Red Indians or even to the Southern States."[17]

Worst of all, the president was standing in his own nation on political ground that the Europeans perceived to be insecure. They could not say to his face that they distrusted his credentials: indeed in the interest of unanimity they took some pains to save his face.[18] They were well aware that what was at stake was the continuing participation of the United States in the affairs of Europe, with all that this implied by way of assurance of peace and prosperity. They knew that to some extent they must play up to America. Nevertheless his detached idealism made it obvious to at least one young American at

---

15. Pierre Renouvin, *Traité de Versailles,* pp. 12–13. "If you have self-determination you cannot have free institutions, the sovereignty of the people (that paraphrase for democracy), self-government or even representative government. To all these renunciation of self-determination and the submission of the minority to the majority, described by John Morley as 'compromise,' are essential." Frank L. Warrin, Jr. to the writer, July 20, 1966.

Wilson was aware of the menace to governments that would result from an immoderate application of the principle of self-determination. "The proper basis," he had said to the British ambassador on January 3, 1918, was "satisfaction of legitimate desires of the separate peoples who had a right to satisfy those desires. They should be allowed to live their own lives according to their own will and under their own laws. In point of logic, of pure logic, this principle which was good in itself would lead to the complete independence of various small nationalities now forming part of various empires. Pushed to the extreme, the principle would mean the disruption of existing governments, to an undefinable extent." Stephen Gwynn, *The Letters and Friendships of Sir Cecil Spring Rice* (Boston, 1929), 2, pp. 422–25.

16. H. Holt, A.L. Lowell, Marburg, and Gadsden to W.W., Nov. 16, 1918, Wilson pa., 2, L.C.; Lansing private memoranda, appendix, Lansing pa., L.C., Dec. 17, 19, 20, 1918; Robert Lansing, *The Peace Negotiations,* pp. 95–97.

17. Nicolson, *Peacemaking,* pp. 194–95.

18. Ibid., p. 205.

Paris that the United States, despite its material power, its moral leadership, and its technical competence, stood as "a strange isolated Parsifal among nations."[19]

When the plenipotentiaries of the victorious powers at last came together on January 12 in an enlarged meeting of the Supreme War Council more than two months had passed since the armistice and almost a month since Wilson and his party had arrived in Europe. While the arbiters of the world's destiny dallied, the general fear of a violent upheaval in the lands of the enemy was not conducive to a deliberate approach to the peacemaking. Surrounded by an atmosphere of dread and importunity the American peacemakers faced grueling negotiations in which they would have to improvise tactics to deal with the war-hardened statesmen of Europe. How would the president fare, it was asked, when he came to close quarters with the premiers of the Allies, who were accustomed to wrangle without breaking off talks. Would these political chiefs measure up to Nicolson's definition of diplomacy: "the art of negotiating documents in a ratifiable and therefore dependable form"?[20] Wilson could also expect bitter opposition from certain senators at Washington and a lack of enthusiasm for an ideal peace on the part of citizens who were concerned only with national prosperity and security.

At Paris, at the beginning of 1919, the scene had been set and the prologue spoken. All mankind was waiting eagerly for the acts that would determine the political direction of the age. The Americans had been swept by a tide of history to the center of the stage, and their president was cast in the leading role. The first of the century's moments of great opportunity for the United States was already at hand. In the prologue of pourparlers at the end of 1918 certain themes appeared that were to persist through the peace conference and were to affect its course. Forces were already alive that were turning the epochal drama toward a tragic denouement.

---

19. Berle diary, Dec. 8, 1918, Franklin D. Roosevelt Library; B.B. Berle and T.B. Jacob (eds.), *Navigating the Rapids, 1918–1971*, p. 8.
20. Nicolson, *Peacemaking*, p. 208.

Appendix A

Official American Commentary on the Fourteen Points

October, 1918

I. Open covenants of peace openly arrived at, after which there shall be no private in-ternational understandings of any kind but diplomacy shall proceed always frankly and in the public view.

The purpose is clearly to prohibit treaties, sections of treaties or under-standings that are secret, such as the Triple Alliance, etc.

The phrase 'openly arrived at' need not cause difficulty. In fact, the Presi-dent explained to the Senate last winter that the phrase was not meant to exclude confidential diplomatic negotiations involving delicate matters. The intention is that nothing which occurs in the course of such confidential ne-gotiations shall be binding unless it appears in the final covenant made public to the world.

The matter may perhaps be put this way: It is proposed that in the future every treaty be part of the public law of the world; and that every nation as-sume a certain obligation in regard to its enforcement. Obviously, nations cannot assume obligations in matters of which they are ignorant; and there-fore any secret treaty tends to undermine the solidity of the whole structure of international covenants which it is proposed to erect.

II. Absolute freedom of navigation upon the seas, outside territorial waters, alike in peace and in war, except as the seas may be closed in whole or in part by international action for the enforcement of international covenants.

This proposition must be read in connection with No. XIV, which pro-poses a League of Nations. It refers to navigation under the three following conditions:

1. General peace;

2. A general war, entered into by the League of Nations for the purpose of enforcing international covenants;

3. Limited war, involving no breach of international covenants.

Under "1" (General peace) no serious dispute exists. There is implied freedom to come and go on the high seas.

No serious dispute exists as to the intention under "2" (a general war entered into by the League of Nations to enforce international covenants). Obviously such a war is conducted against an outlaw nation and complete non-intercourse with that nation is intended.

"3" (A limited war, involving no breach of international covenants) is the crux of the whole difficulty. The question is, what are to be the rights of neutral shipping and private property on the high seas during a war between a limited number of nations when that war involves no issue upon which the League of Nations cares to take sides. In other words, a war in which the League of Nations remains neutral. Clearly, it is the intention of the proposal that in such a war the rights of neutrals shall be maintained against the belligerents, the rights of both to be clearly and precisely defined in the law of nations.

III. *The removal, so far as possible, of all economic barriers and the establishment of an equality of trade conditions among all the nations consenting to the peace and associating themselves for its maintenance.*

The proposal applies only to those nations which accept the responsibilities of membership in the League of Nations. It means the destruction of all special commercial agreements, each nation putting the trade of every other nation in the League on the same basis, the most favored nation clause applying automatically to all members of the League of Nations.

Thus a nation could legally maintain a tariff or a special railroad rate or a port restriction against the whole world, or against all the signatory powers. It could maintain any kind of restriction which it chose against a nation not in the League. But it could not discriminate as between its partners in the League.

This clause naturally contemplates fair and equitable understanding as to the distribution of raw materials.

IV. *Adequate guarantees given and taken that national armaments will be reduced to the lowest point consistent with domestic safety.*

"Domestic safety" clearly implies not only internal policing, but the protection of territory against invasion. The accumulation of armaments above this level would be a violation of the intention of the proposal.

What guarantees should be given and taken, or what are to be the standards of judgment have never been determined. It will be necessary to adopt the general principle and then institute some kind of international commission of investigation to prepare detailed projects for its execution.

V. *A free, open-minded, and absolutely impartial adjustment of all colonial claims, based upon a strict observance of the principle that in determining all such questions of sovereignty, the interests of the populations concerned must have equal weight with the equitable claims of the government whose title is to be determined.*

Some fear is expressed in France and England that this involves the re-opening of all colonial questions. Obviously it is not so intended. It applies clearly to those colonial claims which have been created by the war. That means the German colonies and any other colonies which may come under international consideration as a result of the war.

The stipulation is that in the case of the German colonies the title is to be determined after the conclusion of the war by "impartial adjustment" based on certain principles. These are of two kinds: 1. "Equitable" claims: 2. The interests of the populations concerned.

What are the "equitable" claims put forth by Britain and Japan, the two chief heirs of the German colonial empire, that the colonies cannot be returned to Germany? Because she will use them as submarine bases, because she will arm the blacks, because she uses the colonies as bases of intrigue, because she oppresses the natives. What are the "equitable" claims put forth by Germany? That she needs access to tropical raw materials, that she needs a field for the expansion of her population, that under the principles of peace proposed, conquest gives her enemies no title to her colonies.

What are the "interests of the populations": That they should not be militarized, that exploitation should be conducted on the principle of the open door, and under the strictest regulation as to labor conditions, profits and taxes, that a sanitary régime be maintained, that permanent improvements in the way of roads, etc., be made, that native organization and custom be respected, that the protecting authority be stable and experienced enough to thwart intrigue and corruption, that the protecting power have adequate resources in money and competent administrators to act successfully.

It would seem as if the principle involved in this proposition is that a colonial power acts not as owner of its colonies, but as trustee for the natives and for the interests of the society of nations, that the terms on which the colonial administration is conducted are a matter of international concern and may legitimately be the subject of international inquiry and that the peace conference may, therefore, write a code of colonial conduct binding upon all colonial powers.

VI. *The evacuation of all Russian territory and such a settlement of all questions affecting Russia as will secure the best and freest coöperation of the other nations of the world in obtaining for her an unhampered and unembarrassed opportunity for the independent determination of her own political development and national policy and assure her a sincere welcome into the society of free nations under institutions of her own choosing; and, more than a welcome, assistance also of every kind that she may need and may herself desire. The treatment accorded Russia by her sister nations in the months to come will be the acid test of their good will, of their comprehension of her needs as distinguished from their own interests, and of their intelligent and unselfish sympathy.*

The first question is whether Russian territory is synonymous with territory belonging to the former Russian Empire. This is clearly not so, because

Proposition XIII stipulates an independent Poland, a proposal which excludes the territorial reëstablishment of the Empire. What is recognized as valid for the Poles will certainly have to be recognized for the Finns, the Lithuanians, the Letts, and perhaps also for the Ukrainians. Since the formulation of this condition, these subject nationalities have emerged, and there can be no doubt that they will have to be given an opportunity of free development.

The problem of these nationalities is complicated by two facts: 1. That they have conflicting claims: 2. That the evacuation called for in the proposal may be followed by Bolshevist revolutions in all of them.

The chief conflicts are (a) Between the Letts and Germans in Courland; (b) Between the Poles and the Lithuanians on the northeast; (c) Between the Poles and the White Ruthenians on the east; (d) Between the Poles and the Ukrainians on the southeast (and in Eastern Galicia). In this whole borderland the relation of the German Poles to the other nationalities is roughly speaking that of landlord to peasant. Therefore the evacuation of the territory, if it resulted in class war, would very probably also take the form of a conflict of nationalities. It is clearly to the interests of a good settlement that the real nation in each territory should be consulted rather than the ruling and possessing class.

This can mean nothing less than the recognition by the Peace Conference of a series of *de facto* Governments representing Finns, Esths, Lithuanians, Ukrainians. This primary act of recognition should be conditional upon the calling of National Assemblies for the creation of *de jure* Governments, as soon as the Peace Conference has drawn frontiers for these new states. The frontiers should be drawn so far as possible on ethnic lines, but in every case the right of unhampered economic transit should be reserved. No dynastic ties with German or Austrian or Romanoff princes should be permitted, and every inducement should be given to encourage federal relations between these new states. Under Proposition III the economic sections of the Treaty of Brest-Litovsk are abolished, but this Proposition should not be construed as forbidding a customs union, a monetary union, a railroad union, etc., of these states. Provision should also be made by which Great Russia can federate with these states on the same terms.

As for Great Russia and Siberia, the Peace Conference might well send a message asking for the creation of a government sufficiently representative to speak for these territories. It should be understood that economic rehabilitation is offered, provided a government carrying sufficient credentials can appear at the Peace Conference.

The Allies should offer this provisional government any form of assistance it may need. The possibility of extending this will exist when the Dardanelles are opened.

The essence of the Russian problem then in the immediate future would seem to be:

1. The recognition of Provisional Governments.
2. Assistance extended to and through these Governments.

The Caucasus should probably be treated as part of the problem of the

Turkish Empire. No information exists justifying an opinion on the proper policy in regard to Mohammedan Russia—that is, briefly, Central Asia. It may well be that some power will have to be given a limited mandate to act as protector.

In any case the treaties of Brest-Litovsk and Bucharest must be cancelled as palpably fraudulent. Provision must be made for the withdrawal of all German troops in Russia and the Peace Conference will have a clean slate on which to write a policy for all the Russian peoples.

VII. *Belgium, the whole world will agree, must be evacuated and restored, without any attempt to limit the sovereignty which she enjoys in common with all other free nations. No other single act will serve as this will serve to restore confidence among the nations in the laws which they have themselves set and determined for the government of their relations with one another. Without this healing act the whole structure and validity of international law is forever impaired.*

The only problem raised here is in the word "restored." Whether restoration is to be in kind, or how the amount of the indemnity is to be determined is a matter of detail, not of principle. The principle that should be established is that in the case of Belgium there exists no distinction between "legitimate" and "illegitimate" destruction. The initial act of invasion was illegitimate and therefore all the consequences of that act are of the same character. Among the consequences may be put the war debt of Belgium. The recognition of this principle would constitute "the healing act" of which the President speaks.

VIII. *All French territory should be freed and the invaded portions restored, and the wrong done to France by Prussia in 1871 in the matter of Alsace-Lorraine, which has unsettled the peace of the world for nearly fifty years, should be righted, in order that peace may once more be made secure in the interest of all.*

In regard to the restoration of French territory it might well be argued that the invasion of Northern France, being the result of the illegal act as regards Belgium, was in itself illegal. But the case is not perfect. As the world stood in 1914, war between France and Germany was not in itself a violation of international law, and great insistence should be put upon keeping the Belgian case distinct and symbolic. Thus Belgium might well (as indicated above) claim reimbursement not only for destruction but for the cost of carrying on the war. France could not claim payment, it would seem, for more than the damage done to her northeastern departments.

The status of Alsace-Lorraine was settled by the official statement issued a few days ago. It is to be restored completely to French sovereignty.

Attention is called to the strong current of French opinion which claims "the boundaries of 1814" rather than of 1871. The territory claimed is the Valley of the Saar with its coal fields. No claim on grounds of nationality can be established, but the argument leans on the possibility of taking this territory in lieu of indemnity. It would seem to be a clear violation of the President's proposal.

Attention is called also to the fact that no reference is made to the status of Luxembourg. The best solution would seem to be a free choice by the people of Luxembourg themselves.

IX. *A readjustment of the frontiers of Italy should be effected along clearly recognizable lines of nationality.*

This proposal is less than the Italian claim, less of course, than the territory allotted by the Treaty of London, less than the arrangement made between the Italian Government and the Jugo-Slav State.

In the region of Trent the Italians claim a strategic rather than an ethnic frontier. It should be noted in this connection that Italy and Germany will become neighbors if German Austria joins the German Empire. And if Italy obtains the best geographical frontier she will assume sovereignty over a large number of Germans. This is a violation of principle. But, it may be argued that by drawing a sharp line along the crest of the Alps, Italy's security will be enormously enhanced and the necessity of heavy armaments reduced. It might, therefore, be provided that Italy should have her claim in the Trentino, but that the northern part, inhabited by Germans, should be completely autonomous, and that the population should not be liable to military service in the Italian army. Italy could thus occupy the uninhabited Alpine peaks for military purposes, but would not govern the cultural life of the alien population to the south of her frontier.

The other problems of the frontier are questions between Italy and Jugo-Slavia, Italy and the Balkans, Italy and Greece.

The agreement reached with Jugo-Slavs may well be allowed to stand, although it should be insisted for the protection of the hinterland that both Trieste and Fiume be free ports. This is essential to Bohemia, German Austria, Hungary as well as to the prosperity of the cities themselves.

Italy appears in Balkan politics through her claim to a protectorate over Albania and the possession of Valona. There is no serious objection raised to this, although the terms of the protectorate need to be vigorously controlled. If Italy is protector of Albania, the local life of Albania should be guaranteed by the League of Nations.

A conflict with Greece appears through the Greek claim to Northern Epirus (or what is now Southern Albania). This would bring Greece closer to Valona than Italy desires. A second conflict with Greece occurs over the Ægean Islands of the Dodecanese, but it is understood that a solution favorable to Greece is being worked out.

(Italy's claims in Turkey belong to the problem of the Turkish Empire).

X. *The peoples of Austria-Hungary, whose place among the nations we wish to see safeguarded and assured, should be accorded the freest opportunity of autonomous development.*

This proposition no longer holds. Instead we have to-day the following elements:

1. CZECHO-SLOVAKIA. Its territories include at least a million Germans, for whom some provision must be made.

The independence of Slovakia means the dismemberment of the northwestern counties of Hungary.

2. GALICIA. Western Galicia is clearly Polish. Eastern Galicia is in large measure Ukrainian, (or Ruthenian), and does not of right belong to Poland.

There also are several hundred thousand Ukrainians along the north and northeastern borders of Hungary, and in parts of Bukowina (which belonged to Austria).

3. GERMAN AUSTRIA. This territory should of right be permitted to join Germany, but there is strong objection in France because of the increase of population involved.

4. JUGO-SLAVIA. It faces the following problems:

a. Frontier questions with Italy in Istria and the Dalmatian Coast; with Rumania in the Banat.

b. An internal problem arises out of the refusal of the Croats to accept the domination of the Serbs of the Serbian Kingdom.

c. A problem of the Mohammedan Serbs of Bosnia who are said to be loyal to the Hapsburgs. They constitute a little less than one third of the population.

5. TRANSYLVANIA. Will undoubtedly join Roumania, but provision must be made for the protection of the Magyars, Szeklers and Germans who constitute a large minority.

6. HUNGARY. Now independent, and very democratic in form, but governed by Magyars whose aim is to prevent the detachment of the territory of the nationalities on the fringe.

The United States is clearly committed to the programme of national unity and independence. It must stipulate, however, for the protection of national minorities, for freedom of access to the Adriatic and the Black Sea, and it supports a programme aiming at a Confederation of Southeastern Europe.

XI. *Rumania, Serbia, and Montenegro should be evacuated; occupied territories restored; Serbia accorded free and secure access to the sea; and the relations of the several Balkan states to one another determined by friendly counsel along historically established lines of allegiance and nationality; and international guarantees of the political and economic independence and territorial integrity of the several Balkan states should be entered into.*

This proposal is also altered by events. Serbia will appear as Jugo-Slavia with access to the Adriatic. Rumania will have acquired the Dobrudja, Bessarabia, and probably Transylvania. These two states will have 11 or 12 million inhabitants and will be far greater and stronger than Bulgaria.

Bulgaria should clearly have her frontier in the Southern Dobrudja as it stood before the Second Balkan War. She should also have Thrace up to the Enos-Midia line, and perhaps even to the Midia-Rodosto line.

Macedonia should be allotted after an impartial investigation. The line which might be taken as a basis of investigation is the southern line of the "contested zone" agreed upon by Serbia and Bulgaria before the First Balkan War.

Albania could be under a protectorate, no doubt of Italy, and its frontiers in the north might be essentially those of the London Conference.

XII. *The Turkish portions of the present Ottoman Empire should be assured a secure sovereignty, but the other nationalities which are now under Turkish rule should be assured an undoubted security of life and an absolutely unmolested opportunity of autonomous development, and the Dardanelles should be permanently opened as a free passage to the ships and commerce of all nations under international guarantees.*

The same difficulty arises here, as in the case of Austria-Hungary, concerning the word "autonomous."

It is clear that the Straits and Constantinople, while they may remain nominally Turkish, should be under international control. This control may be collective or be in the hands of one Power as mandatory of the League.

Anatolia should be reserved for the Turks. The coast lands, where Greeks predominate, should be under special international control, perhaps with Greece as mandatory.

Armenia must be given a port on the Mediterranean, and a protecting power established. France may claim it, but the Armenians would prefer Great Britain.

Syria has already been allotted to France by agreement with Great Britain.

Britain is clearly the best mandatory for Palestine, Mesopotamia and Arabia.

A general code of guarantees binding on all mandatories in Asia Minor should be written into the Treaty of Peace.

This should contain provisions for minorities and the open door. The trunk railroad lines should be internationalized.

XIII. *An independent Polish state should be erected which should include the territories inhabited by indisputably Polish populations, which should be assured a free and secure access to the sea, and whose political and economic independence and territorial integrity should be guaranteed by international covenant.*

The chief problem is whether Poland is to obtain territory west of the Vistula which would cut off the Germans of East Prussia from the Empire, or whether Danzig can be made a free port and the Vistula internationalized.

On the east, Poland should receive no territory in which Lithuanians or Ukrainians predominate.

If Posen and Silesia go to Poland rigid protection must be afforded the minorities of Germans and Jews living there, as well as in other parts of the Polish state.

The principle on which frontiers will be delimited is contained in the President's word "indisputably." This may imply the taking of an impartial census before frontiers are marked.

XIV. *A general association of nations must be formed under specific covenants for the purpose of affording mutual guarantees of political independence and territorial integrity to great and small states alike.*

The question of a League of Nations as the primary essential of a permanent peace has been so clearly presented by President Wilson in his speech of September 27, 1918, that no further elucidation is required. It is the foundation of the whole diplomatic structure of a permanent peace.

Wilson's Four Principles of February 11, 1918

First, that each part of the final settlement must be based upon the essential justice of that particular case and upon such adjustments as are most likely to bring a peace that will be permanent;

Second, that peoples and provinces are not to be bartered about from sovereignty to sovereignty as if they were mere chattels and pawns in a game, even the great game, now forever discredited, of the balance of power; but that

Third, every territorial settlement involved in this war must be made in the interest and for the benefit of the populations concerned, and not as a part of any mere adjustment or compromise of claims amongst rival states; and

Fourth, that all well-defined national aspiration shall be accorded the utmost satisfaction that can be accorded them without introducing new or perpetuating old elements of discord and antagonism that would be likely in time to break the peace of Europe and consequently of the world.

Wilson's Five Particulars of September 27, 1918

First, the impartial justice meted out must involve no discrimination between those to whom we wish to be just and those to whom we do not wish to be just. It must be a justice that plays no favorites and knows no standard but the equal rights of the several peoples concerned;

Second, no special or separate interest of any single nation or any group of nations can be made the basis of any part of the settlement which is not consistent with the common interest of all;

Third, there can be no leagues or alliances or special covenants and understandings within the general and common family of the League of Nations.

Fourth, and more specifically, there can be no special, selfish economic combinations within the League and no employment of any form of economic boycott or exclusion except as the power of economic penalty by exclusion from the markets of the world may be vested in the League of Nations itself as a means of discipline and control.

Fifth, all international agreements and treaties of every kind must be made known in their entirety to the rest of the world.

Appendix B

United States Loans to Foreign Governments

*Acts of April 24, 1917, September 24, 1917,
April 4, 1918, and July 9, 1918.*

As of November 25, 1918

	Credits authorized by President	Credits established	Cash advances	Other charges against credits	Balance under established credits
Belgium	153,000,000	141,000,000	139,000,000	—	2,000,000
Belgium	49,220,000	49,220,000	43,520,000	—	5,700,000
Belgium	2,900,000	2,900,000	2,475,000	—	425,000
Belgium	5,000,000	5,000,000	—	—	5,000,000
Brazil	50,000,000	—	—	—	—
Cuba	15,000,000	15,000,000	10,000,000	—	5,000,000
Czecho-Slovak	7,000,000	7,000,000	5,000,000	—	2,000,000
France	2,065,000,000	2,065,000,000	2,010,000,000	—	55,000,000
France	200,000,000	200,000,000	—	200,000,000	—
France	200,000,000	180,000,000	—	—	180,000,000
Great Britain	3,945,000,000	3,945,000,000	3,756,000,000	—	189,000,000
Greece	44,000,000	15,790,000	—	15,790,000	—
Italy	1,150,000,000	1,150,000,000	1,071,000,000	—	79,000,000
Italy	60,000,000	60,000,000	—	—	60,000,000
Liberia	5,000,000	5,000,000	—	—	5,000,000
Roumania	20,000,000	6,666,666	—	5,000,000	1,666,666
Russia	375,000,000	250,000,000	137,729,750	—	112,270,250
Russia	75,000,000	75,000,000	50,000,000	—	25,000,000
Serbia	12,000,000	12,000,000	10,814,697.70	—	1,185,302.30
	8,433,120,000	8,184,576,656	7,235,539,447.70	220,790,000	728,247,218.30

Source: N.A.,R.G. 39, box 220

Abbreviations Used in Footnotes

Baker—Ray Stannard Baker, *Woodrow Wilson: Life and Letters,* Potomac edition, vol. 7

F.R.—*Papers Relating to the Foreign Relations of the United States*

I.P—Charles Seymour, *The Intimate Papers of Colonel House*

P.P.—Ray Stannard Baker and William E. Dodd, eds., *The Public Papers of Woodrow Wilson*

P.P.C.—The thirteen volumes in *F.R.* that pertain to the Paris Peace Conference

A.E.F.—American Expeditionary Force

ACTNP—American Commission to Negotiate Peace

B.D.I.C.—Bibliothèque de Documentation Internationale Contemporaine

B.W.C.—British War Cabinet

f.—fascicule

F.C.—Fonds Clemenceau, Archives Historiques du Ministère de la Guerre, Château de Vincennes

F.O.—British Foreign Office

I.W.C.—Imperial War Cabinet

L.C.—Library of Congress

M.A.E.—Ministère des Affaires Étrangères

N.A.—National Archives of the United States

P.M.—Prime Minister

P.R.O.—Public Records Office, London

R.G.—Record Group

S.W.C.—Supreme War Council

T.R.—Theodore Roosevelt

W.W.—Woodrow Wilson

Y.H.C.—Yale House Collection, Yale University Library

Acknowledgments

There is a certain juncture that seems most favorable to research on an event in recent history. It is the coincidence of that moment at which the important documentary evidence has become available and that moment at which the testimony of participants and eyewitnesses is complete. With respect of the peacemaking at the end of World War I, the past two decades may prove to have been a most fortunate time for a quest for knowledge of what actually transpired. During this period official British and French papers have been released, and important American, German, and Italian collections opened. By the end of the period almost all of the personal records had come into view.

In 1958, after the publication of my biography of Woodrow Wilson, Charles Seymour suggested that I undertake an historical study of American diplomacy at the end of World War I and at the Paris Peace Conference of 1919. He himself had hoped that upon his retirement from the presidency of Yale University he might contribute a sequel to his volume on American diplomacy during the World War, but feeling that his writing years were by, he graciously put at my disposal not only the vast store of documents in the Yale House Collection, of which he was curator, but his knowledge of work of the American peacemakers, of whom he was one. Moreover, while granting complete freedom to use whatever the documents might reveal, he offered to guide my reading and to criticize my work. This he did, faithfully and in detail, almost to the day of his death. Nearly all of the first draft of the present book benefited from his wise and patient counsel.

A few months before he died Charles Seymour put me in touch with Frank Lord Warrin, Jr., law partner and personal assistant to

David Hunter Miller, who was Wilson's legal adviser at Paris. A man
free from the restraint imposed by public office and as much at home in
Europe as in the United States, Warrin was a keen critic of the art of
diplomacy. Until his death he shared with me his recollections of men
and events; furthermore, he brought his finely trained mind to bear
upon the pages of early drafts of this work.

To these men I am deeply indebted. I owe much also to assiduous
and stimulating criticism on the part of Ambassador Rudolf Schoen-
feld. Moreover, I am grateful to the late George Bernard Noble, author of *Policies and Opinions at Paris* and for many years head of the
historical division of the Department of State, as well as to Dr. John
Wells Davidson, Professor Gaddis Smith, and Dr. Kenneth Thompson. These men have read the entire manuscript and made valuable
suggestions.

Professor Samuel F. Bemis, Professor Edward V. Gulick, John W.
Gould, George M. Kendall, George F. Kennan, Professor Ivo J. Lederer, Professor George W. Pierson, Professor Harry R. Rudin, and
Professor Arthur M. Schlesinger, Jr. have read and criticized certain
pages in tentative drafts.

I have been fortunate to have, orally or in writing, recollections
from the following participants in the peacemaking: Philip Noel
Baker, Bernard M. Baruch, William C. Bullitt, François Charles-
Roux, Gilbert F. Close, John W. Davis, Raymond B. Fosdick, Arthur
Hugh Frazier, Robert H. George, Joseph C. Grew, Lord Hankey,
Edith Benham Helm, Herbert C. Hoover, Sir Clement Jones, Jules
LaRoche, Breckinridge Long, Sir Harold Nicolson, George Bernard
Noble, Wallace Notestein, William Phillips, André Portier, Sir Ar-
thur Salter, Francis B. Sayre, James T. Shotwell, Arthur Sweetser,
Charles L. Swem, Sir Charles Webster, Sir Arthur Willert, and Sir
William Wiseman. Cary T. Grayson, Jr., has consulted for me the
record left by his father; and the papers of Stephen Bonsal were
made available by his son, Ambassador Philip Bonsal.

I wish to acknowledge the assistance of Madame Paul Mantoux,
the late Professor Pierre Renouvin, Professor Jean-Baptiste Duroselle, and Professor André Kaspi, and of the staffs of the Bibliothèque de Documentation Internationale Contemporaine, the Archives Historiques of the Ministère de Guerre, and the Archives
Diplomatiques of the Ministère des Affaires Étrangères. I am indebted also to the archivists at the National Archives of Canada in
Ottawa, at the Scottish Record Office in Edinburgh, at the Bodleian
and the library of New College in Oxford, and, in London, those
at the Public Records Office, the Beaverbrook Library, the British
Museum, the Printing House Square collection of *The Times,* and

the libraries of the India Office and the London School of Economics. Professor Agnes Headlam-Morley very kindly permitted me to read papers of her father, Sir James Headlam-Morley; and Geoffrey J. Martin has allowed me to make use of copies of papers of Isaiah Bowman that supplement the file in the library of the Johns Hopkins University.

My work at the Princeton University Library has been facilitated by the cooperation of Alexander P. Clark and his staff, as well as that of Professor Arno J. Mayer and the editors of the Wilson Papers.

At the Yale University Library I have benefited from the good offices of the archivist, the late Herman Kahn, and from the constant help of those who have been in charge of the House Collection and related papers since the death of Charles Seymour: Howard Gotlieb, Judith Schiff, and Nicholas Rizopoulos.

The staffs of the libraries of Harvard University have assisted me often, also those of the libraries of Columbia, Cornell, Duke, and the University of Virginia, and those of the Library of Congress, the National Archives, the Franklin D. Roosevelt Library, and the Hoover Institution of War, Revolution and Peace.

Katharine E. Brand has continued to be, as she was during the writing of *Woodrow Wilson*, an invaluable counselor. Colonel James B. Rothnie has assisted by transcribing notes written in shorthand by Wilson. The lively interest of the late Raymond B. Fosdick was heartening. The Rockefeller Foundation and the American Philosophical Society provided support of far-reaching and protracted research; and Yale University made available the security and the services of its library. Through the years the MacDowell Colony has supplied an ideal setting for revisionary labor.

Bibliography

The American documents that bear upon the ending of World War I, the negotiation of the armistices, and the events of the subsequent two months are of enormous volume, and are located in several archives. Thousands have been printed in one or both of two basic collections: *Papers Relating to the Foreign Relations of the United States,* 1918 and 1919 series and *Lansing Papers,* vol. 2 (Washington, D.C., 1931–1947); and *My Diary,* by David Hunter Miller, twenty-one volumes privately printed by Peter Smith (Gloucester, Mass.). The former compilations include papers that are in the State Department files in the National Archives, the Wilson Collection in the Library of Congress, or the House Collection in the Yale University Library. Miller, in editing his twenty-one volumes, drew upon papers that he brought away from the Paris Peace Conference and that are in the Library of Congress.

I have searched the files from which the documents in these two standard compilations were taken and have made use of some papers not printed heretofore. Moreover, I have drawn upon relevant documents in the archives of the Treasury Department. I have consulted also the following collections:

In the Library of Congress: the papers of these people: Carl Ackerman, Newton D. Baker, Ray Stannard Baker, General Tasker H. Bliss, Stephen Bonsal, Frank I. Cobb, George Creel, Josephus Daniels, Norman H. Davis, Raymond B. Fosdick, Thomas W. Gregory, Charles S. Hamlin, Leland Harrison, Ralph Hayes, Edith Benham Helm, Irwin H. Hoover, Philip C. Jessup, Robert Lansing, Henry Cabot Lodge, Breckinridge Long, Charles O. Maas, William G. McAdoo, Theodore Marburg, David Hunter Miller, John Bassett Moore, Henry Morganthau, Roland S. Morris, General John J. Pershing, Elihu Root, Arthur Sweetser, William Howard Taft, James T. Taylor, Joseph P. Tumulty, William Howard Taft, William Allen White, Henry White, Edith Bolling Wilson, Woodrow Wilson, Robert W. Woolley, and Lester H. Woolsey.

At Yale University in the Sterling Library: the Edward M. House Collection, designated in this book as "Y.H.C." and including the diaries and papers of Edward M. House and Gordon Auchincloss, papers of William C. Bullitt, John W. Davis, Walter G. Davis, Clive Day, Edward M. House, Vance McCormick, Frank L. Polk, Charles Seymour, Sir Arthur Willert, Sir William Wiseman, and William Yale; also at the Yale Library, certain documents of The Inquiry, and microfilms of the papers of Sidney Sonnino, the papers of Willard Straight, the diary of Mark Jefferson, and various collections at the Hoover War Library.

At Princeton University in the Firestone Library: the papers of Bernard M. Baruch, Ray Stannard Baker, Gilbert F. Close, John Foster Dulles, Albert Lamb, Robert Lansing, and Charles L. Swem.

At Harvard University in the Houghton Library: the papers of Ellis L. Dresel, Joseph C. Grew, Walter Hines Page, William Phillips, and Oswald Garrison Villard; in the Widener Library archives, the papers of Archibald Cary Coolidge and Theodore Roosevelt; in the Baker Library, the papers of Thomas W. Lamont.

At Columbia University in the Butler Library: the papers of Sidney E. Mezes and James T. Shotwell, the diaries of George Louis Beer and William L. Westermann, and the Oral History Records of Boris A. Bakhmeteff, William Phillips, DeWitt Poole, James T. Shotwell, and others.

In the Duke University Library: the papers of Thomas Nelson Page.

At the Massachusetts Historical Society: the papers of Henry Cabot Lodge and John T. Morse, Jr.

At the Johns Hopkins University in the Eisenhower Library: the papers of Isaiah Bowman.

In the Franklin D. Roosevelt Library at Hyde Park: the papers of Adolph Berle.

At the University of Virginia in the Alderman Library: the papers of Carter Glass.

At Cornell University in the John M. Olin Library: the papers of Willard Straight.

In the Public Records Office, London, the minutes of the British War Cabinet and the Imperial War Cabinet and the papers of the Foreign Office and its officials pertaining to the ending of the war and the peacemaking.

In the Beaverbrook Library, London, the papers of Lord Beaverbook, David Lloyd George, Andrew Bonar Law, and St. Loe Strachey. These papers are now in the House of Lords Record Office, London.

At Oxford University: in the Bodleian Library, the papers of Viscount Bryce, Gilbert Murray, and Herbert Henry Asquith, Earl of Oxford and Asquith; in the Library of New College, the papers of Alfred, Lord Milner.

In the British Museum, the papers of Arthur James Balfour, Earl of Balfour, and of Lord Robert Cecil.

In the India House Library and Records, the papers of Lord Curzon.

In the Printing House Square Papers of the *Times,* the papers of Geoffrey Dawson, Wickham Steed, and Sir Arthur Willert.

In the British Library of Political and Economic Science, at the London

School of Political and Economic Science, the papers of Sir Charles Webster.

In the Scottish Record Office, Edinburgh, the papers of Philip Henry Kerr, Marquess of Lothian.

In the National Archives of Canada, Ottawa, the papers of Sir Robert L. Borden and Sir G. E. Foster.

In the Archives Diplomatiques of the Ministère des Affaires Etrangères, Paris: *Receuil des Actes de la Conférence de la Paix 1918–20,* 7 vols.; the series "À paix, 1918–1929" and "Europe 1918–29": "Grande-Bretagne," and "L'Amérique."

In the Archives Historiques du Ministère de la Guerre, Château de Vincennes, "Fonds Clemenceau."

In the Bibliothèque de Documentation Internationale Contemporaine, University of Paris, Nanterre, the papers of Paul Mantoux and of André Chéradame.

In the Archives Nationales, Paris, the papers of the Ministry of Commerce and Industry.

A valuable bibliographical guide is Nina Almond and Ralph H. Lutz, *An Introduction to a Bibliography of the Paris Peace Conference,* Stanford, Calif., 1935.

Documents

Albrecht-Carrié, Réné, *Italy at the Paris Peace Conference,* New York, 1938.

Aldrovandi-Marescotti, Luigi, *Guerra Diplomatica,* Milan, 1936. Containing notes on the pre-armistice meetings, Oct. 28–Nov. 6, 1918, many of which are printed in English translation in Albrecht-Carrié's volume. A translation in French, by F. Cravoisier, was published in Paris in 1939.

Baker, Ray Stannard, *Woodrow Wilson: Life and Letters, Armistice 1918,* Potomac edition, New York, 1939.

———, *Woodrow Wilson and World Settlement,* 3 vols., *3,* New York, 1922.

——— and William E. Dodd (eds.), *The Public Papers of Woodrow Wilson,* 6 vols. in *3,* New York, 1925–27.

Bane, Suda L., and Ralph H. Lutz (eds.), *The Blockade of Germany after the Armistice,* 1918–19, Stanford, Calif., 1942.

———, *The Organization of American Relief in Europe,* 1918–19, Stanford, Calif., 1943.

British and Foreign State Papers, vols., 111, 112, London, 1921–22.

I documenti diplomatici italiani, 6th series (Nov. 4, 1918–Jan. 17, 1919), Rome, 1955.

de Launay, Jacques, *Secrets diplomatiques,* 1914–18, Brussels, 1963.

Lutz, Ralph H., *The Fall of the German Empire,* 2 vols., New York, 1940.

Miller, David Hunter, *The Drafting of the Covenant,* 2 vols., New York, 1928.

Scott, James Brown (ed.), *Official Statements of War Aims and Peace Proposals,* Dec. 1916–Nov. 1918, Washington, 1921.

Temperley, Harold W.V. (ed.), *A History of the Peace Conference at Paris,* 6 vols., London, 1920–24.

Terrail, Gabriel (Mermeix), *Les Négotiations Secrètes et les Quatre Armistices, avec Pièces Justificatives,* Paris, 1921.

Diaries, Letters, Memoirs

Baker, Ray Stannard, *American Chronicle,* New York, 1945.

Baruch, Bernard M., *The Public Years,* New York, 1960.

Beaverbrook, William Maxwell Aitken, *Men and Power, 1917–18,* New York, 1956.

Berle, Beatrice B., and Travis B. Jacobs (eds.), *Navigating the Rapids, 1918–1971.* From the papers of A.A. Berle, New York, 1973.

Bonsal, Stephen, *Suitors and Suppliants,* New York, 1946.

———, *Unfinished Business,* New York, 1944.

Borden, R.L., *Robert Land Borden, His Memoirs,* New York, 1938.

Butler, Nicholas Murray, *Across the Busy Years,* 2 vols., *2,* New York, 1939–40.

Callwell, Charles E., *Field Marshal Sir Henry Wilson: His Life and Diaries,* 2 vols., *2,* London, 1927.

Cambon, Paul, *Correspondance,* 3 vols., *3,* Paris, 1946.

Cecil, Lord Robert, *A Great Experiment,* New York, 1941.

Centenaire Woodrow Wilson, 1856–1956, Geneva, 1956.

Charles-Roux, François, *Souvenirs Diplomatiques: Rome—Quirinal,* Paris, 1958.

Clemenceau, Georges, *Grandeur and Misery of Victory,* New York, 1930.

Coolidge, Harold J., and Robert H. Lord, *Archibald Cary Coolidge, Life and Letters,* Cambridge, Mass., 1932.

Creel, George, *Rebel at Large, Recollections of Fifty Crowded Years,* New York, 1947.

Daniels, Josephus, *The Cabinet Diaries of Josephus Daniels,* ed. by E. David Cronon, Lincoln, Neb., 1963.

———, *The Wilson Era,* 2 vols., *2,* Chapel Hill, N.C., 1944, 1946.

Foch, Ferdinand, *Mémoires,* 2 vols., *2,* Paris, 1931.

Grayson, Cary T., *Woodrow Wilson: An Intimate Memoir,* New York, 1960.

Grew, Joseph C., *Turbulent Era,* ed. by Walter Johnson, 2 vols., *1,* Boston, 1952.

Hankey, Maurice, Lord Hankey, *The Supreme Command, 1914–1918,* London, 1961.

———, *The Supreme Control,* London, 1963.

Hardinge of Penshurst, Lord, *Old Diplomacy,* London, 1947.

Hoover, Herbert C., *America's First Crusade,* New York, 1942.

———, *The Memoirs of Herbert Hoover; Years of Adventure, 1874–1920,* New York, 1951.

———, *The Ordeal of Woodrow Wilson,* New York, 1958.

Hoover, Irwin Hood, *Forty-Two Years in the White House,* Boston, 1934.

House, Edward M., *The Intimate Papers of Colonel House and What Really Happened at Paris.* See Seymour.

Hughes, William M., *Policies and Potentates,* Sydney, 1950.

Hurley, Edward N., *The Bridge to France,* Philadelphia and London, 1927.

Jefferson, Mark, *Paris Peace Conference Diary,* ed. by Geoffrey J. Martin, Microfilm, Ann Arbor, Mich., 1966.

Jones, Thomas, *Whitehall Diary,* ed. by Keith Middlemas, 3 vols., *1,* London, 1969.

Keynes, John Maynard, *Two Memoirs,* London, 1949.

Lane, Franklin K., *The Letters of Franklin K. Lane,* ed. by A.W. Lane and L.H. Wall, Boston, 1922.

Lansing, Robert, *The Peace Negotiations: a Personal Narrative,* Boston, 1921.

Lloyd George, David, *The Truth about the Peace Treaties,* 2 vols., London, 1938.

———, *War Memoirs,* 6 vols., Boston, 1937.

Masaryk, Thomas G., *The Making of a State,* New York, 1927.

McAdoo, William G., *Crowded Years,* Boston, 1931.

Mott, Col. Thomas B., *Twenty Years as Military Attaché,* New York, 1937.

Murray, Arthur Cecil, *At Close Quarters,* London, 1946.

Nicolson, Sir Harold, *Peacemaking, 1919,* rev. edn., London, 1943.

Page, Thomas Nelson, *Italy and the World War,* New York, 1920.

Palmer, Frederick, *Bliss, Peacemaker: The Life and Letters of General Tasker Howard Bliss,* New York, 1934.

Percy, Lord Eustace, *Some Memories,* London, 1958.

Pershing, John J., *My Experiences in the World War,* 2 vols., *2,* New York, 1931.

Phillips, William, *Adventures in Diplomacy,* Portland, Me., 1952.

Poincaré, Raymond, *Au Service de la France,* 10 vols., *10,* Paris, 1933; *11,* Paris, 1974.

Recouly, Raymond, *Foch: My Conversations with the Marshal,* New York, 1929.

Riddle, George Allardice, baron, *Lord Riddell's Intimate Diary of the Peace Conference and After, 1918–1923,* New York, 1934.

Seymour, Charles, *The Intimate Papers of Colonel House,* 4 vols., *3, 4,* Boston, 1928.

———, *Letters from the Paris Peace Conference,* New Haven, 1965.

———, *and House, Edward M. (eds.), What Really Happened at Paris,* New York, 1921.

Sharp, William G., *The War Memoirs of William Graves Sharp,* ed. by Warrington Dawson, London, 1931.

Shartle, Samuel G., *Spa, Versailles, Munich,* Philadelphia, 1941.

Shotwell, James T., *At the Paris Peace Conference,* New York, 1937.

Sonnino, Sidney, *Diario, 1916–1922,* Pietro Pastorelli (ed.), 3 vols., *3,* Bari, 1972.

Speranza, Gino Charles, *Gino Speranza's Diary,* New York, 1941.

Steed, Henry Wickham, *Through Thirty Years, 1892–1922,* 2 vols., *2,* New York, 1924.

Tardieu, André, *The Truth about the Treaty,* Indianapolis, 1921.

Tumulty, Joseph P., *Woodrow Wilson as I Know Him,* New York, 1921.

Villard, Oswald Garrison, *The Fighting Years,* New York, 1939.

Wemyss, Lady Victoria Wester, *Life and Letters of Lord Wester Wemyss,* London, 1935.

Weygand, General Maxime, *Mémoires: Mirages et Realité,* 2 vols., *2,* Paris, 1957.

White, William Allen, *The Autobiography of William Allen White,* New York, 1946.

————, *Selected Letters of William Allen White,* ed. by Walter Johnson, New York, 1947.

Willert, Sir Arthur, *Washington and Other Memories,* Boston, 1972.

Wilson, Edith Bolling, *My Memoir,* Indianapolis and N.Y., 1938.

Wilson, Trevor (ed.), *The Political Diaries of C.P. Scott,* Ithaca, NY., 1970.

Secondary Sources

Bailey, Thomas A., *Woodrow Wilson and the Lost Peace,* New York, 1944.

Baumont, Maurice, *La Faillite de la Paix, 1918–1939,* Paris, 1951.

Bell, H.C.F., *Woodrow Wilson and the People,* Garden City, N.Y., 1945.

Berger, Marcel, and Paul Allard, *Les Dessous du Traité de Versailles,* Paris, 1933.

Birdsall, Paul, *Versailles Twenty Years After,* New York, 1944.

Bruun, Geoffrey, *Clemenceau,* Cambridge, Mass., 1943.

Buehrig, Edward H., *Woodrow Wilson and the Balance of Power,* Bloomington, Ind., 1955.

———— (ed.), *Wilson's Foreign Policy in Perspective,* Bloomington, Ind., 1957.

Bullitt, William C., *Thomas Woodrow Wilson,* Boston, 1967.

Churchill, Sir Winston L.S., *The Aftermath,* vol. 4 of *The World Crisis,* New York, 1929.

Clémentel, Étienne, *La France et la Politique Économique Interallié,* Paris, 1931.

Coit, Margaret L., *Mr. Baruch,* Boston, 1957.

Craig, Gordon, and Felix Gilbert (eds.), *The Diplomats, 1919–1939,* Princeton, 1953.

Creel, George, *The War, The World, and Wilson,* New York, 1920.

Devlin, Patrick, Baron Devlin, *Too Proud to Fight,* New York, 1975.

Diamond, William, *The Economic Thought of Woodrow Wilson,* Baltimore, 1943.

Duroselle, Jean-Baptiste, *From Wilson to Roosevelt,* Cambridge, Mass., 1963. See also Huthmacher.

Elcock, Howard J., *Portrait of a Decision,* London, 1972.

Evans, Laurence, *U.S. Policy and the Partition of Turkey,* Baltimore, 1943.

Farnsworth, Beatrice, *William C. Bullitt and the Soviet Union,* Bloomington, Ind., 1967.

Floto, Inga, *Colonel House in Paris,* Copenhagen, 1973.

Fowler, Wilton B., *British-American Relations, 1917–1918: The Role of Sir William Wiseman,* Princeton, 1969.

Fraenkel, Ernest. See Huthmacher.

Garraty, John A., *Henry Cabot Lodge,* New York, 1953.

Gelfand, Lawrence E., *The Inquiry,* New Haven, 1963.

George, Alexander L. and Juliette L., *Woodrow Wilson and Colonel House,* New York, 1956.

Gerson, Louis L., *Woodrow Wilson and the Rebirth of Poland,* New Haven, 1953.

Gollin, Alfred M., *Proconsul in Politics,* London, 1964.

Hammond, J.L.L., *C.P. Scott of the Manchester Guardian,* London, 1934.

Harbaugh, William H., *Lawyer's Lawyer, The Life of John W. Davis,* New York, 1973.

Haskins, Charles H. and Robert H. Lord, *Some Problems of the Paris Peace Conference,* Cambridge, Mass., 1920.

Huthmacher, J. Joseph and Warren I. Susman (eds.), *Wilson's Diplomacy: an International Symposium,* with contributions by Arthur S. Link, Jean-Baptiste Duroselle, Ernest Fraenkel, and H.G. Nicholas, Cambridge, Mass., 1973.

Jordan, W.M., *Great Britain, France, and the German Problem 1918–1939,* London, 1943. Preface by Sir Charles Webster.

Kennan, George F., *Russia and the West,* Boston, 1961.

———, *Soviet-American Relations 1917–1920,* 2 vols.: *1, Russia Leaves the War; 2, The Decision to Intervene,* Princeton, 1956.

Kernek, Sterling J., *Distractions of Peace during War,* Philadelphia, 1975.

Keynes, John Maynard, *The Economic Consequences of the Peace,* New York, 1920.

Lansing, Robert, *The Big Four and Others of the Peace Conference,* Boston, 1921.

Lawrence, David, *The True Story of Woodrow Wilson,* New York, 1924.

Lederer, Ivo J., *Yugoslavia at the Paris Peace Conference,* New Haven, 1963.

Levin, Norman Gordon, Jr., *Woodrow Wilson and World Politics: America's Response to War and Revolution,* New York, 1968.

Link, Arthur S., *Wilson the Diplomatist,* Baltimore, 1957. See also Huthmacher.

Louis, William Roger, *Great Britain and Germany's Lost Colonies, 1914–1919,* Oxford, 1967.

Mamatey, Victor S., *The United States and East Central Europe, 1914–1918, A Study in Wilsonian Diplomacy and Propaganda,* Princeton, 1957.

Marburg, Theodore, *Development of The League of Nations Idea,* ed. by John N. Latané, 2 vols., *2,* New York, 1932.

Marston, F.S., *The Peace Conference of 1919: Organization and Procedure,* London, 1944. Foreword by Sir Charles Webster.

Martin, Geoffrey J., *Mark Jefferson: Cartographer,* Ypsilanti, Mich., 1968.

Martin, Laurence W., *Peace Without Victory: Woodrow Wilson and the British Liberals,* New Haven, Conn., 1958.

Mayer, Arno J., *Political Origins of the New Diplomacy,* New Haven, 1959.

———, *Politics and Diplomacy of Peacemaking: Containment and Counterrevolution at Versailles, 1918–1919,* New York, 1967.

Moore, John Bassett, *Principles of American Diplomacy,* New York, 1930.

Nelson, Harold I., *Land and Power,* London, 1963.

Nevins, Allan, *Henry White: Thirty Years of American Diplomacy,* New York, 1930.

Nicholas, H. G. See Huthmacher.

Nicolson, Harold, *King George V,* London, 1952.

Noble, George Bernard, *Policies and Opinions at Paris, 1919,* New York, 1935.

Notter, Harley, *The Origins of the Foreign Policy of Woodrow Wilson,* Baltimore, 1937.

O'Grady, Joseph P. (ed.), *The Immigrants' Influence on Wilson's Peace Policies,* Louisville, 1967.

Osgood, Robert E., *Ideals and Self-Interest in America's Foreign Relations,* Chicago, 1953.

Parrini, Carl P., *Heir to Empire: U.S. Economic Diplomacy, 1916–1923,* Pittsburgh, 1969.

Pedroncini, Guy, *Les Négociations Secrètes pendant la Grande Guerre,* Paris, 1969.

Perman, Dagmar, *The Shaping of the Czechoslovak State,* Leiden, 1962.

Ratinaud, Jean, *Clemenceau, ou la Colère et la Gloire,* Paris, 1958.

Reading, Gerald Rufus Isaacs, 2nd Marquis, *Rufus Isaacs, 1st Marquess of Reading,* 2 vols., *2,* London, 1945.

Renouvin, Pierre, *L'Armistice de Rethondes,* Paris, 1968.

———, *Les Crises du XXe Siècle,* 2 vols., *1, De 1914 à 1929,* Paris, 1957. English trans. *War and Aftermath,* New York, 1968.

———, *Le Traité de Versailles,* Paris, 1969.

Roskill, Stephen, *Hankey: Man of Secrets,* 3 vols., *1* and *2,* London, 1972.

Rothwell, V.H., *British War Aims and Peace Diplomacy,* Oxford, 1971.

Rowland, Peter, *David Lloyd George,* New York, 1975.

Rudin, Harry R., *Armistice 1918,* New Haven, 1944.

Salter, James Arthur, Lord Salter, *Allied Shipping Control: An Experiment in International Administration,* London, 1921.

Schwabe, Klaus, *Deutsche Revolution und Wilson-Frieden, Die Amerikanische und die deutsche Friedenstrategie zwischen Ideologie und Machtpolitik, 1918–1919,* Göttingen, 1971.

———, *Woodrow Wilson,* Göttingen, 1971.

Seton-Watson, Robert W., *Britain and the Dictators,* New York, 1938.

Seymour, Charles, *American Diplomacy during the World War,* Baltimore, 1934.

———, *Geography, Justice, and Politics at the Paris Peace Conference of 1919,* New York, 1951.

Shelton, Brenda K., *President Wilson and the Russian Revolution,* Monograph in History No. 7, The University of Buffalo Studies, Vol. 23, No. 3, March 1957.

Smith, Arthur D.H., *Mr. House of Texas,* New York, 1940.

Smuts, Jan Christiaan, *The League of Nations, a Practical Suggestion,* London, 1918.

Tardieu, André, *France and America,* Boston, 1927.

Thompson, Charles T., *The Peace Conference Day by Day,* New York, 1920.

Thompson, John M., *Russia, Bolshevism, and the Versailles Peace,* Princeton, 1966.

Tillman, Seth P., *Anglo-American Relations at the Paris Peace Conference,* Princeton, 1961.

The Times History of the War, 21 vols., *21,* London, 1920.

Trask, David F., *Captains and Cabinets: Anglo-American Naval Relations 1917–1918,* Columbia, Mo., 1972.

———, *General Tasker Howard Bliss and the "Sessions of the World," 1919,* Philadelphia, 1966.

————, *The U.S. in the Supreme War Council: American War Aims and Interallied Strategy,* 1917–1918, Middletown, Conn., 1961.

Ullman, Richard H., *Intervention and the War,* Princeton, 1961.

————, *Britain and the Russian Civil War,* Princeton, 1968.

Unterberger, Betty Miller, *America's Siberian Expedition,* 1918–1920, Durham, N.C., 1956.

Walworth, Arthur, *Woodrow Wilson,* one-volume ed., Boston, 1965.

Watt, Richard M., *The Kings Depart,* New York, 1968.

Weill-Raynal, Étienne, *Les Réparations Allemandes et la France,* 3 vols., *1: Des Origines jusqu'à Institution de l'État des Payements* (Nov. 1918–Mai 1921), Paris, 1947.

Willert, Sir Arthur, *The Road to Safety,* London, 1952.

Williams, William A., *Russian-American Relations, 1781–1947,* New York, 1952.

Wilson, Joan Hoff, *Herbert Hoover,* Boston, 1975.

Woodward, Sir Llewellyn, *Great Britain and the War of 1914–1918,* London, 1967.

Zimmern, Sir Alfred, *The American Road to World Peace,* New York, 1953.

Articles

Binkley, Robert C., "New Light on the Paris Peace Conference," *Political Science Quarterly, 46* (1931), 335–61, 509–47.

————, "Ten Years of Peace Conference History," *Journal of Modern History, 1* (1929), 607–29.

Birdsall, Paul, "The Second Decade of Peace Conference History," *Journal of Modern History, 11* (1939), 362–78.

Bliss, Tasker H., "The Armistices," a review of Mermeix, *Les Négotiations Secrètes et les Quatre Armistices,* in *The American Journal of International Law, 16* (1922), 509–22.

Cambon, Jules, "La Paix," *Revue de Paris,* 44th year, 6 (Nov. 1937).

Egerton, George W., "The Lloyd George Government and the Creation of the League of Nations," *American Historical Review,* 79: 2 (April 1974), pp. 419–37.

Gregory, Ross, "Woodrow Wilson and America's Mission," in Frank J. Merli and Theodore A. Wilson (eds.), *Makers of American Diplomacy,* New York, 1974, pp. 359–83.

Holborn, Hajo, "The Reasons for the Failure of the Paris Peace Settlement," *Henry Wells Lawrence Memorial Lectures, 3,* New London, Conn., 1953.

House, Edward M., "The Freedom of the Seas," *The Contemporary Review,* 133:748 (April 1928), 416–21.

Huston, James A., "The Allied Blockade of Germany, 1918–1919," *The Journal of Central European Affairs,* 10:2 (July 1950), 194.

Mayer, Arno J., "Historical Thought and American Foreign Policy in the Era of the First World War," in Francis L. Loewenheim (ed.), *The Historian and the Diplomat,* New York, 1967.

Miller, David Hunter, "Some Legal Aspects of the Visit of President Wilson to Paris," *Harvard Law Review*, 36:1, part 7 (1922).

Safford, Jeffrey J., "Edward Hurley and American Shipping Policy: an Elaboration on Wilsonian Diplomacy, 1918–1919," *The Historian*, 35:4, (August 1973).

Seymour, Charles, "Woodrow Wilson: A Political Balance Sheet," *Proceedings of the American Philosophical Society*, 101:2 (April 1957).

Snell, John L., "Wilson on Germany and the Fourteen Points," *Journal of Modern History*, 26:4 (1954), 364–69.

Wells, Samuel F., Jr., "New Perspectives on Wilsonian Diplomacy: the Secular Evangelism of American Political Economy," *Perspectives in American History*, 6 (1972), Cambridge, Mass., pp. 387–419.

Willis, Edward F., "Herbert Hoover and the Blockade of Germany," in *Studies in Modern European History in Honor of Franklin Charles Palm,* Frederick J. Cox, Richard M. Brace, Bernard C. Weber and John F. Ramsey (eds.), New York, 1956, pp. 265–310.

Dissertations

Ambrosius, Lloyd E., "The United States and the Weimar Republic, 1918–1923," University of Illinois, 1967.

Binkley, Robert C., "Reactions of European Public Opinion to Woodrow Wilson's Statesmanship," Hoover Institution on War, Revolution, and Peace, 1927.

Gould, John W., "Italy and the U.S., 1914–1918," Yale University, 1969.

Helde, Thomas T., "The Blockade of Germany, Nov. 1918–July 1919," Yale University, 1949.

Klachko, Mary, "Anglo-American Naval Competition, 1918–1922," Columbia University, 1962.

Lowry, Francis B., "The Generals, the Armistice, and the Treaty of Versailles, 1919," Duke University, 1963.

Posey, John P., "David Hunter Miller at the Paris Peace Conference, Nov. 1918–May 1919," University of Georgia, 1962.

Rizopoulos, Nicholas X., "Greece at the Paris Peace Conference, 1919," Yale University, 1963.

Schaefer, Ludwig F., "German Peace Strategy in 1918–1919," Yale University, 1958.

Whiteman, Harold B., Jr., "Norman H. Davis and the Search for International Peace and Security, 1917–1944," Yale University, 1958.

Index